Positive Communication
in Health *and* Wellness

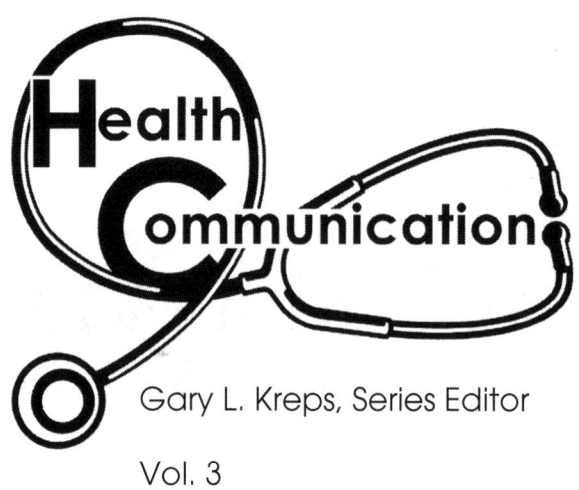

Gary L. Kreps, Series Editor

Vol. 3

The Health Communication series is part of
the Peter Lang Media and Communication list.
Every volume is peer reviewed and meets
the highest quality standards for content and production.

PETER LANG
New York • Washington, D.C./Baltimore • Bern
Frankfurt • Berlin • Brussels • Vienna • Oxford

Positive Communication
in Health *and* Wellness

EDITED BY Margaret J. Pitts & Thomas J. Socha

PETER LANG
New York • Washington, D.C./Baltimore • Bern
Frankfurt • Berlin • Brussels • Vienna • Oxford

Library of Congress Cataloging-in-Publication Data

Positive communication in health and wellness /
edited by Margaret J. Pitts, Thomas J. Socha.
pages cm
Includes bibliographical references and index.
1. Communication in medicine. 2. Interpersonal communication. 3. Health.
I. Pitts, Margaret J. (Margaret Jane). II. Socha, Thomas J.
R118.P67   613—dc23   2012034610
ISBN 978-1-4331-1446-5 (hardcover)
ISBN 978-1-4331-1445-8 (paperback)
ISBN 978-1-4539-0977-5 (e-book)
ISSN 2153-1277

Bibliographic information published by **Die Deutsche Nationalbibliothek**.
Die Deutsche Nationalbibliothek lists this publication in the "Deutsche
Nationalbibliografie"; detailed bibliographic data is available
on the Internet at http://dnb.d-nb.de/.

The paper in this book meets the guidelines for permanence and durability
of the Committee on Production Guidelines for Book Longevity
of the Council of Library Resources.

© 2013 Peter Lang Publishing, Inc., New York
29 Broadway, 18th floor, New York, NY 10006
www.peterlang.com

All rights reserved.
Reprint or reproduction, even partially, in all forms such as microfilm,
xerography, microfiche, microcard, and offset strictly prohibited.

Printed in the United States of America

Contents

Acknowledgments ix

Chapter One. Positive Communication in Creating Healthy Lives,
Healthy Relationships, and Health Institutions 1
Margaret J. Pitts and Thomas J. Socha

Section One
Positive Communication and Health

Chapter Two. Positive Relational Communication: Impact on Health 29
Claire F. Sullivan

Chapter Three. Humor as a Tool, Not the Therapy: A Preliminary
Model of Humor in Health Communication 43
Juliann C. Scholl

Chapter Four. The Social Construction of Hope through
Strengths-Based Health Communication Strategies:
A Children's Mental Health Approach 63
Christine S. Davis, John Mayo, Beth Piecora, and Tessa Wimberley

Chapter Five. Communication in Self-Help Support Groups:
Positive Communication and the Al-Anon Experience 82
Chuck F. Aust

Chapter Six. Healing through Healthy Doses of Positivity:
Mothers' and Daughters' Positive Communication
When Coping with Breast Cancer 98
Carla L. Fisher, Michelle Miller-Day, and Jon F. Nussbaum

Section Two
Positive Communication and Relational Wellness

Chapter Seven. Moving from Positive Thinking to Positive Talk:
Implications for Relational Well-Being 117
Kelly F. Albada and Jessica L. Moore

Chapter Eight. Esteem Support as a Form of Positive Communication:
Connections to Well-Being 133
Amanda J. Holmstrom

Chapter Nine. Relationship Enhancement (RE) as One Approach for
  Improving Health and Wellness, Attaining Communication
  Gratification, and Communicating Positively 148
  Mary Mino

Chapter Ten. Positive Communication, Coaching, and Relational
  Health/Wellness 167
  Jean DeHart

Chapter Eleven. Final Conversations: Positive Communication
  at the End of Life 190
  Maureen Keeley and Paula Baldwin

Section Three
Positive Communication and Healthy Organizations and Institutions

Chapter Twelve. Affirming Communication within
  the Healthcare Organization: Validating Strength through
  Talk in Trauma Medicine 207
  Theodore A. Avtgis, Andrew S. Rancer, and Sherry G. Ford

Chapter Thirteen. Positive Communication and Organizational Crisis:
  Can CEOs Look on the Bright Side? 223
  Sandra L. French

Chapter Fourteen. Communication Joy: Print Journalists and
  the Experience of Flow 238
  Janet Fulton

Chapter Fifteen. Happy Classrooms = Happier Students:
  Making the Case for Positive Communication in Education 252
  Jenny Tatsak and Hollie D. Petit

Chapter Sixteen. Positive Organizations for Older Adults
  in Community Settings.. 266
  Linda M. Johnston and Deanna F. Womack

Chapter Seventeen. *Committed*: Fostering Respect and Well-Being
  through Collaborative Theatrical Performance
  at Piedmont Regional Jail 285
  Claire E. Deal

Coda. Apples and Positive Messages: Towards Healthy Communication
  Habits and Wellness.. 301
  Thomas J. Socha and Margaret J. Pitts

Contributors 307
Author Index 319
Subject Index 333

Acknowledgments

I offer gratitude to Tom Socha, Gary Kreps, Mary Savigar, Sophie Appel, my students Stephanie Smith and Alyssa Apatmos, and the many contributors to this volume. Without them, this volume would not have been realized. This volume is especially important to me because it connects the practice of positive communication with health and wellness. I was introduced to the study of health communication, and most especially the importance of positive communication in health and well-being, by my dear friend Amanda Lee Kundrat. I started graduate school with Amanda who became a very close friend of mine during our years at Penn State. She lived with an invisible illness, but committed herself to make the most out of each day for herself, her family, and her friends. Toward the end of our doctoral training, she passed away. She left behind several works in progress on issues related to health and wellness. I dedicate this volume to Amanda, to her family and friends, and to the ideas that she planted before leaving us. I dedicate this volume to its readers that they may also commit to living each day well.

—MJP

Many thanks to my good friend, co-editor, and co-author Maggie Pitts, and added echos of gratitude to long-time friend and most inspiring communication scholar Gary Kreps, super-editor Mary Savigar, and all of the good folks at Peter Lang Publishing. I too am grateful for all of the authors who see the importance of continuing the important work of positive communication. And I too believe strongly that the field of communication has much to offer in preventing and easing suffering as well as inspiring us to all to live deeply, deliberately, and happily.

—TJS

• CHAPTER ONE •

Positive Communication in Creating Healthy Lives, Healthy Relationships, and Healthy Institutions

Margaret J. Pitts
University of Arizona

Thomas J. Socha
Old Dominion University

In 2012, we organized the first ever collection of scholarship on positive interpersonal communication (Socha & Pitts, 2012). In our open call for contributions to the edited volume, we received so many proposals from communication scholars enthusiastic about the positive communication project it was evident a second volume was needed, one that extended beyond interpersonal relationships to focus on well-being in all domains of life. Therefore, we offer this volume—dedicated to communication and flourishing in health, relationships, and organizations—in response to the growing interest in positive communication scholarship. In the first volume, we conceptualized positive communication as "relational communication facilitative of happiness, health, and wellness" (p. 1). While we agree with positive psychology that interpersonal relationships are key to the development of "the good life," and should feature as central to the study of positive communication, we acknowledge the need to extend studies of positive communication to include our individual health and wellness as well as the health and wellness of organizations/institutions. Thus, this volume considers the multiple levels of communication from individual and relational to organizational and communal in the development of health and well-being.

Underlying this volume is the notion that just as health is not defined by the absence of illness; positive communication is not defined as the absence of negative verbal and nonverbal communication, but rather the presence of positive, enhancing, and facilitative talk and gestures. It should be understood that positive communication is also not about naïvely attending to only good things (i.e., being overly optimistic or avoiding negativity), but rather it is about applying and studying communication that allows us to thrive in the full spectrum of life experiences. Thus, we consider the role of communication in flourishing and question how positive communication, as a developmental and lifespan phenomenon, can be nourished in health, relational, and organizational settings.

This introductory chapter will define and describe positive communication from an interdisciplinary perspective using the movement in positive psychology and positive organizational studies as a foundation. Positive psychology is the science of thriving and optimal functioning of people, groups, and institutions, and represents a broader movement in the social and behavioral sciences toward the study of quality of life and science of human strengths (Gable & Haidt, 2005; Peterson & Seligman, 2004; Seligman, 2003). The field of communication is poised to be an influential voice on the positive scholarship movement. In many ways, communication is the enactment of positive psychology that leads to flourishing. We draw specifically from Seligman's (2011) well-being theory, Peterson and Seligman's (2004) character strengths and virtues, and the three pillars of positive psychology (positive emotion, positive traits, and positive institutions; Seligman, 2002, 2003) to draw parallels between positive communication in health and wellness and positive psychology. This chapter will then outline a rationale for the study of positive communication in three specific domains: individual health and healthcare, healthy relationships, and organizational and institutional wellness. Within each of these domains we offer a preview and brief commentary on the chapters that make up the three sections of this volume. Our chapter concludes with recommendations for generating positive communication and well-being in health, relationships, and institutions.

The Need to Study Positive Communication and Everyday Health and Well-Being

The time is ripe for a turn toward the positive side of communication in generating health and well-being across everyday life domains. Drawing from the field of positive psychology, the communication discipline is positioned well to begin exploring the links between positive communication and health and wellness. This chapter borrows tenets of positive psychology, which has already laid the foundation for the scientific study of human strengths and quality of life, to operationalize positive communication as a fruitful area of study. Positive communication takes as its focus outward expressions and meaning making through talk, language, gesture—communication. Positive communication is unique in its ability to generate physical, social, and psychological health and wellness. It yields the potential to inspire people to achieve higher moments, greater good, and to act selflessly. Moreover, investigating the intersections of positive communication and health allows for a focus on what makes people feel good, what drives people to invest in good health behaviors, and what motivates people to live fully within the parameters of their personal health and life stories. Positive communication in health and wellness offers a focus on what is *going right* physically, mentally, and socially, as well as where care and treatment are needed. It embodies respect, responsibility, higher purpose, and meaning. Moreover, positive communication in the context of health and wellness recognizes that "health" extends well beyond encounters with healthcare professionals and carers. Indeed, it flows throughout our major life domains—relationships, work places, and places of leisure and learning. Healthy people come from and form healthy relationships and healthy institutions and, by extension, healthy institutions and healthy relationships generate healthy individuals (Peterson, 2006). By focusing on health and wellness in communication we acknowledge the intersections of social lives and admonish the false notion that we can study communication in health, relationships, or work as independent features of a person's life when in fact these three domains (and more) are deeply and chaotically entwined.

Communication scholarship has underestimated the importance of positive communication in daily routines that lead to healthy living and healthy living environments. Instead of focusing on communication in enhancing well-being across contexts and generating healthy interpersonal relationships, there has been a focus on *maintaining* status quo in relationships, *managing* communication across diverse encounters, or *achieving* effective and competent communication. A focus on positive communication across life domains (health, relationships, and organizations and institutions) creates a space for thriving and flourishing—important concepts when considering health and wellness. In the health field, for example, the focus on *treatment* or even health *maintenance* leaves room for *enhancing* health. A similar focus on relational maintenance and repair, or maintaining status quo and productivity in organizations and in communities, neglects to consider the power of communication in creating and enhancing health and well-being in these contexts. Admittedly, communication scholars have developed many rich areas that contribute to positive communication across these themes, but there has been no concerted effort to direct these interests in a more focused manner that generates health and wellness through communication. This volume helps to develop an understanding of the ways in which everyday communication in everyday contexts of health, relationships, and organizations generate (or degenerate) possibilities for positive communication and flourishing.

Positive Psychology

Martin Seligman, president of the American Psychological Association in 1998 (www.APA.org) coined the term "positive psychology" to refer to a developing movement in psychology that focused on enhancing quality of life rather than managing pathologies (Seligman, 2003, 2011). Since then, the concept and experiences of well-being, happiness, and flourishing have been central to the movement. The absence of disease, discomfort, distress, or disorder puts an individual at neutral, but what positive psychologists began to question was what pushed individuals toward well-being. The answer, in part, is now what is known as the three pillars of positive psychology: positive emotion, positive traits, and positive institutions (Seligman, 2002, 2003). These same pillars offer a strong structure from which to build the study of positive communication. When the three pillars are present, we see that they not only enhance positive life experiences and quality of life during good times, but more importantly, they also serve us in times of trouble. Indeed, this is what thriving is about—championing character strengths and virtues (e.g., open-mindedness, valor, integrity, leadership, forgiveness, hope, kindness) in the face of deep challenges (Seligman, 2003).

Positive emotions are the *first pillar of positive psychology*. They include positive subjective experiences of the past (i.e., contentment, satisfaction, and well-being), present (i.e., happiness, flow, ecstasy, and sensual pleasures), and future (i.e., optimism and hope; Seligman, 2002, 2003). Positive emotions, like happiness, are important to quality of life and well-being in all life domains. In general, happy people are healthier people. A recent metaanalysis of positive affect studies suggests that happiness brings many more benefits than just feeling good—happy people are likely to acquire favorable life circumstances, are more successful, and are more socially engaged than unhappy people (Lyubomirsky, King, & Diener, 2005; Seligman, Steen, Park, & Peterson, 2005). Positive communication has already contributed significant scholarship in this area, for example, aesthetic relating (Baxter, Norwood, & Nebel, 2012), communication and intimacy (Nussbaum, Miller-Day, & Fisher, 2012), the communication of affection (Floyd & Deiss, 2012), and social and celebratory support (MacGeorge, Feng, Wilkum, & Doherty, 2012; McCullough &

Burleson, 2012). In this volume, several chapters both implicitly and explicitly address the role of communication in generating positive emotions and health and wellness. Sullivan (chapter 2) uses positive relational communication and the positive emotions evoked in the process to address its impact on health. Keeley and Baldwin (chaper 11) demonstrate the importance of final conversations with a Dying loved one in generating positive emotions. Albada and Moore (chapter 7) show how positive thinking and positive talk enhance positive emotions and experiences within relationships. Holmstrom (chapter 8) illustrates the important role of communicating esteem support in generating positive emotions. And Mino (chapter 9) and DeHart (chapter 10) argue that application of interpersonal communication skills (relationship enhancement and life coaching) can lead to positive emotions and individual/relational development.

The *second pillar of positive psychology* is the study of individual strengths and virtues, but also natural abilities and talents such as intelligence and athleticism (Seligman, 2003). Peterson and Seligman (2004) argued that a classification system for measuring and talking about character strengths across the lifespan was a necessary move forward in the development of a science for human strengths. Peterson and Seligman (2004) argued that the "good life is lived over time and across situations, and an examination of the good life in terms of positive traits is demanded. Strengths of character provide the needed explanation for the stability and generality of a life well lived" (p. 12). To this end, Peterson and Seligman, as well as other practitioners of positive psychology, devoted extensive cross-cultural research to the development of a handbook for signature strengths and virtues, a project akin to the *Diagnostic and Statistical Manual of Mental Disorders-IV-TR* (DSM, 2000) but for positive human qualities. In doing so they identified 24 character strengths within six core virtues (see Table 1.1), using the following criteria; Character strengths (a) are ubiquitous across cultures, (b) are individually fulfilling, (c) are morally valued, (d) do not diminish others, (e) have a nonfelicitous opposite (has antonyms that are negative), (f) are traitlike, (g) are measurable, (h) demonstrate distinctiveness, (i) have paragons (i.e., there are examples of people who embody the strength in a striking way), (j) has prodigies (i.e., precociously shown by some children), (k) can be selectively absent in some people, and (l) have institutions (i.e., schools, churches) built to cultivate them (Peterson, 2006; Peterson & Seligman, 2004). Strengths fulfill an individual. And, fulfillment takes effort (Peterson & Seligman, 2004). But, strategies can be put into practice that moves the average person toward greater quality of life through recognition and development of innate strengths and virtues. Indeed, this is the premise of strengths-based discourse in children's mental health (Davis, Mayo, Piecora, & Wimberley, chapter 4) and of the support literature in Al-Anon self-help groups (Aust, chapter 5). Fisher, Miller-Day, and Nussbaum (chapter 6) also establish the healing power of recognizing and validating strengths and virtues among mothers and daughters coping with breast cancer. Scholl (chapter 3) calls upon humor as a character strength in developing a model for the health benefits of health-related humor. Virtuous communication might include communication excellence (Mirivel, 2012), reflective conversation (Miczo, 2012), listening (Bodie, 2012), forgiveness (Kelley, 2012), or humorous (Meyer, 2012), playful (Aune & Wong, 2012), dialogic (Kellett, 2012), and engaged communication (Kreps, 2012).

Table 1.1. Summary of Virtues and Character Strengths in Positive Psychology (Peterson & Seligman, 2004)

Core Virtues	Character Strengths
Wisdom	1. Creativity (originality, ingenuity) 2. Curiosity (interest, novelty-seeking, openness to experience) 3. Open-mindedness (judgment, critical thinking) 4. Love of learning 5. Perspective
Courage	6. Bravery (valor) 7. Persistence (perseverance, industriousness) 8. Integrity (authenticity, honesty) 9. Vitality (zest, enthusiasm, vigor, energy)
Humanity	10. Love 11. Kindness (generosity, nurturance, care, compassion, altruistic love) 12. Social intelligence (emotional intelligence, personal intelligence)
Justice	13. Citizenship (social responsibility, loyalty, teamwork) 14. Fairness 15. Leadership
Temperance	16. Forgiveness and mercy 17. Humility/modesty 18. Prudence 19. Self-regulation (self-control)
Transcendence	20. Appreciation of beauty and excellence (awe, wonder, elevation) 21. Gratitude 22. Hope (optimism, future-mindedness, future orientation) 23. Humor (playfulness) 24. Spirituality (religiousness, faith, purpose)

The study of positive institutions and communities makes up *the third pillar of positive psychology*, including concrete institutions such as places of work and leisure, but also abstract concepts such as family, democracy, or the free press (Seligman, 2003). Here, especially when considering the abstract notions of institutions, Seligman argues that the social sciences need to move beyond the study of disabling conditions—what he terms the "isms" of social interaction, racism, sexism, and agism—and toward the study of what creates positive (not neutral) outcomes. Gable and Haidt (2005) argued that within the first five years of positive psychology scholars have been productive in the areas of positive emotions and positive traits, but significantly less so in their study and creation of positive institutions. They contend that although positive psychology had not yet succeeded in forging similar movements in sister social scientific fields (they note "positive sociology" and "positive anthropology," but clearly "positive communication" should be counted among them), positive psychology itself would have to become "more daring in their theory and their interventions...to actually improve the functioning of schools, workplaces, and even governments" (Gable & Haidt, 2005, p. 108). More recently, the positive movement in the social sciences has begun to make headway in this area. Seligman's application of principles of positive psychology and flourishing in US Army and educational settings are exemplary (Seligman, 2011). The recent development of positive organizational studies (see Linley, Harrington, & Garcea, 2010; Roberts & Dutton, 2009) and humanism in business (see Spitzeck, Pirson, Amann, Khan, & von Kimakowitz, 2009) offer evidence that the positive movement is taking hold at the institutional level. The field of communication has also begun to make significant inroads toward the development of positive institutions, including health and healthcare organizations (Aust, chapter 5; Avtgis, Rancer & Ford, chapter 12; Davis et al., chapter 4; Kreps, 2012; Wilson & Gettings, 2012), within workplaces (see French, chapter 13; Fulton, chapter 14), in education (Tatsak & Petit, chapter 15; Frey & White, 2012), nursing homes (Johnston & Womack, chapter 16), and prisons (Deal, chapter 17; Baesler, Derlega, & Lolley, 2012).

Positive Communication, Quality of Life, and Well-Being

Positive communication as a focused area of study within the field of communication debuted at the 2010 annual convention of the Southern States Communication Association (SSCA) with Socha as the convention planner (Socha, 2012). One year later, in his SSCA Presidential Address, Socha invoked the concept of "savoring" from the positive psychology movement (see Bryant & Veroff, 2007) and applied it to the practice and experience of positive communication. He questioned how the experience of communication might change if we were to "to appreciate, contemplate, mull, muse, linger, ponder, relish, savor, or even wonder about messages" (Socha, 2012, p. 4). Savoring an experience goes beyond physical sensations (such as taste) to attend "to more complex cognitive associations" (Bryant & Veroff, 2007, p. 3).

> Savoring [goes] beyond the experience of pleasure to encompass a higher order awareness or reflective discernment on the part of the individual. We would speak of savoring if people were attending to how much well-being they are deriving from their accomplishments or from their social connections. (Bryant & Veroff, 2007, p. 3)

This leads us to ask, can we savor communication? Can we savor relationships and social connections? And if we can, does savoring, and other communication experiences, increase our quality of life?

Quality of life, as defined by the World Health Organization (1997, p. 1) refers to individuals' perceptions of their position in life in the context of the culture and value systems in which they live and in relation to their goals, expectations, standards and concerns. It is a broad ranging concept affected in a complex way by the person's physical health, psychological state, level of independence, social relationships, personal beliefs and their relationship to salient features of their environment.

This definition encompasses the range of indicators we present in this volume as leading to the life well-lived—especially physical, psychological, and social health within the contexts in which we live (places of work, play, learning, healing, etc.). We argue here that "quality of life" is a communication and psychological construct that develops across the lifespan. And that positive communication holds potential to pave the way to higher quality of life.

In his Presidential Address to the International Communication Association Jon Nussbaum (2007) urged social scientists to start considering the "big," "socially relevant" questions of life. Nussbaum placed quality of life at the center of socially relevant studies and communication at the center of quality of life; "communication across the life span is at the very heart of any reasonable notion of quality of life" (Nussbaum, 2007, p. 2). Communication and quality of life are so entwined that Nussbaum suggests that investigating quality of life without attending to communication across the lifespan is unreasonable. Indeed, as Nussbaum argues "no individual can possibly adapt, maintain, or obtain the necessary requisites of a quality life throughout the life span without competent communication" (p. 3).

Positive communication as a conduit for higher quality of life is grounded in the notion that relationships and the contexts in which we do our relating can move beyond satisfactory or effective to generative, enriching, and enhancing. There are features of communication that can move individuals and groups of people from sufficing to maximizing quality of life across all domains and across the lifespan. Quality of life is equally important during times of health and flourishing as it is during times of sickness and famine, as important during times of temporary ability as disability, and across all contexts—relationships, workplaces, communities, schools, and certainly mental and physical well-being. Quality of life is something that is always with us, but at the same time it is not attainable in the sense that one day we "reach" or "achieve" quality of life. Instead, quality of life is always in a state of "becoming"—something that we can work for regardless of our current state or status from first to last breath (see Keeley & Baldwin, chapter 11).

Quality of life increases subjective well-being, or individual's perception of life satisfaction in important life domains such as work, health, and relationships (Diener & Biswas-Diener, 2008). Subjective well-being "includes their emotions such as joy and engagement, and the relatively rare experience of unpleasant emotions such as anger, sadness, and fear" (Diener & Biswas-Diener, 2008, p. 4). It is also related to the subjective experience of happiness. Happiness can be defined as the frequency (and not intensity) of experiencing positive emotions or positive affect, not the absence of negative emotions (Lyubomirsky et al., 2005). It should be noted that eliminating negative experiences, illness, and pathology does not automatically generate positive affect. However, building positive skills (i.e., positive communication) might aid in reducing or eliminating some negatives and increase quality of life along the way (Burns, 2010).

In his groundbreaking work on happiness, well-being, and positive psychology—*Authentic Happiness*—Seligman (2002) proffered a theory of happiness based on the attainment of three elements (1) positive emotion and pleasure (the pleasant life), (2) engagement (the engaged life), and (3) meaning (the meaningful life). His argument then was that happiness was at the center of positive psychology and could be measured by life satisfaction. The ultimate goal was to increase life satisfaction through principles of positive psychology (Seligman, 2002, 2011). Now, Seligman (2011) argues that it is not happiness, but rather well-being, that should be the driving force behind positive psychology. "Well-being theory" differs significantly from "authentic happiness theory." First, by placing well-being (and not happiness) at the center of positive psychology it becomes scientifically more rigorous. Well-being is a social construct that can be operationalized by several measurable elements—all of which contribute to well-being, but none of which define it (Seligman, 2011). Whereas happiness had one measurement—life satisfaction—well-being is measured by positive emotion, engagement, meaning, positive relationships, and accomplishment (Seligman, 2011). Second, in well-being theory, flourishing, and not life satisfaction, becomes the goal of positive psychology.

Well-being theory maintains the three elements of authentic happiness, (1) positive emotion and pleasure, (2) engagement, and (3) meaning, and adds two additional elements (4) positive relationships, and (5) accomplishment. Thus, Seligman's (2011) pneumonic PERMA encompasses the five elements making up well-being theory. These five elements contribute to "what makes life worth living" and create the opportunities for human flourishing. Here we draw on Seligman's (2002, 2011) and other's (e.g., Peterson, 2006) descriptions of each element.

The *pleasant life* includes the experience positive emotions like happiness, pleasure, joy, and rapture, and includes both pleasures of the body (sensations) and pleasures of the mind. The *engaged life* seeks opportunities for "flow." Flow is a subjective experience that results when a person's skills are optimally matched with a significant or meaningful challenge (Csikszentmihalyi, 1997). During flow, people often lose awareness of time or other nagging pressures such as fatigue or hunger. Instead they are wholly engaged in an activity. The *"relational life"* (our terminology) is one of the new elements Seligman (2011) incorporated into well-being theory, noting that the positive and powerful experiences of profound meaning, purpose, joy, pride, and accomplishment likely all took place within relationships. In fact, Seligman argues that "so basic are positive relationships to the success of *Homo sapiens* that evolution has bolstered them with the additional support of the other [PERMA] elements in order to make damn sure that we pursue positive relationships" (p. 24). Seligman describes the *meaningful life* as "belonging to and serving something that you believe is bigger than the self, and humanity creates all the positive institutions to allow this: religion, political party, being green, the Boy Scouts, or the family" (p. 12). Accomplishment, or the *achieving life*, recognizes that some individuals dedicate a lifetime to achievement or accomplishment just for the sake of achieving it. That is, it can be pursued for its own good even if it does not yield positive emotions, does not result in positive relationships, and/or is not considered meaningful. In other words, people might play a game just for the satisfaction of winning and not for the joy of the game (i.e., flow).

For communication scholars we must now consider how communication can contribute to flourishing in each of these five domains? That is, how can communication enhance the pleasant life, engaged life, relational life, meaningful life, and engaged life across contexts of relationships, health, and institutions. Thus, it is with these questions, and in the pursuit of well-being in health, relational, and organizational/institutional settings, that we introduce the volume.

Introduction to the Volume

This edited volume harnesses a dispersed, developing, yet powerful body of communication scholarship that has at its center a focus on building healthy communication contexts and generating wellness through the development, application, and exploration of positive communication concepts, theories, and strategies. The volume is divided into three communication contexts: Positive Communication and Health, Positive Communication and Relational Wellness, and Positive Communication and Healthy Organizations and Institutions. The first section demonstrates the important role of positive communication in health and health care contexts such as social support, humor, and hope, and includes specialized contexts such as breast cancer, self-help support, and among children diagnosed with serious emotional disturbance. The second section argues for the importance of positive communication in building, maintaining, and enhancing healthy relationships through positive communication. It includes chapters on positive illusions and positive talk, esteem support, relationship enhancements and gratification and life-coaching, and on fostering positive end-of-life conversations. The third section addresses the impact of positive communication on organizational and institutional health and well-being. It includes chapters about building healthy work environments through affirming and validating talk, finding flow in the workplace, and using positive communication to create healthy institutions such as education, nursing homes, prisons, and organizations under crisis.

Positive Communication and Health

We begin with a focus on health communication, as it is the cord that binds together the volume. In the *Handbook of Health Communication,* Cline (2003) argued that everyday, informal, interpersonal communication plays a significant role in health, but is largely under studied as a force in health management in and of itself. In this section, we offer several chapters that address the relationship between everyday communication and health. Many of the practices evident in these chapters demonstrate communicative processes that function to enhance health rather than focus on prevention, maintenance, or correction. This approach helps us to move beyond the notion that health is more than the "absence of disease, distress and disorder" (Peterson & Seligman, 2004, p. 4). Instead, it offers us a focus on what is "right" with people. Positive communication in health contexts is more than just "bedside manner" or compliance gaining. We propose investing in health as potential and not as pathology through positive communication.

The five chapters that make up Section One: *Positive Communication and Health* include health communication processes and contexts that exemplify occasions for and examples of positive communication. In the lead chapter of this section, Sullivan draws from the World Health Organization's definition of health to shape her discussion of health and positive communication. That is, "health is a state of complete physical, mental, and social well-being and not merely the absence of disease or infirmary" (WHO, 1946). Sullivan's review of research in the areas of health, communication, and psychology underscores the important role that communicating social support, gratitude, and humor plays in establishing, maintaining, and enhancing health. Sullivan's review sets the stage for the chapters that follow, each of which addresses these themes in some way. For instance, in the chapter that follows, Scholl (chapter 3) explicitly addresses the importance of humor in health and well-being. In doing so, she not only reveals the numerous health benefits of humor, she takes a conceptual leap forward and proposes a new model of health-related humor comprised of five components: planning, intent, modality, source, and topic. Davis et al. (chapter 4) open with a compelling narrative that demonstrates a "strengths-based approach" within a children's mental health treatment team. Their chapter makes clear the connections between positive communication in health, relationships, and institutions. That is the "institutional" strengths-based approach works toward increasing children's mental health by teaching children and family how to identify, acknowledge, and enhance character strengths through positive communication. Their chapter illuminates the benefits of a strengths-based approach to mental health and offers a typology of 11-strengths-based strategies identified in systems of care for children and families.

Aust (chapter 5) further demonstrates the important connections between health and institutional support. Specifically, Aust examines the member-written publications provided by Al-Anon (a self-help social support group designed to offer support to friends and relatives of alcoholics) for its members. He identifies five themes within the Al-Anon literature (i.e., materials specifically designed to communicate support to members) that map onto positive psychology and character strengths (i.e., a developmental perspective, taking responsibility, gratitude, courage, and forgiveness). In the chapter that concludes this section, Fisher et al. (chapter 6) present recent findings on the role of positive communication in mothers' and daughters' ability to adjust to cancer and promote a healthy healing environment. Fisher et al. found that mothers and daughters reported using positive communication in various forms (e.g., encouragement, assurance, having a positive attitude, preventing negative talk, telling survivor stories), but that in a few cases positive communication functioned as a hindrance in their wellness rather than promoting it. Their findings highlight both the power and complexity of positive communication in health and wellness.

Positive Communication and Relational Wellness

Relationships (Seligman's, 2011, "relational life") are the capstone of our lives. This is no doubt the reason we have already completed a volume focused entirely on positive interpersonal communication (Socha & Pitts, 2012) and still wish to give them prominence in this volume. Positive communication in health and wellness focuses on relationships and processes that are marked by their abundance and resource-producing capabilities (Ragins & Dutton, 2007). This is in stark contrast to what Gable and Haidt (2005) reveal as an imbalance in the study of close relationships. They argue, for example, there is a significant amount of scholarship that focuses on how couples use social support during times of difficulty, how couples respond to "bad" relational behavior, how families resolve conflict, and how individuals cope with negative emotions. Yet, there is very little evidence about how people respond to other's triumphs, respond to good relational behavior, how families and couples play, laugh, and have fun with each other, and how people respond to positive moral emotions such as gratitude (Gable & Haidt, 2005). Duck (2007) notes that "it is important to recognize that positivity is not a perpetual state, but merely a predominant form of relationship. One cannot expect individuals to view all positive relationships as positive all the time" (p. 183). The potential for positive communication in understanding and fostering relational well-being is particularly salient. Interpersonal communication has already made great leaps forward in this area to contribute to the science of well-being. Communication concepts such as aesthetic relating (Baxter et al., 2012), interpersonal synchrony in intercultural communication (Young, 2012), communication excellence

(Mirivel, 2012), communication virtue (Miczo, 2012), listening (Bodie, 2012), forgiveness (Kelley, 2012), and celebratory support (McCullough & Burleson, 2012) are but a few examples of positive communication in relationships.

In this volume, five chapters contribute to the section on *Positive Communication and Relational Wellness*. Albada and Moore (chapter 7) provide the opening chapter for this section with an in-depth look at the role positive illusions and positive cognitions play in creating relational wellness. They demonstrate that by communicating (via expressive writing, affirmation, and storytelling) their relational experiences, people move beyond just thinking positively about their partner to actually developing, maintaining, and enhancing their relationships. Through the expression of positive communication, relational partners engender trust, intimacy, and may even inspire each other to strive to meet their partner's idealized image—becoming better relational partners. In chapter eight, Holmstrom conceptualizes esteem support as a form of positive relational communication that has positive relational and health outcomes. This chapter nicely follows Albada and Moore by demonstrating the importance of recognizing, acknowledging, and sometimes enhancing a person's self-esteem, or sense of self and identity. Holmstrom's chapter demonstrates the links between esteem support and mental, physical, and relational health as she lays out a theory of esteem support messages designed to improve momentary losses of state self-esteem: The cognitive-emotional theory of esteem support messages.

In the two chapters that follow, Mino (chapter 9) and DeHart (chapter 10) offer strategic application of positive communication for the enhancement of personal relationships. Mino presents the relationship enhancement (RE) approach as a form of positive communication that is grounded in principles of rhetorical sensitivity, communication competence, and communication enrichment. Using her pedagogical experience with the RE approach, Mino provides a preliminary foundation for a practical guide for training and application of the RE approach. She makes clear connections between the communication practices involved in RE and the development of positive emotions and well-being through the enactment of communication excellence and virtues (gentleness, generosity, courage, justice, and compassion; see Miczo, 2012; Mirivel, 2012). DeHart draws from her experience in the new and evolving area of life coaching and as an interpersonal communication scholar to argue for the importance of using positive communication strategically to achieve relational and personal goals. Life coaching begins by examining "what is right with me" and "what is right with our relationship" and then considers the client's goals for enhancing "what is right" as well as what the client determines to achieve in the future. Her chapter centers on ten widely used empowerment practices: goal setting, accountability, ability to look at the well-being of the whole person, reframing, practice in message design and delivery, identifying values/priorities, validation, listening, celebrating-encouraging, and positive language.

Relationships are a lifespan phenomenon and the different events we experience over the life course present us with numerous opportunities to engage in positive communication and demonstrate strength of character, but perhaps none more difficult than managing relationships at the end of life. Keeley and Baldwin (chapter 11) conclude the section on positive communication and relational wellness by offering insight into the importance of final conversations between loved ones for the development of relational wellness in the present (with the Dying loved one) and in the future (without a loved one). By interviewing adults and children who have engaged in end-of-life conversations, Keeley and Baldwin identify important conversational themes that become memorable messages to the Living inspiring hope, positivity, happiness, peacefulness, and empowerment after the loved one has died.

Positive Communication and Healthy Institutions

Much of our adult lives and the majority of our days are spent at work. Similarly, for most of us, much of our childhood is spent at school. It makes sense then, that a volume on positive communication would include workplace relationships, organizations, and educational and other institutions. As Ragins and Dutton (2007) note, work relationships are too often ignored in the pursuit of "what makes life worth living." Indeed, for many reasons (economic, social, epistemic) workplace relationships have a significant influence on quality of life. In *creating* the meaningful life, a term we prefer to "searching" for the meaningful life because it draws attention to individual agency in this process, we should attend to our workplace and other organizational/institutional settings with as much fervor as we do personal and relational health and wellness. Indeed, there is a reciprocal relationship between healthy institutions, healthy relationships, and healthy individuals (Peterson, 2006). Positive organizational scholars, Ragins and Dutton (2007) note, "relationships represent not only the essence of meaning in people's lives, but they also reside deep in the core of organizational life; they are the means by which work is done and meaning is found in organizations" (pp. 4–5).

Duck (2007) suggests that in considering positive workplace relationships, intimacy is a relevant issue that perhaps has not been given enough scholarly attention. Intimacy in the work place likely takes a very different shape than, say, intimacy in voluntary romantic or friendship relationships, or intimacy within families, but is none-the-less an important contributor to what moves workplace interactions from mundane and mechanistic to enjoyable relationships. Moreover, as Duck notes, workplace interactions are often brief, task-focused, and not generally geared toward long-term relational development or satisfaction. The "lifespan" of workplace relationships is very different from our other voluntary and involuntary relationships.

Six chapters round out our third section: *Positive Communication and Healthy Organizations and Institutions.* All of them draw from principles and practices of positive psychology and positive organizational scholarship (see, Dutton & Ragins, 2007; Lopes, Cunha, Kaiser, & Müller-Seitz, 2009; Roberts & Dutton, 2009) to make an argument for the importance of studying and applying positive communication in these contexts. Three chapters consider workplace organizations and relationships, while one chapter centers on education as an institution. The remaining two chapters are unique in that they consider intersections of living space and institutions, nursing homes on one hand and a prison on the other.

Avtgis, Rancer, and Ford (chapter 12) lead the section on positive communication in organizations and institutions with their chapter on affirming communication in workplaces. Affirming communication includes recognizing and responding to the face needs of all communicators and demonstrating value and respect to organizational members. For example, people with an affirming communicator style present a relaxed, friendly, and attentive style of communication that opens up potential for positive outcome even in conflict situations. Avtgis et al. present two organizational healthcare studies (i.e., trauma medical teams during inter-hospital transfer) to demonstrate that the mindful practice of positive/affirming communication significantly reduced the total amount of time to care for and transfer the patient. Their results confirm that affirmative communication is a skill that can be taught and successfully implemented as a communication intervention in high-stakes work environments such as trauma medical teams.

French (chaper 13) calls upon work in positive psychology and positive organization scholarship to ask why some organizations flourish and others fail during time of organizational crises. French uses examples of CEOs of organizations under crisis, and specifically the case of Malden Mills (a knitting mill that CEO Aaron Feuerstein brought from bankruptcy to financial success) to examine the role positive communication and the virtues of hope, optimism, and resiliency, in turning organizational crises into opportunities for growth.

Fulton (chapter 14) applies the concept of flow (e.g., Csikszentmihalyi, 1997) to the workplace in generating happiness and well-being. Specifically, she draws upon interviews and observations of print journalists (as well as other documents) to address positive forces in the workplace such as creativity, motivation, and flow. Her chapter offers an in depth look at the workplace features that create opportunities for flow among print journalists, including the challenges of working within the journalistic structures (e.g., continued presence of strict deadlines) and the necessary skill set.

With the chapter by Tatsak and Petit (chapter 15) we focus our attention toward what could arguably be one of the most important institutions of modern day—the educational system. Seligman (2011) argues that for more than a century the educational system in the US has done little more than pave the way for adult work. He argues, however, that schools could incorporate positive education strategies to teach the skills of achievement as well as the skills of well-being. Tatsak and Petit agree. Their chapter exposes the problems associated with achievement skills which are often benchmarked by outcome goals such as success, money, prestige, power, etc. They argue that teaching well-being skills in the classroom will result in the pursuit of happiness and not achievement.

As noted previously, the final two chapters consider institutional living spaces. In chapter sixteen, Johnston and Womack present best practices for positive communication among the elderly, and within their relationships with family and staff, in nursing homes and assisted living facilities. Their findings come from in-depth interviews with residents, family, and staff designed to produce instances of positive communication and the institutional practices that foster positive communication. Johnston and Womack present their findings within the framework of positive organizational studies (e.g., Richardson & West, 2010; Youssef & Luthans, 2010).

The section culminates with a chapter by Deal (chapter 17) that explores positive communication within what would seem a most difficult institutional setting, and yet, the health and wellness outcomes for self, relationships, and the institution are strong. Deal's chapter is situated within two institutional contexts—a prison and a college—in which prisoners and students worked collaboratively to script and perform a community theatre piece based on a synthesis of students' and prisoners' personal narratives. Interviews with prisoners and students, as well as community responses, revealed the transformative power of theater in giving voice to people in marginalized statuses, the rewards that come from civic engagement, and the empowerment prisoners experienced by the process of re-creating their "selves" through narrative performance and the many positive comments about their work. The organization and effort involved in creating the performance easily met Seligman's (2011) PERMA elements of well-being: The program resulted in several pleasant experiences (from retrospective interviews of "good" times to feelings of pride and happiness associated with the project), actors had to fully engage in the rehearsal process and performance, they fostered new and positive relationships between inmates and students, actors found meaning in the experience, and they experienced achievement with a successful performance.

Communication Strategies for Building Health and Wellness

As we begin to wrap up our chapter, we would like to take a cue from many of the works in positive scholarship and offer specific suggestions for ways to enhance well-being in healthcare, relational, and organizational contexts. We offer these with the idea that human beings are always a work in progress—we can continually practice the verbal and nonverbal communication skills that help create optimal experiences in health encounters, relationships, and institutions.

Early in the development of positive psychology, Seligman (2003) articulated the importance of assessment, intervention, and lifespan development in building the field and strengthening the three pillars. We reiterate their importance here and suggest their application to the field of positive communication. That is, we can use positive communication to (a) assess our strengths, (b) ask which strengths can be built and how, and (c) learn how to identify, nurture, and enhance each across the lifespan and within the domains of health, relationships, and organizations. Within the health domain, for example, health professionals incorporating a positive communication approach might use optimism to promote health and longevity, use intake interviews that help healthcare professionals identify signature strengths and ask questions about hope, love, joy, and vitality, and communicate in ways that encourage feelings of enrichment and empowerment. Diener and Biswas-Diener (2008) suggest for example that along with prescribing medication for physical limitations such as diabetes or high blood pressure, physicians can also probe patients for levels of happiness and when necessary "prescribe" activities that can help patients raise their happiness level (e.g., exercises on gratitude and savoring training; see Peterson, 2006). Seligman, Steen, Park, and Peterson (2005) found that positive exercises such as the gratitude visit, three good things in life, and using signature strengths in a new way (particularly the last two for long-term, sustained improvement) contributed to individual well-being. The strategies listed below have clear connections to the health communication field, but can also be successfully applied in relational and organization settings.

Take a "What Is Right" Orientation

Adopting a "what is right" orientation to annual or regular health check ups, toward relationships, and within organizations can be a powerful way to identify strengths. A "what is right" orientation is like a well-baby exam—probe for positive health, growth, and happiness indicators while at the same time identifying any trouble areas (Erickson, 2010). This orientation focuses on function rather than dysfunction across all life domains; strengths as well as weaknesses. Ask a patient, student, child, romantic partner, client, co-worker, or employee "what is right?"

Probe for Happiness

This is especially important in health encounters where we know that happiness and healthiness are related. "Probing your happiness is one of the most important things your doctor can do to predict your health and longevity, and to offer you advice on how to live healthier and longer. Yet few physical exams actually include this easy assessment" (Diener & Biswas-Diener, 2008, p. 29). Practitioners can also ask about other positive emotions and the extent to which they are experienced, like hope, love, joy, and vitality. Conversations that assess a person's feelings of hope and vitality could have strong implications for health and healing, but also work place satisfaction, ingenuity, and productivity.

Practice "Strength Spotting"

Positive communication, like positive psychology is more than repairing what is wrong, but also about identifying and nurturing what is good (Seligman, 2003). "Strength spotting" is a practice for positive psychology wherein the psychologist *listens* for character strengths and virtues in a presenting patient (Linley & Burns, 2010). In addition to listening for strengths in a short narrative, for example, the doctor/friend/interviewer can probe for strengths through direct questioning (see Table 1.2), as well as note nonverbal cues that might indicate true strengths (such as increased interest and enthusiasm talking about a an experience using a strength) and keying into signals that indicate a person has tapped into a particular strength (loss of time, increased vitality, rapid learning, high levels of repeated success, yearning to use the strength in different contexts, etc.; Linley & Burns, 2010). Strength spotting is important because people who report using their strengths also report higher self-esteem, self-efficacy, subjective well-being (or happiness), psychological well-being and vitality (Linley & Burns, 2010).

Table 1.2. Strength Spotting Questions (Linley & Burns, 2010, p. 10)

1.	What sort of everyday things do you enjoy doing?
2.	What makes for a really good day for you? Tell me about the best day that you remember having.
3.	What would you describe as your most significant accomplishment?
4.	When you are at your best, what are you doing?
5.	What gives you the greatest sense of being authentic and who you really are?
6.	What do you think are the most energizing things that you do?
7.	Where do you gain the most energy from? What sorts of activities?
8.	What are you doing when you feel at your most invigorated?
9.	Tell me about a time when you think that "the real me" is most coming through.
10.	Do you have a vision for the future? What is it about?
11.	What are you most looking forward to in the future?
12.	Thinking about next week, what will you be doing when you are at your best?

Consider Strengths

In generating health and wellness in all life domains. When we experience our strengths, we feel we are tapping into our authentic self. Our strengths are natural to us, helping us to achieve optimal functioning (Burns, 2010). Readers can assess their own strengths by going to the authentic happiness website (www.authentichappiness.com) and taking the on-line strengths tests. There are tests/questionnaires for adults and for children to assess strengths. Readers can also access questionnaires that measure work-life satisfaction, optimism, forgiveness, happiness, life meaningfulness, and life satisfaction. Taking a moment to identify individual strengths may also lead to better capacity to recognize strengths in others.

Identify Opportunities for Optimal Functioning and "Flow"

Identifying, using, and maximizing strengths can contribute to more frequent "flow" experiences. "Flow" is the state of being in an optimal experience where there is a perfect or near perfect match between skills, tasks, challenge, interest/motivation, and goals (see Csikszentmihalyi, 1997). Csikszentmihalyi writes that flow experiences "act as a magnet for learning – that is, for developing new levels of challenges and skills" (p. 33). Flow experiences often occur when there is a clear goal that requires specific attention and when outcomes produce immediate feedback. Csikszentmihalyi argues "if work and relationships are able to provide flow, the quality of everyday life is bound to improve" (p. 115). Flow is relevant across all life domains, as its presence increases quality of life in sickness and in health, in our relationships, and within our workplaces. Finally, creating opportunities for flow experiences in all three domains has the potential to exponentially increase quality of life.

Identify and Articulate Meaningful Life Goals

Hone in on important life goals; especially in discussing care options—quality of life, quality of living (Street, 2010). In health encounters, questions about life goals can help the patient and provider work together to create a treatment plan. For example, what can we do to maximize the good aspects of your health and well-being right now? In the future? What would you like to be able to do that can be reasonably achieved? Questions such as these place quality of life at the center of a treatment plan and foster a sense of empowerment. Emmons (2003) sums up this practice succinctly, "meaningful living, expressed as the pursuit of personally significant goals, contributes to positive experience and to a positive life" (p. 105). Emmons (2003) reports three types of goal strivings that consistently contribute to subjective well-being: intimacy goals (i.e., goals for close, reciprocal relationships), generativity goals (goals demonstrating interest in future generations), and spirituality goals (goals toward personal transcendence).

Set Manageable "Approach" Goals

An "approach" goal is one that is specific, achievable, and conceptualized as something "to do" rather than "to avoid" (Emmons, 2003). Emmons writes,

> goals are the concretized expression of future orientation and life purpose, and provide a convenient and powerful metric for examining these vital elements of a

positive life...goals are signals that orient a person to what is valuable, meaningful, and purposeful (pp. 106–107).

Moreover, goals research has demonstrated higher quality subjective well-being with intrinsic (e.g., personal growth) as compared to extrinsic (e.g., financial success) goals (see Emmons, 2003).

Conclusion

This edited volume makes a singularly important contribution to the practice of communication in three major life domains: health, relationships, and organizations/institutions. These life domains can be thought of as concentric circles, emanating from personal health, to relational well-being, and extending to the communities and contexts in which we doing our "living." Few texts cover such a range of communication contexts, and none with a focus on creating positive and healthy life domains. This volume is at once specific, generating communicative and interpersonal health and well-being through positive communication, and broad, tapping into three core areas of living and communicating. As such, this is an ideal text for both scholars and laypersons interested in surveying the fertile land of studies in positive communication. We invite the reader to now explore these areas.

References

Aune, K. S., & Wong, N. C. H. (2012). Fun with friends, pranks with partners: How we play in our closest relationships. In T. J. Socha & M. J. Pitts (Eds.), *The positive side of interpersonal communication* (pp. 143–159). New York: Peter Lang.

Baesler, E. J., Derlega, V. J., & Lolley, J. (2012). Positive religious/spiritual coping among African American men living with HIV in jails and/or prisons. In T. J. Socha & M. J. Pitts (Eds.), *The positive side of interpersonal communication* (pp. 259–276). New York: Peter Lang.

Baxter, L. A., Norwood, K. M., & Nebel, S. (2012). Aesthetic relating. In T. J. Socha & M. J. Pitts (Eds.), *The positive side of interpersonal communication* (pp. 19–38). New York: Peter Lang.

Bodie, G. D. (2012). Listening as positive communication. In T. J. Socha & M. J. Pitts (Eds.), *The positive side of interpersonal communication* (pp. 109–125). New York: Peter Lang.

Bryant, F. B., & Veroff, J. (2007). *Savoring: A new model of positive experience*. Mahwah, NJ: Lawrence Erlbaum.

Burns, G. W. (Ed.). (2010). *Happiness, healing, enhancement: Your casebook collection for applying positive psychology in therapy*. Hoboken, NJ: John Wiley & Sons.

Cline, R. J. W (2003). Everyday interpersonal communication and health. In T. L. Thompson, A. M. Dorsey, K. I. Miller, & R. Parrott (Eds.), *Handbook of health communication* (pp. 285–313). Mahwah, NJ: Lawrence Erlbaum.

Csikszentmihalyi, M. (1997). *Creativity: Flow and the psychology of discovery and invention* (1st ed.). New York: HarperCollins.

Diagnostic and statistical manual of mental disorders-IV-TR. (2000). Arlington, VA: American Psychiatric Association.

Diener, E., & Biswas-Diener, R. (2008). *Happiness: Unlocking the mysteries of psychological wealth.* Malden, MA: Blackwell

Duck, S. (2007). Commentary: Finding connections at the individual/dyadic level. In J. E. Dutton, & B. R. Ragins (Eds.), *Exploring positive relationships at work: Building a theoretical and research foundation* (pp. 179–186). Mahwah, NJ: Lawrence Erlbaum.

Dutton, J. E., & Ragins, B. R. (Eds.). (2007). *Exploring positive relationships at work: Building a theoretical and research foundation.* Mahwah, NJ: Lawrence Erlbaum.

Emmons, R. A. (2003). Personal goals, life meaning, and virtue: Wellsprings of a positive life. In C. L. M. Keyes & J. Haidt (Eds.), *Flourishing: Positive psychology and the life well-lived* (pp. 105–128). Washington, DC: American Psychological Association.

Erickson, B. A. (2010). What is right with him? Ericksonian positive psychotherapy in a case of sexual abuse. In G. W. Burns (Ed.), *Happiness, healing, enhancement: Your casebook collection for applying positive psychology in therapy* (pp. 29–39). Hoboken, NJ: John Wiley & Sons.

Floyd, K., & Deiss, D. M. (2012). Better health, better lives: The bright side of affection. In T. J. Socha & M. J. Pitts (Eds.), *The positive side of interpersonal communication* (pp. 128–142). New York: Peter Lang.

Frey, L. R., & White, A. B. (2012). Promoting personal, interpersonal, and group growth through positive experiential encounter communication pedagogy. In T. J. Socha & M. J. Pitts (Eds.), *The positive side of interpersonal communication* (pp. 297–312). New York: Peter Lang.

Gable, S. L., & Haidt, J. (2005). What (and why) is positive psychology? *Review of General Psychology, 9,* 103–110.

Kellett, P. M. (2012). The bright side of conflict: Dialogic communication, telesmatic moments, and deep narrative learning. In T. J. Socha & M. J. Pitts (Eds.), *The positive side of interpersonal communication* (pp. 179–191). New York: Peter Lang.

Kelley, D. L. (2012). Forgiveness as restoration: The search for well-being, reconciliation, and relational justice. In T. J. Socha & M. J. Pitts (Eds.), *The positive side of interpersonal communication* (pp. 193–209). New York: Peter Lang.

Kim, Y. Y. (2012). Being in concert: An explication of synchrony in positive intercultural communication. In T. J. Socha & M. J. Pitts (Eds.), *The positive side of interpersonal communication* (pp. 39–56). New York: Peter Lang.

Kreps, G. L. (2012). Engaging health communication. In T. J. Socha & M. J. Pitts (Eds.), *The positive side of interpersonal communication* (pp. 249–258). New York: Peter Lang.

Linley, P. A., & Burns, G. W. (2010). Strengthspotting: Finding and developing client resources in the management of intense anger. In G. W. Burns (Ed.), *Happiness, healing, enhancement: Your casebook collection for applying positive psychology in therapy* (pp. 3–14). Hoboken, NJ: John Wiley & Sons.

Linley, P. A., Harrington, S., & Garcea, N. (2010). *Oxford handbook of positive psychology and work.* New York, NY: Oxford University Press.

Lopes, M. P., Cunha, M. P. E., Kaiser, S., & Müller-Seitz, G. (2009). Positive organizational scholarship: Embodying a humanistic perspective on business. In H. Spitzeck, M. Pirson, W. Amann, S. Khan, & E. von Kimakowitz, E. (Eds.), *Humanism in business* (pp. 278-298). New York, NY: Cambridge University Press.

Lyubomirsky, S., King, L., & Diener, E. (2005). The benefits of frequent positive affect: Does happiness lead to success? *Psychological Bulletin, 131*(6), 803–855.

MacGeorge, E., Feng, B., Wilkum, K., & Doherty, E. (2012). Supportive communication: A positive response to negative life events. In T. J. Socha & M. J. Pitts (Eds.), *The positive side of interpersonal communication* (pp. 211–228). New York: Peter Lang.

McCullough, J. D., & Burleson, B. R. (2012). Celebratory support: Messages that enhance the effects of positive experience. In T. J. Socha & M. J. Pitts (Eds.), *The positive side of interpersonal communication* (pp. 227–245). New York, NY: Peter Lang.

Meyer, J. C. (2012). Humor as personal relationship enhancer: Positivity for the long term. In T. J. Socha & M. J. Pitts (Eds.), *The positive side of interpersonal communication* (pp. 162–177). New York: Peter Lang.

Miczo, N. (2012). Reflective conversation as a foundation for communication virtue. In T. J. Socha & M. J. Pitts (Eds.), *The positive side of interpersonal communication* (pp. 73–89). New York: Peter Lang.

Mirivel, J. C. (2012). Communication excellence: Embodying virtues in interpersonal communication. In T. J. Socha & M. J. Pitts (Eds.), *The positive side of interpersonal communication* (pp. 57–72). New York: Peter Lang.

Nussbaum, J. F. (2007). Life span communication and quality of life [Presidential Address]. *Journal of Communication, 57,* 1–7.

Nussbaum, J. F., Miller-Day, M., & Fisher, C. L. (2012). "Holding each other all night long": Communicating intimacy in older adulthood. In T. J. Socha & M. J. Pitts (Eds.), *The positive side of interpersonal communication* (pp. 92–105). New York: Peter Lang.

Peterson, C. (2006). *A primer in positive psychology.* New York: Oxford.

Peterson, C., & Seligman, M. E. P. (2004). *Character strengths and virtues: A handbook and classification.* New York: Oxford University Press.

Ragins, B. R., & Dutton, J. D. (2007). Positive relationships at work: An introduction and invitation. In J. D. Dutton & B. R. Ragins (Eds.), *Exploring positive relationships at work: Building a theoretical and research foundation* (pp. 3–25). Mahwah, NJ: Lawrence Erlbaum.

Richardson, J., & West, M. A. (2010). Dream teams: A positive psychology of team working. In P. A. Linley, S. Harrington, & N. Garcea (Eds.), *Oxford handbook of positive psychology and work* (pp. 235–250). New York: Oxford University Press.

Roberts, L. M., & Dutton, J. E. (2009). *Exploring positive identities and organizations: Building a theoretical and research foundation.* New York, NY: Routledge.

Seligman, M. E. P. (2002). *Authentic happiness.* New York: Free Press.

Seligman, M. E. P. (2011). *Flourish: A visionary new understanding of happiness and well-being.* New York: Free Press.

Seligman, M. E. P. (2003). Foreword: The past and future of positive psychology. In C. L. M. Keyes & J. Haidt (Eds.), *Flourishing: Positive psychology and the life well-lived* (pp. xi – xx). Washington, DC: American Psychological Association.

Seligman, M. E. P., Steen, T. A., Park, N., & Peterson, C. (2005). Positive psychology progress: Empirical validation of interventions. *American Psychologist, 60*(5), 410–421.

Socha, T. J. (2012). In a Southern minute: Messages, mindfulness, and pie—The 2011 Southern States Communication Association President's Address. *Southern Communication Journal, 77,* 2-9.

Socha, T. J., & Pitts, M. J. (Eds.). (2012). *The positive side of interpersonal communication.* New York: Peter Lang.

Spitzeck, H., Pirson, M., Amann, W., Khan, S., & von Kimakowitz, E. (2009). *Humanism in business*. New York, NY: Cambridge University Press.

Street, H. (2010). The why, not the what: The positive power of intrinsic motivations in client goal setting and pursuit. In G. W. Burns (Ed.), *Happiness, healing, enhancement: Your casebook collection for applying positive psychology in therapy* (pp. 40–50). Hoboken, NJ: John Wiley & Sons.

Wilson, S. R., & Gettings, P. E. (2012). Nurturing children as assets: A positive approach to preventing child maltreatment and promoting healthy youth development. In T. J. Socha & M. J. Pitts (Eds.), *The positive side of interpersonal communication* (pp. 277–295). New York: Peter Lang.

World Health Organization. Preamble to the Constitution of the World Health Organization as adopted by the International Health Conference, New York, 19–22 June, 1946; and signed on 22 July, 1946 by the representatives of 61 States (Official Records of the World Health Organization. No, 2. p. 100) and entered into force on 7 April, 1948.

World Health Organization (1997). *Measuring quality of life: The World Health Organization Quality of Life instruments*. Division of Mental Health and Prevention of Substance Abuse of the World Health Organization. WHO/MSA/MNH/PSF/97.4

Youssef, C. M., & Luthans, F. (2010). An integrated model of psychological capital in the workplace. In P. A. Linley, S. Harrington, & N. Garcea (Eds.), *Oxford handbook of positive psychology and work* (pp. 277–288). New York: Oxford University Press.

Section One
Positive Communication and Health

• CHAPTER TWO •

Positive Relational Communication: Impact on Health

Claire F. Sullivan
University of Maine

Positive psychology is a new field of study that focuses attention on the sources of psychological health and wellness as opposed to a focus on mental disorder and the dark side of life (e.g., Lopez, 2008; Seligman, 2011; Seligman & Csikszentmihalyi, 2000). Receiving inspiration from this new focus, positive communication scholars (e.g., see Socha & Pitts, 2012) are setting out to understand the impact of communication on health and well-being. A commonly cited definition of health was formulated by the World Health Organization (WHO) more than sixty years ago. It states, "Health is a state of complete physical, mental, and social well-being and not merely the absence of disease or infirmary" (WHO, 1946).

The link between relationships and health is complex. In 1977, George Engel, Professor of Psychiatry and Medicine at the University of Rochester, openly criticized the reductionist, disease–focused medical model, proposing instead the biopsychosocial model of health. This model illustrated that one's health could be influenced by diverse, interdependent factors from the social to the biological. Today, more than thirty years later, researchers find that close relationships do indeed have a profound impact on our health (e.g., Uchino, 2004, 2006; Umberson, Crosnoe, & Reczek, 2010). House, Landis, and Umberson (1988) summarized research showing that the association between negative social relationships and health is comparable with health risk factors such as smoking, high blood pressure, and lack of physical activity. People in close relationships, especially in large networks, tend to be healthier, happier, and live longer than those who are socially isolated (House et al., 1988; Umberson & Montez, 2010).

Both positive and negative relationships shape health outcomes throughout the life course and have a cumulative impact on health over time (Umberson et al., 2010). Early research tended to focus on negative processes in relationships (Uchino, 2004). More recently, researchers have been investigating the independent effects of both negative and positive processes in relationships (Reis & Gable, 2002). Although relationships have costs and benefits for health, in this chapter I will focus on the health benefits of positive communication and relationships. The chapter will highlight research on social support and communication within close interpersonal relationships, including important communication important to relational development and maintenance: self-disclosure, expressions of gratitude, and humor.

Social Support and Health

Positive communication in the form of social support has been found to protect individuals from numerous health problems, ranging from mild depression to cardiovascular disease and cancer (Cohen, Underwood, & Gottlieb, 2000). Hundreds of studies have established that relational support benefits mental and physical health (e.g., see Uchino, 2004). Much of the early research focused on how people maintained or restored their well-being in the face of negative events or stressors (Folkman, Lazarus, Dunkel-Schetter, Delongis, & Gruen, 1986). Emotional support in the form of social ties enhances psychological well–being, which, in turn, may reduce the risk of unhealthy behaviors and poor physical health (Kiecolt-Glaser, McGuire, Robles, & Glaser, 2002). Cobb (1976) defined social support as information leading one "to believe that he is cared for and loved, esteemed, and a member of a network of mutual obligations" (p. 300).

In a review of eighty-one studies of social support, Uchino and colleagues (1996) reported relatively strong and reliable evidence linking social support to aspects of endocrine, cardiovascular and immune systems. Later, Cohen and colleagues (2003) found that sociability was associated with greater resistance to developing the common cold when persons were experimentally exposed to a cold virus. This association was found even after entering multiple controls, such as preexisting immunity, age, season of the year, body mass index, and type of virus. Both the quality and quantity of social ties have been reliably related to morbidity and mortality (Cobb, 1976; House et al., 1988).

Social Support and Mortality

One of early findings of the health-support connection using mortality data was derived from an epidemiological study in Alameda County, California

(Berkman & Breslow, 1983; Berkman & Syme, 1979) that examined several types of social connections including marriage, contact with family and friends, and memberships in religious and other voluntary organizations. It was reported that social integration of healthy people was negatively related to later mortality. These researchers found that healthy adults who were socially integrated at the beginning of the study were more likely to be living nine years later than those who were more socially isolated. Those who lacked social ties were more likely to die compared with those who had more contacts. Findings persisted even after a variety of healthy behaviors and habits were considered.

The association between social support and mortality has been replicated in numerous community-based studies (Uchino, 2004). Brown and colleagues (2003) found that in older adults, providing emotional support to one's spouse was related to reduced-mortality over a 5–year period. Also, helping others, as opposed to receiving help, was found to be associated with improved longevity. The study was replicated in 2005 using a large ethnically diverse sample of older adults (Brown, Consedine, & Magai, 2005).

A few studies have examined the link between cancer mortality and social support (e.g., Fawzy, Canada, & Fawzy, 2003; Fawzy et al., 1993). In a landmark study, David Spiegel and colleagues (1989) found metastatic breast cancer patients with support group intervention lived an average of 18 months longer than did individuals given standard oncological care. Other studies have found beneficial effects of support groups but not survival differences (Chow, Tsao, & Harth, 2004; Coyne, Stefanek, & Palmer, 2007).

More recently, Holt-Lunstad, Smith, and Layton (2010) conducted a meta-analysis of 148 studies. The analysis included data from 303,849 men and women followed for an average of 7.5 years. The analysis indicated a 50% increased likelihood of survival for participants with stronger social relationships compared with those who had poor or insufficient social relationships. This finding remained consistent across age, sex, initial health status, and cause of death. The magnitude of the effect was comparable to smoking and alcohol consumption and exceeded other known risk factors for mortality including obesity and physical inactivity.

Cardiovascular Benefits and the Stress Response

Researchers have also investigated the impact of support on the stress–response system. Stressors can activate the sympathetic nervous system that elicits elevations in heart rate, blood pressure and secretion of the catecholamines, epinephrine, and norepinephrine, in response to certain stressful conditions. During stress, the hypothalamic-pituitary-adrenal (HPA) axis can become activated, leading to the release of the hormone cortisol. Prolonged activation of the stress–response systems can have severe impact on the body. Chronic exposure to stressors and the resulting exposure to stress hormones have been associated with a range of negative outcomes including, suppression of the immune system, damage to neurons, and increased depressive symptomology (Uchino, Kiecolt-Glaser, & Glaser, 2000).

In contrast, Uchino (2006) contends that supportive social ties may result in reduced blood pressure, heart rate, and stress hormones. A meta-analysis of twenty-one correlational studies found a small but reliable association between higher levels of social support and lower resting blood pressure (Uchino et al., 1996). Further, supportive communication appears to be beneficial for individuals after the clinical diagnosis of cardiovascular disease (Brummett et al., 2001). Only a few studies have been conducted on social support and cortisol responses to stress. However this literature suggests that social support could dampen HPA responses. In a video-relayed emotional support study, participants showed reductions in cortisol levels and heart rate during a cognitive challenge compared to those in the no–support condition (Thorsteinsson, James, & Gregg, 1998). In another laboratory study, individuals who had frequent interactions with supportive persons during a 10–day period showed reduced cortisol responses to a stressor (Eisenberger, Taylor, Gable, Hilmert, & Lieberman, 2007).

The fear of being negatively evaluated by others can interfere with the benefits associated with support attempts (Lepore, 1998). Researchers found that when there was no threat of being evaluated, the presence of a friend buffered cardiovascular reactivity (Kamarck, Annunziato, & Amateau, 1995; Kamarck, Manuck, & Jennings, 1990). It has been shown that a supportive partner does not have to be physically present to reduce cardiovascular responses to stressors. Just thinking about a close friend prior to a stressor can reduce systolic blood pressure responses in comparison to those who call an acquaintance on the phone (Smith, Ruiz, & Uchino, 2004).

Self–Disclosure and Celebratory Support

Within supportive relationships, self-disclosure affects health and well-being. Sharing personal information, not only results in increased affection but also reduced feelings of loneliness and isolation (Pennebaker, 1995). Using self-disclosure effectively is an important everyday skill and is significantly related to relationship success, marital satisfaction, and mental health (Jourard, 1971; Pennebaker, 1995). Disclosure of traumatic experiences also reduces stress as well as physical and mental health problems. Pennebaker and O'Heeron (1984) studied nineteen spouses who had been recently bereaved due to suicide or accidents. They found that people who talked more about the unexpected death of a spouse had better physical health during the year following bereavement than those who talked less. The more the participants talked with friends, the less they ruminated about their spouse's death. These findings remained intact even after controlling for the number of close friends one had before and after the death.

Disclosing personal information that had not previously been shared appears to have particularly important health ramifications. Pennebaker, Kiecolt–Glaser, and Glaser (1988) conducted a study on fifty healthy undergraduate students who were asked to write for 20 minutes about either personal, traumatic events or trivial topics for four consecutive days. Immunological data was collected at baseline, at the end of 4 days, 6 weeks, and again after 3 months. Autonomic measures (blood pressure, heart rate, skin conductance) were also collected at the same times. There were no differences at baseline between the two groups. Findings suggested improvements in health were associated with disclosing traumatic events. At the end of the study, the traumatic group had improved immunological response following the baseline compared with the trivial group. Further, high disclosers, who had not previously discussed the topic with others, showed a greater decline in both systolic and diastolic blood pressure compared with low disclosers. Therefore, those who wrote about topics that they previously held back appeared to reap the most benefit. The traumatic events group also had fewer health center visits compared with the preceding months after. These results supported an earlier study by Pennebaker and Beall (1986) suggesting that the disclosure of traumas is associated with improvements in immune function and physical health. Not only does talking impact health, but the act of writing and revealing traumatic disclosures can also impact both physical and psychological health (Pennebaker, 1993; Pennebaker & Beall, 1986).

A new genre of supportive communication has focused attention on the health benefits of disclosure of personal triumphs and good news to others (see McCullough & Burleson, 2012, for a new study of celebratory support). Gable and colleagues (2001, 2010) suggest that research on the social sharing of positive events is important to the overall understanding of the impact of self–disclosure on health and well-being. Capitalization (Langston, 1994), the process of sharing positive events with others, has received relatively little research attention compared with work on negative events. Personal health benefits linked to capitalization processes include increased positive emotions, subjective well-being, and self-esteem, and decreased loneliness (Tesser, Millar, & Moore, 1988). Relationship benefits associated with capitalization processes include satisfaction, intimacy, commitment, trust, liking, closeness, and stability (Gable & Reis, 2010). In close relationships, a partner's good fortune may be psychologically experienced as one's own. Langston (1994), found that when people shared positive events with others or celebrated that event in some way, they experienced greater positive affect, beyond increases associated with the positive event itself. Further, positive events communicated to others may be remembered better than positive events not communicated by helping to relive the positive event (Gable & Reis, 2010).

Recent work also suggests that processes linked to positive events may have independent associations with well-being and health compared with findings of traumatic events research (Ryff & Singer, 1998). The independent effects of positive and negative events on well-being are consistent with extensive research demonstrating the independence of appetitive and aversive processes (Gable & Reis, 2001). According to Carver and colleagues (2000) approach behaviors and positive affect (appetitive) are managed by one regulatory system while avoidance (aversive) and negative affect are managed by another. These two processes may be rooted in separate neurological processes (Sutton & Davidson, 1997). Further, positive emotions are distinct from negative emotions and are independently linked to health and well-being (Gable & Reis, 2010). Appetitive processes characterize behavior, motivation and affect associated with rewarding aspects of interpersonal relationships (Gable & Reiss, 2010). Sharing positive events with others may build social resources by fostering positive social interactions and strengthening relationships. A partner's response of genuine pleasure to one's capitalization attempts may increase a sense of connection. The greatest benefits of capitalization appear to occur when the person hearing the news reacts actively, constructively, and with enthusiasm (Gable, Reiss, Impett, & Asher, 2004). The benefits were even more pronounced when the partners recognized and validated the good news (Reis & Patrick, 1996). More negative responses such as stating the downside of a positive event or minimizing its importance can dampen or reverse the benefit produced by the positive event. Capitalization serves a different relational function with different outcomes distinct from that found in traditional social support research. The sharing of positive events in one's life are not thought to mirror the sharing of negative events (Gable & Reiss, 2010). According to Gable and Reiss (2010) successful social support leads to alleviation of negative outcomes, whereas successful capitalization leads to growth of positive outcomes. Not only do capitalization interactions positively impact the provider, there is reason to believe that this type of communication positively impacts the responder as well. Positive benefits are likely tied to gratitude and expressed appreciation (Algoe & Haidt, 2009; Gable & Reiss, 2010).

Gratitude

Gratitude is a positive emotion that can be thought of as the pleasant reaction that can occur when someone has intentionally and gratuitously done something costly and of value for us (McCullough, Kilpatrick, Emmons, & Larson, 2001). Wood and colleagues (2010) suggested that gratitude is part of a life orientation in which people notice and appreciate the positive in the world. With gratitude, it is not necessary for that action to be successful; it is often the "thought that counts." Thus, intention is one of the most essential components of gratitude (Emmons & Crumpler, 2000). The experience of gratitude has the potential to positively affect an individual's mental and physical health and may work to strengthen social bond

Although gratitude is often conceptualized as an internal psychological characteristic, through the expression of gratitude it can be viewed as having strong altruistic and collective benefits. Expressing gratitude can be rewarding to the benefactor and motivate people to do further good deeds (McCullough et al., 2001; McCullough & Tsang, 2004). When we feel gratitude we are more likely to return the favor to the original benefactor and expand the giving to others (Tsang 2006, 2007).

Only a few studies have examined the relationship between gratitude and physical health, but these studies give an early indication of an association. Gratitude may generally relate to health through the mechanism of stress reduction (Wood, Maltby, Gillett, Linley, & Joseph, 2008). In their experimental study, Emmons and McCullough (2003) found that those participants who kept weekly gratitude journals reported fewer physical symptoms, exercised more regularly, were more optimistic about the upcoming week, and felt better about their lives as a whole compared with those who recorded hassles or neutral life events.

Some data suggests that women compared with men show evidence of a more grateful disposition and derive greater benefits from the experience and expression of gratitude (Kashdan, Mishra, Breen, & Frohs, 2009). This may occur because of women's tendencies to view the experience of gratitude in a positive light. Research shows that men are less likely to seek help from friends, family, or medical professionals due to fears of being evaluated negatively and the embarrassment of being dependent on others (George & Fleming, 2004). As a result, women are expected to derive greater benefits from the experience and expression of gratitude, including building strong and satisfying relationships. The overall data indicate that women compared with men are at an advantage to reap more benefits, such as personal and relational well-being, social capital, and physical resources, from the experience and expression of gratitude (Kashdan et al., 2009).

Humor and Laughter

The final form of positive communication touched upon in this chapter is humor and laughter (e.g., see Meyer, 2011). Bennett and Lengacher (2006) make a distinction between humor, laughter and sense of humor. According to their definitions humor refers to as a mental process or as a stimulus intended to produce a humorous response while laughter is considered to be a psycho-physiological response to humor. A sense of humor refers to a variable psychological trait that allows people to respond to different types of humorous stimuli. Although mixed findings have been reported (Martin, 2001), humor and laughter have been shown to positively impact health and well-being. The work of Cousins (1979), Fry (1992), and Berk, Tan, Napier, and Evy (1989) along with the field of psychoneuroimmunology have frequently been cited to support the role that humor and laughter play in impacting one's health. According to these studies, the health benefits of laughter include improved cardiovascular and respiratory status and increased cognitive functioning and immune system performance. Humor and laughter have been shown to aid immunity by increasing the number of helper T-cells as well as the ratio of helper to suppressor T-cells (Berk et al., 1989). Humor has been shown to elevate mood and enhance the ability to cope with stressful situations while lessening the effects of depression (Lefcourt & Martin, 1986).

Research has shown that humor can have a positive impact on one's communication (Wanzer, Booth-Butterfield, & Booth–Butterfield, 1995) and relationships (Honeycutt & Brown, 1998). Those who use humor effectively are seen as attractive mates (Buss, 1988) and desirable friends (Wanzer et al., 1996). Humor is also related to quality of life (Thorson, Powell, Sarmany-Schuller, & Hampes, 1997). It has been found to be associated with less loneliness (Wanzer, Booth-Butterfield, & Booth–Butterfield, 1996) and higher self–esteem (Kuiper & Martin, 1993).

Humor research has shed light on the role humor plays in male's relationships. Research findings indicated that humor impacts men's level of self–disclosure (Olsson, Backe, Sorensen, & Kock, 2002). Humor is a common feature in male interactions, most commonly taking the form of competition–based joking made at the expense of others (Lampert & Ervin-Tripp, 1998) as well as self–deprecating humor (Lampert & Ervin-Tripp, 2006). An interview study of men with testicular cancer indicated that these men preferred joking to expressions of sympathy. They also showed that humor provided a means to disclose their illness and vent their feelings (Chapple & Ziebland, 2004). Men also used humor to distance themselves from the illness and to reduce their level of anxiety.

Conclusion

Many researchers from various disciplines have contributed to our understanding of the link between social ties and health. We know that people in close relationships tend to be healthier, happier, and live longer than those who are more isolated (Umberson & Montez, 2010).

Social support has been found to protect individuals from numerous health problems, ranging from mild depression to cardiovascular disease, stress–related disorders, and cancer (Cohen et al., 2000). Both the giving and receiving of emotional support appears to be important in building and maintaining social ties. Further, self-disclosure and expressions of gratitude and humor may be particularly important in building close, intimate bonds, resulting in health benefits. Finally, gender appears to play an important role in the strength of health benefits associated with positive communicative acts. The impact of gender differences in communication as well as other aspects of diversity on health outcomes should continue to be explored.

The link between communication and health is multi-faceted and complex. The independent effect of negative and positive communication in relationships must continue to be studied. It is important to understand the divergent processes in order to develop a more holistic view on the impact of communication on health and well-being.

Celebratory support and capitalization are important new areas of research worthy of increased scholarly attention. There are noticeable individual differences in people's ability and willingness to disclose personal information. Therefore, helping to increasing one's comfort level and skill in disclosing personal information may bring about further improvements in health. Continued research on both positive and negative self-disclosure is important to the development of integrated theories and models explaining the overall benefits of relational communication on health and well-being.

Communication skills are important in the process of mobilizing support and experiencing the health benefits of positive communication. Interventions can be developed to help people understand the important impact of positive communication in their lives. Participants can learn the skills needed to develop positive interactions and to help others to see how their ways of communicating impact their own health and the health of others. During these interventions, participants would practice the communication skills needed to create positive interactions and develop more satisfying personal relationships whether it is at work, at home, or in everyday encounters.

In this volume, communication scholars have set out to research, describe, and explore the role of positive communication in generating individual health and creating healthy relationships and organizations. In this chapter, I offered an overview of the health impact of positive communication behaviors including, social support, self-disclosure, gratitude, and humor.

References

Algoe, S. B., & Haidt, J. D. (2009). Witnessing excellence in action: The "other-praising" emotions of elevation, gratitude, and admiration. *Journal of Positive Psychology, 4*, 105–127.

Bennett, M. P., & Lengacher, C. A. (2006). Humor and laughter may influence health: History and background. *Evidence-Based Complementary and Alternative Medicine, 3*(1), 61–63.

Berk, L., Tan S., Napier, B., & Evy, W. (1989). Eustress of mirthful laughter modifies natural killer cell activity. *Clinical Research, 37*, 115A.

Berkman, L. F., & Breslow, L. (1983). *Health and ways of living: The Alameda County Study.* New York: Oxford University Press.

Berkman, L. F., & Syme, L. (1979). Social networks, host resistance, and mortality: A nine-year follow-up study of Alameda County residents. *American Journal of Epidemiology, 117*, 1003–1009.

Brown, S. L., Nesse, R .M., Vinokur, A. D., & Smith, D. M. (2003). Providing social support may be more beneficial than receiving it: Results from a prospective study of mortality. *Psychological Science, 14*, 320–327.

Brown, W. M., Consedine, N. S., & Magai, C. (2005). Altruism relates to health in an ethnically diverse sample of older adults. *Journals of Gerontology: Series B: Psychological Sciences & Social Sciences, 60*, 143–152.

Brummett, B. H., Barefoot, J. C., Siegler, I. C., Clapp–Channing, N. E., Lytle, B. L., Bosworth, H. B., Williams, R. B., & Mark, D. B. (2001). Characteristics of socially isolated patients with coronary artery disease who are at elevated risk for mortality. *Psychosomatic Medicine, 63*, 267–272.

Buss, D. M., (1998). The evolution of human intrasexual competition: Tactics of mate attraction. *Journal of Personality and Social Psychology, 54*, 616–628.

Chapple, A., & Ziebland, S. (2004). The role of humor for men with testicular cancer. *Qualitative Health Research, 14*, 1123–1139.

Chow, E., Tsao, M. N., & Harth, T. (2004). Does psychosocial intervention improve survival in cancer? A meta–analysis. *Palliative Medicine, 18*, 25–31.

Cobb, S. (1976). Social support as a moderator of life stress. *Psychosomatic Medicine, 38*, 300–314.

Cohen, S., Doyle, W.J., Turner, R. B., Alper, C. M., & Skoner, D. P. (2003). Sociability and susceptibility to the common cold. *Psychological Science, 14*, 389–395.

Cohen, S., Underwood, L. G., & Gottlieb, B. H. (2000). *Social support measurement and interventions.* New York: Oxford University Press.

Cousins, N. (1979). *Anatomy of an illness perceived by the patient.* Toronto: Bantam Press.

Coyne, J. C., Stefanek, M., & Palmer, S. C. (2007). Psychotherapy and survival in cancer: The

conflict between hope and evidence. *Psychological Bulletin, 133*(3), 367–394.
Eisenberger, N. I., Taylor, S. E., Gable, S. L., Hilmert, C. J., & Lieberman, M. D. (2007). Neural pathways link social support to attenuated neuroendocrine stress response. *Neuro-Image, 35*, 1601–1612.
Emmons, R. A., & Crumpler, C. A. (2000). Gratitude as human strength: Appraising the evidence. *Journal of Social and Clinical Psychology, 19*, 56–69.
Emmons, R. A., & McCullough, M. E. (2003). Counting blessings versus burdens: An experimental investigation of gratitude and subjective wellbeing. *Journal of Personality and Social Psychology, 84*, 377–389.
Engel, G. L. (1977). The need for a new medical model: A challenge for biomedicine. *Science, 196*, 129–136.
Fawzy, F. I., Canada, A. L., & Fawzy, N. W. (2003). Malignant melanoma: Effects of a brief, structured psychiatric intervention on survival and recurrence at 10-year follow-up. *Archives of General Psychiatry, 60*, 100–103.
Fawzy, F. I., Fawzy, N. W., Hyun, C. S., Elashoff, R., Guthrie, D., & Fahey, J. L. (1993). Malignant melanoma: Effects of an early structured psychiatric intervention, coping, and affective state on recurrence and survival 6 years later. *Archives of General Psychiatry, 50*, 681–689.
Folkman, S., Lazarus, R. S., Dunkel–Schetter, C., Delongis, A., & Gruen, R. J. (1986). Dynamics of a stressful encounter: Cognitive appraisal, coping, and encounter outcomes. *Journal of Personality and Social Psychology, 50*, 992–1003.
Fry, W. F. (1992). The psychological effects of humor, mirth and laughter. *Journal of the American Medical Association, 207*, 1857–1858.
Gable, S. L., & Reis, H. T. (2001). Appetitive and aversive social interaction. In J. Harvey & A. Wenzel (Eds.), *Close romantic relationships: Maintenance and enhancement* (pp. 169–194). Mahwah, NJ: Erlbaum.
Gable, S. L., & Reis, H. T. (2010). Good news! Capitalizing on positive events in an interpersonal context. In M. P. Zanna (Ed.), *Advances in experimental social psychology* (vol. 42, pp. 195–257). San Diego, CA: Elsevier Academic Press.
Gable, S. L., Reis, H. T., Impett, E., & Asher, E. R. (2004). What do you do when things go right? The intrapersonal and interpersonal benefits of sharing positive events. *Journal of Personality and Social Psychology, 87*, 228–245.
George, A., & Fleming, P. (2004). Factors affecting men's help–seeking in the early detection of prostate cancer: Implications for health promotion. *Journal of Men's Health and Gender, 1*, 345–352.
Glynn, L. M., Christenfeld, N., & Gerin, W. (1999). Gender, social support, and responses to stress. *Psychosomatic Medicine, 61*, 234–242.
Holt–Lunstad J., Smith T. B., & Layton, J. B. (2010). Social relationships and mortality risk: A meta–analytic review. *PLoS Medicine 7*(7): e1000316.doi:10.1371/ journal.pmed. 1000316
Honeycutt, J., & Brown, R. (1998). Did you hear the one about?: Typological and spousal differences in the planning of jokes and sense of humor in marriage. *Communication Quarterly, 46*, 342–352.
House, J. S., Landis, K. R., & Umberson, D. (1988). Social relationships and health. *Science, 241*, 540–545.
Jourard, S. M. (1971). *Self–disclosure: An experimental analysis of the transparent self.* Oxford, England: Wiley.

Kamarck, T. W., Annunziato, B., & Amateau, L. M. (1995). Affiliation moderates the effects of social threat on stress–related cardiovascular responses: Boundary conditions for a laboratory model of social support. *Psychosomatic Medicine, 57*, 183–194.

Kamarck, T. W., Manuck, S. B., & Jennings, J. R. (1990). Social support reduces cardio-vascular reactivity to psychological challenge: A laboratory model. *Psychosomatic Medicine, 52*, 42–58.

Kashdan, T. B. Mishra, A., Breen, W. E., & Frohs, J. J. (2009). Gender differences in gratitude: Examining appraisals, narratives, the willingness to express emotions, and changes in psychological needs. *Journal of Personality 77*, 691–730.

Kiecolt–Glaser, J. K., McGuire, L. Robles, T. F., & Glaser, R. (2002). Emotions, morbidity, and mortality: New perspectives from psychoneuroimmunology. *Annual Review of Psychology, 53*, 83–107.

Kuiper, N. A., & Martin, R. A. (1993). Humor and self–concept. *Humor: International Journal of Humor Research, 6*(3), 251–270.

Lampert, M. D., & Ervin-Tripp, S. M. (1998). Exploring: The study of gender and sense of humor near the end of the twentieth century. In W. Ruch (Ed.), *The 'sense' of humor: Explorations of a personality dimension* (pp. 231–270). London: Mouton deGruyter.

Lampert, M. D., & Ervin-Tripp, S. M. (2006). Risky laughter: Teasing and self–directed joking among male and female friends. *Journal of Pragmatics, 38*, 51–72.

Langston, C. A. (1994). Capitalizing on and coping with daily–life events: Expressive responses to positive events. *Journal of Personality and Social Psychology, 67*, 1112–1125.

Lefcourt, H. M., & Martin, R. A. (1986). *Humor and life stress: Antidote to adversity*. New York: Springer.

Lepore, S. J. (1998). Problems and prospects for the social support–reactivity hypothesis. *Annuals of Behavioral Medicine, 20*, 257–269.

Lopez, S. J. (2008), *Positive psychology: Exploring the best in people* (pp. ix–xi). Westport, CT: Greenwood Publishing Group.

Martin, R. (2001). Humor, laughter and physical health: Methodological issues and research findings, *Psychological Bulletin, 127*(4), 504–519.

Martin, R. A. (2007). *The psychology of humor: An integrative approach*. Burlington, MA: Elsevier Academic Press.

McCullough, J. D., & Burleson, B. R. (2012). Celebratory support: Messages that enhance the effects of positive experience. In T. J. Socha & M. J. Pitts (Eds.), *The positive side of interpersonal communication* (pp. 229–245). New York: Peter Lang.

McCullough, M. E., Kilpatrick, S. D., Emmons, R. A., & Larson, D. B. (2001). Is gratitude a moral affect? *Psychological Bulletin, 127*, 249–266.

McCullough, M. E., & Tsang, J. (2004). Parent of the virtues? The prosocial contours of gratitude. In R. A. Emmons & M. E. McCullough (Eds.), *The psychology of gratitude* (pp. 123–141). New York: Oxford University Press.

Meyer, J. C. (2012). Humor as personal relationship enhancer: Positivity for the long term. In T. J. Socha & M. J. Pitts (Eds.), *The positive side of interpersonal communication* (pp. 161–178). New York: Peter Lang.

Olsson, H., Backe, H., Sorensen, S., & Kock, M. (2002). The essence of humor and its effects and functions: A qualitative study. *Journal of Nursing Management, 10*, 21–26.

Pennebaker, J. W. (1993). Putting stress into words: Health, linguistic and therapeutic implications. *Behaviour Research and Therapy, 31*, 539–548.
Pennebaker, J. W. (Ed.). (1995). *Emotion, disclosure and health*. Washington, DC: American Psychological Association.
Pennebaker, J. W., & Beall, S. K. (1986). Confronting a traumatic event: Toward an understanding of inhibition and disease. *Journal of Abnormal Psychology, 95,* 274–281.
Pennebaker, J. W., Kiecolt–Glaser, J., & Glaser, R. (1988). Disclosure of traumas and immune function: Health implications for psychotherapy. *Journal of Consulting and Clinical Psychology, 56*, 239–245.
Pennebaker, J. W., & O'Heeron, R. C. (1984). Confiding in others and illness rates among spouses of suicide and accidental death. *Journal of Abnormal Psychology, 93,* 473–476.
Reis, H. T., & Gable, S. L. (2002). Toward a positive psychology of relationships. In C. L. Keyes & J. Haidt (Eds.), *Flourishing: The positive person and the good life* (pp. 129–159). Washington, DC: American Psychological Association.
Reis, H. T., & Patrick, B. C. (1996). Attachment and intimacy: Component processes. In E. T. Higgins & A. W. Kruglanski (Eds.), *Social psychology: Handbook of basic principles* (pp. 523–563). New York: Guilford Press.
Ryff, C. D., & Singer, B. (1998). The contours of positive human health. *Psychological Inquiry, 9*, 1–28.
Seligman, M. E. P. (2011). *Flourish: A visionary new understanding of happiness and well-being*. New York: Free Press.
Seligman, M. E. P., & Csikszentmihalyi, M. (2000). Positive psychology: An introduction. *American Psychologist, 55*, 5–14.
Smith, T. W., Ruiz, J. M., & Uchino, B. N. (2004). Mental activation of supportive ties, hostility, and cardiovascular reactivity to laboratory stress in young men and women. *Health Psychology, 23*, 476–485.
Socha, T. J., & Pitts, M. J. (Eds.). (2012). *The positive side of interpersonal communication.* New York: Peter Lang.
Spiegel, D., Bloom, J. R., Kramer, H. C., & Gottheil, E. (1989). Effect of treatment on the survival of patients with metastatic breast cancer. *Lancet, 2*, 888–891.
Sutton, S. K., & Davidson, R. J. (1997). Prefrontal brain asymmetry: A biological substrate of the behavioral approach and inhibition systems. *Psychological Science, 8*, 204–210.
Tesser, A., Millar, M., & Moore, J. (1988). Some affective consequences of social comparison and reflection processes: The pain and pleasure of being close. *Journal of Personality and Social Psychology, 54*, 49–61.
Thorson, J. A., Powell, F. C., Sarmany-Schuller, I., & Hampes, W. P. (1997). Psychological health and sense of humor. *Journal of Clinical Psychology, 53*, 605–619.
Thorsteinsson, E. B., James, J. E., & Gregg, M. E. (1998). Effects of video-relayed social support on hemodynamic reactivity and salivary cortisol during laboratory-based behavioral challenge. *Health Psychology, 17*, 436–444.
Tsang, J. (2006). Gratitude and prosocial behavior: An experimental test of gratitude.

Psychology, 3, 157–167.

Uchino, B. N. (2004). *Social support and physical health: Understanding the health consequences of relationships.* New Haven, CT: Yale University Press.

Uchino, B. N. (2006). Social support and health: A review of physiological processes potentially underlying links to disease outcomes. *Journal of Behavioral Medicine, 29,* 377–387.

Uchino, B. N., Cacioppo, J. T., & Kiecolt–Glaser, J. K. (1996). The relationship between social support and physiological processes: A review with emphasis on underlying mechanisms and implications for health. *Psychological Bulletin, 119,* 488–531.

Uchino, B. N., Kiecolt–Glaser, J. K. & Glaser, R. (2000). Psychological modulation of cellular immunity. In J. T. Cacioppo, L. G. Tassinary, & G. G. Berntson (Eds.), *Handbook of psychophysiology* (pp. 397–424). New York: Cambridge University Press.

Umberson, D., Crosnoe, R., & Reczek, (2010). Social relationships and health behaviors across the life course. *Annual Review of Sociology, 36,* 139–157.

Umberson, D., & Montez, J. K. (2010). Social relationships and health: A flashpoint for health policy. *Journal of Health and Social Behavior, 51,* S54–S66.

Wanzer, M. B., Booth-Butterfield, M., & Booth-Butterfield, S. (1995). The funny people: A source–orientation to the communication of humor. *Communication Quarterly, 43,* 142–154.

Wanzer, M. B., Booth–Butterfield, M., & Booth–Butterfield, S. (1996). Are funny people popular? An examination of humor orientation, loneliness, and social attraction. *Communication Quarterly, 44,* 42–52.

World Health Organization. Preamble to the Constitution of the World Health Organization as adopted by the International Health Conference, New York, 19–22 June, 1946; and signed on 22 July, 1946 by the representatives of 61 States (Official Records of the World Health Organization. No, 2. p. 100) and entered into force on 7 April, 1948.

Wood , A. M., Froh, J. J., & Geraghty, J. (2010). Gratitude and well-being: A review and theoretical integration. *Clinical Psychology Review, 30,* 890–905.

Wood, A. M., Maltby, J., Gillett, R., Linley, P. A., & Joseph, S. (2008). The role of gratitude in the development of social support, stress, and depression: Two longitudinal studies. *Journal of Research in Personality, 42,* 854–871.

• CHAPTER THREE •

Humor as a Tool, Not the Therapy: A Preliminary Model of Humor in Health Communication

Juliann C. Scholl
Texas Tech University

Many medical professionals associate humor with positive well-being, and humor has become a prevalent component in holistic health (Horowitz, 2009), which takes into account physical, emotional, psychological, and spiritual issues that affect one's wellness. Humorous messages can enhance persuasion and compliance (Coopman & Applegate, 2000; Meyer, 2000), increase one's likability (Lyttle, 2001; Meyer, 2012), gain cooperation (Simmons-Mackie & Schultz, 2003), enhance satisfaction (Wrench & Booth-Butterfield, 2003), and establish open relationships between providers and patients (Beck, 1997a; Bellert, 1989; Simmons-Mackie & Schultz, 2003). The use of humor even distinguishes physicians and surgeons who do not receive malpractice claims from those who do (Levinson, Roter, Mullooly, Dull, & Frankel, 1997). Humor can be a positive force in relationships (Meyer, 2012), and relationships between patients and providers are not exceptional in this regard.

Although health websites and practitioners stress, anecdotally, the need for humor in the healing process, very little empirical research exists to support humor's measurable impacts (although see Babrow & Dinn, 2005; Resnick, 1996; Wanzer, Booth-Butterfield, & Booth-Butterfield, 2005). In particular, research has yet to measure extensively humor's impact on physical health outcomes (Babrow & Dinn, 2005; Simmons-Mackie & Schultz, 2003). Given that different kinds of humor appeal to various audiences (Linn & DiMatteo, 1983; Sala, Krupat, & Roter, 2002; Simon,

1990), there could be some confusion as to what effects humor actual has, and conceptualizations of health-related humor could be as varied as the contexts in which in occurs.

Despite the extensive research addressing the physical, cognitive, and behavioral issues of therapeutic humor, much still needs to be learned about how decisions regarding humor use relate to positivity of mind and subsequently affect health outcomes, especially when its use needs to be adapted for different medical settings and individuals. To serve this end, this paper reviews various studies and literature examining therapeutic and medical humor in order to put forth a five-component model of health-related humor. These components of humor are *planning* (planned and spontaneous), *intent* (benevolent and malevolent), *modality* (verbal and nonverbal), *source* (provider- and patient-initiated), and *topic* (related and not related to the health issue). A humorous message that reflects certain levels of these components might result in an increased (or decreased) level of rapport between patient and provider, an enhanced level of physical wellness, or a more positive attitude resulting from the humorous exchange. Many interactions in the health setting, especially those between providers and their patients, are often emotional and stressful (Kreps, 2012). Humor can ameliorate the effects of these high-stakes situations by enhancing positivity and creating more feelings of unity (Meyer, 2012) and partnership between parties.

By acknowledging and incorporating various levels of each of these components, we might discover more concrete ways of using humor to affect more directly patients' health and well-being and bring about more positivity in health-related practice. Humor is not just for its own sake; it is the tool with which people in the medical setting can facilitate happiness and be advocates for patients' and medical team members' well-being. The preliminary model in this chapter is presented with the intent to move beyond understanding how health-related humor works and to encourage practitioners and scholars to see humor as a process to achieve a greater outcome, that is, to promote more positivity in the health care setting.

Humor as a Tool: The Benefits to Health

Health-Related Humor Defined

As construct, humor in the medical context can be very difficult to define; sometimes we do not know what humor is until we actually see or hear it. "Humor can be many things to many people, and a limited definition would include words such as amusing, caprice, or a funny state of mind" (Hunt, 1993, p. 35). Norman Cousins (1979, 1989) was among the first to popularize therapeutic humor, claiming that he was able to treat his own debilitating disease using laughter. We know far less about what humor *is* than we do about its effects—respiratory, cardiovascular, nervous, immune, muscle, and digestive (Buxman, 2000). To some, more important than a definition of humor might be that laughter reduces pain (Davidhizar & Shearer, 1996; Franzini, 2001), provides cardiovascular benefits (Arnett, 1998); relaxes muscles (Van Wormer & Boes, 1997), increases the release of beneficial hormones (Berk et al., 1989; Franzini, 2001; Lambert & Lambert, 1995; Martin & Dobbin, 1988), and instigates stimulation and relaxation (Herth, 1993).

Benefits of Health-Related Humor

There are many social and psychological benefits to humor and laughter in the health setting. Humor is positively related to self-esteem and the reduction of stress (Buxman, 2000; Franzini, 2001; Thorson, Powell, Sarmany-Schuller, & Hampes, 1997), and can add novelty and imagination to otherwise dull and mechanical communication efforts on the part of healthcare providers (Kreps, 2012). Psychologists, psychotherapists, and physicians use humor to decrease psychological distance (Bellert, 1989; Buckman, 1994; Simmons-Mackie & Schultz, 2003) and to promote openness (Minden, 2002) and connectedness (Marshall, 2004) between them and their patients. Moran (1996) observes that humor can help reframe an otherwise aversive medical situation. Humor can break the ice in situations where patients and families, faced with life-threatening illnesses, have to build fast relationships with the people who are helping them through a difficult time (Bellert, 1989; Buckman, 1994; Franzini, 2001; Marziah, McDonald, & Donahue, 2008; Merz et al., 2010). Humor can also strengthen relationships. Even when laughing at oneself or the other person, mutually shared experiences can enhance the immediacy both parties feel for each other (Meyer, 2012). This immediacy is just one path to happiness, which often represents the pursuit and achievement of a general sense of satisfaction (Socha & Pitts, 2012)—which is one of the key goals of providers and healthcare organizations. Although not synonymous with happiness, humor is a mechanism that can cultivate happiness and positivity within health-based relationships.

Humor has been proven valuable to psychotherapeutic interventions (Minden, 2002). Humorous banter can be used to treat obsessive-compulsive disorders by encouraging patients to recognize and appreciate the absurdity of their behaviors (Buckman, 1994). Paradox or absurdity can be especially helpful in allowing marginalized individuals to express their needs and to cope with mental illness (Buckman, 1994; Cardeña, 2003). Paradox therapy can help patients detach from such symptoms as insomnia, depression, or anxiety (Newton & Dowd, 1990; Simmons-Mackie & Schultz, 2003) by allowing them to entertain illogical notions (Buckman, 1994). The medical humor literature suggests that health care providers make sure patients are receptive to humor (Herth, 1993; Leiber, 1986; Schultes, 1997); make sure that the content of the humor suits the patient's age group or personal interests (Leiber, 1986; Robinson, 1983; Wender, 1996); get to know the patient's personality, age, interests, and so on; adapt the humor accordingly (Leiber, 1986; Robinson, 1983; Scholl & Ragan, 2003; Wender, 1996); and avoid sarcastic, aggressive, or abusive forms of humor (McGuire, 1999).

Whether humor is used as a tool to treat mental disorders or simply applied to ease tension during difficult medical interactions, it makes sense to draw connections between medical humor and the study of positivity and positive psychology. Among other things, positivity has been conceptualized in terms of the pleasant life, the engaged life, and the meaningful life (Duckworth, Steen, & Seligman, 2005), and has practical implications in most social contexts (Kristjánsson, 2010), some of which are health-related. For instance, Evans' (2005) found that the application of these and other positive psychological principles (e.g., building what's strong versus fixing what's wrong) could be applied to exercises used during brain injury rehabilitation. As part of Evans' study, patients engaged in such exercises as expressing gratitude to a helpful friend of family member, listing three good things in life, and identifying personal strengths. The relevance of positivity to these exercises were in patients' increased awareness in brain changes as well as a more coherent framework for developing therapy goals, addressing emotional issues such as guilt or anger, and accepting limitations after the injury.

Many of these exercises are related to exercises that can elicit humor and laughter. In their studies of a skilled nursing unit utilizing humor, Scholl (2007) and Scholl and Ragan (2003) found that as a result of such activities as storytelling, cooking, and board games, patients reported many spontaneous funny moments and the increase in positive attitudes. Such activities are consistent with psychologists Foster and Lloyd (2007) who direct their workplace clients to arrange positive experiences with family and friends, or to take part regularly in hobbies or other pleasant activities. Positivity entails a sense of well-being in both positive and negative circumstances. "Everyone who is seeking and striving for something is after some kind of well-being—something that makes them feel good and something that is evaluated as good and satisfying" (Wong, 2011, p. 75). Health-related humor has the potential to serve these ends.

Conceptualizing and Theorizing about Humor

Some researchers have developed and used measures to assess humor in coping with stressful and high-stakes circumstances. For example, the 21-item *Situational Humor Response Questionnaire* (Martin & Lefcourt, 1984) survey measures emotion-based coping by determining how people perceive humor in stressful situations (Lefcourt, Davidson, Prkachin, & Mills, 1997). The *Coping Humor Scale* (Martin & Lefcourt, 1983) is a more pragmatic measure of how one uses humor to alter a potentially stressful situation as opposed to taking a defensive stance to lessen a response (Lefcourt et al., 1997). There are also scales designed to be more specific to culture, such as the *Chinese Humor Scale* (Hsieh, Hsiao, Liu, & Chang, 2005), which indexes "humorous creativity," "tendency to laugh," "perceptivity to humor," and "humorous attitude."

Besides instruments that measure perceptions of or tendencies toward humor, other scholars have studied and classified different forms of humor. For instance, there are jokes, wit, laughter, joking, comedy, kidding, teasing, clowning, mimicking, and satire (Davidhizar & Giger, 1995; Robinson, 1999). Humor might also be viewed in terms of its different uses or functions, such as coping and expressing frustration (Minden, 2002; Sala et al., 2002; Sayre, 2001; Simon, 1990).

Theories exist to explain how humor operates and manifests itself in certain contexts. For instance, Freud (Freud, 1909, cited in Robinson, 1999) contended that many of our impulses become repressed by society; however, humor allows us to indulge those impulses in a socially acceptable manner (Freud, 1960). This idea is also expressed through Berlyne's (1969) Arousal-Relief theory, which posits that emotional energy is generally arousing and that humans have an innate need to release this energy, often resulting in laughter. Something that is funny brings about increased arousal (e.g., pleasure) and is then followed by a punch line or resolution, thus decreasing the arousal.

Other theories of humor include superiority theory and disparagement theory (Wolff, Smith, & Murray, 1934; Zillman, 1983). Laughing at mistakes or stupidity often makes us feel superior, which might appear derogatory and malicious (Robinson, 1999). However, laughing at imperfections—especially our own—might be uplifting as well as elicit feelings of empathy (Sayre, 2001). du Pré (1997) refers to this process as liberation. Related to liberation is the notion of surprise or revelation (Goshen-Gottstein, 1994) or a respite from the current aversive situation (Robinson, 1999; Simmons-Mackie & Schultz, 2003). Surprise lowers one's defenses and clears the way for new observations and sensitivities. To put forward a more unifying theory of humor, du Pré (1997) proposes surprise liberation theory, which argues that, "to consider something funny, we must begin with an expectation, perceive a surprising deviation from that expectation, and experience the deviation as pleasurable and liberating" (p. 60).

The notion of surprise liberation might be related to incongruence or incongruity theory (Berlyne, 1960; Goshen-Gottstein, 1994; Sayre, 2001). Incongruity refers to pairing or connecting objects, ideas, or constructs that appear not to belong together at face value (e.g., thinking and saying, "This is fun" while at the same time experiencing an embarrassing medical procedure). However, a violated expectation or otherwise unfunny statement, gesture, or thought might seem humorous if placed in an incongruous context (Simmons-Mackie & Schultz, 2003) in a disjointed way (Robinson, 1999), especially if it is done to relieve embarrassment, pain or stress. For instance, in a qualitative study of couples' use of humor, Meyer (2012) concludes that incongruity helped explain couples' ability to cope with and adapt to unexpected life events, which allowed many of them to grow closer in their relationships. The notion of incongruity might transfer to patient-provider relationships such that both parties who are dealing with bad news, bleak prognoses, or unexpected problems might use humor to work through the difficult medical situation; such coping could be done to deal with unexpected events or uncomfortable circumstances in which patients might feel they otherwise do not belong.

Another perspective of humor is that of dual process (Cupchik & Leventhal, 1974; Leventhal & Cupchik, 1975), which stresses the outcomes of environmental cues (one process) and self-perception (the other process) on one's views of and reactions to humor. du Pré (1997) says, "The presence of other people laughing, for instance, is said to enhance the perceived humor of a stimulus" (p. 57). According to dual process, environmental cues might have a causal or indirect effect on the perception of humor. While some argue against making causal connections between the environment and laughter (du Pré, 1997), hearing other people laugh possibly encourages one to laugh as well (Provine, 2002). Scholl and Ragan (2003) found this to be the case during group activities in the skilled nursing unit. Patients themselves reported times when they felt compelled to chuckled or laugh when hearing or seeing other patients or volunteers express mirth and amusement.

Humor typologies or coding schemes can be useful in analyzing people's humorous talk. Simon (1990) utilized a framework of situational and coping humor in an attempt to find correlates of humor with certain indicators of health and morale among older adult patients. Among Simon's sample, situational and coping humor were found to correlate positively with perceived health and morale, but not life satisfaction. Coping humor was found to be the strongest predictor of morale, followed by socioeconomic status. Sala, Krupat, and Roter (2002) used a humor coding scheme to categorize humorous talk within patient-provider conversations. The humor was coded as positive, negative, or general humor. Their study revealed that physicians within highly satisfying visits used tension release, light humor, and self-disparaging humor—all of which were coded as positive. Negative humor was used more often patients in visits with low levels of satisfaction.

Despite the fact that there are over 100 theories and concepts of humor (Ziv, 1988) and about 80 psychological explanations for laughter (Provine, 2002), more situational theories of humor are warranted, particularly those that account for the multiple components of a humorous message executed in different medical settings. Such dimensions or aspects include motivation of the message source, verbal and nonverbal aspects of the communication, as well as the extent to which the humor is spontaneous versus contrived. Due to the high-stakes and emotional nature of the interpersonal health setting, it would be advantageous to explore the types of humor that yield the most benefits in the medical context. Treating humor as a health-promoting and positive factor in health-care communication might allow for more specific testing of the use of humor to enhance physical functioning and psychological health (Cernerud & Olsson, 2004). Moreover, clear conceptualizations of humor types might shed light on when and how specific tactics can be implemented, as well as with whom those tactics should be practiced.

A Preliminary Model of Health-Related Humor

The health-related humor model is the latest development in a line of research looking at humor as it occurs when patients and providers interact with each other. The first investigation (Scholl & Ragan, 2003) involved a grounded theory approach to understand how members of a hospital unit (which adopted a humor approach) came to understand humor and how humor emerged in this particular setting. In general, the results suggested that humor was more about positive attitudes and well-being rather than mere laughter, and that what facilitated good humor was extensive knowledge and personal interest in patients. These results spurred a subsequent investigation

(Scholl, 2007) which revealed evidence of humor as a means toward enhanced patient-centeredness.

Healthcare practitioners interested in using humor serve themselves professionally when they consider the underlying mechanisms that might drive a humorous message. The subsequent discussion of the health-related humor model does not just address what might elicit laughter, but also implies how one might respond to a situation and adapt the message to achieve greater positivity in health-related relationships and overall sense of wellness. The following model presents humor as a tool, which is merely one path toward the overall goals of health, happiness, and positivity.

Health-related humor can take the form of a joke or riddle, absurdity, accidental pun, mannerism, illogical reasoning example, exaggeration or hyperbole, or self-deprecating comment (Franzini, 2001). From here on, health-related humor refers to humor—spontaneously emergent or contrived—that is communicated during interactions within various healthcare settings (e.g., patient-provider interactions). When deemed appropriate, a care provider might use any of these tools in a variety of health settings to achieve positive physical outcomes. Humor is most likely beneficial when it is used in the right form and amount. "Valid and reliable measurement tools...need to be developed in order to quantify the subjective quality of humor" (Bellert, 1989, p. 69). To make more sense of these various humor tools and to progress toward measurement and conceptualization of humorous communication in healthcare, this paper proposes a five-part preliminary model that presents mechanisms that inspire most humorous messages. Organizing the underlying motives and meanings behind humorous communication might shed additional light on how humor is adapted for various health-related contexts.

Like all messages, humorous messages contain components that fluctuate based on the situation. The components in this preliminary model refer to aspects that vary or fluctuate based on amount, intensity, magnitude, or scope based on a communicator's assessment of and reaction to the person (e.g., patient) and/or context (e.g., routine medical examination). With further research and development of this preliminary model, these components could be measured and observed. With respect to humor, these components or aspects include: *planning, intent, modality, source,* and *topic*.

Each component of the model can be likened to different settings of a stereo equalizer (see Figure 3.1). A lover of alternative rock would alter an equalizer's settings to improve the sound quality of music and to bring out the qualities that are unique to this genre. If the listener is unhappy with how the treble sounds, he or she would adjust a component to change the quality of the sound. As with an equalizer, so too might the components of each humorous message be adjusted to fit each individual situation and produce quality, health-enhancing messages. If a communicator tells a sarcastic joke and does not like the nonverbal reaction of his or her conversational partner, she or he might adjust one or more things (e.g., adjust vocal tone, change the sarcastic tone to a friendlier one).

During the adjustment process, attention to particular components might vary according to the person with whom one is interacting, the constraints of the physical environment, or the demands of the social situation. These assumptions are in keeping with Waldron's (1997) interactive planning approach, which argues that plans are created and maintained when people socialize and communicate with each other. Interactive planning is a dyadic process that encompasses the "the management of goals through discourse, the role of relationships in message selection; the communicative mechanisms which facilitate coordination" (Waldron, 1997, p. 212). Specific to the medical context, some doctors have the goal of enhancing patient compliance, and they would be wise to adjust certain communicative mechanisms (use a playful instead of judgmental tone) to increase the likelihood of achieving that goal. The ultimate result might be the preservation of a relationship based on trust and respect. The mechanisms to which Waldron refers could be the five components, which are subsequently explained.

Figure 3.1. Health-Related Model of Humor

PLANNING
Planned- ----------|||---Spontaneous
INTENT
Benevolent ----------------------------|||---Malevolent
MODALITY
Verbal ---|||----Nonverbal
SOURCE
Provider-initiated --|||---Patient-initiated
TOPIC
Health-related --|||---Not Health-related

Figure 3.1. Health-related model of humor: Variations on the five components. The symbol ||| represents a level or degree at which a component is represented in a particular health-related humorous message.

Planning—as a component of the preliminary model and not to be confused with Waldron's (1997) interactive approach—in humor ranges from the contrived to the spontaneous (Franzini, 2001; Herth, 1993). Contrived humor examples include jokes, stories, or scheduled showings of comedy movies, funny quizzes, magic tricks, or puppetry (Franzini, 2001; Herth, 1993; Hunt, 1993). Compared to contrived humor, spontaneous humor is thought to be executed with much less forethought, if any (Herth, 1993). Spontaneous humor often emerges as unexpected mannerisms, clowning around, or elements of a situation that surprise individuals with their humorous implications (du Pré, 1997; Beck, 1997b; Goshen-Gottstein, 1994; Robinson, 1999; Simmons-Mackie & Schultz, 2003).

Exploring spontaneous forms of humor more in depth, Scholl's (2007) ethnographic study of humor in a hospital setting suggests that spontaneous forms of humor influenced patients' positive attitudes more than those messages that were "imposed" on the patients (e.g., knock-knock jokes, scheduled skits, etc.). Herth's (1993) in-depth interviews of 60 older adults living in a variety of home situations (e.g., private home, nursing care facility) yielded the theme of *preferred sources of humor*, which referred to comical everyday-life experiences, such as antics of pets and children. Perhaps play (Berlyne, 1969; Goffman, 1974) and incongruence (Goshen-Gottstein, 1994; Simmons-Mackie & Schultz, 2003) suggest the superiority of unplanned humor over more contrived types, especially when it comes to communicating with patients. Drawing attention to the light-sided aspects of everyday life might allow patients to focus more on their healthier days than on their current conditions, which could have positive effects on a patient's holistic health (Scholl, 2007).

Intent refers to the beneficial (positive) or harmful (dark side) impetus behind a humorous message. For instance, there is benevolent and prosocial humor (e.g., builds up one's self-esteem, elevates mood) as well as harmful humor, which often diminishes the other person's status or self-esteem (Herth, 1993; Simmons-Mackie & Schultz, 2003). According to Buxman (2000), helpful humor "raises self-esteem, includes people, reduces tension, is supportive, stimulates laughter with others, confronts stereotypic ideas, stimulates new ideas, and creates energy and a positive atmosphere" (p. 122). In this sense, positive humor serves as an invitation for the patient to be open and take part in the medical interaction. Hunt (1993) argues that positive or beneficial humor situations are those in which providers and patients can laugh together and no one is ridiculed.

Individuals vary in their perceptions of whether a particular humorous message is helpful or harmful, or how receptive they are to them. Receptivity is the extent to which one likes or appreciates the message, is inclined toward it, or even finds it useful and beneficial. For example, females have been shown to desire caring humor whereas males favor more aggressive humor (Crawford & Gressley, 1991). In general, ensuring patients' receptivity to humor is important for positive communicative outcomes (Abel, 1998; Bellert, 1989; Buxman, 2000; Franzini, 2001; Scholl, 2007; Scholl & Ragan, 2003) and demonstrates patient-centeredness by giving patients the final authority on the appropriateness of the humor (Scholl, 2007). Receptivity gives patients a voice in their care, even if just to satisfy psychological or interpersonal needs (Cooper et al., 2003; McCabe, 2004; Wanzer et al., 2004). Receptivity might also be enhanced when humor diminishes hierarchical differences between providers and patients (Sala et al., 2002; Saunders, 1998). In this sense, malevolent humor has serious implications in the health setting where status differences between patients and their providers are particularly conspicuous (Nussbaum, Pecchioni, & Crowell, 2001; Nussbaum, Pecchioni, Grant, & Folwell, 2000). Although not fail-proof, the de-emphasis of power disparities can help when patients anticipate painful or embarrassing procedures (du Pré, 1997).

Harmful humor includes ridicule, exclusionary messages, and comments that contain sexist or foul language (Herth, 1993). Harmful humor "lowers self-esteem, excludes or belittles others, creates tension, stimulates laughter at someone, perpetuates a stereotype, closes off creative thought, and focuses on negatives" (Buxman, 2000, p. 122). Additionally, more negative types of humor might contribute to lower levels of patient satisfaction (Sala et al., 2002). Another type of harm results when humor is used to deny or avoid a problem (Minden, 2002; Rosenberg, 1989). This might be cracking a joke to evade talking about a particular health condition or avoid an issue by saying, "I was only joking." In this case, a patient's humor might be an initial ploy to put attention on serious problem or illness, and should be interpreted as an invitation to the provider to discuss it. Unfortunately, such cues often escape detection (Sparks, Travis, & Thompson, 2005).

Some forms of humor that appear to be negative might actually be received positively. Simmons-Mackie and Schultz (2003) observed mild teasing and self-deprecation in aphasia therapy sessions that were often perceived as constructive or benign. The unexpected positive reaction to teasing or deprecation might reflect the lowering of one's resistance, hostility, or defensiveness (du Pré, 1997). Notwithstanding the potential risks of sarcastic humor, conceptualizing intent has implications for ridicule or sarcasm as masterful coping strategies (Robinson, 1999). Even when malicious humor is used to vent frustrations, health professionals and those charged with the care of patients need to recognize the potentially devastating effects of these humor types on the ability to administer treatment (Sayre, 2001). As with any humorous attempt, it might be advantageous to pre-test a message or activity before relying on it as a humor tool (Houston, McKee, & Marsh, 1998). For instance, some patients might be willing to provide their feedback on or initial reaction to a joke, story, or activity that a provider is considering using for therapeutic benefit.

Modality describes a method of conveying a message—verbal, nonverbal, or both. Humor that is more verbal could take the form of requests, questions, or descriptions, stories, or jokes (Scholl, 2007; Scholl & Ragan, 2003; Simmons-Mackie & Schultz, 2003). Often accompanying verbal forms are nonverbal cues, such as animated facial expressions, gestures, paralinguistic cues, body positioning, or pantomimes. Simmons-Mackie and Schultz (2003) reported aphasia therapy patients playfully sticking out their tongues at clinicians and therapists putting their hands to their faces in exaggerated gestures of exclamation. Additionally, providers' humorous nonverbal displays (e.g., scowls, eye rolling) could be coded as humor if they are normally uncharacteristic of their typical professional demeanor, which imply surprise (du Pré, 1997) or play (Berlyne, 1969). Incongruence (Berlyne, 1960; Goshen-Gottstein, 1994) could also explain the humorous impact of nonverbal cues. While verbal-nonverbal incongruity is sometimes interpreted as deception (Bavelas, Black, Chovil, & Mullett, 1990; Burgoon, 1985), such a clash might elicit laughter in the form of subtle sarcasm. For instance, a female patient might roll her eyes and joke, "That was fun," at the conclusion of her annual pelvic exam.

Eliciting laughter often requires both verbal and nonverbal cues (Linn & DiMatteo, 1983; Simmons-Mackie & Schultz, 2003). Soliciting a grimace might require a corny joke with exaggerated eyebrow and hand gestures. This combination might compel a patient to respond with an eye roll (nonverbal) and an, "Oh, brother" (verbal), which might reveal a patient's physical or emotional state. In Scholl's (2007) study of older adults, such reactions were often interpreted by staff as an indication that a patient was almost recovered from his or her illness (c.f., Sparks, Travis, & Thompson, 2005). In this case, modality does not just refer to the means (e.g., facial cues, playful verbal tactics) with which a message is conveyed, but how a recipient communicates his or her reaction (e.g., receptivity) to the message. Attention to modality can provide insight into the impact of health-related humor and its perceived effectiveness.

The *source* or originator of the humor is another component of health-related humor. In this preliminary model, source refers to the individual (e.g., nurse) who decides to initiate some form of humor to engage the other (e.g., patient). To illustrate, Simmons-Mackie & Schultz (2003) found that 82 percent of the humor in their study was initiated by clinicians. The source or originator might simply utter a joke to get a chuckle or attempt a message that spurs a more elaborate exchange in which the other person becomes involved. Their observations revealed that various nonverbal and verbal cues were used to elicit laughter from the client. Sala et al.'s (2002) study found that patients initiated humor attempts more often than physicians, and this finding was correlated with high levels of satisfaction during the patient-doctor visit. Some patients studied by Minden (2002) used or initiated humor to lash out at the health care system or to deny psychiatric problems.

Given that many patients feel hesitant to take a more active communicative role in their medical interactions (Nussbaum et al., 2000, 2001), it might surprise both parties when a patient says something outspoken or even teases the provider. This was evident in Scholl and Ragan's (2003) ethnographic observations of a skilled nursing unit. On many occasions, patients playfully teased the volunteer staff; other patients who observed the setting often reacted with surprise and subsequent delight. Dual process (Cupchik & Leventhal, 1974; Leventhal & Cupchik, 1975) might also explain how patients react to their cohorts' attempts to gain control through humor. A patient in a group setting might engage in humorous behavior and be observed by other patients. When the other patients witness positive reactions to the behavior, they might also interpret the attempt as funny and socially acceptable.

The mutual initiation of humor—when both interactants participate in initiating the exchange—can help patients and providers cope with face threats and taboo topics (Beck, 1997b; Saunders, 1998). For instance, Beck (1997b) discusses paradoxes in patient identity during gynecological exams. During one pelvic examination, the doctor asked the patient if she was doing okay, and the patient responded with, "Yeah"; the patient subsequently laughed at the question's absurdity. The doctor responded in kind and acknowledged the patient's discomfort and temporary violation of her personal space. In such an exchange, the mutual acknowledgment of the absurdity compelled both patient and provider to create humor through their talk.

Topical or *nontopical* refers to the extent to which humor pertains to the medical issue at hand. Topical humor might emerge as self-disclosure of anxiety about the illness (Sparks et al., 2005). Humor might be the only way patients feel comfortable talking about their medical condition. Nontopical humor—that which relates little or not at all to a patient's medical issue—

might be a spontaneous joke or lighthearted comment about the patient's family, which can be very effective in making the encounter more informal, help break the ice, and minimize any feelings of intimidation on the part of patients who those are feeling vulnerable (Scholl, 2007).

Humorous communication likely has underlying motivations that reflect the issues and context surrounding the message. Suppose a nurse is caring for a female patient about to undergo a breast biopsy. The patient has already been briefed about the procedure. She is lying face-down on the table awaiting anesthesia and the Valium the nurse gave her is starting to take effect. In a helpful gesture, the nurse decides to tell the patient a lawyer joke to liberate her momentarily from the upcoming procedure. The nurse might somehow consider the following factors: *Planning*—The nurse remembers hearing the joke the day before and decides on the spot to tell it, but makes sure she has the punch line memorized. *Intent*—The nurse knows the patient is a lawyer and assumes the patient enjoys a good jab at her own profession. *Modality*—The punch line is a play on words, so nonverbal cues are not important. *Source*—The nurse initiates the joke. *Topic*—In the nurse's mind, there is nothing in the joke about a breast biopsy or breast cancer. In the previous example, the nurse chose a joke she thought would require little effort for the patient to process. Also, the joke had to be planned just enough to avoid ruining the punch line and was intended to be playful. Despite the nurse's original intent, however, if the patient does not get the joke and/or becomes agitated, the humorous attempt might be judged inappropriate or detrimental.

Conclusion and Implications for Future Inquiry

The preliminary health-related humor model introduced in this chapter illustrates how humor might be understood as a decision-making process within various medical contexts. Individuals might apply these components to increase the likelihood of a positive outcome, even if it is simply to put the patient in a positive mood. As it currently stands, however, the model does not include an overt reference to outcomes, but rather, focuses on the planning and execution on the part of the person considering the humorous message. As studies examine this model further, and we understand more the potential impacts and outcomes of health-related humor, this greater understanding will likely lend itself to a more developed model that can account for the outcomes of health-related humor. Additionally, the outcomes go beyond the immediate satisfaction derived from a healthy laugh; they include an increased general well-being and sense of positivity and happiness that can be a part of virtually any patient-provider relationship. While the preliminary model primarily focuses on antecedent conditions for health-related humor, the model can be developed and be applied as an adaptable conversational tool. Evans (2011) notes, "In recent years, there has been a shift in the focus of [positivity] from understanding the factors that contribute to wellbeing to developing and evaluating interventions to improve wellbeing" (p. 117).

It is likely that the components contained in this preliminary conceptual model might serve as both outcome and predictor variables in future studies. One goal might be to develop generalizable claims about what demographic, psychographic, or communicative factors best predict the desired levels of one or more of the humor components. The five components might also serve as independent variables tested for their effects on such patient factors as mood, motivation, physiological response, and stress level. Just as Sala et al. (2002) found that satisfaction predicted the use of certain types of humor, it is possible that different types of humor will have an effect on satisfaction and other variables.

Health-related humor is something that virtually anyone can utilize and benefit from, regarding of individuals might think about their own tendencies toward humor or laughter. Humor in the medical setting is not so obscure that it can't be understood and measured for its potential impacts. Additionally, humor is a skill that might require practice in some settings to be effective and positively received. Nonetheless, rigorously tested typologies and extensive knowledge of humor might not guarantee positive outcomes, and the problems sometimes resulting from humor can be further exacerbated when misunderstandings from cultural differences emerge (Chiang-Hanisko, Adamle, & Chiang, 2009). Hunt (1993) argues, "A[n]...intervention cannot be effective if the attitudes of [providers] are obstructive or if positive reinforcement for the use of humor is absent" (p. 36). Rather, humor should always be appreciated and viewed as an inexact science. What we might be able to count on is the notion that humor can be most effective when it accommodates individual differences and is used with sensitivity.

Humor "is not a waste of time or a frivolous endeavour [sic]; rather it is a subtle and powerful method of furthering a positive experience...and relieving tension or frustration" (Simmons-Mackie & Schultz, 2003, p. 763). Continued research into the types and functions of humor in the health setting can improve communication and enhance positivity for everyone involved. Being able to predict the positive and negative outcomes of particular types of humor might prove valuable to individuals who are constantly searching for more methods of caring. Such advances can help us develop and improve a multidimensional tool that is a noninvasive, cost-effective, and reassuring method that can be used at the individual and group level (Horowitz, 2009).

The preliminary model introduced in this chapter can enable scholars and practitioners to develop and test humor-based tools that can have positive impacts on people's health as well as bring about more positive experiences with the healthcare system. Health-related humor is an easily-accessible tool that can facilitate not just laughter but general satisfaction and happiness in many medical encounters. Based on the preliminary model presented in this chapter, an understanding of the planning that might go into a humorous attempt can potentially produce a sense of positivity and happiness that is ultimately pro-social, spiritual, character building (Socha & Pitts, 2012). To conclude in the words of Buckman (1994), "Humor has the potential to enhance the development of basic trust so necessary to a relationship; it is upon this trust that we begin to truly communicate and build therapeutic relationships" (p. 13).

References

Abel, M. H. (1998). Interaction of humor and gender in moderating relationships between stress and outcomes. *The Journal of Psychology, 132*(3), 267–276.

Arnett, N. (1998). A laugh a day. *Surgical Services Management, 4*, 23–24.

Babrow, A. S., & Dinn, D. (2005). Problematic discharge from physical therapy: Communicating about uncertainty and profound values. In E. B. Ray (Ed.), *Health communication in practice: A case study approach* (pp. 27–38). Hillsdale, NJ: Erlbaum.

Bavelas, J. B., Black, A., Chovil, M., & Mullett, J. (1990). *Equivocal communication*. Newbury Park, CA: Sage.

Beck, C. T. (1997a). Humor in nursing practice: A phenomenological study. *International Journal of Nursing Studies, 34*, 346–352.

Beck, C. T. (1997b). *Partnership for health: Building relationships between women and health caregivers*. Mahwah, NJ: Lawrence Erlbaum Associates.

Bellert, J. L. (1989). Humor: A therapeutic approach in oncology nursing. *Cancer Nursing, 12*(2), 65–70.

Berk, L. S., Tan, S. A., Fry, W. F., Napier, B. J., Lee, J. W., Hubbard, R. W., Lewis, J. E., & Eby, W. C. (1989). Neuroendocrine and stress hormone changes during mirthful laughter. *American Journal of the Medical Sciences, 298*, 390–396.

Berlyne, D. E. (1960). *Conflict, arousal, and curiosity*. New York: McGraw-Hill.

Berlyne, D. E. (1969). Laughter, humor, and play. In G. Lindsey & E. Aronson (Eds.), *The handbook of social psychology* (2nd ed., Vol. 3, pp. 795–852). Menlo Park, CA: Addison-Wesley.

Buckman, E. S. (1994). Review of literature: Historical, theoretical perspective. In E. S. Buckman (Ed.), *The handbook of humor: Clinical applications in psychotherapy* (pp. 1–23), Malabar, FL: Krieger Publishing Company.

Burgoon, J. K. (1985). Nonverbal signals. In M. L. Knapp & G. R. Miller (Eds.), *Nonverbal communication: The unspoken dialogue* (pp. 344–319). New York: Harper & Row.

Buxman, K. (2000). Humor in critical care: No joke. *AACN Clinical Issues, 11*(1), 120–127.
Cardeña, I. (2003). On humour and pathology: The role of paradox and absurdity for ideological survival. *Anthropology and Medicine, 10*(1), 115–142.
Cernerud, L., & Olsson, H. (2004). Humour seen from a public health perspective. *Scandinavian Journal of Public Health, 32*, 396–398.
Chiang-Hanisko, L., Adamle, K., & Chiang, L. (2009). Cultural differences in therapeutic humor in nursing education. *Journal of Nursing Research, 17*(1), 52–61.
Cooper, L. A., Roter, D. L., Johnson, R. L., Ford, D. E., Steinwachs, D. M., & Powe, N. R. (2003). Patient-centered communication, ratings of care, and concordance of patient and physician race. *Annals of Internal Medicine, 139*(11), 907–916.
Coopman, S. J., & Applegate, J. L. (2000). Social-cognitive influences on the use of persuasive message strategies among health care team members. *American Communication Journal, 3*(2), available at http://acjournal.org.
Cousins, N. (1979). *Anatomy of an illness as perceived by the patient: Reflections on healing and regeneration.* New York, NY: W. W. Norton & Company.
Cousins, N. (1989). *Head first: The biology of hope.* New York: E. P. Dutton.
Crawford, M., & Gressley, D. (1991). Creativity, caring, and context: Women's and men's accounts of humor preferences and practices. *Psychology of Women Quarterly, 15*, 217–231.
Cupchik, G., & Leventhal, H. (1974). Consistency between expressive behavior and the evaluation of humorous stimuli: The role of sex and self-observation. *Journal of Personality and Social Psychology, 30*, 429–442.
Davidhizar, R., & Giger, J. N. (1995). Humor-care for the caregiver. *Caring, 14*(3), 64–66.
Davidhizar, R., & Shearer, R. (1996). Using humor to cope with stress in home care. *Home Healthcare Nurse, 14*, 825–830.
du Pré, A. (1997). *Humor and the healing arts: A multimethod analysis of humor use in health care.* Mahwah, NJ: Lawrence Erlbaum.
Duckworth, A. L., Steen, T. A., & Seligman, M. E. P. (2005). Positive psychology in clinical practice. *Annual Review of Clinical Psychology, 1*, 629–651.
Evans, J. J. (2011). Positive psychology and brain injury rehabilitation. *Brain Impairment, 12*(2), 117–127.
Foster, S. L., & Lloyd, P. J. (2007). Positive psychology principles applied to consulting psychology at the individual and group level. *Consulting Psychology Journal: Practice and Research, 59*(1), 30–40.
Franzini, L. R. (2001). Humor in therapy: The case for training therapists in its uses and risks. *The Journal of General Psychology, 128*(2), 170–193.
Freud. S. (1960). *Jokes and their relation to the unconscious.* New York: Norton.
Goffman, E. (1974). *Frame analysis: An essay on the organization of experience.* New York: Harper Colophon.
Goshen-Gottstein, E. R. (1994). The absurd statement in psychotherapy: The treatment of individual adults. In E. S. Buckman (Ed.), *The handbook of humor: Clinical applications in psychotherapy* (pp. 103–109), Malabar, FL: Krieger Publishing Company.
Herth, K. A. (1993). Humor and the older adult. *Applied Nursing Research, 6*(4), 146–153.
Horowitz, S. (2009). Effect of positive emotions on health. *Alternative and Complementary Therapies, 15*(4), 196–202.
Houston, D. M., McKee, K. J., & Marsh, C. (1998). Using humour to promote psychological wellbeing in residential homes for older people. *Aging and Mental Health, 2*(4), 328–332.

Hsieh, C., Hsiao, Y., Liu, S., & Chang, C. (2005). Positive psychological measure: Constructing and evaluating the reliability and validity of a Chinese humor scale applicable to professional nursing. *Journal of Nursing Research, 13*(3), 206–215.

Hunt, A. H. (1993). Humor as a nursing intervention. *Cancer Nursing, 16*(1), 34–39.

Kreps, G. L. (2012). Engaging health communication. In T. J. Socha & M. J. Pitts (Eds.), *The positive side of interpersonal communication* (pp. 249–258). New York: Peter Lang.

Kristjánsson, K. (2010). Positive psychology, happiness, and virtue: The troublesome conceptual issues. *Review of General Psychology, 14*(4), 296–310.

Lambert, R. B., & Lambert, N. K. (1995). The effects of humor on secretory immunoglobulin A levels in school-aged children. *Pediatric Nursing, 21*, 16–19.

Lefcourt, H. M., Davidson, K., Prkachin, K. M., & Mills, D. E. (1997). Humor as a stress moderator in the prediction of blood pressure obtained during five stressful tasks. *Journal of Research in Personality, 31*, 523–542.

Leiber, D. B. (1986). Laughter and humor in critical care. *Dimensions of Critical Care Nursing, 5*, 162–170.

Leventhal, H., & Cupchik, G. C. (1975). The informational and facilitative effects of an audience upon expression and evaluation of humorous stimuli. *Journal of Experimental Social Psychology, 11*, 363–380.

Levinson, W., Roter, D. L., Mullooly, J. P., Dull, V. T., & Frankel, R. M (1997). Physician-patient communication: The relationship with malpractice claims among primary care physicians and surgeons. *Journal of the American Medical Association, 277*, 553–559.

Linn, L. S., & DiMatteo, R. (1983). Humor and other communication preferences in physician-patient encounters. *Medical Care, 21*(12), 1223–1231.

Lyttle, J. (2001). The effectiveness of humor in persuasion: The case of business ethics training. *The Journal of General Psychology, 128*(2), 206–216.

Marshall, R. J. (2004). Getting even on the jest propelled couch: Humor and play in psychoanalysis. *Modern Psychoanalysis, 29*(1), 63–75.

Martin, R. A., & Dobbin, J. P. (1988). Sense of humor, hassles, and immunoglobulin A: Evidence for a stress-moderating effect of humor. *International Journal of Psychiatry in Medicine, 18*, 93–105.

Martin, R. A., & Lefcourt, H. M. (1983). Sense of humor as a moderator of the relation between stressors and moods. *Journal of Personality and Social Psychology, 45*, 1313–1324.

Martin, R. A., & Lefcourt, H. M. (1984). Situational humor response questionnaire: Quantitative measure of sense of humor. *Journal of Personality and Social Psychology, 47*, 145–155.

Marziah, E., McDonald, L., & Donahue, P. (2008). The role of coping humor in the physical and mental health of older adults. *Aging and Mental Health, 12*(6), 713–718.

McCabe, C. (2004). Nurse-patient communication: An exploration of patients' experiences. *Journal of Clinical Nursing, 13*, 41–49.

McGuire, P. A. (1999). Therapists see new sense in use of humor. *APA Monitor, 30*, 1, 10–11.

Merz, E. L., Malcarne, V. L., Hansdottir, I., Furst, D. E., Clements, P. J., & Wiesman, M. H. (2010). A longitudinal analysis of humor coping and quality of life in systemic sclerosis. *Psychology, Health and Medicine, 14*(5), 553–666.

Meyer, J. C. (2000). Humor as a double-edged sword: Four functions of humor in communication. *Communication Theory, 10*(3), 310–331.

Meyer, J. C. (2012). Humor as personal relationship enhancer: Positivity for the long term. In T. J. Socha & M. J. Pitts (Eds.), *The positive side of interpersonal communication* (pp. 161–177). New York: Peter Lang.

Minden, P. (2002). Humor as the focus point of treatment for forensic psychiatric patients. *Holistic Nursing Practice, 16*(4), 75–86.

Moran, C. C. (1996). Short-term mood change, perceived funniness, and the effect of humor stimuli. *Behavioral Medicine, 22*(1), 36–42.

Newton, G. R., & Dowd, E. T. (1990). Effect of client sense of humor and paradoxical interventions on text anxiety. *Journal of Counseling and Development, 68*, 668–672.

Nussbaum, J. F., Pecchioni, L., & Crowell, T. (2001). The older patient-health care provider relationship in a managed care environment. In M. L. Hummert & J. F. Nussbaum (Eds.), *Aging, communication, and health: Linking research and practice for successful aging* (pp. 23–42). Mahwah, NJ: Lawrence Erlbaum Associates.

Nussbaum, J. F., Pecchioni, L., Grant, J., & Folwell, A. (2000). Explaining illness to older adults: The complexities of the provider-patient interaction as we age. In B. B. Whaley (Ed.), *Explaining illness: Research, theory, and strategies* (pp. 171–194). Mahwah, NJ: Lawrence Erlbaum Associates.

Provine, R. R., (2002). Contagious yawning and laughter: Significance for sensory feature detection, motor pattern generation, imitation and the evolution of social behavior. In C. M. Heyes & B. G. Galef (Eds.), *Social learning in animals: The roots of culture* (pp. 179–208). New York: Academic Press.

Resnick, B. (1996). Motivation in geriatric rehabilitation. *Journal of Nursing Scholarship, 28*(1), 41–45.

Robinson, V. M. (1983). Humor and health. In P. E. McGhee & J. H. Goldstein (Eds.), *Handbook of humor research Vol. II. Applied studies* (pp. 109–128). New York: Springer-Verlag.

Robinson, V. M. (1999). *Humor and the health professions: The therapeutic use of humor in health care.* Thorofare, NJ: SLACK Incorporated.

Rosenberg, L. (1989). A delicate dose of humor. *Nursing Forum, 24*(2), 3–7.

Sala, F., Krupat, E., & Roter, D. (2002). Satisfaction and the use of humor by physicians and patients. *Psychology and Health, 17*(3), 269–280.

Saunders, P. A. (1998). "You're out of your mind!": Humor as a face-saving strategy during neuropsychological examinations. *Health Communication, 10*, 357–372.

Sayre, J. (2001). The use of aberrant humor by psychiatric unit staff. *Issues in Mental Health Nursing, 22*(7), 669–689.

Scholl, J. C. (2007). The use of humor to promote patient-centered care. *Journal of Applied Communication Research, 35*(2), 156–176.

Scholl, J. C., & Ragan, S. L. (2003). The use of humor in promoting positive provider patient interactions in a hospital rehabilitation unit. *Health Communication, 15*(3), 319–330.

Schultes, L. S. (1997). Humor with hospice clients: You're putting me on. *Home Healthcare Nurse, 15*, 561–566.

Simmons-Mackie, N., & Schultz, M. (2003). The role of humor in therapy for aphasia. *Aphasiology, 17*(8), 751–766.

Simon, J. M. (1990). Humor and its relationship to perceive health life satisfaction and morale in older adults. *Issues in Mental Health Nursing, 11*(1), 17–31.

Socha, T. J., & Pitts, M. J. (2012). Toward a conceptual foundation for positive interpersonal communication. In T. J. Socha & M. J. Pitts (Eds.), *The positive side of interpersonal communication* (pp. 1–15). New York: Peter Lang.

Sparks, L., Travis, S. S., & Thompson, S. R. (2005). Listening for the communicative signals of humor, narratives, and self-disclosure in the family caregiver interview. *Health and Social Work, 30*(4), 340–343.

Thorson, J. A., Powell, F.C., Sarmany-Schuller, I., & Hampes, W. P. (1997). Psychological health and sense of humor. *Journal of Clinical Psychology, 53*, 605–619.

Van Wormer, K., & Boes, M. (1997). Humor in the emergency room: A social work perspective. *Health & Social Work, 22*, 87–92.

Waldron, V. R. (1997). Toward a theory of interactive conversational planning. In J. O. Greene (Ed.), *Message production: Advances in communication theory* (pp. 195–220). Mahwah, NJ: Lawrence Erlbaum Associates.

Wanzer, M., Booth-Butterfield, M., & Booth-Butterfield, S. (2005). "If we didn't use humor, we'd cry": Humorous coping communication in health care settings. *Journal of Health Communication, 10*, 105–125.

Wender, R. C. (1996). Humor in medicine. *Primary Care, 23*, 141–154.

Wolff, H. A., Smith, C. W., & Murray, H. A. (1934). The psychology of humor: A study of responses to race-disparagement jokes. *Journal of Abnormal and Social Psychology, 28*, 341–365.

Wong, P. T. P. (2011). Positive psychology 2.0: Towards a balanced interactive model of the good life. *Canadian Psychology, 52*(2), 69–81.

Wrench, J. S., & Booth-Butterfield, M. (2003). Increasing patient satisfaction and compliance: An examination of physician humor orientation, compliance-gaining strategies, and perceived credibility. *Communication Quarterly, 51*(4), 482–503.

Zillman, D. (1983). Disparagement humor. In P. McGhee & J. H. Goldstein (Eds.), *Handbook of humor research* (Vol. 1, pp. 85–108). New York: Springer-Verlag.

Ziv, A. (1988). *National styles of humor.* New York: Greenwood Press.

• CHAPTER FOUR •

The Social Construction of Hope through Strengths-Based Health Communication Strategies: A Children's Mental Health Approach

Christine S. Davis
University of North Carolina at Charlotte

John Mayo
Beth Piecora
Tessa Wimberley
Success 4 Kids & Families, Tampa, Florida

I crossed the street in front of a burned-out church building, walked past the group of pot smokers, and rang the buzzer at the group home door. The case manager, Irene,[1] greeted me warmly and led me in. Roger, from the local community center and Brisa, the house manager, shook my hand as I introduced myself. Within a minute Maria, the youth with whom the team was working, slouched in.

"We're here to check Maria's progress," Irene began. She looked toward Maria, but Maria's eyes remained downcast, her hands folded in her lap. Irene pointed to the agenda. "First we'll talk about the strengths of Maria and our team. What strengths does Maria have?" "She's tenacious," offered Roger. Irene wrote on the flip chart. "She can follow through on things." He gave a recent example. "Here's one," said Brisa. "Just this morning, I came in the recreation room and she was sitting on the couch, reading. I said 'hello,' and she responded, 'I don't want to talk to you right now.' This is a

---

1. Names and identifying details have been changed.

strength because instead of getting angry at the interruption, she was honest with her feelings. I really appreciated that." She smiled warmly at Maria, and Maria responded with slight eye contact.

"Good!" Irene affirmed as she wrote on the flip chart. She directed the next question to Maria. "What strengths do you think you have?" Maria shook her head, but Irene gently pressed. "What about yesterday, when you were going to buy that CD but decided it wasn't worth the money? I'd say you were good at decision-making. What do you think?" Maria kept her eyes downcast, but she nodded, so Irene added that to the list before continuing. "What about strengths of the team? What is one strength each of you brings to this team?" "I have good access to resources," Roger offered. "I care about Maria," suggested Brisa. I noticed Maria had begun looking directly at the team members as they spoke.

This opening narrative offers an example of what's called a "strengths approach" as it is used in a children's mental health treatment team meeting within a children's mental health system of care (SOC). In contrast to traditional social service systems that focus on deficits when working with children, a strengths approach is a positive one which concentrates on the family's resources and talents, and uses them as vehicles for positive change as they help families help themselves. This approach takes a similar philosophy to the fields of positive psychology and psychotherapy, which suggest that building on positive things already in a patient's life (positive characteristics, emotions, engagement, meanings, talents, and institutions) rather than focusing on repairing and fixing negative attributes, is a more effective treatment for depression and other pathologies (Seligman, Steen, Park, & Peterson, 2005; Seligman, Rashid, & Parks, 2006; Seligman & Csikszentmihalyi, 2000). The strengths approach also has a philosophy similar to that of positive communication which is defined as "communication that promotes positive emotions and attitudes and benefits interpersonal relationships" (e.g., Socha & Pitts, 2012). However, the use of strengths in children's mental health treatment planning moves beyond both of these perspectives by moving past feelings and thoughts into the realm of using communication to enhance not just mood, satisfaction, and emotion, but the more tangible, day-to-day *functioning* of a person's life.

Thus, this chapter provides a practical understanding of the use of strengths in family service planning in SOC teams. This chapter will first explain the history and characteristics of the strengths approach in the field of children's mental health, particularly as it contrasts with more traditional medical models of care. We will then introduce our research which suggests a typology, or categories, of strengths-based communication strategies and examine the language that service providers use as they follow a strengths approach. We'll next talk about the strengths-deficit dialect and how this tension problematizes the use of a strengths philosophy when working with children and families. Finally, we'll discuss how strengths discourse can construct hope with children, families, and their providers.

Introduction to a Strengths-Based Approach

The SOC philosophy in children's mental health was developed in the past decade in response to criticisms of the health, social, mental health, and educational systems (Friedman, 1994). Mental health care systems following this approach take a holistic, contextual view of treating the child and family. This philosophy encompasses, among other characteristics, a collaborative interagency planning team which includes the child and family as full team members and—within that team context—a strengths orientation (Lourie, Katz-Leavy, & Stroul, 1996; Stroul & Friedman, 1986).

Practicing in a strengths manner—identifying strengths and using them as part of interventions for change—is an approach to treating children and families that differs significantly from more traditionally based ones, partly because the strengths perspective is a departure from the medical model's reliance on deficit language (Laveman, 2000). Providers practicing in this manner seek to develop the family's strengths by focusing on family talents, skills, possibilities, values, culture, and competencies that promote and enhance family functioning, instead of focusing on deficits and problems (Dunst, Trivette, & Mott, 1994; Durrant & Kowalski, 1993; Saleebey, 1996). When moving from deficiency (what's wrong with the child and family that needs to be fixed) to capability (what's right with the child and family that can be enhanced and built upon) language transcends problems and reframes an individual's (and family's) identity to a more positive one (Bronfenbrenner, 1979; Saleebey, 1996).

There is some criticism of the strengths approach to mental illness (Taylor, 2006), including that some adherents of this philosophy oppose the use of accepted diagnostic evaluation measures such as the DSM. However, people practicing this philosophy don't ignore problems, they just look at them a different way: they assess the needs but rather than focusing on them, they focus on strengths as pathways to solutions. While positive psychology advocates suggest that they are supplementing, not replacing, the deficit-based approach, some admit they are "challenging" the deficit model of traditional psychology (Peterson, 2006, p. 5), and Peterson and Seligman (2004) have actually developed their own DSM-modeled book that classifies virtues rather than disorders. Positive psychology advocates suggest what's good about your life is as important as what's bad and a focus on simply alleviating symptoms results in short-lived and less effective outcomes (Peterson, 2006; Seligman, Rashid, & Parks, 2006; Seligman, Steen, Park, & Peterson, 2005). Treating problems as personal deficiencies contributes to dependence, passivity, and disempowerment. Along with others, we argue focusing on strengths does just the opposite: helps empower and enable children and families (Dunst & Trivette, 1996).

Most children's mental health providers who attempt to follow a strengths orientation do so by conducting a "strengths discovery"—an exercise in which strengths of each team member are elicited and written down in a formal, rote manner. Simply listing strengths can be a good assessment tool, but by itself, does not effectively address family's needs. Providers are most effective when they use strengths to strategically move the family and team forward in a positive direction (Davis, 2006, 2008, 2012). Prior research identified a typology of seven strengths that, when used in child and family treatment planning, yields a strategic use of strengths: child and family talents, child and family resilience, child and family possibilities, available family and team resources, borrowed strengths, past or historical strengths, and hidden strengths (Davis, Mayo, Sikand, Kobres, & Dollard, 2007).

We next discuss our most recent research on how service providers using a strengths approach do so discursively.

Methodology

This research is based on an SOC site for children's mental health services in a major Southeastern city. This site, like over 100 others throughout the U.S., was funded by a grant from the Child and Family Branch of the Center for Mental Health Services (CMHS) in the Federal Substance Abuse and Mental Health Services Administration (SAMHSA) to implement and enhance systems of care (SOC). This site has been a graduated site since 2004, which means that they have completed their six years of funding from this program, and have since maintained the practice of SOC values through training, supervision, and implementation of strengths techniques at the direct service level.

These SOC programs are community-based initiatives intended to integrate mental health, social, and human services for children with serious emotional disturbances (SED) and their families. At the time of the CMHS grant, the children enrolled in services at this site ranged in age from 4 to 18 years, and had a history of psychiatric hospitalizations, physical abuse, sexual abuse, running away, suicide attempts, and substance abuse. Their biological family histories included family violence, mental illness, psychiatric hospitalization, criminal convictions, and substance abuse. Their diagnoses included ADHD, depression, disruptive disorder, adjustment disorder, and other major psychiatric disorders, with many children identified with multiple diagnoses.

Extending from our earlier research which identified a typology of seven strengths that can be used in child and family planning (Davis, Mayo, Sikand,

Kobres, & Dollard, 2007), this study sought to build on those results by correcting some shortcomings of that study's methodology, to validate or amend that typology, and then understand how actual discourse is used in construction of strengths.

The prior research (referenced above) was a longitudinal study measuring outcomes of children and families enrolled in CMHS funded services, which included observation of 118 SOC child and family team meetings and a case review of 65 child and family teams across four different agencies to assess fidelity to SOC principles (Davis, Sikand, Mayo, Kobres, & Dollard, 2007). While the sample was large and extensive, analysis was retrospective and based on field notes gathered for a different purpose, yielding information that was less detailed than ideal and that did not allow for analysis of actual discourse. In the research reported here, we gathered new data by observing and video recording ten recent children's mental health treatment team meetings in the originally studied CMHS-funded community. For this project, we used a volunteer and convenience sample of client families who had children with SED and who were recruited by referrals from case managers. The participants were purposefully chosen to provide a variety of child and family teams.

The ten meetings observed were with one independent case management agency. Two parents were in attendance in five of the meetings, one parent (the mother) in the other four, and one grandparent as caregiver was in one. From one to four youth attended the meetings. Most parents were married, although a few were never married and one was widowed. About half of the families were white (not Latino), and the rest were black (not Latino), Latino, Asian, and Native American. Most parents attending had less than a high school education, and the treated children were in elementary or middle school. About half of the families had been receiving mental health services for less than a year; the rest, from one to nine years.

Half of the meetings observed were maintenance meetings, that is, meetings with ongoing teams, but two were the initial meeting for the teams, and three were final team meetings, preparing the families for discharge. Most of the meetings were held at the family's home, but one was held at the agency office. The meetings were approximately one hour long, and the transcripts ranged from five to fifty-one pages long. Two of the meetings were conducted in Spanish. On average, the meetings had just five attendees, ranging from four to seven. In addition to the parents and children, meetings were always attended by a case manager (who served as team leader). Two meetings also included a therapist/psychologist, and three meetings also included one or two mentors.

Observers had little interaction with meeting participants and primarily videotaped the meetings from positions in the room removed from the discussion. The tapes were transcribed verbatim with non-verbal behaviors noted. Meetings conducted in Spanish were translated into English for coding and analysis. Participants gave informed consent and the study was approved by UNC-Charlotte's IRB. Participating team members were paid a stipend for their participation.

Data Analysis

For this research, we conducted a qualitative content analysis and subsequent discourse analysis of transcripts from ten treatment team meetings to identify strengths, validate or amend our original typology of strengths, and understand how actual discourse is used in construction of strengths. For the purposes of this research, we defined "strengths discourse" as *language used which refers to, suggests, or acknowledges something positive in the child, parent, family, team, or environment which can be used to move them forward in a positive direction.*

Qualitative content analysis describes elements in a message based on an existing coding scheme, and for our analysis, we began with the coding scheme of seven types of strengths developed in our prior research (child and family talents, child and family resilience, child and family possibilities, available family and team resources, borrowed strengths, past or historical strengths, and hidden strengths). Although we began our coding process with the existing typology, using an inductive approach to the data we left ourselves open to the possibility of revising categories or identifying additional ones.

To identify strengths and develop the typology of strengths, four coders conducted line-by-line coding of the meeting transcripts, as follows:

1. The first author examined the transcripts to identify instances of strengths discourse (times when strengths were mentioned or discussed). She compared these instances to the original typology, and noted when they did not fit into the proposed categories. From this she proposed a revised typology of 11 categories (see Table 4.1).

2. All four researchers met and jointly coded two transcripts, using the revised typology. They conducted line-by-line coding to identify instances of strengths discourse, then made a second pass through the transcripts to identify the category of the discourse. They conducted a negative case analysis to determine if additional categories should be added or revised, and made revisions to the code book definitions.

3. The four coders split into dyads to code the remaining eight transcripts, with each dyadic partner coding separately then each dyad comparing codes. Rather than attempting to reach a specific percentage of interrater reliability as in quantitative content analysis, taking a social constructionist point of view, we used a collaborative coding process called "peer debriefing" (Harris, Pryor, & Adams, 2012; Lincoln & Guba, 1985) in which individual coding differences were discussed and jointly resolved within the dyads.

Table 4.1. Strengths-Based Health Communication Strategies

Strategy	Description	Example
Identifying/ acknowledging positive child or family skills, talents, or competencies.	Skills, or things in which the child or family (or team members) have excelled in the past, or do excel in the present.	A child's math ability.
Mentioning positive (recent) past behaviors.	Specific behavioral examples of strengths exhibited in the past usually recent past).	When a child buckled down and did well on his assignment.
Finding positive interests for the child/family.	Things a child or family is interested in doing that would move them in a positive direction. (Interest strengths are often manifested in behavioral strengths, if a person is interested in something then does it).	A child's interest in crafts.
Identifying possibilities for the child/family.	Goals or dreams set in the *future* toward which the family and team are working. Goals which are *stated in the positive*— "What will it look like when things are better?"	A new home for the family.
Identifying available resources.	Financial, time, and knowledge resources available to help the family and team achieve their goals.	Assistance budget: re- source provided by community mental healthcare system. Psychological testing: school provides. Other types: environmen-tal, food/clothing, medical, vocational, transportation, educational, recreational emotional, cultural, social resources.
Borrowing strengths.	Positive characteristics taken from another person, or by the strengths of the intervention or treatment itself.	A teacher's intervention borrowed from other work done in other schools.

Continued on next page

Table 4.1. Strengths-Based Health Communication Strategies *continued*

Strategy	Description	Example
Uncovering hidden strengths.	Strengths that, on the surface, look like deficits, but could be turned around into strengths.	A child's aggressiveness could be a positive thing if he learned to channel it in a good direction.
Identifying strengths in the environment.	Positive things in the environment.	The fact that the family has a home with a mother *and* a father at home.
Identifying feelings, attitudes, or values that are positive/ helpful.	Attitudes or beliefs that are helpful for a family (or team member) to have (other than resiliency).	A family's desire to keep their family intact is a value strength.
Pointing out family resiliency.	Personality traits that enable a child or family to have survived so far in the face of difficult life circumstances.	A parent's persistence in obtaining help for her family. A parent's ability to remain calm in the midst of ongoing crisis.

Discourse analysis studies the content, delivery, and context of discourse, to understand how people use language to construct meaning. To conduct the discourse analysis, once the discourse was categorized into the revised typology (themes), we analyzed how language was used to construct meaning within each theme.

Results and Discussion

Typology of Strengths-Based Communication Strategies

In this research, we've revised and expanded the original typology of seven types of strengths and have now identified eleven tangible ways team members (including family members) enact a strengths approach to family services. Reminiscent of the "three pillars" of positive psychology, "positive emotion," "positive traits," and "positive institutions" (Seligman, 2002, p. xiii), together these categories comprise a preliminary typology of what might be called strengths-based health communication strategies. Overlap and interaction across the eleven identified strategies exists, yet this typology provides a framework with which we can approach training of case managers and other healthcare providers and from which we can develop and further test communication-based hypotheses. We will next discuss each theme, give a description and examples of each, and discuss how discourse is used to construct a strengths approach.

Identifying positive talents, competencies, or skills. The first theme, or strength-based communication strategy we identified, is to acknowledge positive talents of the child or family members. Talents include, for example, scholastic, musical, and sports talents (Dunst, Trivette, Davis, & Cornwell, 1994). Focusing on competencies supports the value that children and families are greater than their problems, and gives a foundation upon which to build goals and plans. Related to Csikszentmihalyi's (1990, 1999) concept of "flow," acknowledging their competencies provides opportunities for families and youth to use their talents, have enjoyable experiences, and feel in control. This communication strategy is the one most frequently identified in team meetings, and is elicited typically through a formal "strengths discovery" process in which the case manager goes around the table and asks each participant to list a strength of each other participant. With this strategy, the rote listing of strengths certainly has "feel good" qualities but does not appear to contribute much to positive progress.

> Case Manager: I guess grandma can read [Youth's] strengths.
> Grandmother: helpful, smart.
> Case Manager: Especially in—
> Grandmother: Especially in math.
> Case Manager: Yeah.
> Grandmother: Quick learner, good at video games...

Giving specific examples of positive behaviors. The second strengths-based communication strategy is to mention specific behavioral examples of positive things a family member, usually the "targeted" child, has done in the recent past. This type of strategy is a way team members tangibly reinforce actual behaviors, often of the youth, and frequently do so in "real time" as it occurs in the team meeting. This example shows how pointing out specific positive behaviors soon after they occur reinforces and acknowledges them:

> Therapist: I want to say [youth] has done an amazing turnaround since last Friday. ...We're seeing some changes and I was talking with [school counselor] today and she said you were much more receptive to talking to her. [Addresses youth] You were willing to talk to her. She...told me there was a problem in class today where one of the kids was trying to give you a hard time and you were [trying] to step away from it....I just think that's wonderful. I've seen some real big changes in that area. I think you're moving in the right direction. I'm really proud of you and I want you to know that.

Finding interests that move children or families in a positive direction. The next strengths-based communication strategy is to find things a child or family is interested in doing that would move them in a positive direction, such as having an interest in playing or watching sports. Interests are often manifested in talents or specific positive behaviors as a person interested in something is likely to do it. Distinct from possibilities (mentioned next), interests are short term or immediate things a person might want to do, as opposed to bigger picture, longer term dreams. While not goals or dreams, interests may be turned into goals that might lead a child or family toward a possibility or dream.

Identifying possibilities for the child or family. The fourth strengths-based communication strategy is to identify possibilities. Similar to "solution talk" (Berg & DeShazer, 1993; Fanger, 1993), this refers to goals or dreams set in the future toward which the family and team are working. This type of discourse uses imagery to orient the family toward what they have to look forward to, or what they can accomplish (Fanger, 1993). In this example, the mentor uses future tense language to move from the youth's problems to a vision of what life like will look like when those problems are improved.

> Mentor: When you start a family, you will know how to lead and guide your family in a positive way so that you will be able to provide what's best for them....One day you are going to be a man, you're going to have a house, you're going to have a wife, you're going to have children, and that those are things that you're going to have to learn to do.

Identifying available resources in the family, team, and community. The fifth strengths-based communication strategy is to point out financial, time, and knowledge resources that are available to the family, either from within the family unit, the team, or the community. Resources mentioned in the meetings include educational tools, information, recreational activities and organizations, community resources, formal supports (therapist, school counselor, police), and informal supports (mom, dad, grandma, step-parents, siblings). Recent research reports expansion of family resources (such as informal support and community resources), enhances the parent-child relationship, and reduces parenting strain (Cook & Kilmer, 2010; Kilmer, Cook, Munsell, & Salvador, 2010). Positive psychology (Peterson, 2006) suggests that "enabling institutions" (pp. 275-303) contribute to the fulfillment, purpose, safety, fairness, humanity, and dignity (p. 298) of the people with whom they are working. Of course, "supportive communication" within these institutions is what makes them a resource—providing instrumental support such as advice, for example, that is high in person-centeredness (acknowledgment of feelings in a sensitive manner), politeness, and appropriateness for the situation (MacGeorge, Feng, Wilkum, & Doherty, 2012). Teams often mention resources as part of goal setting—as a listing of what resources are available or needed in order to move toward the goal. Family members can serve as resources for other family members, which is an empowering acknowledgement.

Borrowing strengths. The sixth strengths-based communication strategy is to borrow strengths from an exemplary other person, or by the strengths of the intervention or treatment itself, such as in medical treatments (Groopman, 2004). This strategy differs rhetorically from simply listing a resource by actually lifting elements or characteristics of that resource and holding them up as an example, suggestion, or lesson. So, for example, strengths can be borrowed from the successes, failures, or mistakes of a mentor, another child or family who has overcome similar circumstances, or from a service provider. A teacher's intervention in a classroom could be borrowed from other work he or she had done in other schools, and a school staff's success in controlling a child's behavior could be borrowed from their experience with other children at their school. Strengths can be borrowed from a person who has overcome similar experiences, such as in the example below:

> Therapist : The other thing I asked (father) to do – and he has been doing it – is to talk about when he was a young man and people tried him or said things to him to try to get him going. How did he ignore it? How was he able to walk away from it and still have his pride intact and everything? So he's also been addressing that.

Remembering past or historical strengths. The seventh strengths-based communication strategy is to remember past or historical strengths. These are events or memories that are actually borrowed from the family's own history, such as "coming from a home that was stable," and "we stayed in one place." This category differs from the previous one—borrowing strengths from a person's past experiences in that—in this category—the past strengths are from within the family itself. This distinction is important, because past strengths help remind the family how they came to have their current strengths, what they did to achieve their goals and successes, and that these skills can generalize to the future. The following example is an exchange between two parents and the case manager reminiscing about what the family has done in the past to remain close despite their problems:

> Parent 2: We normally have this big Easter thing that we do, our family is so big with all of my kids and grandkids. We do relay races. All kinds of fun things. I've got videos that you cannot believe, doing three-legged races together, and stuff.
>
> Case Manager: And that goes back to the culture thing too of your family. Those are things that you remember.
>
> Parent 1: It's just one big happy family, if one needs something the other one's right there, it's all tight-knit.

Uncovering hidden strengths. The eighth strengths-based communication strategy is to uncover hidden strengths—strengths manifested, at least apparently, through undesirable behaviors, or which are hidden by negative behaviors or communication. The challenge is to identify these strengths and help the child channel them into more productive activities, or identify how the traits manifesting these undesirable behaviors can be redirected to become constructive. The opening narrative in the introduction to this chapter gives an example of a hidden strength. The youth said "I don't want to talk to you right now" and, rather than labeling this as antisocial behavior, the service provider acknowledged it as a strength. ("This is a strength because instead of getting angry at the interruption, she was honest with her feelings").

In this next example, this parent tells a story of resisting a teacher's attempt to label her child as learning disabled. She reframes the situation as one of the child being intelligent but not manifesting (hiding) those strengths because the youth is exhibiting resistance behavior.

> Parent: [The teacher] was very frustrated that she doesn't think [youth] was placed right....[Youth]'s placed just fine, she's very intelligent, and she could do the work, she's just not doing for her, because she's resisting because the teacher's demeanor.

Sometimes past strengths are hidden when—due to current difficulties—people have forgotten about strengths exhibited in their past. In one specific instance, reminding a woman of her past strengths re-energized her and helped her achieve progress toward her goals.

Identifying strengths in the environment. The ninth strengths-based communication strategy is to uncover acknowledge positive things in the family's own environment or culture. Characteristics such as "stable household" and "solid home," living in a community with resources, and being on a team with caring people remind team members, including family, there are beneficial things in their lives that can be built upon. In an environment where children can be removed from the home if child welfare (frequently involved in these teams) deems the home environment to be unsuitable or unsafe, acknowledging strengths in the environment is a very powerful statement.

Identifying positive feelings, attitudes, or values. The tenth strengths-based communication strategy is to identify positive feelings, attitudes, beliefs, values, "virtues" (Seligman, 2002, p. 133), or "character strengths" (Peterson, 2006, p. 142) helpful for a family (or team member) to have because they contribute to feelings of well-being, as well as eudemonic and hedonic happiness (see Socha & Pitts, 2012), and lead to future positive actions (Peterson, 2006), and perhaps therefore, a longer life (Seligman, 2002). Usually listed in the strengths discovery process, these include attributes such as "loves her family," "loving, genuine, concerned, and spiritual," "trusting," "generous," "motivated," and "he always puts his family first." Seligman (2002) and Peterson (2006) suggest the helpfulness of developing a grateful outlook on life, a will to be happy, and an attention to the positive.

Reinforcing family resiliencies. One specific positive attitude is called resiliency, and the final strengths-based communication strategy is to point out a family's resiliency. Resiliency is a personality trait that enables a child or family to have survived so far in the face of difficult life circumstances (Dunst, Trivette, Davis, & Cornwell, 1994; Richardson, 2002), such as the ability to survive in the face of chronic stressful situations, a sense of humor, a mother's desire to keep her family intact, a parent's persistence in obtaining help for her family, and a strong spiritual or religious faith. While life circumstances play a role in individual happiness, it resiliency in the face of negative circumstances that has been shown to have a powerful and positive impact (Socha & Pitts, 2012).

In the following example, family resilience is mentioned conversationally, as justification for believing the family's situation will get better, rather than in a rote listing. This conversational tone embraces the strengths orientation rather than simply complying with a mandate, and thus, is a more positive acknowledgment of the family.

> **Case Manager:** It's because of all these strengths that you guys have gotten through some rough patches. Because…you guys are very stable; if you weren't as stable as you are, it might be a little harder road.

Strengths-Deficit Dialectic

Evident in our past research about children's mental health treatment teams (e.g, Davis, 2008, 2012), and reinforced in the current study, is the struggle with the strengths-deficit dialectic. Dialectical theory says that individuals struggle with dialectical contradictions, relational phenomenon that are interdependent yet functionally incompatible (Montgomery & Baxter, 1998). This tension problematizes the use of a strengths philosophy when working with children and families. Team members, frequently including family members, have difficulty moving away from the child's problems. This makes sense, if strengths are seen as a rote listing of "nice things" that a parent who has come for help with a child might wish to move quickly through in order to address the presenting problem(s). This next example shows how difficult this shift can be for team members who are ensconced in a deficit paradigm—frequently, strengths language is cancelled out by deficit language, often in the same breath.

> Behavioral Analyst: [Youth] has exceptional skills.
>
> Case Manager: I know [youth] has exceptional skills. His want is lacking but he has exceptional skills.

In this next example, the parent both acknowledges a strength of the child and a deficit in the same sentence.

> Parent: He's smarter than he lets on, but a lot of stuff he thinks he knows 'cause he don't like learning new things.

In another strengths-deficit dance, this parent is stating a child's strength (being naturally intelligent and getting good grades) negatively as a deficit:

> Parent: One of his problems when he was at [school] was that he was not doing class work. The only reason he kept his grades up was because he can ace the test. He didn't do his homework, they didn't get turned in, he didn't participate in class work, but when it came to the test he would ace [it] which kept his grades up. So he's smart, he just wasn't always doing, if he had done the work he'd be a straight A student.

The following conversation is also interesting as the case manager seems to be scaling back the dream the child and family have by reducing the goal from "going to college" or even "graduating" to just "finishing school."

> Case Manager: Now what goal can we attach to be successful?...I think that you had just mentioned to graduate, to finish school.
>
> Parent: He wants to graduate. He wanted to go to college; he told me forever ago that he wanted to go to college.
>
> Case Manager: Okay, so [to] be successful...the goal would be to finish school.
>
> Parent: (As Case Manager writes "to finish school" on board) To graduate.

Strengths Discourse as Hope-Building

In this last section, we'll discuss how strengths discourse can help construct hope with children, families, and their providers. Hope can be defined as the ability to see beyond limitations toward dreams, possibilities, and desired goals, and to imagine one's ability to reach those desires (Kearney & Griffin, 2001; Snyder, 2002). We suggest teams—including family members and youth—use the language of strengths to construct hope for each other and themselves (see Davis, 2012). Hope theory (Snyder, 2000) sees hope as types of thoughts and suggests that hope results from the combination of motivation to move forward (agency) and the ability to find ways to reach goals (pathways). Hope theory also suggests that positive thoughts result in pursuit of goals and then positive emotions, and the more alternative paths people have to reach their goals, the more hope they have. We suggest that hope is not only a way of thinking but a way of communicating, and strength-based communication strategies construct hope because they discursively contribute to agency thoughts (resiliencies, possibilities, past strengths, positive feelings/attitudes/values) and pathway thoughts. Taken together, our array of strengths-based communication strategies reflect "pathways thinking"—the practice of "attach[ing] oneself to positive outcomes or goals" (Snyder, 2000, p. 6) by constructing visions of a positive future and creating ways to reach them. They move the attention from the past and present (away from problems or deficits) to the future, toward positive, concrete alternatives, options, and solutions (Lipchik, 1994).

Hope theory suggests that hope is learned (Snyder, 1994) and we suggest that strengths-based language contributes to the lesson: strengths-based language shows the child or family is good at something (or multiple things) they can use to help themselves and develop alternative pathways; is a reminder the situation is not completely bleak; moves the family out of a present-time focus—which is often problem and deficit laden—into a future-time focus; reminds everyone working with the family they're not in this alone—there are resources they can all rely on for help; and reminds everyone the family accomplished something before, therefore they can do it again. Borrowing strengths is hopeful because this also borrows hope—someone else could do this; this helped in another situation, therefore this will help here. While deficits and problems frequently reside in the past and present, hope resides in the future, and hope discourse resides in the future also. Hope moves children with mental illness and their families forward (Kearney & Griffin, 2001; Snyder, 1994, 2000, 2002).

Discussion

As this analysis shows, fully adhering to a strengths approach in providing services for children and families is quite a challenge. In the "real world," attempts to do this are derailed by problem-saturated language and the difficulty in seeing family and child strengths in the midst of the deficits, problems, and challenges with which the team is bombarded. Child and family teams exist because of the family's problems, but if those problems remain the main focus of the team, positive psychology suggests help will be fleeting.

We suggest using strengths language can help families construct hope by introducing ways of reframing problems and challenges. Our characterization of 11 strengths-based health communication strategies suggests useful ways providers can focus on family strengths. Overlap and interaction across the 11 identified strategies exists, and in fact, many of these strategies can lead to others. For example, interests lead to talents which lead to positive behaviors and goal attainment. This suggests that starting somewhere—beginning to identify and build upon strengths of some sort—is the key to constructing hope for the family. Focusing on a positive future leads to hopeful feelings, which leads to forward momentum, positive motivation, and more hopeful feelings (Averill, Catlin, & Chon 1990; Groopman, 2004).

Strengths language can be thought of as "hope discourse." Effectively used, strengths direct the team toward a future where hope resides; they provide resources, ideas, and suggestions the family and team can use; and they remind everyone positive change is possible. Focusing on strengths reminds everyone they are greater than their problems and provides a foundation on which to build goals and plans. Positive psychology suggests thinking constructs reality (Kelley, 2004), and people feel less stressed and more positive about problems or challenges when they know what they are working toward and believe they have the traits, capacity, and resources necessary to deal with the problems (Aspinwall & Tedeschi, 2010; Csikszentmihalyi, 1993; Seligman & Csikszentmihalyi, 2000). In fact, research has found positive beliefs and self-affirmations can actually be induced by others in people who do not already have them (Aspinwall & Tedeschi, 2010). We suggest strengths discourse constructs hope.

Implications

After ten years, many of the SOC sites throughout the United States have progressed toward a strengths-orientation. An SOC approach has become a standardized philosophy, and in some child-serving systems, has even become institutionalized. However, most case managers still are operating from a deficit approach and require reframing to a strengths orientation. This is a paradigm shift not only for the professionals but also for the families who are accustomed to their traditional "sick" roles. Our typology of strengths-based health communication strategies is being effectively used in training of case managers and other mental healthcare providers. Re-training a strengths approach sets up a positive experience for training participants as well as the families that will eventually be served by them.

References

Aspinwall, L. G., & Tedeschi, R. G. (2010). The value of positive psychology for health psychology: Progress and pitfalls in examining the relation of positive phenomena to health. *Annals of behavioral medicine, 39*(1), 4–15.

Averill, J. R., Catlin, G., & Chon, K. K. (1990). *Rules of hope.* New York: Springer-Verlag.

Berg, I. K., & DeShazer, S. (1993). Making numbers talk: Language in therapy. In S. Friedman (Ed.), *The new language of change: Constructive collaboration in psychotherapy* (pp. 5–24). New York: Guilford Press.

Bronfenbrenner, U. (1979). Beyond the deficit model in child and family policy. *Teachers College Record, 81*, 95–104.

Cook, J. R., & Kilmer, R. P. (2010). The importance of context in fostering community systems: Supports for families in systems of care. *American Journal of Orthopsychiatry, 80*(1), 115–123.

Csikszentmihalyi, M. (1990). *Flow.* San Francisco: Harper-Collins.

Csikszentmihalyi, M. (1993). *The evolving self: A psychology for the third millennium.* San Francisco: Harper-Collins.

Csikszentmihalyi, M. (1999). If we are so rich, why aren't we happy? *American Psychologist, 54*, 821–827.

Davis, C. S. (2006) Sylvia's story: Narrative, storytelling, and power in a children's community mental health system of care. *Qualitative Inquiry, 12*(6), 1–24.

Davis, C. S. (2008). Dueling narratives: How peer leaders use narrative to frame meaning in community mental health care teams. *Small Group Research: An International Journal of Theory, Investigation, and Application, 39*(6), 706–727.

Davis, C. S. (2012). *Constructing the future with hope: Inside a children's mental health system of care.* Walnut Creek, CA: Left Coast Press.

Davis, C. S., Mayo, J., Sikand, C., Kobres, M., & Dollard, N. (2007). A typology and narrative illustration of procedures for following a strengths-based approach in a children's mental health system of care. In C. Newman, C. Liberton, K. Kutash, & R. M. Friedman (Eds.), *The 19th annual research conference proceedings, A system of care for children's mental health: Expanding the research base.* Tampa: University of South Florida, The Louis de la Parte Florida Mental Health Institute, Research and Training Center for Children's Mental Health.

Dunst, C. J., & Trivette, C. M. (1996). Empowerment, effective helpgiving practices and family-centered care. *Pediatric Nursing, 22*, 334–337.

Dunst, C. J., Trivette, C. M., Davis, M., & Cornwell, J. C. (1994). Characteristics of effective help-giving practices. In C. J. Dunst, C. M. Trivette, & A. G. Deal (Eds.), *Supporting and strengthening families: Methods, strategies and practices* (pp. 171–185). Cambridge, MA: Brookline Books.

Dunst, C. J., Trivette, C. M., & Mott, D. W. (1994). Strengths-based family-centered intervention practices. In C. J. Dunst, C. M. Trivette, & A. G. Deal (Eds.), *Supporting and strengthening families: Methods, strategies and practices* (pp. 115–131). Cambridge, MA: Brookline Books.

Durrant, M., & Kowalski, K. (1993). Enhancing views of competence. In S. Friedman (Ed.), *The new language of change: Constructive collaboration in psychotherapy* (pp. 107–137). New York: Guilford Press.

Fanger, M. T. (1993). After the shift: Time-effective treatment in the possibility frame. In S. Friedman (Ed.), *The new language of change: Constructive collaboration in psychotherapy* (pp. 85–106). New York: Guilford Press.

Friedman, R. M. (1994). Restructuring of systems to emphasize prevention and family support. *Journal of Clinical Child Psychology, 23*(Suppl.), 40–47.

Groopman, J. (2004). *The anatomy of hope: How people prevail in the face of illness.* New York: Random House.

Harris, J., Pryor, J., & Adams, S. (2012). Intercoder agreement: The challenge of intercoder agreement in qualitative inquiry. Retrieved from http://emissary.wm.edu/templates/content/publications/intercoder-agreement.pdf.

Kearney, P. M., & Griffin, T. (2001). Between joy and sorrow: Being a parent of a child with developmental disability. *Journal of Advanced Nursing, 34*(5), 582–592.

Kelley, T. M. (2004). Positive psychology and adolescent mental health: False promise or true breakthrough? *Adolescence, 39*(154), 257–278.

Kilmer, R. P., Cook, J. R., Munsell, E., & Salvador, S. (2010). Factors associated with positive adjustment in siblings of children with Severe Emotional Disturbance: The role of family resources and community life. *American Journal of Orthopsychiatry, 80*(4), 473–481.

Laveman, L. (2000). The Harmonium Project: A macrosystemic approach to empowering adolescents. *Journal of Mental Health Counseling, 22*, 17–31.

Lincoln, Y. S., & Guba, E. G. (1985). *Naturalistic inquiry.* Beverly Hills, CA: Sage.

Lipchik, E. (1994). "Both/And" solutions. In S. Friedman (Ed.), *The new language of change: Constructive collaboration in psychotherapy* (pp. 25–49). New York: Guilford Press.

Lourie, I. S., Katz-Leavy, J., & Stroul, B. A. (1996). Individualized services in a system of care. In B. A. Stroul (Ed.), *Children's mental health: Creating systems of care in a changing society* (pp. 23–39). Baltimore, MD: Paul H. Brookes.

MacGeorge, E., Feng, B., Wilkum, K., & Doherty, E. (2012). Supportive communication: A positive response to negative life events. In T. Socha & M. Pitts, (Eds.), *The positive side of interpersonal communication* (pp. 211–228). New York: Peter Lang.

Montgomery, B. M., & Baxter, L. A. (1998). A guide to dialectical approaches to studying personal relationships. In B. M. Montgomery & L. A. Baxter (Eds.), *Dialectical approaches to studying personal relationships.* Mahwah, NJ: Lawrence Erlbaum Associates.

Peterson, C. (2006). *A primer in positive psychology.* New York: Oxford University Press.

Peterson, C., & Seligman, M. E. P. (2004). *Character strengths and virtues: A handbook and classification.* New York: Oxford University Press.

Richardson, G. E. (2002). The metatheory of resilience and resiliency. *Journal of Clinical Psychology, 58*, 307–321.

Saleebey, D. (1996). The strengths perspective in social work practice: Extensions and cautions. *Social Work, 41*, 296–305.

Seligman, M. E. P. (2002). *Authentic happiness: Using the new positive psychology to realize your potential for lasing fulfillment.* New York: Free Press.

Seligman, M. P., & Csikszentmihalyi, M. (2000). Positive psychology: An introduction. *American Psychologist, 55*(1), 5–14.

Seligman, M. P., Steen, T. A., Park, N., & Peterson, C. (2005). Positive psychology progress: Empirical validation of interventions. *American Psychologist, 60*(5), 410–421.

Seligman, M. P., Rashid, T., & Parks, A. C. (2006). Positive psychotherapy. *American Psychologist, 6*(8), 774–899.

Snyder, C. R. (1994). *The psychology of hope: You can get there from here.* New York: Free Press.

Snyder, C. R. (2000). Hypothesis: There is hope. In C. R. Snyder (Ed.), *Handbook of hope: Theory, measures, and applications* (pp. 3–21). San Diego, CA: Academic Press.

Snyder, C. R. (2002). Hope theory: Rainbows in the mind. *Psychological Inquiry, 13*(4), 249.

Socha, T. J., & Pitts, M. J. (2012). Toward a conceptual foundation for positive interpersonal communication. In T. J. Socha & M. J. Pitts (Eds.), *The positive side of interpersonal communication* (pp. 1–18). New York: Peter Lang.

Stroul, B. A., & Friedman, R. M. (1986). *A system of care for children and youth with severe emotional disturbances (Rev. ed.).* Washington, DC: Georgetown University Child Development Center, CASSP Technical Assistance Center.

Taylor, E. H. (2006). The weaknesses of the strengths model: Mental illness as a case in point. *Best Practice in Mental Health, 2*(1), 1–30.

• CHAPTER FIVE •

Communication in Self-Help Support Groups: Positive Communication and the Al-Anon Experience

Charles F. Aust
Kennesaw State University

A support group is a gathering of individuals on a recurring basis around similar concerns with the purpose of sharing experiences, thoughts, and feelings (du Pré, 2010). One of the purposes for which support groups form and operate is to promote health and well-being. Health-promoting communication takes place in these groups (du Pré, 2010; *How Al-Anon Works*, 2008; Schopler & Galinsky, 1993; Withorn, 1980).

Because self-help support groups have the power to promote growth and change lives, it is logical to expect that elements of positive psychology would be at work in the beneficial communication that takes place in these life-enhancing interpersonal arenas. This chapter describes an analysis undertaken to determine if elements of positive psychology appeared in member-written literature of one of the largest support groups in the world, Al-Anon.[1] In particular, the analysis employed a taxonomy called the "Classification of Strengths and Virtues" (Peterson & Seligman, 2004; Seligman, 2011) compiled by leaders of the positive psychology movement Indeed, numerous applications of the 24 character strengths and virtues of the classification were found in the literature of Al-Anon. This chapter details numerous excerpts and how they reflect the positive communication that flows from practice of those character strengths and virtues.

The Worldwide Support Groups of Al-Anon

Founded in 1951 in the United States, Al-Anon is an international organization with a vast number of local support groups. Al-Anon exists to help family and friends recover from the effects of someone else's drinking. Starting with 87 groups in the 1950s, Al-Anon "has grown to many thousands of groups meeting in over 130 countries around the world" (*How Al-Anon Works*, 2008, p. 146). The following describes the purpose and operation of Al-Anon groups, from the *Al-Anon/Alateen Service Manual* (2010):

> The Al-Anon Family Groups are a fellowship of relatives and friends of alcoholics who share their experience, strength, and hope in order to solve their common problems. We believe alcoholism is a family illness and that changed attitudes can aid recovery. Al-Anon is not allied with any sect, denomination, political entity, organization, or institution; does not engage in any controversy; neither endorses nor opposes any cause. There are no dues for membership. Al-Anon is self-supporting through its own voluntary contributions. Al-Anon has but one purpose: to help families of alcoholics. We do this by practicing the Twelve Steps, by welcoming and giving comfort to families of alcoholics, and by giving understanding and encouragement to the alcoholic. (p. 12)

A similar support group for teenagers of alcoholics called Alateen is part of the Al-Anon program, but because of space limitations, this chapter will focus only on Al-Anon.

It is estimated that there are 17.6 million alcoholics in the United States (National Library of Medicine/National Institutes of Health, 2011). If just four other people are affected by each alcoholic, probably a rather modest estimate, that would put the number of people trying to cope with an alcoholic in their lives at more than 68 million. This represents a significant number of people in need of support in order to cope with the alcoholic who struggles with a disease described as "cunning, baffling, and powerful" (*Alcoholics Anonymous*, 2001, p. 58). With these large numbers, then, it is not surprising that Al-Anon is one of the largest self-help support groups. In addition to the hundreds of groups in the United States, Al-Anon has groups meeting in 130 countries and its books have been translated into 30 languages (*How Al-Anon Works*, 2008). For example, *Courage to Change* (1992), first published in 1992, has been translated into seven languages, with approximately 1.9 million copies in print (Tom C., personal communication, May 2009).

In the Al-Anon program, the main goal is called "recovery," which involves finding strength, guidance and support by reaching out to others who have the same problems and coming together at meetings to provide a "nourishing source of compassion and support" (*How Al-Anon Works*, 2008, p. 11). In this recovery process they share their "experience, strength and hope" (*How Al-Anon Works*, 2008, p. 11) with one another in order to build a more fulfilling life, a life of virtue and strength. They speak of regaining hope and finding ways to effectively deal with difficulties. Recovery involves the opportunity to learn what makes relationships healthy and ways to develop and enhance them (*Discovering Choices*, 2008).

Positive Psychology, Positive Communication, and Support Groups

Application of positive psychology can be found in numerous types of self-help support groups. An example is identified in the research of Resnick and Rosenheck (2006). They investigated the use of the Values in Action Inventory of Strengths (VAIS) in a psychiatric rehabilitation program. VAIS is based on 24 character strengths of the "Classification of Strengths and Virtues" (Peterson & Seligman, 2004; Seligman, 2011). Those 24 strengths are organized into six broad virtues—wisdom and knowledge, courage, humanity, justice, temperance, and transcendence. In the program these researchers examined, the focus of development was on the self and not other-directed. Participants were encouraged to build on strengths rather than dwell on deficiencies or weaknesses. They assessed their strengths using the VAIS, a process which resembles the Al-Anon idea of taking an inventory (detailed self-examination). This vital process is suggested in Al-Anon's Step 4, "Made a searching and fearless moral inventory of ourselves" (see Table 5.1). Strengths and virtues are to be considered as part of that inventory-taking, not just what are called "defects of character" (Table 5.1, end of chapter), which are the problem behaviors that members identify and seek to change or lessen.

The *Wise Ways Program* (The Wise Ways Fellowship, 2011) is another example of application of positive psychology in support groups. Like Al-Anon, this group is patterned after the 12 Steps of Alcoholics Anonymous.[2] The preamble that is read at the beginning of each meeting contains this: "Wise Ways Happiness Support Groups are a fellowship of persons gathered together to study perennial wisdom and positive psychology principles. We believe happiness is an inside job and that changed attitudes and perceptions can lead to greater life satisfaction" (p. 4). Another example of the manifestation of positive psychology in self-help recovery programs is found in a study of Alcoholics Anonymous by Emmons and Shelton (2005). They document the cultivation and promotion of gratitude.

From these examples it is evident that positive communication that occurs in support groups parallels themes of positive psychology.

The Power of Symbols for Positive Communication

The numerous books and pamphlets of the Al-Anon program are among the innumerable symbolic expressions humans have created for communication. Symbolic Interactionism (Mead, 1934; Shibutani, 1961) provides a frame in which to understand these life-enhancing communications of Al-Anon and other support groups that form over time an empowering discourse. Symbolic interactionism posits that humans are equipped with the ability to think in symbolic ways. We convert thoughts into language that can be shared within a community that socially constructs meaningful experience. Symbolic interaction makes it possible for us to understand ourselves and others, and our thoughts, feelings, and actions (Mead, 1934). With these symbolic tools we are capable of reflecting on the past, imagining the future, formulating plans and contemplating actions and goals which we can then carry out.

Table 5.1. The Twelve Steps of Al-Anon Family Groups

"...Because of their proven power and worth, A.A.'s Twelve Steps have been adopted almost word for word by Al-Anon. They represent a way of life appealing to all people of goodwill, of any religious faith or of none. Note the power of the very words!"

1. We admitted we were powerless over alcohol—that our lives had become unmanageable.
2. Came to believe that a Power greater than ourselves could restore us to sanity.
3. Made a decision to turn our will and our lives over to the care of God *as we understood Him*.
4. Made a searching and fearless moral inventory of ourselves.
5. Admitted to God, to ourselves, and to another human being the exact nature of our wrongs.
6. Were entirely ready to have God remove all these defects of character.
7. Humbly asked Him to remove our shortcomings.
8. Made a list of all persons we had harmed, and became willing to make amends to them all.
9. Made direct amends to such people wherever possible, except when to do so would injure them or others.
10. Continued to take personal inventory and when we were wrong promptly admitted it.
11. Sought through prayer and meditation to improve our conscious contact with God as we understood Him, praying only for knowledge of His will for us and the power to carry that out.
12. Having had a spiritual awakening as a result of these steps, we tried to carry this message to others, and to practice these principles in all our affairs.

Table 5.1 is excerpted from *Al-Anon/Alateen Service Manual 2010-2013* (pp. 13–14).

Symbolic interaction asserts that it is possible, even necessary, to have the creative ability to move back and forth between the concrete and the abstract. Charon (1995) says it well: "We learn what is known, we understand it, and we go further than what we have been taught. We create our own reality. And some of us produce great creations in literature, science, music, and art through playing with the understanding we have learned through symbols" (p. 63).

Humans create and use symbols in great variety and complexity to imagine and convey abstract situations, scenarios, goals, and ideals that take on important and meaningful value in their minds. They can create and imagine mental statements they might consider making to others. They can imagine the other's responses to their communication. They can think about and adjust expectations they have of themselves and of others in imagined future scenarios. Literature contributes to these thoughts and imaginings and is used to bridge the gap between abstract thinking and concrete action.

A symbolic-interpretive perspective offered by Frey and Sunwolf (2004) explains how group experience is both a process and a product. Members of the group engage in a symbolic-management process as they use words, actions and objects to communicate and support one another. At the same time a symbolic-constitutive process unfolds, in which the group experience exists as a product or outcome of symbolic interaction. Frey and Sunwolf explain:

> The linking together of processes and products, as opposed to treating them as separate entities, highlights their recursive and reflexive relationship....Symbolic predispositions, practices, processes, and products, thus, emerge and merge continually during group formation and throughout the course of a group's life. (p. 286)

Al-Anon members start with their own raw and vivid experiences about a very difficult social challenge. As they enter into the abstract by writing and reading the narratives in the Al-Anon literature, they construct and discover language, thoughts, and meanings that assist in connecting their concrete experience with abstract ideals and aspirations for better health and well-being. The Al-Anon literature offers symbolic tools members can use as both product and process to learn, inculcate, and apply the ideals and aspirations of Al-Anon.

The human capacity to create and use symbols makes it possible for us to learn from one another, to empathize with one another, and to engage in and benefit from group participation. It is at such times that the tools of meetings and literature in support groups such as Al-Anon take on poignant and practical value. The importance of these tools to generate positive communication and build community comes into stark relief for the person who has felt isolated and defeated and is reaching out for help.

Literature as a Vital Communication Connection

The main goal of a self-help support group, according to Withorn (1990), is the experience of helpful communicative connections: "mutual sharing, support, advice-giving, and the pooling of group resources and information" (p. 20). While keeping in mind the primacy of meetings in the support group process, literature is thought to play an essential role as a way for members to communicate with one another. Self-help literature connects the members with others who are not part of their day-to-day contacts but who share their struggles (Grodin, 1991).

Although group meetings are integral to Al-Anon, literature plays a key role in experiencing the benefits of Al-Anon, as mentioned in the welcome statement used at group meetings: "The loving interchange of help among members and daily reading of Al-Anon/Alateen literature thus make us ready to receive the priceless gift of serenity" (*Al-Anon/Alateen Service Manual*, 2010, p. 11). Books and pamphlets written by the members of Al-Anon help them to "continue their recovery between meetings, and gain insight into themselves and the principles of the Al-Anon/Alateen program" (*Al-Anon/Alateen Service Manual*, 2010, p. 56).

More than 100 books and pamphlets have been published by Al-Anon. Literature is approved only after a stringent review by the World Service Conference of Al-Anon (*Al-Anon/Alateen Service Manual*, 2010). Members are encouraged to write about their experience of applying the program to their lives and to submit those writings to the Literature Service at Al-Anon's World Service Office (WSO). Members submit writing to the WSO spontaneously or in response to a specific call for sharing from the WSO (*How Al-Anon Works*, 2008). The amount of responses to such calls can be high. For example, when a call for sharing was announced for a new daily reading book called *Hope for Today* (2002), the WSO received over 1,100 writings from members (Tom C., personal communication, May 20, 2009).

Proposed content is reviewed by a literature committee comprised of Al-Anon members who have long-term experience of participating in and benefitting from the program. In addition, the executive director, the chairperson of the policy committee, and four other members of that committee also review all new content and any major revisions to previously-published material. This "approval process guarantees the fellowship that the material is an expression of Al-Anon principles" (*Al-Anon/Alateen Service Manual*, 2010, p. 91). It ensures that the literature is conference-approved and reflects what the WSO calls "an informed group conscience" and "a unified view of Al-Anon/Alateen to professionals, other individuals, and outside agencies" (*Al-Anon/Alateen Service Manual*, 2010, p. 101).

Members are encouraged to read recovery literature on a daily basis. For those who do so, literature then becomes a regular part of their communication link with others who have the same challenges. "Al-Anon/Alateen literature and service materials help members to continue their recovery between meetings and gain insight into themselves and the principles of the Al-Anon/Alateen program" (*Al-Anon/Alateen Service Manual*, 2010, p. 56). The literature also offers members the flexibility to access the support of other members, their ideas, and encouragement at a time of the reader's own choosing, whether in a public sphere, in the company of others, or in private, quiet, solitary ways.

The literature is a source of testimonials from members, contains self-reports of their shared struggles, describes progress, and recounts achievements that writers deem satisfactory or successful as a result of applying the principles of Al-Anon (*How Al-Anon Works*, 2008). Two examples of daily readings books are *One Day at a Time in Al-Anon* (2002) and *Courage to Change* (1992). In addition to daily readings books, more detailed stories written by members are contained in *How Al-Anon Works* (2008). Here is a sample of titles of personal stories from the 44 contained in the book:

Surviving Personal Tragedy

A Wife Copes With Physical Abuse

A Husband Learns to Detach With Love

A War Veteran Makes Life and Death Decisions

A Parent Sets Boundaries

A Gay Man Copes With Sexual Intimacy

Alcoholism Crosses Racial Lines

Daily use of literature is encouraged as a way to experience the shared wisdom of members as they apply the program to their relationship with the alcoholic and also to themselves, regarding their self-concept, self-understanding and intrapersonal communication (i.e., self-talk). But members are also encouraged to practice the principles of the program in all facets of their lives, as mentioned in Step 12: "Having had a spiritual awakening as the result of these steps, we tried to carry this message to others, and to practice these principles in all our affairs" (see Table 5.1). This broadens the usefulness of the literature by encouraging members to apply the wisdom and knowledge they derive from the literature to all areas of their lives, including all relationships.

Using Member-Written Literature as Empirical Evidence

This section explains why literature was chosen for analysis. Anonymity is considered the most important principle in the Al-Anon approach because it promotes trust (*How Al-Anon Works*, 2008). The adherence to anonymity among members (i.e., only first names are used in the program) encourages people to speak freely and openly at meetings. It assures people that their identity and that of the alcoholic will not be revealed, thereby removing one of the major concerns that some people have about appearing at and interacting at meetings. The trust that anonymity establishes then fosters willingness to self-disclose. Freely self-disclosing and having those disclosures acknowledged and accepted can engender unconditional positive regard. Also, the recognition from others that the person self-disclosing is not the only one experiencing such thoughts, feelings and behaviors fosters self-acceptance and a bond with those to whom the person is self-disclosing.

Because confidentiality and anonymity are essential, the presence of a researcher at support group meetings to record audio or write notes and then disseminate those statements in a public venue could inhibit interactions, erode trust and be considered a violation of anonymity and confidentiality (Frey & Sunwolf, 2004). Since freely sharing personal experience with one another is a vital feature of self-help support groups (Withorn, 1980), the recording of such interactions during meetings would affect the authenticity of those interactions and undermine the validity of such data.

Therefore, the member-written literature was chosen as an alternative. Using this source of evidence overcomes the limitation imposed by anonymity, respects the privacy of members, avoids inhibiting sharing during meetings, and taps into a rich source of detailed testimonials that have been carefully vetted and selected for publication (see above) by those who are most familiar with the Al-Anon program. In addition to the careful vetting, several other factors suggest that the literature has validity as a source for empirical analysis. The huge volume of books and pamphlets sold and their wide distribution among the millions who have used the literature, the span of time during which this literature has been used, the longevity of the 12 Step programs of Al-Anon (1951) and Alcoholics Anonymous (1935), and the formation and continuation of these support groups throughout the world all suggest that the literature is valid and does indeed represent Al-Anon principles and the genuine experience of its members.

Connections between Positive Communication and Positive Psychology

Leaders of the positive psychology movement compiled a list of 24 character strengths called the "Classification of Strengths and Virtues" (Peterson & Seligman, 2004; Seligman, 2011). Those 24 strengths are organized into six broad virtues—wisdom and knowledge, courage, humanity, justice, temperance, and transcendence. Among the themes discovered in this study of the Al-Anon literature are courage (one of the six broad virtues), gratitude and forgiveness (associated with the virtue of transcendence), and taking responsibility for one's actions and attitudes (associated with two strengths: social intelligence, which is related to the virtue of wisdom and knowledge, and self-control, which is related to the virtue of temperance). Character strengths are manifested in the narratives of Al-Anon members and the actions those narratives describe. The remaining sections of the chapter provide excerpts from the Al-Anon literature that illustrate various character strengths.

 A developmental perspective. Realizing that individual strengths emerge and build over time (Seligman & Czikszentmihalyi, 2000), positive psychology reflects a developmental perspective. In Al-Anon, slogans have been created that provide clear and direct application of a thought, attitude, or action that can quickly help a member cope in the moment. Slogans include, "First Things First," "One Day at a Time," "Keep an Open Mind," and "Live and Let Live" (*How Al-Anon Works*, 2008).

 The slogan "Progress Not Perfection" (p. 340) captures the developmental theme while at the same time acknowledging that the development will not result in a complete and resolved end that no longer needs to be revisited or further developed or renewed. Members seem to be saying that they never finish the quest for complete wholeness and total serenity (*How Al-Anon Works*, 2008). This slogan also helps Al-Anon members to consider more realistic expectations about the alcoholic in their lives, knowing that alcoholics too have a lifelong challenge, even if they maintain sobriety. Character strengths of perspective, perseverance, prudence and hope from the Classification of Strengths and Virtues are reflected in these slogans.

 In their advocacy of positive psychology, Seligman and Czikszentmihalyi (2000) propose that one does not have to wait for stability, harmony, or prosperity before focusing on and fostering the positive, the healthy, the constructive aspects of behavior and attitudes that help one to flourish in the midst of struggles. The positive can be experienced in the midst of the negative. As Seligman and Czikszentmihalyi (2000) point out, the existence of problem behaviors, or what Al-Anon members would call their "defects of character" (see Table 5.1), should not preclude a focus also on what is healthy. When members take Step 4 in their recovery process, it involves making a "searching and fearless moral inventory" (Table 5.1). In this process Al-Anon encourages its members to recognize strengths, virtues and healthy tendencies as well as weaknesses, shortcomings, and unhealthy behaviors (*Courage to Change*, 1992, p. 181; *How Al-Anon Works*, 2008, p. 51). Persevering (one of the character strengths) toward a worthwhile goal in the midst of adversity or difficulties is another of the qualities of flourishing in positive psychology, according to Seligman (2011), and is reflected in the goal of self-examination and self-improvement promoted by Al-Anon.

Taking responsibility for actions and attitudes. Another way positive psychology manifests itself in the literature is to consider how members respond to adversity and the difficulties caused by alcoholism. Instead of giving in to defeat, despair, or self-pity, members encourage one another not to lose sight of those positive aspects of their lives that are flourishing or the good that they could emphasize and build upon.

As part of the work of recovery, members are encouraged to reflect on how they choose to react to situations. The literature contains reminders that they have the power to decide how to respond to people and situations instead of reacting without thinking. And in that decision-making they encourage one another to choose healthy, constructive ways to respond. For example, a member writes: "I have choices about how I react to what happens....I stopped making excuses for my self-pity and inertia, and began to consider what I could do about changing my attitudes in order to make my day more pleasant and constructive" (*How Al-Anon Works*, 2008, p. 297). This resonates with numerous strengths in the Classification of Strengths and Virtues, among them the strengths of judgment, social intelligence, perspective, and self-control (Seligman, 2011).

An excerpt from *Hope for Today* (2002) challenges the reader to think not in terms of running away from a negative but rather moving toward a positive:

> I choose how I act, how I think, and how I feel about any situation that arises. I can choose fear, or I can choose love. Fear keeps me shut off and unhealed. Love opens me up and heals me. Today I choose love (p. 104).

Awareness of self-defeating thinking is an important effort the program encourages. But as this member writes, it also helps to move beyond awareness and take action: "I must do more than just dismiss the negative thoughts. I must replace them with something positive or I am likely to slide right back into my negative thinking" (*Courage to Change*, 1992, p. 105).

Being aware of choices about one's attitude is a major theme of the literature. In fact, an entire chapter titled "Changed Attitudes" in *How Al-Anon Works* (2008) is devoted to examining the importance of attitudes. In addition, the suggested welcome used by groups to begin meetings contains the statement "So much depends on our own attitudes, and as we learn to place our problem in its true perspective, we find it loses its power to dominate our thoughts and our lives" (*Al-Anon/Alateen Service Manual*, 2010, pp. 10-11). Experts in the recovery movement believe that taking responsibility for oneself is an essential aspect of effective recovery (Resnick & Rosenheck, 2006), and the Al-Anon literature echoes that belief. Parallels exist between this mindset and the character strengths and virtues approach of positive psychology.

Gratitude. An example of the manifestation of positive psychology in self-help recovery programs is the encouragement to cultivate gratitude. Seligman (2011) relates the strength of gratitude with the virtue of transcendence. He suggests several activities to assist in fostering gratitude, such as the "what-went-well" exercise or the "hunt the good stuff" activity. Al-Anon members challenge themselves to cultivate this powerful attitude. A member writes: "What am I doing with what I've got? Instead of crying over what I don't have, and wishing my life were different, what am I doing with what I've got? ...Am I using my capabilities well? Do I recognize and appreciate all I have to be grateful for?" (*One Day at a Time in Al-Anon*, 2000, p. 253). Al-Anon members are encouraged to foster "an attitude of gratitude" (*How Al-Anon Works*, 2008, p. 78).

Gratitude is emphasized in many places in the member-written literature of Al-Anon and is indexed numerous times (e.g., 13 entries in *Courage to Change* and 9 in *One Day at a Time in Al-Anon*). A member writes about the importance of a time for meditation every day, and to contemplate gratitude for the good: "I have much more to be grateful for than I realize. Too often I don't remember to give thought to all the things in my life that I could enjoy and appreciate" (*One Day at a Time in Al-Anon*, 2000, p. 126). The recovery process is meant to be a healing process and gratitude can be an ingredient in that nurturing of health and well-being. One member describes gratitude as a "healing force" (*One Day at a Time in Al-Anon*, 2000, p. 319). Gratitude is also suggested as an antidote to envy and self-pity (*One Day at a Time in Al-Anon*, 2000).

Courage. Positive psychology recognizes courage as an important element of healthy and adaptive functioning (Seligman & Czikszentmihalyi, 2000). It is one of the six virtues in Peterson and Seligman's Classification of Strengths and Virtues (2004). Courage is also a major theme in Al-Anon literature. The word even occurs in the title of one of the daily readings books, *Courage to Change* (1992), which states in the preface: "This book, like its companion volume *One Day at a Time in Al-Anon*, is designed to keep our focus on today and give us the courage to change the things we can" (Preface). One member writes in *Courage to Change* (1992): "I don't have to feel threatened by the future. I can take life one day at a time" (p. 351). Another shares this: "It takes courage to step beyond what is comfortable, predictable, and known" (p. 219).

In *Hope for Today* (2002) a member describes an act of maturity that requires courage: "Do I have the courage to take responsibility for my own feelings and actions?" (p. 167). Countering fear with this thought, a member writes: "Reminding myself that I always have choices gives me hope and courage to leave fear and passivity behind" (*Hope for Today*, 2002, p. 189).

Courage can be needed to face a frightening past and work through it to begin a healing process. A member wrote in *The Forum*, a monthly magazine of Al-Anon, that the book *From Survival to Recovery* (1994) "helped me to address the ugliness of my childhood sexual abuse" (How Al-Anon Conference, 2010, p. 20). In that same issue of *The Forum*, a member wrote: "It is truly a blessing to read the experience of others and to be able to identify myself with their experience, strength, and hope" (Grateful for *The Forum*, 2010, p. 4).

While the Al-Anon program encourages patience and perseverance in what is a long-term process of learning and applying the principles of the program effectively, it takes a clear-eyed and realistic approach to immediate threats of violence. In *How Al-Anon Works* (2008) the program delivers an exhortation on the very first page for members who are confronted with violence. Ensuring one's safety and the safety of children should be the most immediate concern, it advises readers. The first priority is to get out of harm's way. This can take tremendous courage. "Anyone who has been physically or sexually abused or even threatened may be terrified of taking action at all. It can require every ounce of courage and faith to act decisively. But no one has to accept violence. No matter what seems to trigger the attack, we all deserve to be safe" (Preface).

Forgiveness. Peterson and Seligman (2004) associate the character strength of forgiveness with the virtue of transcendence in the tenets of positive psychology. Likewise, forgiveness is a major theme in Al-Anon literature, as evidenced by numerous entries in several books (e.g., eight in each of the books *Hope for Today* and *Discovering Choices: Recovery in Relationships*, and six in *Opening Our Hearts: Transforming Our Losses*). Entries about forgiveness encourage members to forgive themselves for past mistakes and wrongs they have committed. Recognizing that self-forgiveness might also involve coming to terms with past actions toward others, the program also asks members to make amends to other people. Step 9 (Table 5.1) states: "Made direct amends to such people wherever possible, except when to do so would injure them or others."

A member writes in *Courage to Change* (1992) about self-forgiveness: "Today I seek to become a little more accepting of myself, a little more comfortable in my own skin....Condemning my imperfections has never enhanced my appreciation of life or helped me to love myself more" (p. 19). The writer also states that the recovery process is gradual and self-improvement takes time, and concludes with the thought that "Al-Anon is a gentle, healing program. I will remember to be gentle with myself today, trusting that the healing will come" (p. 19). Another writes that "It takes time for old doubts to fade and wounds to heal....With practice, we learn to treat ourselves with gentleness and compassion" (p. 183).

Forgiving others is also encouraged. In *How Al-Anon Works* (2008) is the statement "Resentment will do nothing except tear us apart inside. No one ever found serenity through hatred" (*How Al-Anon Works*, 2008, p. 85). Al-Anon acknowledges that this can be a monumental task because actions of others might have caused great physical, emotional, or material harm. Some offenses may seem unforgivable, but ultimately, this is about the member's recovery, it advises. In *Opening Our Hearts, Transforming Our Losses* (2007) members are told that forgiveness does not mean the past is forgotten, nor does forgiveness imply that continued mistreatment is to be overlooked or tolerated. The person may choose to forgive and work to repair the relationship, or forgive but take steps to limit or end contact in order to prevent further abuse.

The section about forgiveness in *How Al-Anon Works* (2008) concludes by saying: "Although we may despise what others have done, if we keep in mind that everything we are now trying to do has the goal of healing us, we are bound to decide that the best thing we can do for ourselves is forgive" (p. 86). This is reflected in a member's writing in *Hope for Today* (2002): "In Al-Anon I learned that forgiveness is for me. I realized how much of my energy was drained by maintaining my resentment and by reminding myself that I was angry" (p. 95). The member also ponders the cost of harboring resentments: "Have I ever tried to tally the time I take every day to feed resentful thoughts and feelings? What else could I be doing with that energy?" (p. 95).

Forgiveness developed in a member's heart after he was able to embrace the idea that his father's alcoholism was not an intentional act to make his life miserable but instead was a disease. With this new awareness he felt compassion for his father and along with that, forgiveness: "I was able to forgive him and love him for the first time since my childhood. I was given back a father who was simply a man with a disease, deserving of my compassion, forgiveness, and love" (*Discovering Choices*, 2008, p. 292).

Conclusion

This analysis of Al-Anon literature was undertaken to determine if elements of positive psychology appeared in member-written narratives. Indeed, that is the case. This chapter details numerous excerpts from the narratives. The themes illustrated include gratitude, courage, forgiveness, and taking responsibility for one's actions. These themes reflect tenets of positive psychology and, in particular, nine of the 24 character strengths of the "Classification of Strengths and Virtues" (Peterson & Seligman, 2004; Seligman, 2011). They include judgment, social intelligence, perspective, perseverance, self-control, prudence, gratitude, hope and forgiveness. These results contribute to our knowledge of the extent to which positive psychology manifests itself in the positive communication that enhances the emotional and psychological well-being of support group members, and in this particular investigation, those who practice the Al-Anon program. Resnick and Rosenheck (2006) suggest that positive psychology should be integrated into the recovery movement. This exploration has found evidence to suggest that the self-help support groups of Al-Anon already do this, at least implicitly.

Al-Anon members face difficult, sometimes tragic and traumatizing circumstances. Seligman titles a chapter in *Flourish* (2011) "Turning Trauma Into Growth." That, in fact, is what Al-Anon encourages its members to do, and that is what members describe over and over again in their narratives as they work to recover from the harmful effects of someone's drinking. Seligman captures it well: "renewed appreciation of being alive, enhanced personal strength, acting on new possibilities, improved relationships, and spiritual deepening" (p. 169).

A bright side of communication reveals itself in the supportive and hopeful communication of Al-Anon members. This exploration of positive psychology in the literature of this worldwide self-help support group begins to fill a gap in our knowledge about the melding of these two valuable facets of human activity, self-help support group communication and positive psychology, and their beneficial impact on the health and wellness of those seeking recovery.

Notes

1. Quotations from Al-Anon literature copyright by Al-Anon Family Group Headquarters, Inc. Permission to reprint these excerpts does not mean that Al-Anon Family Group Headquarters, Inc. has reviewed or approved the contents of this publication, or that Al-Anon Family Group Headquarters, Inc. necessarily agrees with the views expressed herein. Al-Anon is a program of recovery for families and friends of alcoholics—use of this excerpt in any non Al-Anon context does not imply endorsement or affiliation by Al-Anon.

2. The Twelve Steps as adapted by Al-Anon with permission of Alcoholics Anonymous Services World, Inc. ("AAWS") are reprinted with permission of Al-Anon and AAWS. AAWS's permission to reprint Al-Anon's Steps does not mean that AAWS has reviewed or approved the contents of this publication, or that AAWS necessarily agrees with the views expressed therein. Alcoholics Anonymous is a program of recovery from alcoholism only—use or permissible adaptation of A.A.'s Twelve Steps in connection with programs and activities which are patterned after A.A., but which address other problems, or in any other non-A.A. context, does not imply otherwise.

References

Al-Anon/Alateen service manual 2010 –2013 (2010). Virginia Beach, VA: Al-Anon Family Group Headquarters.

Alcoholics anonymous: The big book (4th ed.). (2001). New York: Alcoholics Anonymous World Services.

Courage to change (1992). Virginia Beach, VA: Al-Anon Family Group Headquarters.

Discovering choices: Recovery in relationships (2008). Virginia Beach, VA: Al-Anon Family Group Headquarters.

du Pré, A. (2010). *Communicating about health: Current issues and perspectives.* New York: Oxford University Press.

Emmons, R.A., & Shelton, C.M. (2005). Gratitude and the science of positive psychology. In C.R. Snyder & S.J. Lopez (Eds.), *Handbook of positive psychology* (pp. 459–471). New York: Oxford University Press.

Frey, L.R., & Sunwolf (2004). The symbolic-interpretive perspective on group dynamics. *Small Group Research, 35,* 277–306.

From survival to recovery (1994). Virginia Beach, VA: Al-Anon Family Group Headquarters.

Grateful for *The Forum* (2010, December). *The Forum,* 4.

Grodin, D. (1991). The interpreting audience: The therapeutics of self-help book reading. *Critical Studies in Mass Communication, 8,* 404–420.

Hope for today (2002). Virginia Beach, VA: Al-Anon Family Group Headquarters.

How Al-Anon conference approved literature helped me (2010, December). *The Forum,* 20.

How Al-Anon works for families & friends of alcoholics (2008). Virginia Beach, VA: Al-Anon Family Group Headquarters.

Mead, G.H. (1934). *Mind, self and society.* Chicago: University of Chicago Press.

National Library of Medicine/National Institutes of Health. (2011). *Alcoholism.* Retrieved from http://vsearch.nlm.nih.gov/vivisimo/cgi-bin/query- eta?v%3Aproject=medlineplus&query=alcoholism.

One day at a time in Al-Anon (2000). Virginia Beach, VA: Al-Anon Family Group Headquarters.

Opening our hearts: Transforming our losses (2007). Virginia Beach, VA: Al-Anon Family Group Headquarters.

Peterson, C., & Seligman, M.E.P. (2004). *Character strengths and virtues: A handbook and classification.* Washington, DC: American Psychological Association.

Resnick, S.G., & Rosenheck, R.A. (2006). Recovery and positive psychology: Parallel themes and potential synergies. *Psychiatric Services*, 57, 120–122.

Schopler, J.H., & Galinsky, M.J. (1993). Support groups as open systems: A model for practice and research. *Health and Social Work, 18,* 195–207.

Seligman, M.E.P., (2011). *Flourish: A visionary new understanding of happiness and well-being.* New York: Free Press.

Seligman, M.E.P. & Czikszentmihalyi, M. (2000). Positive psychology: An introduction. *American Psychologist, 55*, 5–14.

Shibutani, T. (1961). *Society and personality: An interactionist approach to social psychology.* Englewood Cliffs, NJ: Prentice-Hall.

The Wise Ways Fellowship. (2011). *The wise ways program.* Retrieved from http://wiseways.org/12traditionsofwiseways/supportgroupprogram.html.

Withorn, A. (1980). Helping ourselves: The limits and potential of self-help. *Social Policy, 11*(3), 20–27.

• CHAPTER SIX •

Healing through Healthy Doses of Positivity: Mothers' and Daughters' Positive Communication When Coping with Breast Cancer

Carla L. Fisher
George Mason University

Michelle Miller-Day
Chapman University

Jon F. Nussbaum
Pennsylvania State University

Since the early 1980s, researchers have explored connections between coping with and surviving cancer and positivity. Positivity has been framed in a variety of ways in psychological scholarship and, in an illness context, could include having a positive attitude about one's disease, thinking positively particularly about one's circumstances or future, and engaging in positive talk that might be considered hopeful or enlightened (e.g., Fredrickson, 2001; Greer, Morris, & Pettingale, 1979). For patients (and their support network), positivity has been classified as a healthy means of coping with cancer, particularly for those individuals with advanced stages of the disease. Moreover, positivity is often juxtaposed with any form of negativity, whether it be negative feelings (e.g., anger, sadness), thinking, or talk (e.g., disclosing one's fears). Some scholars even claim links between cancer mortality and pessimism or conversely between cancer survivorship and optimism, thereby advocating that a "fighting spirit" predicts cancer survival (e.g., Greer, 1991). Other scholars suggest a positive outlook buffers cancer-related distress and enhances a cancer patient's psychological well-being (e.g., Shelby et al., 2008). Psycho-oncology scholars have also demonstrated that to fully understand the implications of positivity when coping, it is vital to conceptualize positivity as an interactive process and not merely the patient's cognitive thought process about his or her cancer-related experiences (Wilkinson & Kitzinger, 2000).

This notable, widespread attention to positivity and cancer is certainly tied to the fact that "thinking positive" has become a prevalent social moral norm (Wilkinson & Kitzinger, 2000). Positivity as fundamental to surviving cancer is a prominent fixture in popular culture (Wilkinson & Kitzinger, 2000). This belief is evidenced by many self-help books geared toward cancer patients such as Winograd's (1992), *Get help, get positive, get well: How to survive cancer*, that infer this moral social norm is a key to beating the disease. One might also then presume that anything negative would work against survival. There is a clear societal push for cancer patients to be positive at all times. Cancer patients encounter a "moral and psychological pressure to 'think positively' about their disease" (de Raeve, 1997, p. 249). In fact, some patients seek help from psychologists and other mental health professionals fearing they are not positive enough (Gray & Doan, 1990). Yet, this linkage between optimistic thinking and behavior is not *always* positive. Rather, positivity might not always result in healthy coping and instead result in feelings of forced optimism or restrictions in how one can cope. Scholars have identified the controversy created by a push for positivity in cancer care (e.g., Spiegel, 2001) and some self-help books even attend to this quandary by attempting to integrate some sense of reality into the cancer-positivity connection. For instance, Kahane (1995) writes to cancer patients about letting go of the "shoulds" that include pressure to be positive.

As Wilkinson and Kitzinger (2000) advocated we need to "think differently" about positivity (as it too can have a dark side). In this chapter, we explore the healing potential of positive communication further and attempt to address it holistically to further understand how it can be used to heal. Specifically, we examine breast cancer patients' interactive experiences within mother-daughter relationships. We begin by exploring breast cancer coping and its connection to the societal ideal of "being positive" including the interactive nature of positivity, or the experience of positive communication, in cancer coping.

Positive Communication in Coping with Breast Cancer

Positivity and coping is largely conceptualized as a cognitive phenomenon even though cancer patients' coping experiences are largely *interactive*.

Optimism is often categorized as a critical form of support, a resource for patients, and a means for loved ones to help patients cope (Bloom, Stewart, Johnston, Banks, & Fobair, 2001). In other words, the healing potential of positivity must also be considered as an interactive experience within support networks, rather than just a thought process experienced by individuals. The idea of "being positive" is often communicated by loved ones to patients, or vice versa, and patients' ability to *be* positive is tied to their coping-related interactions within supportive relationships. Hence, an interaction approach more so than an individual approach will be useful in determining the extent to which positive communication is helpful and adaptive for patients.

A considerable amount of research has focused on the nature of positive communication and health effects among cancer patients that demonstrates a range of health-promoting effects as diagnosed women learn to manage traumatic changes within a complex world that becomes their new "normal." Communicating a positive outlook, encouragement or reassurance, as well as being humorous are all positive or optimistic behaviors family members and patients engage in to cope with this life-threatening disease (Helgeson & Cohen, 1999). The scholarship shows that communicating positivity in these ways can be helpful to patients' adjustment and overall wellness.

Although positive communication is linked with healthier coping and wellness outcomes, studies also suggest this approach may not always result in health-promoting outcomes. Patients may not always perceive positive communication as supportive. For instance, breast cancer patients describe "forced optimism" (e.g., pressure to be cheery when not ready) as insufficient support (Lichtman, Taylor, & Wood, 1987) that can prompt feelings of dismay (Peters-Golden, 1982).

Chalmers, Thomson, and Degner (1996) found that breast cancer patients' perceptions of the helpfulness of positive communication from family may be influenced by two communication dimensions. First, positive communication patterns between patients and loved ones were either restricted (talk about physical or technical cancer experiences) or unrestricted (talk of emotional aspects of cancer). Second, positivity was either realistic or unrealistic. Unrestricted, realistic positive communication was the least common experienced by patients although this type of interaction helped facilitate disease adjustment. Communicating realistic positivity in an unrestricted manner promoted congruent communication between patients and family, minimizing regrets, enhancing understanding about disease risk, and facilitating coping. Interestingly, restricted, unrealistic positive communication was most common, yet most problematic. Patients and family members viewed this pattern as interfering with the patient's disease adjustment and hindering their ability to come to terms with their illness or disease risk. This pattern was also linked to fear, anxiety, family conflict, remorse about interactions, and lack of preparation for the patient's death.

Collectively, past research suggests that merely *being* positive does not automatically equate with better health, coping, or disease adjustment. To actually engage in positive communication in a *healing* manner is undoubtedly complex. And yet, doing so in a competent manner that meets patients' needs is a vital part of helping them adapt. Many studies demonstrate that family communication influences patients' ability to adjust, maintain well-being, and manage challenges they face (Helgeson & Cohen, 1999). Without healthy kin support, patients have more depressive symptoms, troubled relationships, and cancer-related symptoms (Helgeson & Cohen, 1999). Unfortunately, families facing cancer sometimes engage in unhealthy behaviors that inhibit well-being because they lack the resources and life experiences necessary to help them engage in healthy positive coping behavior given that competent communication develops across the life span with life experience and maturity (Pecchioni, Wright, & Nussbaum, 2005). Thus, families need help learning healthy ways of communicating after a diagnosis.

Leading psycho-oncology scholars and the National Cancer Institute (NCI) have called for research that can provide families with a "psychosocial map" for coping with cancer (see Rolland & Williams, 2005). Families need psychosocial resources that help them communicate in ways that maximize wellness. For women diagnosed with breast cancer, the mother-daughter bond is especially critical to their adjustment.

Mothers, Daughters, and Breast Cancer Coping

For many breast cancer patients, their illness is a mother-daughter experience. Mothers and daughters are often described as having "linked lives" (Fischer, 1991), linked through their role as women and linchpins of communication and family. Though not without tension, mothers and daughters encounter a range of changes across the life span that can intensify emotional closeness and enhance communication competence (Fisher & Miller-Day, 2006; Miller-Day, 2004). As breast cancer patients cope with traumatic changes, they are simultaneously concerned about their mothers' and daughters' well-being (and disease risk) and vice versa. Together they encounter challenging relational, psychological, and physical changes. For instance, daughters of diagnosed women can face a role reversal as they provide support and caregiving to their mother, often for the first time in their relationship (Berlin, 2008). In addition, having a mother with cancer increases a daughter's cancer risk. As such, daughters battle a chronic psychological disease risk for themselves and also of recurrence for their mothers (Kenen, Ardern-Jones, & Eeles, 2003). It is not entirely surprising then that mothers' and daughters' stress responses are highly correlated both psychologically and physiologically. When mothers experience post-traumatic stress disorder symptoms, elevated stress hormones, or decreased immunological functioning, so too do their daughters (e.g., Boyer et al., 2002; Cohen & Pollack, 2005). The mother-daughter cancer experience is acutely unique. Unlike other kin, they cope with personal risk and, concurrently, want to support one another.

Previous research by the first author explored how mothers and daughters cope with the disease at various points in the life span. Fisher (2008, 2010, 2011, in process) examined how they coped with the disease through emotional support communication and identified whether the support was helpful, hence adaptive, in patients' disease adjustment (see Fisher, 2008, 2010). A notable theme that emerged across all ages was that women described "positive communication" (e.g., encouragement, assurance, a positive attitude) as talk that centered on remaining positive as they struggled with changes. Their descriptions of this support capture the complex nature of positive communication and its potential for healing.

Research Questions

The women in this study described the potential healing value of positive communication. First we seek to offer a description of the emergent theme of positive communication from the original study to capture how this type of communication is enacted by mothers and daughters, across adulthood, in an adaptive manner. Second, we also ask about what was perceived as unhelpful positive communication. Two research questions guided our analysis:

> RQ1: For mothers/daughters coping with breast cancer, what constitutes adaptive positive communication?
>
> RQ2: For mothers/daughters coping with breast cancer, what constitutes maladaptive positive communication?

Method

Sample

The original study sampled women diagnosed in young, middle, and later adulthood and their mothers or adult daughters. Purposive sampling was used since predefined groups were needed. Women were recruited through a university newswire and database of students, hospitals, and support groups. Women with a diagnosis and who had received treatment within the last 36 months were eligible. Diagnosed women were asked to recruit their mother or daughter. Each woman received $25 and/or research credit.

This study consisted of 40 diagnosed women: 8 young[1] adults (ages 30-39), 20 midlife adults (44-52), and 12 later-life adults (57–69). In addition, 38 of their mothers/daughters participated: 25 young adults (18–37), 5 midlife adults (51–56), and 8 later-life adults (58–83). A total of 35 dyads participated (78 women). Three dyads had an additional daughter participate whereas five diagnosed women participated without a partner. Most were Caucasian (98.7%), from the East Coast (85.3%) with a college-level education, and half were married.

Procedures

As this is part of a larger study, only procedures relevant for the current analysis are outlined. All women participated in individual, in-depth, semi-structured, script-guided interviews. The Interviewer used a life-span recall method by asking interviewees to describe their communication prior to diagnosis and up to the present day. Participants were asked specifically about enacting or receiving emotional support and their perceptions of what was helpful or unhelpful in facilitating adjustment. Full transcriptions resulted in 2,434 single-spaced pages of data.

Analyses

Glaser and Strauss's (1967) and Strauss and Corbin's (1998) grounded theory approach was used. Forms of emotional support termed "positive communication" were analyzed with special attention paid to how positive communication could function adaptively and maladaptively in diagnosed women's adjustment. If participants perceived the support as helpful in their ability to cope with cancer, then the support was coded as adaptive and helpful in maximizing women's quality of life. If participants perceived the support as unhelpful (i.e., not helpful to them in coping), the support was coded as maladaptive. Illuminating the participants' communicative experiences required repeated examination until theoretical saturation occurred; that is, no new patterns were evident. Using the qualitative management computer program ATLAS.ti.5.2, diagnosed women and their mothers' and daughters' perspectives were combined so that the presentation of themes was according to both perspectives The analytical process involved (1) discovery of concepts through open coding, (2) discovery of categories via thematic salience, and (3) developing and refining the categories by identifying each category's properties and dimensions (Strauss & Corbin, 1998). According to Owen (1984), thematic salience is reflected in recurrence, repetition, and forcefulness (i.e., linguistic traces of emphasis and importance). In the last analytical step, the categories were reviewed again to identify similar descriptions, quotations, and ideas while making a note of these for descriptive purposes. Using thick rich description in the presentation of analyses is an important verification strategy to ensures transferability of the study's findings.

Findings

Adaptive Positive Communication

Across every age group, the primary motivation to engage in positive communication was to change or elevate one's affective state. Namely, mothers' and daughters' use of positive communication was enacted in an effort to alleviate a diagnosed woman's negative emotional states (sadness, fear, anger, anxiety). Diagnosed women often described this support functioning adaptively because "she picks me up" or "makes me feel better." As a diagnosed mother stated, "She's very in tune to how I feel. Picks me up, you know?" Mothers/daughters of diagnosed women described actively trying to "pump up" their daughter/mother's feelings as they coped with stressful changes, such as struggling with body image after a mastectomy, losing hair during chemotherapy, coping with physical treatment side effects like nausea and pain, and dealing with uncertainty about the future while waiting for test results. Daughters/mothers of diagnosed women also disclosed that they talked positively about the stress or disease when they did not know what to say or do. Some women also used positive talk because they felt their diagnosed mother/daughter needed "tough love," either because she had been talking "negative" for a prolonged period or was not aware that things "could be worse."

Mothers and daughters enacted positivity in many ways. For example, they used reassurances (e.g., "I know you'll be okay" or "You're doing the right treatment") that seemed particularly important early in the disease trajectory when uncertainty was high. Additionally, encouragement was used to motivate diagnosed women to keep moving forward, particularly during debilitating treatment. For example, a daughter recalled her mother encouraging her as she struggled with continuing chemotherapy saying,

"Honey, you've gone this far. I think you could do it ... you got that far you can do two more." Women also felt that compliments about how they looked or were coping helped them feel better. A daughter recalled this form of positivity moments after having surgery: "The first thing I said to my mom is, 'Give me your lipstick. I need some lipstick' [Mom said] 'My God, you look good. You just don't look like you had any surgery!'" Women also talked about sharing survivor stories or reading daily affirmations together. For instance, one daughter discussed how every morning she and her diagnosed mother would read from an affirmation book. She felt that this form of positive communication was critical to healthy coping – "It kind of helped us wake up and at least think 'Okay! Today's going to be better.'"

Mothers and daughters also tried to talk positively by reframing situations to highlight the "positive side." Reframing seemed to be particularly uplifting. For example, one mother reframed her daughter's anxiety about the "what-ifs" by telling her to focus only on what they knew for sure. Another mother reframed her daughter's complaints about her husband (who was not helping with the children and housework during her chemotherapy) by telling her of worse situations. A third mother reframed the seriousness of her daughter's disease by focusing on how happy she was that the diagnosis was not terminal (a revelation she had after the Virginia Tech tragedy). Reframing seemed to help diagnosed women feel better and appraise their situations more realistically: For instance, one diagnosed daughter recalled: [Mom said] "let's just focus on all of what we know, and it is very scary, and I don't want you to die. And that would be horrible so let's just focus on what we know." And she kind of went through all the positives.

Many women also stressed that positive communication was more than just supportive talk during distress or the opposite of negative talk. Rather, many women perceived their positive behavior was also a philosophy of living or a way to survive cancer. As a mother of a diagnosed women stated,

> I've learned from experience. I am 70 years old and I've learned from experience that it doesn't do any good to think about it and sit around and mope ...you have to get up and go out and do something to make you feel better.

Similarly a daughter of a diagnosed mom stated,

> I think that when something like this happens, if you're not positive everybody suffers....The person who has it suffers because you're not really supporting them because all you're doing is talking negative. That doesn't make them feel better and it makes them feel worse about themselves. If you're positive, they have a better outlook

on it, like, "Okay—You're right. I am almost done [with treatment]."…They want to get it done and they want to be fine when it's done.

Diagnosed women perceived this communication functioning adaptively for their adjustment because it helped change their mood to be less negative, made them feel better, gave them hope about the future, made them realize things could be worse, or motivated them to keep fighting. Positive communication seemed especially helpful in managing stressful uncertainty. One diagnosed daughter waiting for a test result stated:

If I say, "Oh my gosh! I got to go through this test. I hope everything's okay. Oh my gosh! I hope it doesn't come back!" And she'll be like "[Daughter's name], don't even worry! Everything's going to be fine. You'll be fine. If it is something, we'll deal with it." … Sometimes I just need to hear that.

Moreover, mothers and daughters felt that positive communication had a reciprocal health-promoting effect. It helped set the tone for daughters/mothers of diagnosed women and reassured diagnosed women that their mother/daughter was okay. As one diagnosed mother stated, "I was positive about it. That made them feel positive about it. Or maybe I felt so positive about it because they talk positively about it." Similarly a daughter with a diagnosed mom said, "She was very, very positive and very upbeat right away…That was a really good thing to hear right off the bat."

While there were many similar experiences, one notable age difference emerged. Midlife diagnosed mothers who had young-adult or late adolescent daughters at the time of diagnosis were the only age group of diagnosed women who did *not* describe positive communication in a maladaptive manner. In other words, these diagnosed mothers always felt it was helpful when their daughters talked positively. Diagnosed moms felt their daughters' positivity reassured them that their daughter was coping okay. It is important to note that this age group of dyads were also the only group to experience extreme avoidance or withdrawal on the part of daughters (see Fisher, 2010). This age group of daughters often avoided talking about cancer, a finding that has emerged in other studies demonstrating that for adolescent daughters, breast cancer is especially traumatic (e.g., Stiffler, Barada, Hosei, & Haase, 2008). Thus, it is likely that for diagnosed women with young daughters, positive talk alleviated concerns they had about their daughter's welfare.

Maladaptive Positive Communication

Regardless of age, mothers and daughters also described positive communication as not always supportive or meeting their needs. Like adaptive positive communication, maladaptive positive support took various forms (e.g., encouragement, assurance, positive reframing) across cancer-related contexts (e.g., body image, dealing with treatment side effects) and was used to alter negative moods. A common feature in women's descriptions of unhelpful positive communication was a silencing effect that centered around three interpretations about why the support was not helpful: (1) *minimizing or not validating feelings or concerns;* (2) *preventing them from expressing negative emotions;* and (3) *not allowing for ups and downs across the cancer trajectory.* These maladaptive functions are described below.

Minimizing or Not Validating Feelings or Concerns. Positive talk was maladaptive when diagnosed women felt their mother or daughter was dismissive of their feelings. As one diagnosed young-adult daughter stated, "As long as it's just talking positive and not crossing over [my feelings], it's helpful. Once [she] crosses over something then it's not helpful." In this case, the daughter recalled her mother minimizing her concerns about recurrence: "Sometimes she goes, 'You don't really have to worry about that because you're young and your doctors are on top of things.'" When women felt positive communication dismissed their concerns or feelings, they also inferred that their mother/daughter did not understand what they were dealing with. A diagnosed daughter described this effect when her mother's positive communication undermined her struggles with her new body image after her mastectomy:

> I have a big divot under my arm [from surgery]. The first time I went bathing suit shopping I was with my mom and that was one time I remember [her saying] "Well it doesn't look too bad." And I'm standing there. I came home bawling that really upset me. ... I think that was one of those [instances] where you don't understand. Like I remember saying to her she didn't understand because she wasn't the one going through it.

Another daughter recalled that her mother's positivity, right after she disclosed her diagnosis, made her feel as though her mother did not realize how serious this was. She recalled: "I think my initial reaction to her being so positive was almost like 'No it's not! What do you mean? How can you think like that?'" Although this interpretation emerged across ages, feeling unsupported was most prominent for diagnosed women who were daughters. In these instances, it seemed critical for mothers and daughters to validate the diagnosed woman's feelings while also engaging in positivity.

Preventing One from Venting. Diagnosed women also perceived that positive communication was not helpful when it shut down their ability to vent. These women described their mother/daughter using positive talk to prevent negative talk. Although both diagnosed mothers and daughters experienced this outcome, diagnosed mothers described this more prevalently. One diagnosed mother asserted that "negative talk" was just not in her daughter's vocabulary.

> If someone would ask me how I felt or whatever and if I would talk about it in a negative way, she would not be happy about that. She wants that positive attitude. She would say, "Don't dwell on the negative." She still tells me if I start being negative.

Although women seemed to appreciate the consistency of being positive as they coped (and often defended their mother/daughter's positive support), they also talked about wanting to just vent at various points. A diagnosed woman recalled feeling silenced when her daughter's positive communication worked in this manner saying, "Let me get it out of my system, kind of thing!" It seemed critical that diagnosed women also have an opportunity to vent their negative affect in order for positive communication to function as health-promoting. As one mother stated, "I wish sometimes they'd allow me to talk more than they do…They don't want to hear it."

Not Allowing for Ups and Downs. At times, positive communication seemed to infer that having ups and downs across the cancer trajectory was not "normal." As such, mothers and daughters used positive support to silence the down times. For instance, one diagnosed daughter mentioned not really wanting to hear her mother's positive talk when she was feeling debilitated from treatment. Rather, she just wanted to "lay there." This silencing effect was interconnected to the previous two themes in that it was critical for positive communication to both validate negative feelings and allow diagnosed women to vent about them.

Women sometimes recognized that having ups and downs while coping with breast cancer was realistic. When mothers and daughters normalized ups and downs, this seemed to facilitate supportive positive communication. One mother of a diagnosed daughter explained the importance of this reality:

> Sometimes when she was down [and I was] trying to convince her that it was going to be okay, you know, it was going to get better. I think sometimes she was very, very tired and down….You know, you can't go through something like that and not have the ups and downs.

Discussion and Practical Implications

As mothers and daughters in this study shared, positive communication can play a profound role in helping diagnosed women adapt to a diagnosis.

Mothers and daughters engage in positive talk in many ways, and this support seemed most helpful in altering a woman's mood, giving her motivation to move forward and find happiness. Given that the original study sought to highlight diversity in women's experiences across the life span, it is vital to note that regardless of women's age at diagnosis, they all perceived positive communication could be instrumentally helpful to them as they coped with the disease. It is also important to note that across age, women found that sometimes this support was *not* helpful. In addition, while some of the women's experiences is in line with previous research on positive support enacted in a cancer context (e.g., encouragement, assurances, affection, and reframing) other forms (e.g., sharing survivor stories or reading daily affirmations) may be more unique to the mother-daughter or woman-to-woman bonds. Further research that compares positive communication across family relationships may provide insight.

The findings provide some insight that can be helpful to mothers and daughters by enriching their interactions as they cope together. We summarize some of these findings below and bring to the surface some practical implications for families and professionals helping them.

Preventing the Silencing Effect

Positive communication may not be helpful when it also results in women feeling silenced. In this case, the potential benefit of this communication seems to backfire. Rather than uplift or change a woman's perspective or mood (mothers' and daughters' original intentions), positive communication can result in women feeling invalidated about their fears, concerns, and emotions. For some women, it led them to believe their mother or daughter did not understand what they were going through. And, in effect, restricted their communication.

According to Wilkinson and Kitzinger (2000), thinking positive needs to be understood not just as an individual coping style but as "a conversational device which is interactionally useful in enabling cancer patients to talk about their suffering and distress" (p. 806). The emergent themes in the present study about the maladaptive functioning of positive communication support this statement. Talking about suffering may include releasing distressful emotions—what women described as "negative." These women often felt it was important *not* to talk "negatively." Yet, this interpretation may lead to a silencing effect. When mothers and daughters do not recognize that positive thinking or talk should also enable patients to talk about distress and not exclude negative talk, it restricts their interaction. In other words, negative and positive communication might be connected in the coping process rather than polar opposites that need to be separated.

We reframe these findings as communication tips to help mothers and daughters enact helpful positive support. We offer these as tips for families but also as tools practitioners can use when providing families with a "psychosocial map" of coping with cancer. These guiding principles seem to also reiterate Chalmers et al.'s (1996) work in that for positive communication to be health-promoting, it should also be unrestrictive and realistic.

First, it is important to validate feelings and concerns when using positive support. If positive talk "glosses over" women's distress or concerns, patients can feel that their mother or daughter does not understand or appreciate what they are experiencing. As Chalmers et al. (1996) noted, families sometimes restrict cancer-related talk to exclude the emotional aspects of the disease. However, validating concerns or feelings, including distress, is a verbal technique that is known to be helpful to patients in promoting healthy adjustment (Helgeson & Cohen, 1999). Thus, while positive communication can be used to reframe one's anxiety or negative affect, if mothers and daughters do not also validate the diagnosed woman's feelings, it could be perceived as unsupportive. Validating feelings and concerns should be used with positive communication simultaneously.

Second, by validating a diagnosed mother or daughter's concerns and feelings, one also opens the door for releasing negative emotions. Women in our study expressed that they wished their family would let them talk, particularly when it was negative. Restricting what someone can say can result in a patient feeling silenced or that her voice is unimportant. Moreover, restricted communication patterns are associated with less healthy adaptation (Chalmers et al., 1996). Thus, it is vital that positive communication still allow women an opportunity to vent. Unrestricted communication includes talk about the emotional side of cancer (Chalmers et al., 1996). Hearing patients' fears, sadness, anger, or anxiety is not easy for loved ones and can be distressing. Nevertheless, like validating feelings, having the opportunity to talk about negative emotions is just as valuable to patients' adjustment (Helgeson & Cohen, 1999). It may be helpful for family to reframe how they perceive their loved one's talk about distress, viewing it instead as part of the coping process because it is an opportunity to release stress.

Finally, by recognizing that positive communication is a conversational experience, and one that might also include an opportunity to talk about distress, we can understand the role of positivity in the coping process more realistically. In essence, it is okay to have ups and downs. Realistic positivity is important. Mothers and daughters need to refine the balancing act of being positive by viewing it in conjunction with the opportunity to express emotions that are viewed as "negative."

There is a clear juxtaposition between being positive and talking negative that continues to prevail in scholarship, popular culture, and moral social assumptions. Rather than contrasting these two experiences as different coping styles or ways of life, mothers and daughters may benefit from viewing positive and negative communication as *connected*. Doing so can ease the societal and moral pressure put on patients to be positive, no matter what, and help families to realistically visualize how positivity, negativity, and coping all go hand in hand. In sum, it is okay to have ups and downs and those negative feelings are warranted. It is helpful to vent that distress, talk about it, have it validated by a loved one and, at the same time, positive communication can be a way to reframe those feelings and concerns and lift one back up.

Note

1. According to Arnett (2000), developmental phases of adulthood have evolved due to sociocultural changes in society affecting aging. Emerging adulthood precedes young adulthood which can extend into one's 30s.

References

Arnett, J. J. (2000). Emerging adulthood: A theory of development from the late teens through the twenties. *American Psychologist, 55,* 469–480.

Bloom, J. R., Stewart, S. L., Johnston, M., Banks, P., & Fobair, P. (2001). Sources of support and the physical and mental wellbeing of young women with breast cancer. *Social Science & Medicine, 53,* 1513–1524.

Berlin, K. L. (2008). *Psychological and biological stress during mother-daughter communication about breast cancer risk.* Unpublished doctoral dissertation, Vanderbilt University. Retrieved June 1, 2009.

Boyer, B. A., Bubel, D., Jacobs, S. R., Knolls, M. L., Harwell, V. D.,Goscicka, M., & Keegan, A. (2002). Posttraumatic stress in women with breast cancer and their daughters. *The American Journal of Family Therapy, 30,* 323–338.

Chalmers, K., Thomson, K., & Degner, L. F. (1996). Information, support, and communication needs of women with a family history of breast cancer. *Cancer Nursing, 19,* 204–213.

Cohen, M., & Pollack, S. (2005). Mothers with breast cancer and their adult daughters: The relationship between mothers' reaction to breast cancer and their daughters' emotional and neuroimmune status. *Psychosomatic Medicine, 67,* 64–71.

De Raeve, L. (1997). Positive thinking and moral oppression in cancer care. *European Journal of Cancer Care, 6,* 249–256.

Fischer, L. R. (1991). *Linked lives.* New York: Harper and Row.

Fisher, C. L. (2008). *Adaptive communicative behavior of mothers and their adult daughters after a breast cancer diagnosis.* Unpublished doctoral dissertation, The Pennsylvania State University.

Fisher, C. L. (2010). Coping with breast cancer across adulthood: Emotional support communication in the mother-daughter bond. *Journal of Applied Communication Research, 38,* 386–411.

Fisher, C. L. (2011). "Her pain was my pain": Mothers and daughters communicatively sharing the breast cancer journey. In M. Miller-Day (Ed.), *Going through this together: Family communication, connection, and health transitions* (pp. 57–76). New York: Peter Lang.

Fisher, C. L. (in process). *Coping together, side by side: Enriching mother-daughter communication during the breast cancer journey.* Cresskill, NJ: Hampton Press.

Fisher, C. L., & Miller-Day, M. (2006). Communicating over the life span: The mother-adult daughter relationship. In K. Floyd & M. T. Morman (Eds.), *Widening the family circle: New research on family communication* (pp. 3–20). Thousand Oaks, CA: Sage.

Fredrickson, B. L. (2001). The role of positive emotions in positive psychology: The broaden-and-build theory of positive emotions. *American Psychologist, 56,* 218–226.

Glaser, B. G., & Strauss, A. L. (1967). *The discovery of grounded theory: Strategies for qualitative research.* New York: Aldine de Gruyter.

Gray, R. E., & Doan, B. D. (1990). Heroic self-healing and cancer: Clinical issues for the health professions. *Journal of Palliative Care, 6,* 32–41.

Greer, S. (1991). Psychological response to cancer and survival. *Psychological Medicine, 21,* 43–49.

Greer, S., Morris, T., & Pettingale, K.W. (1979). Psychological response to breast cancer: Effect on outcome. *The Lancet II* (October 13), 785–787.

Helgeson, V. S., & Cohen, S. (1999). Social support and adjustment to cancer: Reconciling descriptive, correlational, and intervention research. In R. M. Suinn & G. R. VandenBos (Eds.), *Cancer patients and their families: Readings on disease course, coping, and psychological interventions* (pp. 53–79). Washington, DC: American Psychological Association.

Kahane, D. H. (1995). *No less a woman: Femininity, sexuality and breast cancer,* 2nd ed. Alameda, CA: Hunter House.

Kenen, R., Ardern-Jones, A., & Eeles, R. (2003). Living with chronic risk: Healthy women with a family history of breast/ovarian cancer. *Health, Risk & Society, 5,* 315–331.

Litchman, R. R., Taylor, S. E., Wood, J. V. (1987). Social support and marital adjustment after breast cancer. *Journal of Psychosocial Oncology, 5,* 47–74.

Miller-Day, M. (2004). *Communication among grandmothers, mothers, and adult daughters: A qualitative study of maternal relationships.* Mahwah, NJ: Erlbaum.

Owen, W. F. (1984). Interpretive themes in relational communication. *Quarterly Journal of Speech, 70,* 274–287.

Pecchioni, L. L., Wright, K., & Nussbaum, J. F. (2005). *Life-span communication.* Mahwah, NJ: Erlbaum.

Peters-Golden, H. (1982). Breast cancer: Varied perceptions of social support in the illness experience. *Social Science and Medicine, 16,* 483–491.

Rolland, J. S., & Williams, J. K. (2005). Toward a biopsychosocial model for 21st-century genetics. *Family Process, 44,* 3–24.

Shelby, R. A., Crespin, T. R., Wells-Di Gregorio, S. M., Lamdan, R. M., Siegel, J. E., & Taylor, K. L. (2008). Optimism, social support, and adjustment in African American women with breast cancer. *Journal of Behavioral Medicine, 31,* 433–444.

Spiegel, D. (2001) Mind matters: Coping and cancer progression, *Journal of Psychosomatic Research, 50,* 287–290.

Stiffler, D., Barada, B., Hosei, B., & Haase, J. (2008). When mom has breast cancer: Adolescent daughters' experiences of being parented. *Oncology Nursing Forum, 35,* 933–940.

Strauss, A., & Corbin, J. (1998). *Basics of qualitative research: Techniques and procedures for developing grounded theory.* Thousand Oaks, CA: Sage.

Wilkinson, S., & Kitzinger, C. (2000). Thinking differently about thinking positive: A discursive approach to cancer patients' talk. *Social Science & Medicine, 50,* 797–811.

Winograd, S. (1992). *Get help, get positive, get well: How to survive cancer.* Highland City, FL: Rainbow Books.

Section Two
Positive Communication and Relational Wellness

• CHAPTER SEVEN •

Moving from Positive Thinking to Positive Talk: Implications for Relational Well-Being

Kelly F. Albada
North Carolina State University

Jessica L. Moore
North Carolina State University

Many scholars consider the ways we think and talk about close relationships, as well as communicate within close relationships, to be important indicators of individual and relational well-being. Though our relational thoughts and behavior may seem to come to us naturally, we are frequently making cognitive and communicative *choices* (Miller & Perlman, 2009). Notably, it is these choices that have the capacity to inhibit or enhance our individual and relational well-being. This chapter examines connections between close relationships and well-being by considering the ways in which cognition and communication contribute to the development, maintenance, and enhancement of close relationships. Moreover, this chapter confers special attention to the function of positivity in cognitive and communicative processes through examining research on positive illusions, expressive writing, affirmations, and storytelling. Ultimately, this chapter conveys that close relationships are important to human health and well-being and that positive thinking and talking facilitate the establishment and preservation of rewarding relationships if enacted prudently.

Close Relationships and Well-Being

It has been argued that frequent and positive interactions with intimate partners are a necessity for humans to function normally (Baumeister & Leary, 1995). What's more, researchers have established that high-quality social ties contribute to physical (Berscheid & Reis, 1998) *and* psychological wellness (Argyle, 1987). For instance, receiving social support is associated with improved cardiovascular, endocrine, neuroendocrine, and immune system functioning (Seeman, 1996; Uchino et al., 1996). Research additionally indicates that people with histories of economic hardship often have elevated allostatic loads, a risk factor for various health problems and earlier morbidity; however, people who have hardship histories *and* positive social relationships evidence lower prevalence of elevated allostatic load (Russek & Schwartz, 1997). As Ryff and Singer (2000) explained, positive social relationships may buffer people from the negative impact of other life hardships on physical health. Ultimately, the physiological impact of maintaining positive social ties is conclusive—people who establish and preserve close relationships have better physical health and lower mortality rates that those who do not maintain close social ties (Berkman & Glass, 2000).

In addition to physical health benefits, the quality of our connections with others can have profound affects on our psychological health. Alcoholism, eating disorders, schizophrenia, and depression, among other psychological health disorders, are more likely to afflict people with inadequate social ties (Segrin, 1998). Generally speaking, people in committed intimate relationships are happier than those who are not in committed relationship (Diener, Gohm, Suh, & Oishi, 2000), and the presence of such positive feelings about close relationships has been linked to psychological well-being (Fletcher & Fitness, 1990). Paradoxically, people who cope well with life's stressors tend to be those who enlist social support (Veroff, Kulka, & Douvan, 1981), and successfully coping with life stressors is critical in maintaining healthy relationships (Weisman & Worden, 1972). Being able to read others, communicate thoughts and feelings, and effectively manage emotions in social situations often creates a positive impression for others, and these positive impressions serve as the building blocks for successful relationships (Segrin & Taylor, 2007). In sum, the quality of our relationships contributes significantly and profoundly to our happiness and outlook on life.

Positive patterns of thinking and communicating are often described as key factors for individual and relational health; however, research on "thinking" and "talking" is multifaceted. Such research is explored below.

Positive Thinking and Well-Being

Most people like to think of their significant other as being kind, smart, attractive, trustworthy and by and large, a likable person. The fact of the matter is that what people get in a relational partner is usually something less. So how do we maintain happy close relationships with people who possess some positive traits, but don't exactly measure up to our idealized standards? Research suggests that people develop positive illusions that portray their partner *and* relationship in the best possible light (Murray, Holmes, & Griffin, 1996; Taylor & Brown, 1994).

As a way of shaping relationship confidence, individuals weave stories that depict their partner's faults in the best possible light. The illusions that people create are not altogether false insofar that they are usually an amalgamation of idealized perceptions and realistic knowledge (Murray & Holmes, 1994, 1999). It is not that we overlook the negative elements of our partner or relationship altogether, but that we consider negative characteristics less significant while concomitantly emphasizing and amplifying the positive ones. For instance, research shows that people in committed relationships will accommodate divergent behaviors by assigning benign attributions (Rusbult, Yovetich, & Verette, 1996) and will integrate positive behavioral anomalies into coherent schemas of each other's worthiness (Murray & Holmes, 1996). Such positive construal of potentially negative attributes may strengthen positive feelings people have about their partners. Research also reveals that people often consider their partners' positive qualities as being more socially rare and unique than their deficiencies (Goodfriend, 2004). Regardless of the underlying mechanism, growing evidence supports that positive illusions are critical for individual and relational well-being (Taylor & Brown, 1988).

Several scholars contend that a certain degree of idealization is critical for satisfying close relationships (Murray, Holmes, & Griffin, 1996). "The allure of a partners' virtues draws individuals into their relationships, creating feelings of confidence and hope that belie the lack of more representative experiences" (p. 80). It is the reconfiguration or amplification of such virtues that may assist couples in managing their relational wellness over time. Taylor and Brown (1988) posit that constructing illusions about the self and others increase perception of control and functions as a buffer, protecting self-esteem in the face of threats. Studies show that self-esteem is bolstered when we believe that we are needed and loved by partners who we perceive to be highly desirable (Murray et al., 2000). Believing that a partner mirrors one's image of the relational ideal allows one to feel safe and secure in one's commitments (Murstein, 1971), thereby reducing experiences of cognitive uncertainty. Holmes and Remple (1989) speculate that seeing oneself in a partner fosters a sense of certainty, predictability, and assumed similarity. Positive illusions promote psychological well-being as well as "higher motivation, greater persistence, more effective performance, and ultimately, greater successes" (Taylor & Brown, 1988, p. 199). The National Institute for Mental Health report (1995) concludes that "considerable evidence suggest positive psychological benefits for people who believe their future will be rosier than they have any right to expect. Such optimism keeps people in a positive mood, motivates them to work toward future goals. . .and gives them a sense of being in control of their destiny" (p. 182). Interestingly, it seems that positive idealization of our partners not only makes *us* feel good, it seems to improve *their* esteem as well (Murray et al., 1996). Over time, it seems, *our partners* slowly become convinced that they are the wonderful people we have judged them to be, and *we* revise what it is we want such that our ideal standards reflect our current partner. As noted by Miller and Perlman (2009), we conveniently decide that the qualities our partners have are the one's we want. In sum, evidence suggests that positive illusions in close relationships are associated with greater satisfaction, love, trust, and, ultimately, longer lasting relationships (Miller, Niehuis, & Huston, 2006).

Research suggests that positive illusions have the potential to assist in the healthy construction, maintenance, and enhancement of close relationships. In line with these findings, research on the psychological, physiological, and potential relational benefits of expressive writing is promising.

Expressive Writing and Well-Being

Confronting personal issues via thinking and talking, among other processes, has been found to promote physical health and subjective well-being. Pennebaker (1999) posits that the act of constructing stories is a natural human process that not only allows people to understand their experiences, but *themselves*. Putting thoughts into narrative form seems to assist people with maintaining a sense of predictability and control over their lives (Pennebaker & Seagal, 1999), particularly during times of uncertainty. Research has revealed that when people are able to put their emotional experiences into narrative form, physical and mental health typically improves.

A multitude of studies provide evidence to support expressive writing as a useful tool for physical and psychological health management. Expressive writing researcher indicates positive outcomes for blood pressure, liver enzymes, lung function, the immune system, and other biological markers (Baikie & Wilhelm, 2005; Slatcher & Pennebaker, 2007). The benefits of expressive writing for emotional health outcomes, such as mood (Pennebaker, Kiecolt-Glaser, & Glaser, 1988), psychological well-being

(Park & Blumberg, 2002), and communication behavior (Pennebaker & Graybeal, 2001), are also supported. To date, the findings for physical health have been more consistent and robust than psychological health, and it has been noted that expressive writing has failed to associate with positive outcomes across all psychological and physical health conditions (Baikie & Wilhelm, 2005).

Researchers have extended studies on expressive writing to close relationships. Researchers pose that the application of the expressive writing paradigm to couples may help partners communicate difficult feelings to one another and experience empathic understanding in return (Snyder, Gordon, & Baucom, 2006). Moreover, they argue, expressive writing in a relational context "provides an opportunity for restoring or creating the shared cognitive schema essential to intimacy and trust" (p. 155). For example, when people write expressively about recent relationship dissolutions, they are more likely than control groups to reunite with their partners (Gordon, Baucom, & Snyder, 2004). Likewise, when married couples that experience infidelity engage in expressive writing with their partners, they report reductions in anger, depression, PTSD-related symptoms, and marital distress (Snyder et al., 2004). Researchers noted, "The exchange of written disclosures [expressive writing] facilitated greater understanding and effected a substantial shift in their attitudes toward their partners" (p. 157). Other studies have explored the social effects of expressive writing among couples that are not distressed. Slatcher and Pennebaker (2006) found couples were significantly more willing to use positive and negative emotion words during routine instant messaging exchanges when exposed to relational expressive writing conditions compared to control conditions. Moreover, their study revealed that higher levels of positive emotion words were associated with higher levels of relationship stability; participants in the expressive writing group were also more likely to be dating their partner three months after the study regardless of the content of their messages. Research also reveals that expressive writing about one's partner has a positive impact on relational perceptions (Moore & Middleton, 2008). Participants in this investigation who engaged in positive expressive writing (i.e., writing about their partner's positive qualities or positive memories associated with their partner) reported greater levels of relationship stability, quality, and commitment, than did control groups.

Taken together, research findings on expressive writing in close relationships appear promising for those interested in the processes through which close relationships are initiated, sustained, and enhanced. Moreover, such findings shed light on potential opportunities for the application of expressive writing within the context of individual and relational well-being. Expressive writing as a tool for relational enhancement could be applied to a broad range of relationships, including friendships and families. Regardless of how narratives are formed or the mechanisms that underlie them, it is clear that they serve a critical function in people's lives and have implications for general well-being (Pennebaker & Seagal, 1999).

Positive Talking and Well-Being

As Rempel, Ross, and Holmes (2001) argue, thinking positively and communicating positively are strongly linked processes. In the simplest of characterizations, individuals express—verbally and nonverbally—their positive (or negative) thoughts to their relational partners, as well as respond in various ways to their partner's positive (or negative) messages. The reciprocal relationship between positive thinking and positive talking about one's partner, self, or relationship is explored in this section.

Positive Narratives and Affirmations

The ways in which we think positively about ourselves, our partners, and our relationship are manifested, altered, and reinforced through communication. Whether the messages are direct or indirect, verbal or nonverbal, or recounted or spontaneous, research on close relationships highlights the importance of relational communication in the establishment and maintenance of high-quality relationships. Relational narratives and affirmations are two communicative acts that reveal much about the interwoven processes of positive thinking and positive talking in close relationships.

Relational narratives. Segrin and Flora (2001) argue that one way to study a couple's reality is to examine the stories that they tell. Relational narratives may serve as an indirect method for assessing the affective state and motivational processes within romantic relationships (Holmberg, Orbuch, & Veroff, 2004). For instance, Fincham, Bradbury, and Scott (1990) suggest that past events are organized by what is most salient in the present; happy couples, so the argument goes, are likely to recount more positive events than unhappy couples within their stories. Moreover, happy couples are likely to recast negative events in positive light; whereas, unhappy couples may reflect positive events in a negative, or at least neutral, light. In other words, happy couples not only see each other in the best possible light, they also commonly express these positive or idealized notions of their partner and relationships in the relational narratives they tell.

Relational narratives may reveal the nature of the relational bond through both story content and the process of storytelling. The narrative content includes the topic of the story, events or beliefs that are emphasized, and degree of coherence between the partners., The narrative process involves the demonstrated affect during the storytelling, nonverbal feedback during storytelling (both when self or other are speaking) and coordination between the partners (e.g., finishing each other's sentences, interrupting). For instance, using this type of analysis, Carrere et al. (2000) were able to classify which newlywed couples would divorce within 4-6 years of marriage with 87% accuracy. Other researchers have similarly found that a spouse's affection and fondness for their partner and the unity within the relationship, as evidenced in the relational narrative, was predictive of marital satisfaction (Honeycutt, 1999) and family cohesion and warmth (Doohan, Carrere, Siler, & Beardslee, 2009). Doohan, Carrere, and Riggs (2010) propose that a couple's identity is negotiated through the telling of a story, thus narratives could be used as a "diagnostic tool in an effort to improve the communicative abilities of couples and their relational well being" (p. 74).

Positive affirmations. As discussed in the positive illusions and idealization section of this chapter, happy people tend to produce attributions that portray their partners positively. Specifically, happy people often perceive their partner's positive behavior as caused by internal, permanent, global characteristics and negative behavior as more contextually determined, less stable, and less general (Grigg, Fletcher, & Fitness, 1989). To this end, happy people produce attributions that enhance their relationship and dismiss those associated with negative events. Conversely, unhappy people produce attributions that distress or maintain distress in the relationship; they dismiss the implications of positive events and readily accept negative events (Grigg et al., 1989). Moreover, they also express more positive attributional statements (Rempel, Ross, & Holmes, 2001). Ironically, Holmes and Rempel (1989) found that positive attributional statements occurred most frequently in discussions about a past, negative behavior committed by their partner. The authors reason that the communication of positive attributions fosters the continued expression of positive behavior by the partner and, as a result, enhances relational well-being. It appears then that when we think positively about our partners we are more likely to communicate positively with the partner, which promotes future positive behavior.

Another factor in this process involves responding positively to a partner's communication. For instance, behaviorally affirming one's partner is important for relational well-being when it comes to a partner's goals or public presentation of self. In Rusbult and colleagues (2005) summary of the Michelangelo phenomenon, the authors articulate the key processes by which partner communication influences the movement of the self towards the ideal self. When partners are judged to display more insightful and affirming behaviors during a discussion of an important and personal goal, self-confidence increases, as does reports of individual and relational well-being. In several studies, researchers have found that behavioral affirmation from the partner is just as important, or more so, than any *actual* movement towards that ideal self. Longitudinal data further reveals that early partner affirmation predicts changes over time towards the ideal self and that early partner affirmation and movement towards the ideal predicts change over time in personal well-being and relational well-being (Drigotas et al., 1999; Rusbult et al., 2005).

Perceiving one's partner positively, supporting partner achievement towards his/her goals, and communicating this positive regard and support are integral pieces of high quality, satisfying relationships. However, the caveat may lie in the aspects of the partner that are supported. Generally, people prefer to be affirmed on aspects congruent with their ideal self, rather than normatively desirable aspects. People also like partners who, as Rusbult et al. (2005) describe, "let you be the real you" and "help you become the ideal you" (p. 383). Therefore, there may be a subtle, but important, difference in seeing your partner in the best light and seeing your partner in the best *possible* light for him or her. The task requires an understanding of what is important to the partner, an ability to communicate in an affirmatively effective and appropriate way, and a motivation to see these actions as salient for individual and relational well-being.

Sharing Positive Events

Sharing positive events is an area of research that is garnering increased interest by scholars. Hicks and Diamond (2008) found that participants reported greater positive affect on days when they told their partner about the most positive event of their day. Participants also reported greater positive affect on days when their partner shared their most positive event. Similar to expressive writing outcomes, talking about stressors was not associated with greater negative affect. Gable, Reis, Impett, and Asher (2004) similarly found that daily positive affect was higher on days when participant's communicated about the day's most positive event, over and above the event itself and the day's negative events. Moreover, life satisfaction was reportedly higher on these days as well. Reminiscing about positive events is linked to similar outcomes for the relationship (Shumway & Wampler, 2002). For instance, reminiscing about laughter has a more potent influence on relationship well being than reminiscing about other positive events (Bazzini, Stack, Martincin, & Davis, 2007).

Why does talking about something positive in one's day or about a time that made you laugh improve individual and relational well-being? One theory is that the retelling of events related to a specific emotion causes the storyteller to experience the emotion, as indicated by emotion-specific automatic nervous system activity (Levenson, Carstenson, Friesen, & Ekman, 1991). Laughter is also correlated with relationships satisfaction (Ziv & Gadish, 1989), and the elaboration and rehearsal of shared emotions continues to strengthen the relationship by increasing the salience and accessibility of those emotions and events in memory.

Another theoretical explanation advanced by Langston (1994) is capitalization. People seek additional advantage from the positive event by marking them and enhancing them. In Bryant's (1989) words, retelling positive events allows them to be savored. Other researchers have argued that people are more likely to share positive events if they perceive a favorable reception from their partners. Gable et al. (2004) found that dating and married participants were more likely to engage in capitalization if they anticipated that their partners would respond with active enthusiasm. In a subsequent study, Gable and colleagues (2006) demonstrated that the perception of positive partner reactions were positively associated with relational well-being. Yet, receivers of the positive event message may not respond in the desired way, if the disclosure incites envy, conflict, or indifference. A positive listener response, one that is attentive and supportive, is an important part of the process if the benefits of this type of positive message are to be realized. Gable et al. (2004) found that partners who perceive each other as supportive of personal good fortune have relationships that are higher in commitment, satisfaction, trust, intimacy, and daily positive activities and lower in daily conflict. Reis et al. (2010) experimentally tested many of the ideas above with some notable outcomes.

First, they found that recounting a positive event increased ratings of the positivity of that event but not of another event that was positive but not retold. Retelling the event also produced a greater increase in perceived positivity than writing about the event in private. Second, they confirmed the important role of the listener's responsiveness and enthusiasm, with the impact on the rating of the event lasting up to 17 days when the retelling experience was met with enthusiasm and support. These interactions led to greater felt closeness, liking, trust, and willingness to sacrifice and accommodate a partner.

Discussion

Though culture or social grouping may play some part, what constitutes positive thinking and communicating is largely contextually constituted. As such, what qualifies as positive thinking and talking varies widely across individuals, relationships, and situations. This signifies a need to discuss the multifaceted role of positivity on individual and relational well-being.

Positive Illusions

The research suggests that idealization and positive illusions are critical for relational and individual well-being (Taylor & Brown, 1988). Yet, it is *not* the unwavering acceptance of reality that contributes to well-being; rather, the ability to position the self and others in the best possible light. Indeed, it is reasonable to believe that people in close relationships will experience disappointment if they stretch reality too far. Positive illusions and idealization have limits that need to be explored. For example, if positive illusions are being constructed out of disappointing realities, such idealization could lead to relational difficulties over time. It is also possible that idealizing one's partner in lieu of engaging in problem solving may undermine feelings of efficacy when problems become severe (Holmes & Murray, 1996). And there may be relational contexts in which positive illusions are simply maladaptive. Despite these caveats, current research suggests that positive illusions may be an effective buffer against the inevitable relational vicissitudes.

Similarly, putting thoughts into narrative form assists people with maintaining a sense of predictability and control over their lives (Pennebaker & Seagal, 1999). Research indicates that when people are put their emotional experiences into narrative form, their physical and mental health typically improves (Baikie & Wilhelm, 2005; Petrie, Fontanilla, & Thomas, 2004). In spite of the general positive features associated with narratives, some studies have cautioned for possible short-term increases in negative affect for those who engage in expressive storytelling. Others studies have failed to demonstrate significant health improvements as a result of engaging in the storytelling process altogether, which points toward potential contextual constraints in need of greater examination. The degree of responsive communication by the partner represents one of these contextual constraints. Couples who relate stories that contain more positive than negative events and who engage in responsive communication—affirming each other's positive qualities and supporting each other's goals—are typically happier and more stable.

But where is the tipping point between positive and negative communicative behaviors? Gottman (1998) argued that the key to relational well-being lay in the balance between positive and negative interactions, demonstrating that a ratio of 5:1 is ideal for relational health. Other studies found that negative patterns of interaction more strongly differentiate the distressed from the non-distressed couples than positive patterns (Gottman, Markman, & Notarius, 1977). However, the relationship between these valenced interaction qualities is not that simple. Many researchers have moved to considering them as separate predictors and to examining their interdependence in ongoing relationships. For example, negative communication predicts declines in relationship satisfaction when lower levels of positive communication are present (Johnson et al., 2005). Moreover, high levels of positive affect mitigate the predictive power of the negative patterns on relational well-being. In a longitudinal study of premarital communication and marital distress, Markman, Rhoades, Stanley, Ragan, and Whitton (2010) note that non-distressed couples experienced a decline in negative communication over a 5-year period. Distressed couples experienced a decline in positive communication over that same period; the authors conclude that the negatives tend to erode the positives over time.

Sharing Positive Events

Sharing and reminiscing about positive events and emotions seem to consistently produce positive well-being for individuals and relationships, regardless of the theoretical explanation. However, what constitutes a positive event is defined more by perception than by an objective set of criteria. For instance, Bazzini and colleagues noted that the events that couples recalled involving shared laughter were not objectively more positive (as judged by raters) than other recalled events. What makes people laugh can be far from positive circumstances, and yet, the ability to laugh about neutral and negative events may have a beneficial impact on relationship well-being. Gottman, Katz, and Hooven (1996) proposed that negative emotions are fundamental to healthy social relationships, yet how the emotions are discussed and responded to differentiates healthy from less healthy relationships. Young (2010) describes the "bright side" of hurtful communication, noting some conditions under which hurtful communication is perceived in a favorable manner by the recipients. Similarly, evoking jealousy may be construed positively if the outcome is that the partner pays more attention to the evoker and responds supportively to the evoker's needs (Cayanus & Booth-Butterfield, 2004). Thus, the benefits accrued from positive communication is dependent on the reciprocal processes within the relationship. This body of research raises some interesting issues regarding the conceptualization and operationalization of "positive" communication in relationship research, and the complex ways in which negative and positive experiences are blended together in ways that promote psychological, relational, and physical well-being.

Taken together, these studies call into question straightforward definitions of positive communication in close relationships. Considering communication as an ongoing, dialogic process points to the need to place positive communication within the context of the relationship and within a relationship trajectory. Additional research is needed to understand the evolving nature of positive communication in ongoing close relationships. Future research may also investigate the situations and conditions under which communication takes a "positive" turn. Moreover since relational communication is at the very base dyadic, understanding the implications of positive thinking and positive communication requires some teasing out of the benefits for individual, partner, and relationship. For instance, one may imagine a situation where a message is perceived as positive by one partner but was not necessarily intended to be, yet the relationship benefits in any case. Due to these complexities and desirability to understand positive communication within and across relationships and situations, it behooves communication researchers to employ multiple and mixed methods, as well as to explore new methodological approaches. We also need to recognize the limitations of positive communication, much like the psychologists have begun to do within the positive cognition literature (see McNultry, 2009). Positive communication may harm relational well-being in the long run if relationship issues go unaddressed and if the communication masks important emotions and thoughts that become harmful to the individual and/or relationship. On other hand, if thinking positively results in communicating positively, and communicating positively results in feeling and thinking more positively about our partners, our relationships, and ourselves, we can all pursue "happily ever after."

References

Argyle, M. (1987). *The psychology of happiness*. London: Methuen.
Baikie K., & Wilhelm, K. (2005). Emotional and physical health benefits of expressive writing. *Advances in Psychiatric Treatment, 11*, 338–346.

Baumeister, R., & Leary M. (1995). The need to belong: Desire for interpersonal attachments as a fundamental human motivation. *Psychological Bulletin, 117*, 497–529.

Bazzini, D., Stack, E., Martincin, P., & Davis, C. (2007). The effect of reminiscing about laughter on relationship satisfaction. *Motivation and Emotion, 31*, 25–34.

Berkman L. F., & Glass T. (2000). Social integration, social networks, social support, and health. In L. F. Berkman & I. Kawachi (Eds.), *Social epidemiology* (pp. 137–173). New York: Oxford Press; 2000.

Berscheid, E., & Reis, H. T. (1998). Attraction and close relationships. In D. Gilbert, S. Fiske, & G. Lindzey (Eds.), *Handbook of social psychology* (Vol. 2, 4th ed., pp. 193–281). Boston: McGraw-Hill.

Bryant, F. B. (1989). A four-factor model of perceived control: Avoiding, coping, obtaining, and savoring. *Journal of Personality, 57*, 773–797.

Cayanus, J., & Booth-Butterfield, M. (2004). Relationship orientation, jealousy, and equity: An examination of jealousy evoking and positive communicative responses. *Communication Quarterly, 52*(3), 237–250.

Doohan, E. M., Carrere, S., & Riggs, M. L. (2010). Using relational stories to predict the trajectory toward marital dissolution: The oral history interview and spousal feelings of flooding, loneliness, and depression. *Journal of Family Communication, 10*, 57–77.

Doohan, E. M., Carrere, S., Siler, C., & Beardslee, C. (2009). The effect of the marital bond on the future triadic family interactions. *Journal of Marriage and Family, 71*, 892–904.

Diener, E., Gohm C.L., Suh E., & Oishi, S. (2000). Similarities of the relations between marital status and subjective well-being across cultures. *Journal of Cross-Cultural Psychology, 31*, 419–436.

Drigotas, S., Rusbult, C., Wieselquist, J., & Whitton, S. (1999). Close partner as sculptor of the ideal self: Behavioral affirmation and the Michelangelo phenomenon. *Journal of Personality and Social Psychology, 77*, 293–323.

Fincham, F. D., Bradbury, T. N., & Scott, C. K. (1990). Cognition in marriage. In F. D. Fincham & T. N. Bradbury (Eds.), *The psychology of marriage* (pp. 118–149). New York: Guilford.

Gable, S. L, Reis, H. T., Impett, E. A., & Asher, E. R. (2004). What do you do when things go right? The intrapersonal and interpersonal benefits of sharing positive events. *Journal of Personality and Social Psychology, 87*, 228–245.

Goodfriend, W. (2004). *Partner-esteem: Romantic partners' biased perceptions of each other's faculties and flaws.* Paper presented at the meeting of the Society for Personality and Social Psychology, Austin, TX.

Gordon, K. C., Baucom, D. H., & Snyder, D. K. (2004). An integrated intervention for promoting recovery from extramarital affairs. *Journal of Marital and Family Therapy, 30*, 213–231.

Gottman, J. M. (1998). Psychology and the study of marital processes. *Annual Review of Psychology, 49*, 169–197.

Gottman, J. M., Katz, L. F., & Hooven, C. (1996). Parental meta-emotion philosophy and the emotional life of families: theoretical models and preliminary data. *Journal of Family Psychology, 10*(3), 243–268.

Gottman, J. M., Markman, H. J., & Notarius, C. I. (1977). The topography of marital conflict: A sequential analysis of verbal and nonverbal behavior. *Journal of Marriage and the Family, 39*, 461–477.

Grigg, F., Fletcher, G. J., & Fitness, J. (1989). Spontaneous attributions in happy and unhappy dating relationships. *Journal of Social and Personal Relationships, 6*(1), 61–68.

Hicks, A. M., & Diamond, L. M. (2008). How was your day? Couple affect when telling and hearing daily events. *Personal Relationships, 15*(2), 205–228.

Holmes, J. G., & Rempel, J. K. (1989). Trust in close relationships. In C. Hendrick (Ed.), *Review of personality and social psychology* (Vol. 10, pp. 187–220). Beverly Hills, CA: Sage.

Holmberg, D., Orbuch, T., & Veroff, J. (2004). *Thrice told tales: Married couples tell their stories.* Mahwah, NJ: Lawrence Erlbaum.

Honeycutt, J. (1999). Typological differences in predicting marital happiness from oral history behaviors and imagined interactions. *Communication Monographs, 66*(3), 276–291.

Johnson, M., Cohen, C., Davila, J., Lawrence, E. Rogge, R. D., Karney, B., & Bradbury, T. (2005). Problem-solving skills and affective expression as predictors of change in martial satisfaction. *Journal of Consulting and Clinical Psychology, 73*, 15–27.

Langston, C. (1994). Capitalizing on and coping with daily life events: Expressive responses to positive events. *Journal of Personality and Social Psychology, 67*, 1112–1125.

Levenson, R. W., Carstensen, L. L., Friesen, W. V., & Ekman, P. (1991). Emotion, physiology, and expression in old age. *Psychology and Aging, 6*, 28–35.

Markman, H. J., Rhoades, G. K., Stanley, S. M., Ragan, E. P., & Whitton, S. W. (2010). The premarital communication roots of marital distress and divorce: The first five years of marriage. *Journal of Family Psychology, 24* (3), 289–298.

Miller, R. S., & Perlman, D. (2009). *Intimate relationships* (5th ed.). New York: McGraw Hill.

Miller, P. J., Niehuis, S., & Huston, T. L. (2006). Positive illusions in marital relationships: A 13–year longitudinal study. *Personality and Social Psychology Bulletin, 32,* 1579–1594.

Moore, J. L., & Middleton, A. (2008). *The effects of intrapersonal communication: Thinking and writing about romantic partners.* Paper presented at the meeting of the International Association for Relationship Researchers Convention, Providence, RI.

Murray, S. L., & Holmes, J. G. (1994). Storytelling in close relationships: The construction of confidence. *Personality and Social Psychology Bulletin, 20*, 650–663.

Murray, S. L., & Holmes, J. G. (1996). The construction of relationship realities. In G. J. O. Fletcher & J. Fitness (Eds.), *Knowledge structures in close relationships: A social psychological approach* (pp. 91–120). Mahwah, NJ: Lawrence Erlbaum.

Murray, S. L., & Holmes, J. G. (1999). The (mental) ties that bind: Cognitive structures that predict relationship resilience. *Journal of Personality and Social Psychology, 77*, 1228–1244.

Murray, S. L., Holmes, J. G., Dolderman, D., & Griffin, D. W. (2000). What the motivated mind sees: Comparing friends' perspectives to married partners' views of each other. *Journal of Experimental Social Psychology, 36*, 600–620.

Murray, S. L., & Holmes, J. G., & Griffin, D. W. (1996). The benefits of positive illusions: Idealization and the construction of satisfaction in close relationships. *Journal of Personality and Social Psychology, 70*, 79–98.

National Institute for Mental Health. (1995). *Basic behavioral science research for mental health* (NIH Publication No. 95–3682). Washington, DC: U.S. Government Printing Office.

Park, C. L., & Blumberg, C. J. (2002) Disclosing trauma through writing: Testing the meaning-making hypothesis. *Cognitive Therapy and Research, 26*, 597–616.

Pennebaker, J. W. (1999). Psychological factors influencing the reporting of physical symptoms. In A. Stone, J. Turkkan, C. Bachrach, J. Jobe, H. Kurtzman, & V. Cain (Eds.),

The science of self-report: Implications for research and practice (pp. 299–316). Mahwah, NJ: Erlbaum.

Pennebaker, J. W., Kiecolt-Glaser, J. K., & Glaser, R. (1988). Disclosure of traumas and immune function: Health implications for psychotherapy. *Journal of Consulting and Clinical Psychology, 56,* 239–245.

Pennebaker, J. W., & Seagal, J. D. (1999). Forming a story: The health benefits of narrative. *Journal of Clinical Psychology, 55,* 1243–1254.

Petrie, K. J., Fontanilla, I., & Thomas, M. G. (2004). Effect of written emotional expression on immune function in patients with Human Immunodeciciency Virus infection. A randomized trial. *Psychosomatic Medicine, 66,* 272–275.

Reis, H. T, Smith, S. M., Carmichael, C. L., Caprariello, P.A., Tsai, F., Rodrigues, A., & Maniaci, M. (2010). Are you happy for me? How sharing positive events with others provides personal and interpersonal benefits. *Journal of Personality and Social Psychology, 99*(2), 311–329.

Rempel, J. K., Ross, M., & Holmes, J. G. (2001). Trust and communicated attributions in close relationships. *Journal of Personality and Social Psychology, 18*(1), 57–64.

Rusbult, C. E., Kumashiro, M., Stocker, S. L., Kirchner, J. L., Finkel, E. J., & Coolsen, M. K. (2005). Self processes in interdependent relationships: Partner affirmation and the Michelangelo phenomenon. *Interaction Studies, 6*(3), 375–391.

Rusbult, C. E., Yovetich, N. A., & Verette, J. (1996). An interdependence analysis of accommodation processes. In G. J. O. Fletcher & J. Fitness (Eds.), *Knowledge structures in close relationships: A social psychological approach* (pp. 63–90). Hillsdale, NJ: Erlbaum.

Russek, L. G., & Schwartz, G. E. (1997). Feelings of parental caring predict health status in midlife: A 35-year follow-up of the Harvard Mastery Study of Stress. *Journal of Behavioral Medicine, 30,* 1–13.

Ryff, C.D., & Singer, B. (2000). Biopsychosocial challenges of the new millennium. *Psychotherapy and Psychosomatics, 69,* 170-177.

Seeman, T. E. (1996). Social ties and health: The benefits of social integration. *Annals of Epidemiology, 6,* 442–451.

Segrin, C. (1998). Disrupted interpersonal relationships and mental health problems. In B. H. Spitzberg & W. R. Cupach (Eds.), *The dark side of close relationships* (pp. 327–365). Mahwah, NJ: Erlbaum.

Segrin, C., & Flora, J. (2001). Perceptions of relational histories, marital quality, and loneliness when communication is limited: An examination of prison inmates. *Journal of Family Communication, 1*(3), 151–173.

Segrin, C., & Taylor, M. (2007). Positive interpersonal relationships mediate the association between social skills and psychological well being. *Personality and Individual Differences, 43,* 637–646.

Shumway, S. T., & Wampler, R. S. (2002). A behaviorally focused measure for relationships: The Couple Behavior Report (CBR). *The American Journal of Family Therapy, 30,* 311–321.

Slatcher, R. B., & Pennebaker, J. W. (2006). How do I love thee? Let me count the words: The social effects of expressive writing. *Psychological Science, 17,* 660–664.

Slatcher, R. B., & Pennebaker, J. W. (2007). Emotional expression and health. In S. Ayers, A. Baum, C. McManus, S. Newman, K. Wallston, J. Weinman, & R. West (Eds.), *Cambridge handbook of psychology, health & medicine* (2nd ed., pp. 84–86). Cambridge, UK: Cambridge University Press.

Snyder, D. K., Gordon, K., & Baucom, D. H. (2004). Treating affair couples. Extending the written disclosure paradigm to relationship trauma. *Clinical Psychology: Science and Practice, 11,* 155–159.

Taylor, S. E., & Brown, J. D. (1988). Illusion and well-being: A social psychological perspective on mental health. *Psychological Bulletin, 103,* 193–210.

Uchino, B. N., Cacioppo, J. T., & Kiercolt-Glaser, J. K. (1996). The relationship between social support and physiological processes: A review with emphasis on underlying mechanisms and implications for health. *Psychological Bulletin, 119,* 488–531.

Veroff, J., Kulka, R. A., & Douvan, E. (1981). *Mental health in America: Patterns of help-seeking from 1957-1976.* New York: Basic Books.

Young, S. (2010). Positive perceptions of hurtful messages: The packaging matters. *Communication Research Reports, 27*(1), 49–57.

Ziv, A., & Gadish, O. (1989). Humor and marital satisfaction. *The Journal of Social Psychology, 129,* 759–768.

• CHAPTER EIGHT •

Esteem Support as a Form of Positive Communication: Connections to Well-Being

Amanda J. Holmstrom
Michigan State University

In Western culture, possessing a healthy degree of self-esteem is considered essential. In fact, feeling good about who we are is so important to living a productive life that it ranks behind only food, safety, and belonging in Maslow's (1954) famous hierarchy of human needs. Conversely, having low self-esteem is so personally and socially debilitating that several countries have targeted it as a root of social crisis (Furlong, 2005; Laurance, 2005). Another prominent example of society's focus on healthy self-esteem is the Dove Self-Esteem Fund, which promotes young women's self-esteem through workshops, videos, and other materials (http://www.dove.us/).

These campaigns share an underlying assumption: that self-esteem is of real import. Research supports this assumption. Possessing healthy self-esteem is associated with various significant outcomes, including effective performance in school and at work, some indices of mental and physical health, happiness, and success at creating and maintaining mutually satisfying, lasting personal and social relationships (e.g., Aron, 2003; Guindon, 2010; Rosenberg & Owens, 2001). Extensive previous research provides a good understanding of the agents and processes that shape children's self-esteem over the course of primary socialization (see Bowlby, 1982; Gecas, Calonico, & Thomas, 1974; Harter, 2003). However, although adults' self-esteem is relatively stable, there are situations in which it may become less so. For example, life transitions (e.g., changing jobs or communities, getting married or divorced, starting or leaving college) can upturn a stable sense of self and challenge one's self-esteem. Losses and disappointments characteristic of the adult years (e.g., failed relationships, job loss, professional disappointments) may also undermine what had been a stable level of self-esteem.

During such times of transition and loss, individuals may seek support from their social networks to buffer the negative impact of events on their feelings about themselves. Empirical evidence suggests that esteem support may aid in enhancing individuals' self-esteem, particularly after an acute threat to the self (e.g., Holmstrom, 2012; Holmstrom & Burleson, 2011). Esteem support is a unique form of emotional support that is provided to others with the intent of enhancing how they feel about themselves and their attributes, abilities, and accomplishments. Evidence suggests that esteem support may contribute to outcomes in addition to enhanced self-esteem, such as mental and physical well-being (e.g., King, Reis, Porter, & Norsen, 1993; Swift & Wright, 2000). Research also indicates that esteem support has the potential to improve the quality of interpersonal relationships (Carels & Baucom, 1999; Cutrona, 1986).

Despite its apparent importance, however, little work has sought to develop a theoretical understanding of esteem support as a communicative process, especially as it plays out in interactions between adults. This chapter (a) frames esteem support as a form of positive communication, (b) outlines a theory of esteem support messages and discusses results of two tests of the theory, and (c) identifies challenges and future directions for research on the communication of esteem support.

The Communication of Esteem Support

Research suggests that esteem support can buffer individuals from the negative effects of esteem threats and chronic low self-esteem (e.g., Holmstrom & Burleson, 2011; King et al., 1993; Swift & Wright, 2000). However, is it a form of positive communication? Positive communication research was inspired by work in positive psychology. There are three pillars of positive psychology (Seligman, 2002): positive traits, positive emotion, and positive institutions (for example, "democracy, strong families, and free inquiry," p. xiii). I argue that esteem support has links with each of these pillars. One of the positive traits noted by Seligman and his colleagues (e.g., Seligman & Csikszentmihalyi, 2000) is interpersonal skill. The ability to provide sophisticated esteem support may be defined as one such interpersonal skill, a skill that may be enhanced through appropriate training. With respect to positive emotion, the most proximal goal of esteem support is enhanced positive emotion. More specifically, the goals of esteem support are to enhance state self-esteem, or how the recipient feels about himself or herself in the moment, and to decrease negative, self-conscious emotions like shame, guilt, and embarrassment. In turn, esteem support has the potential for other positive effects, including improved physical, mental, and relational well-being. The final pillar of positive psychology is positive institutions. Sophisticated esteem support interactions in relationships, families, and workplaces have the potential to enhance the quality of these institutions. For example, the receipt of high-quality esteem support messages is associated with greater feelings of acceptance and belongingness for the recipient (Holmstrom, 2009; Holmstrom & Burleson, 2011). Other benefits of effective esteem support include enhanced relational satisfaction and stability for both helper and recipient (Carels & Baucom, 1999; Cutrona, 1986).

Not only does esteem support correspond with positive psychology, it also links clearly to the field of positive communication. "Positive communication is unique in its ability to generate physical, social, and psychological health and wellness. It yields the potential to inspire people to achieve higher moments, greater good, and to act selflessly" (Pitts & Socha, chapter 1, pp. 2–3). Providing esteem support is often a difficult task. Helpers are faced with a number of obstacles, including their own distress at the upsetting situation, lack of knowledge about how to provide support, pre-existing tension in the relationship, and reluctance to support someone who has committed a perceived transgression. As such, the provision of esteem support may indeed call upon a person to achieve "higher moments, greater good, and to act selflessly." Seligman's research on positive psychology indicates that people who encounter and master challenge are often stronger, and experience greater well-being, than those who do not (see Seligman, 2011, for a review). Thus, helpers who take up the challenge of providing esteem support may experience greater well-being as a result. Those who receive sophisticated esteem support may also benefit from the challenge, if not in the short term, then perhaps in the long term, in the form of enhanced relational satisfaction, enhanced self-esteem, and ability to cope with future threats.

Thus, esteem support has connections with each of the three pillars of positive psychology and exemplifies the editors' definition of positive communication. Furthermore, it is a form of positive communication that exhibits links to various indices of well-being.

Cognitive-Emotional Theory of Esteem Support Messages

Though mounting evidence suggests the importance of esteem support, to date little research has focused on how the esteem support process unfolds, particularly among adults. In this section of the chapter, I will lay out a theory of esteem support messages. The cognitive-emotional theory of esteem support messages (CETESM) is informed by theories of emotion, self-esteem, and the general process of emotional support, and identifies (a) conceptual dimensions along which better and worse esteem support messages can be scaled, (b) mechanisms through which sophisticated esteem support messages should have their effects, and (c) outcomes associated with the receipt of support varying in quality.

This theory addresses acute threats or injuries to self-esteem, that is, those that may arise from particular unfavorable circumstances, rather than those that may originate from socialization experiences or from chronic conditions in adulthood, such as an abusive spouse or long-term unemployment. Thus, esteem support messages are primarily focused on improving state versus trait self-esteem; state self-esteem refers to self-feelings that may fluctuate in response to daily upsets and triumphs, whereas trait self-esteem is a more stable component of personality (James, 1890).

Theoretical Background

The CETESM is rooted in cognitive theories of emotion, particularly attribution and appraisal theories (Lazarus, 1991; Weiner, 1986). According to these theories, it is not events themselves that predict emotional reactions, but rather it is the cognitions one has about those events that determine how one will feel. These varying cognitions explain why it is possible for one person to be devastated by an event, whereas another person, in the same situation, is hopeful for the future.

Causal attributions vary on several dimensions, including locus, stability, controllability, and globality (e.g., Abramson, Seligman, & Teasdale, 1978; Weiner, 1986). Locus refers to whether the cause is perceived as internal (i.e., caused by the actor) vs. external (i.e., caused by someone or something other than the actor). Stability refers to the extent to which the cause is seen as lasting as opposed to temporary. Perceptions of controllability refer to beliefs about whether a cause may be altered (by the actor or someone else). Finally, globality refers to whether the cause is viewed as general or specific. Attribution theories suggest that threats to self-esteem are particularly likely when people perceive that events have been caused by an internal, stable, uncontrollable, global feature, like general IQ (Abramson et al., 1978; Weiner, 1986).

Appraisal theories distinguish between primary and secondary event appraisals (e.g., Lazarus, 1991). Primary appraisals, or initial cognitions about an event, include perceptions of goal relevance and goal congruence.

When events are seen as goal relevant, emotion is more likely to occur, and when events are viewed as incongruent with relevant goals, the emotion is likely to be negative. Secondary appraisals determine the type of positive or negative emotion likely to be experienced and involve perceptions of accountability, coping potential (both problem-focused and emotion-focused), and future expectancy. State self-esteem may be negatively affected when individuals perceive that they are accountable for goal-relevant, goal-incongruent events (Smith & Lazarus, 1993), particularly when coping potential and future expectancy appear to be poor (Lazarus, 1991).

Thus, the CETESM proposes that lowered self-esteem is a consequence of esteem-threatening attributions and appraisals of events. Burleson and Goldsmith (1998) note that since appraisal theories indicate that emotional distress is predicted by how events are interpreted by individuals (as opposed to the events themselves), the only way to alter a distressed emotional state is by changing those appraisals, or by making reappraisals of events. Others can help an individual make such reappraisals through a process called conversationally-induced reappraisal (Burleson & Goldsmith, 1998). Consistent with this thinking, the CETESM asserts that a goal of esteem support should be to facilitate modifications in targets' attributions and appraisals about the threatening event and its impact on the self. That is, this theory posits that effective esteem support will promote conversationally induced reappraisals and reattributions of the event. When esteem support conversations prompt new attributions and appraisals by targets for esteem-threatening events (and especially the impact of those events on the self), targets' self-esteem may be enhanced.

The Emotion-Focused and Problem-Focused Dimensions of Esteem Support

The CETESM posits that messages may vary on three dimensions: emotion focus, problem focus, and induction/assertion. Attribution and appraisal theories suggest two of these three dimensions: an emotion-focused dimension and a problem-focused dimension (Table 8.1 summarizes the three dimensions of the CETESM and provides message examples). The emotion-focused and problem-focused dimensions concern the content of esteem support messages, that is, what the message attempts to do. Emotion-focused strategies (Lazarus, 1991) attempt to alter cognitions. In contrast, problem-focused strategies represent efforts to change the target's behavior as a way of improving self-esteem.

Attribution and appraisal theories (Lazarus, 1991; Weiner, 1986) maintain that emotion, including how we feel about ourselves, stems from cognitions. Thus, emotion-focused strategies for esteem support are theorized to be better at improving targets' self-esteem than problem-focused strategies.

Table 8.1. Definitions of Levels of Message Extensiveness and Examples

Low problem focus: Focuses on few, less relevant behaviors and promotes false reassurance about the efficacy of advocated actions (e.g., "Why don't you go out to the bars and hang out —the relaxation will help you do better on your next exam!")

High problem focus: Focuses on multiple, more relevant behaviors and makes no empty promises about the efficacy of behaviors (e.g., "You could consider talking to the professor about retaking the class – maybe he can suggest some people for tutoring, or you could get a study group together?")

Low emotion focus: Focuses on few, less relevant cognitions; denies the reality of the esteem threat and makes unsubstantiated appraisals (e.g., "Don't worry about failing your exam – it'll be fine. Hey, what do you think about your new boyfriend/girlfriend? Isn't he/she great?")

High emotion focus: Focuses on multiple, relevant attributions and appraisals and makes positive yet substantiated appraisals (e.g., "You haven't failed before, and this test was particularly difficult. You have what it takes to bounce back from this.")

High assertive: Commands, demands, and orders target what to do (i.e., bald-on-record imperatives) (e.g., "you must," "start studying right now, period")

Low assertive: Uses politeness strategies to mitigate the face threat of directives (e.g., "maybe," "it's just a suggestion")

Low inductive: Asks targets closed-ended questions about the nature of their current or anticipated actions or thoughts/feelings; gives provider's own perspective with limited input from target (e.g., "You can bounce back from this, right?")

High inductive: Asks a series of more open-ended questions designed to help targets explore their current or anticipated thoughts/feelings (e.g., "What do you think about this situation?")

Note: Example messages pertain to a hypothetical situation in which the recipient has failed his or her last pre-major course.

Dimension Extensiveness

The CETESM posits that esteem support strategies may be more or less extensively emotion focused and/or more or less extensively problem focused; that is, emotion focus and problem focus are both dimensions on which a given message may fall. More extensively emotion-focused messages fulfill three conditions, derived from attribution and appraisal theories of emotion (Lazarus, 1991; Weiner, 1986). First, more extensively emotion-focused messages attempt to alter relevant appraisals and attributions; less extensively emotion-focused messages focus on less relevant cognitions. Relevant cognitions are thoughts about the problem situation that impact or may impact self-esteem (that is, causal attributions and appraisals about the esteem-threatening event). For example, in a situation in which a person has lost her job, a relevant cognition may be that she will not be able to find another job (a stable, esteem-threatening attribution). In this situation, a less relevant thought may be how successful she is with one of her hobbies.

Esteem-threatening cognitions may vary in number, but it is likely that in truly threatening situations, targets exert relatively substantial cognitive effort in determining the cause of the event and its effect on the self. As such, they are likely to make multiple appraisals about and attributions for the event. Thus, the second condition for extensively emotion-focused messages is that they address more of these relevant attribution and appraisals than do less extensively emotion-focused messages. Third, more extensively emotion-focused esteem support advocates truthful, realistic attributions and appraisals about the past, present, and future. Less truthful messages make false reattributions and unsubstantiated claims about emotion-focused and problem-focused coping potential and future expectancy. Since they focus on multiple, esteem-threatening cognitions in a truthful manner, high emotion-focused messages are predicted to be more effective than low emotion-focused messages.

With problem-focused strategies, message extensiveness refers to the behaviors providers address as opposed to the cognitions they attend to. More extensively problem-focused messages also fulfill three conditions, parallel to those laid out for emotion-focused messages. First, a more extensively problem-focused message addresses relevant behaviors. Relevant behaviors are those that may conceivably address the cause of the esteem threat, and are determined by the nature of the esteem-threatening situation. For example, when an individual fails an exam, it is generally more relevant to speak to one's professor about improving course performance than it is to drink one's cares away. Second, a more extensively problem-focused message centers on more, rather than fewer, relevant behaviors. Finally, more extensively problem-focused messages provide realistic assessments of the future or of the efficacy of advocated actions and implicitly or explicitly accept that an esteem-threatening situation has, in fact, occurred. Less extensively problem-focused messages promote false assessments of the reality of the event, the future, and/or the efficacy of advocated actions. As such, high problem-focused messages are predicted to be more effective than low problem-focused messages; however, high emotion-focused messages are predicted to be the most effective form of esteem support.

The Assertive-Inductive Dimension

The third dimension of the CETESM is the style dimension, on which all messages (i.e., problem-focused, emotion-focused, or both) fall. Whereas the emotion focus and problem focus dimensions describe the content of an esteem support message, this dimension explains how the message is presented. More specifically, this dimension is defined by the degree to which providers attempt to force versus induce alterations in targets' cognitions and/or affect (with emotion-focused support) and/or behaviors (with problem-focused support). According to the CETESM, the assertion-induction dimension arises from people's underlying conceptions about how communication produces lasting changes in others' self-esteem. More assertive strategies rely on exhortation, and are based on the assumption that the helper can force the target to think, feel, or act a certain way. On the other hand, more inductive strategies are based on the belief that for real change to occur, recipients must be active participants in the esteem support interaction.

Research indicates that directives (such as those associated with assertive strategies), are not "magic bullets" or a "salve" that can be applied directly to distress (Burleson & Goldsmith, 1998). Though more assertive strategies may achieve temporary results, it is predicted that lasting changes in self-esteem stem from more inductive strategies. Inductive processes actively invoke targets' reflective and reasoning processes, and as such, targets are more likely to "own" the outcome of inductive processes and recreate them when faced with future esteem threats.

Dimension extensiveness. As with the problem-focused and emotion-focused dimensions, messages vary in the style in which they are presented. More specifically, they range from highly assertive to highly inductive. Extensively (highly) assertive messages tell targets what to do (with problem-focused support), or what to think or feel (with emotion-focused support). They are coercive and contain bald-on-record demands, directives, and threats. Less extensive (low) assertive messages include hedges, qualifiers, and other politeness forms to soften their directives. Low assertive messages are less face threatening than bald-on-record messages (e.g., MacGeorge, Lichtman, & Pressey, 2002), and as such, are predicted to be more helpful than highly assertive messages at alleviating esteem threat. However, all assertive messages are predicted to be less effective than messages that are inductive.

Less extensively (low) inductive messages tend to use more closed-ended questioning to guide targets to a particular conclusion. Extensively (highly) inductive messages encourage targets to engage in a greater degree of cognitive effort by considering and analyzing varied aspects of the situation. Messages high in induction are posited to be more effective than low inductive messages because they promote a higher degree of participation and reflection by the recipient. This careful, reflective process may also benefit the esteem support provider, as it indicates positive regard for his or her perspective (see, for example, Bodie, 2012; Mirivel, 2012).

To summarize, the CETESM posits three dimensions on which esteem support messages may vary. First, messages may have problem-focused and/or emotion-focused content. Content may be high or low in problem focus and/or high or low in emotion focus. All messages have a particular style which ranges from highly assertive to highly inductive. The CETESM maintains that messages that are high in emotion focus and induction are the most theoretically sophisticated strategies because of what they try to change and how they try to change it. These strategies are more sophisticated than alternative forms of esteem support because they focus on the proximal cause of negative self-feelings—the attributions and appraisals that are particularly relevant in a given circumstance, and seek to bring about functional changes in these cognitions that are grounded in honest judgments about the past, present, and future. Second, these strategies are more sophisticated because they seek to induce change in the target's cognitions by using questions, reflections, and probes that encourage the target to articulate, examine, and reason through relevant attributions and appraisals (and, perhaps, associated underlying cognitions). Changes in cognitions that emerge from this inductive, reflective process should be comparatively stable since the target can review and retrace the reasoning that led to these revised cognitions as needed. Thus, they should be less likely to decay over time and should also be more resistant to future esteem threats.

Applications of the CETESM

Several empirical studies have been conducted to test the CETESM. Below, I summarize the results of two of these studies and their implications for the study of the communication of esteem support and well-being.

Initial test of the CETESM. In an initial test of the CETESM (Holmstrom & Burleson, 2011), the merits of the model were evaluated in a study (N = 506) examining esteem support messages provided in response to three types of esteem threat: failure, rejection, and transgression. The study examined two general forms of esteem support messages that are of special theoretical interest: Emotion-focused/inductive messages (with no problem-focused content) and problem-focused/assertive messages (with no emotion-focused content). Emotion-focused/inductive strategies are predicted to do a better job at enhancing state self-esteem, as they stem from providers' correct beliefs that diminished self-esteem is caused by appraisals of and attributions for problematic events. They also reflect the understanding that long-lasting changes in appraisals and attributions may be achieved when targets develop their own reattributions and reappraisals. Problem-focused/assertive messages, on the other hand, are predicted to be less effective esteem support strategies, as they stem from the erroneous beliefs that events themselves cause diminished self-esteem, and that to improve self-esteem, targets must be forced to change their behavior.

Participants in this initial study were randomly assigned to read one of 24 hypothetical situations representing one of three types of esteem threat: failure (e.g., failing one's last pre-major course), rejection (e.g., getting dumped by one's significant other), and transgression (e.g., cheating on one's significant other). They then read eight esteem support messages created by crossing the problem-focused/assertive dimensions and emotion-focused/inductive dimensions. Finally, participants rated each message for the degree to which they believed that message would enhance various facets of state self-esteem.

Generally, results were consistent across type of esteem threat, and for the most part, as predicted, (a) emotion-focused/inductive messages were rated as better than problem-focused/assertive messages, (b) high emotion-focused messages were rated as better than low emotion-focused messages, (c) high problem-focused messages were rated as better than low problem-focused messages, and (d) low assertive messages were rated as better than high assertive messages.

One hypothesis that was not supported was that high inductive messages would be rated as better than low inductive messages. For the most part, there was no significant difference in ratings of high and low inductive messages, and in some cases, low inductive messages were rated as significantly better. It is possible that methodological limitations explain the lack of support for this hypothesis. Here, participants simply read a series of messages, a procedure that does not allow for the most realistic depiction of the inductive process, which unfolds with helpers asking questions and targets responding, and targets making reattributions and reappraisals in a slow, directed fashion. This process cannot be modeled in a one-shot message. If future studies with more valid operationalizations of induction still show a preference for low inductive messages, the theory may need to be modified.

Though emotion-focused/inductive messages were mostly perceived as better than problem-focused/assertive messages, in some situations, there was no difference in the ratings of these two types of messages. This finding suggests that perhaps in some events, esteem support should place greater emphasis on targets' desires to engage in action where such behaviors are relevant and feasible. This hypothesis was tested in the next study.

Job search study. In a following study, relationships between esteem support messages varying in quality (as defined by the CETESM), job search self-efficacy, and job search behaviors were examined. Unemployment rates in recent years have increased (Bureau of Labor Statistics, 2010). Because employment serves as an important source of social legitimacy (Fryers, 2006) and self-esteem (Eden & Aviram, 1993) for many adults, job loss and the job search process can be esteem-threatening experiences (Vuori & Vinokur, 2005). Research indicates that high self-esteem can promote coping with the job search process (Tharenou, 1979), and high self-esteem individuals may be more successful in achieving employment (Blau, 1994; Ellis & Taylor, 1983). The abundant evidence of a link between employment and self-esteem suggests that esteem support may be a relevant form of social support for those involved in the job search process.

The results reported here involve a sample of unemployed, underemployed, and displaced individuals (N = 290) seeking work in a particularly economically depressed state (Holmstrom, Russell, & Clare, 2012). Participants were recruited at one-stop career centers, which are the result of the Workforce Investment Act (WIA) of 1998 which restructured resources for job seekers to provide a variety of federally funded programs available at one location. Participants ranged from 17 to 66 years old (M = 33.78, SD = 11.40). On average, they had obtained a high school or two-year college degree. Participants had been unemployed for a median of 5 months, but they ranged from currently still employed to unemployed for 208 months (M = 10.79 months). Participants had been searching for a job for an average of 9.93 months (SD =12.49), ranging from just starting the job search to job searching for 120 months.

Participants read and rated five esteem support messages derived from the CETESM: a high emotion-focused message, a low emotion-focused message, a high problem-focused message, a low problem-focused message, and one message that was high in both problem and emotion focus (all messages were low in induction). They were asked to rate each message for the extent to which they believed it would improve their state self-esteem, job search self-efficacy, and intention to persist in the job search.

Results indicate that for all dependent variables, high emotion-focused messages were rated as significantly better than any of the four other messages, including the message that included both high emotion-focused and high problem-focused content. These findings suggest that, at least with respect to these particular outcomes, messages that focus on making multiple, relevant, truthful reattributions and reappraisals for the esteem threat (in this case, the job search and associated issues) are viewed as most helpful.

The two studies summarized here have several implications for the field of positive communication. First, they indicate that esteem support may be an important way to help a friend or family member who is experiencing common, esteem-threatening phenomena like failure, transgression, and rejection—and even job loss. Various aspects of well-being were associated with the receipt of sophisticated support, including enhanced state self-esteem and job search self-efficacy. Though not measured in the studies described here, findings from another study suggest that the esteem support exchange may also have a beneficial influence on the quality of the relationships in which it occurs (Holmstrom, 2008).

Furthermore, the results of these studies indicate that not all esteem support is equally effective. Helping the recipient to make less esteem-threatening attributions and appraisals appears to be a more successful strategy than problem-focused strategies or even messages that combine both problem-focused and emotion-focused content, as tested in the job search study.

Future Challenges and Directions for Esteem Support Research

An understanding of esteem support communication is critical, because it has the potential to influence a fundamental component of well-being: how we feel about who we are. Esteem support also has the potential to contribute directly or indirectly to the mental, physical, and relational health of the recipient. Esteem support may provide benefits not only for the recipient, but for the provider as well, in terms of improved skill in this positive trait, enhanced positive emotion, and a positive relationship with the recipient.

The CETESM shows promise in theorizing about this phenomenon. With this line of research, interventions and pedagogies designed to enhance individuals' esteem support skills may be developed. However, questions remain about some tenets of the theory. For example, it is unknown whether a better operationalization of high inductive messages will result in higher ratings for those messages than for low inductive messages. Also, though the job search study suggests that high problem-focused content is not a helpful addition to high emotion-focused content, this hypothesis should be tested with respect to other types of esteem threat (e.g., moral transgression; other forms of failure or rejection). Finally, both studies reported here represent paper-and-pencil tests of the CETESM. An important next step in this research program is a study in which participants engage in esteem support exchanges in the laboratory, in order to assess the theory's claims in face-to-face settings.

In their article introducing the science of positive psychology, Seligman and Csikszentmihalyi (2000) outline a number of potential challenges for the field. Two related challenges they note suggest issues that esteem support researchers may want to consider. First, they point out the potential tension between individual happiness and collective happiness. For example, they note that what may make one person happy (motor boating on a lake for one hour) may impair others' (in their example, sunbathers') happiness. Similarly, it is important to note that there may sometimes be tension between individual self-esteem and collective well-being. For example, suggesting that a person is not responsible for his or her transgressions may help the transgressor to feel better, but it may also inhibit his or her desire to apologize for those transgressions or even suggest permission to transgress again, which may have a negative impact on others' well-being.

Seligman and Csikszentmihalyi also note the tension between realism and happiness; that is, sometimes being realistic (e.g., accepting one has been diagnosed with a fatal disease) can impair happiness, whereas being unrealistically optimistic (e.g., believing that one will certainly thwart the disease), can promote happiness. Similarly, believing that one is not responsible for an esteem threat might promote positive self-esteem, but what if that belief is not realistic? The CETESM tends to assume that it will be possible to make truthful, esteem-enhancing reattributions and reappraisals for events. However, how does one best provide esteem support to someone who truly is guilty or actually does not have the ability, motivation, or resources to succeed at a given task? While it may not be up to social scientists to decide when it is factually correct or morally right to provide esteem support, research should consider the more and less effective ways to provide esteem support given the potential complexities these two tensions entail.

The studies presented here suggest that esteem support can enhance the mental, physical, and relational well-being of both provider and recipient. It is a form of communication that can be considered a positive trait that leads to positive emotion and positive institutions, the three pillars of positive psychology. Research in this area should continue to explore the best forms of esteem support, as well as the mechanisms by which they may have their short-term and long-term benefits.

References

Abramson, L. V., Seligman, M. E. P., & Teasdale, J. D. (1978). Learned helplessness in humans: Critique and reformulation. *Journal of Abnormal Psychology, 87*, 49–74.

Aron, A. (2003). Self and close relationships. In M. R. Leary & J. P. Tangney (Eds.), *Handbook of self and identity* (pp. 442–461). New York: Guilford.

Blau, G. (1994). Testing a two-dimensional measure of job search behavior. *Organizational Behavior and Human Decision Processes, 59*, 288–312.

Bodie, G. (2012). Listening as positive communication. In T. J. Socha & M. J. Pitts (Eds.), *The positive side of interpersonal communication* (pp. 109–125). New York: Peter Lang.

Bowlby, J. (1982). *Attachment and loss: Vol 1: Attachment* (2nd ed.). New York: Basic Books.

Bureau of Labor Statistics. (2010). *News release: The employment situation—September 2010*. Retrieved from http://www.bis.gov/news.release/pdf/empsit.pdf.

Burleson, B. R., & Goldsmith, D. J. (1998). How the comforting process works: Alleviating emotional distress through conversationally induced reappraisals. In P. Anderson & L. K. Guerrero (Eds.), *Handbook of communication and emotion: Research, theory, applications, and contexts* (pp. 245–280). San Diego, CA: Academic Press.

Carels, R. A., & Baucom, D. H. (1999). Support in marriage: Factors associated with on-line perceptions of support helpfulness. *Journal of Family Psychology, 13*, 131–144.

Cutrona, C. E. (1986). Behavioral manifestations of social support: A microanalytic investigation. *Journal of Personality and Social Psychology, 51*, 201–208.

Eden, D., & Aviram, A. (1993). Self-efficacy training to speed reemployment: Helping people to help themselves. *Journal of Applied Psychology, 78*, 352-360.

Ellis, R. A., & Taylor, M. S. (1983). Role of self-esteem within the job search process. *Journal of Applied Psychology, 68*, 632–340.

Fryers, T. (2006). Work, identity and health. *Clinical Practice and Epidemiology in Mental Health, 2*(12), http://www.cpementalhealth.com/content/2/1/12.

Furlong, R. (2005, September 29). *Ad campaign to lift German morale*. BBC News. Retrieved from http://www.bbc.co.uk/news/world/europe/.

Gecas, V., Calonico, J. M., & Thomas, D. L. (1974). The development of self-concept in the child: Mirror theory versus model theory. *Journal of Social Psychology, 92*, 67–76.

Guindon, M. H. (Ed.). (2010). *Self-esteem across the lifespan: Issues and interventions*. New York: Routledge.

Harter, S. (2003). The development of self-representations during childhood and adolescence. In M. R. Leary & J. P. Tangney (Eds.), *Handbook of self and identity* (pp. 610–642). New York: Guilford.

Holmstrom, A. J. (2008). *The development and assessment of a theory of esteem support messages.* Unpublished doctoral dissertation, Purdue University, West Lafayette, IN.

Holmstrom, A. J. (2009, May). *Who, what, and when: A naturalistic study of esteem support messages.* Paper presented at the annual meeting of the National Communication Association, Chicago, IL.

Holmstrom, A. J. (2012). What helps—and what doesn't—when self-esteem is threatened?: Retrospective reports of esteem support. *Communication Studies, 63,* 77–98.

Holmstrom, A. J., & Burleson, B. R. (2011). An initial test of a theory of esteem support messages. *Communication Research, 38,* 326–355.

Holmstrom, A. J., Russell, J. C., & Clare, D. D. (2012, May). *Esteem support messages and the job search: An application of a cognitive-emotional theory of esteem support messages.* Paper presented at the annual meeting of the International Communication Association, Phoenix, AZ.

James, W. (1890). *The principles of psychology.* New York: Holt.

King, K. B., Reis, H. T., Porter, L. A., & Norsen, L. H. (1993). Social support and long-term recovery from coronary artery surgery: Effects on patients and spouses. *Health Psychology, 12,* 56–63.

Laurance, J. (2005, September 12). Unhappiness 'is Britain's worse social problem.' *The Independent.* Retrieved from http://news.independent.co.uk

Lazarus, R. S. (1991). *Emotion and adaptation.* New York: Oxford University Press.

MacGeorge, E. L., Lichtman, R. M., & Pressey, L. C. (2002). The evaluation of advice in supportive interactions: Facework and contextual factors. *Human Communication Research, 28,* 451–463.

Maslow, A. (1954). *Motivation and personality.* New York: Harper & Row.

Mirivel, J. C. (2012). Communication excellence: Embodying virtues in interpersonal communication. . In T. J. Socha & M. J. Pitts (Eds.), *The positive side of interpersonal communication* (pp. 57–72). New York: Peter Lang.

Rosenberg, M., & Owens, T. J. (2001). Low self-esteem people: A collective portrait. In T. J. Owens, S. Stryker, & N. Goodman (Eds.), *Extending self-esteem theory and research: Sociological and psychological currents* (pp. 400–436). New York: Cambridge University Press.

Seligman, M. E. P. (2002). *Authentic happiness.* New York: Free Press.

Seligman, M. E. P. (2011). *Flourish: A visionary new understanding of happiness and well-being.* New York: Free Press.

Seligman, M. E. P., & Csikszentmihalyi, M. (2000). Positive psychology: An introduction. *American Psychologist, 55,* 5–14.

Smith, C. A., & Lazarus, R. S. (1993). Appraisal components, core relational themes, and the emotions. *Cognition & Emotion, 7,* 233–269.

Swift, A., & Wright, M. O. (2000). Does social support buffer stress for college women: When and how? *Journal of College Student Psychotherapy, 14*(4), 23–42.

Tharenou, P. (1979). Employee self-esteem: A review of the literature. *Journal of Vocational Behavior, 15,* 331–346.

Vuori, J., & Vinokur, A. D. (2005). Job-search preparedness as a mediator of the effects of the Tyohon Job Search Intervention on re-employment and mental health. *Journal of Organizational Behavior, 26,* 275–291.

Weiner, B. (1986). *An attributional theory of motivation and emotion.* New York/Berlin: Springer-Verlag.

• CHAPTER NINE •

Relationship Enhancement (RE) as One Approach for Improving Health and Wellness, Attaining Communication Gratification, and Communicating Positively

Mary Mino
Pennsylvania State University DuBois

In order to minimize the ambiguity associated with establishing and maintaining relationships, self-help books, popular magazines, and websites offer relationship advice that purport to solve relationship problems through unique insights. Unlike communication scholars, as credentialed academic authorities, authors who provide this relationship advice may or may not conduct or cite research to support their claims about communication. Lack of research validity is surprising given the volume of communication studies that have examined the wide ranging and diverse aspects of human interactions. In fact, in 2009 with the celebration of the Eastern Communication Association's Centenary anniversary, we see that for more than a century communication experts have offered reliable research about the practices, the processes, and the intricacies of human communication (see the Eastern Communication Association website, www.ecasite.org).

Gratification, feeling pleasure or satisfaction, is one emotion people strive to experience. Additionally, this feeling is related directly or indirectly to the quality of their relationships. Communicating, speaking with and listening to others, is an inevitable and ongoing part of life. As Eubanks (1952) has affirmed, "speech has always been used to create, to alter, or to destroy some type of social relationship" (p. 9). Accordingly, in most cases, individuals want to understand how to communicate capably to foster those relationships they hope will endure.

Positive communication has been associated with improving relational health and wellness (see Socha & Pitts, 2012). This chapter identifies several positive communication concepts, such as communication gratification, rhetorical sensitivity, communication competence, and communication enrichment, and demonstrates their connections to the RE Approach. The chapter also explains the origin of employing this approach for interpersonal communication instruction and offers a description of a course that specifically applies RE by providing training in communicating positively.

RE's Role in Positive Communication, Communication Gratification, and Health and Wellness

Interpersonal communication, expressing one's attitudes, feelings, ideas, thoughts, or needs, has been discussed consistently in the communication literature. Interpersonal communication requires perceiving the verbal and nonverbal subtleties and variations that are involved while interacting in these contexts. As such, communicating positively not only includes acquiring the proper attitude and learning theoretical concepts but also necessitates applying these concepts by demonstrating them regularly, effectively, and consciously.

Communication scholars have focused on gaining a better understanding of ways to enhance communication experiences by conceptualizing positive communication (Socha & Pitts, 2012). For example, positive communication enhances communication competence (Mizco, 2012), creates opportunities for communication excellence (Mirivel, 2012), and involves deep and appreciative listening (Bodie, 2012).

Although those communication professionals who study positive communication have developed theories and shared cogent examples that further clarify this construct, one successful approach to positive communication, RE, has been underemphasized. The RE Approach features nine basic relational skills. Through these skills, individuals learn to improve the quality of their interpersonal communication (Ginsberg, 2004; Scuka, 2005).

Research conducted on the RE Approach has supported its effectiveness in teaching skills that help individuals communicate positively. Specifically, RE has enriched marital (Jesse & Guerney, 1981, 1984; Rapport, 1976; Snyder & Guerney, 1993) and family communication (Guerney, 1985, 1990; Guerney, Guerney, & Sebes, 1984) and has improved couples' and children's communication after divorce (Avery & Thiessen, 1982; Guerney & Jordon, 1980).

The RE Approach also has been used successfully with college roommates (Waldo, 1989), wife batterers (Waldo, 1988), alcoholics and addicts (Matter, McAllister, & Guerney, 1984; Waldo & Guerney, 1983), those who are diagnosed with borderline personality (Waldo & Harman, 1993), and community residential rehabilitation staff and clients (Accordino & Guerney, 1993). Moreover, Gibin, Sprenkle, and Sheehan's (1985) meta-analysis of premarital, marital, and family interventions that was conducted with 3,000 couples and compared over a dozen approaches concluded the maintenance of individual gains found over time revealed far greater improvement with the RE Approach than with any of the other approaches studied.

Researchers who have studied RE have applied the approach to a variety of relational contexts. The significant findings reported in these studies conclude that the RE Approach teaches individuals to improve their oral communication skills. Improved communication skills create feelings of gratification and produce additional positive outcomes. Each positive outcome serves to motivate individuals to discuss and to address further their interpersonal issues or problems. These discussions result in more successful completion of relational goals (Guerney, 1989).The ability to manage close interpersonal relationships through positive communication can improve individual's physical and psychological health and increase feelings of happiness and wellness (see, for example, Pitts & Socha, chapter 1; Socha & Pitts, 2012). In short, the RE Approach translates communication theory into practice that results in positive communication outcomes.

A Description of the RE Approach

In the 1960s, Bernard J. Guerney Jr., Ph.D., a Pennsylvania State University professor emeritus of Individual and Family Studies (IFS) and Psychology, conceived of, designed, and first implemented the RE Approach as a couples-therapy system. RE is based on the "special strengths" (Guerney, 1990, p.117) of client-centered, interpersonal, behavior modification, and psychodynamic theories (Guerney, 1977; Scuka, 2005). However, the approach primarily relies on an educational model (Guerney, 1977, 1985). As RE evolved beyond a couples-therapy approach, its objective became to teach nine basic skills to enrich any relationship.

When used efficaciously, RE significantly enriches personal and professional relationships, effectively assists individuals when expressing themselves and when responding to others' attitudes and needs, and helps individuals to manage interpersonal issues skillfully or to solve problems expeditiously (Guerney, 1984). In order to accomplish its objectives, the RE approach focuses on the study and practice of Empathic (Listening), Expressive (Speaking), Discussion-Negotiation (Conversing), Problem-Conflict Resolution, Self-Change, Helping Others Change, Teaching or Facilitation, Generalization, and Maintenance Skills (see Table 9.1; see Mino, 2012).

Table 9.1. An Overview of Relationship Enhancement (RE) Skills

RE Skill	Goals	Guidelines
The Empathic or Listening Skill	Apply effective listening behaviors	Focus all attention on the other by demonstrating appropriate nonverbal behaviors. Concentrate on the other's statements by identifying with the emotions, perceptions, needs, or wants the other is expressing and without considering one's own emotions, perceptions, needs, or wants. Mentally formulate a tentative statement(s). Declaratively state to the other, without including one's own viewpoints or using the other's words, his or her emotions, perceptions, needs, or wants. Accept any corrections the other makes to the response.
The Expressive (Speaking) Skill	Utilize effective speaking behaviors	Empathically respond to the other before expressing one's own feelings, wants, or needs with others. Use "I" statements when sharing one's own emotions, perceptions, needs, or wants with others. Avoid using generalities, like "always" or "never," or personality, motives, or character, such as "selfish," "jealous," or "insincere," when describing one's perception(s) of the other. Select the most appropriate time to request a change in the other's behavior. Be specific about any behavioral changes desired and state the positive effects the change(s) would have on the relationship.
The Discussion-Negotiation (Conversing) Skill	Apply conversational turn-taking to ensure speaker-listener define themselves as equal partners while communicating	Use empathic skills and goals as guidelines during interpersonal interactions. Either person may be the Expresser. However, before expressing, an accurate empathic response is required and must be approved and/or adjusted. Cues for Mode Switching or changing from the Empathic Responder to the Expresser occur when one person is experiencing significantly stronger emotions; important thoughts have been shared at least twice; the Empathic Responder's viewpoint is requested; one's thoughts impair him or her from being empathic; or information can be shared that will favorably influence the situation or resolve the issue.

Continued on next page

Table 9.1. An Overview of Relationship Enhancement (RE) Skills
continued

RE Skill	Goals	Guidelines
The Problem-Conflict Resolution Skill	Employ conversational skills to discuss interpersonal needs and issues and to detail an agreed-upon plan that provides the best and most equitable remedies for parties involved	Incorporate Discussion-Negotiation Skills' Goals and Guidelines to resolve interpersonal issues positively, solve relational problems, or satisfy individual needs. Select or schedule the most appropriate time to introduce a problem or engage in an extended discussion. Share, through Expressive and Empathic Skills, the topic to be discussed and decide if both parties need more time to think about the issue or the discussion can begin. Present and listen to solutions that come close to meeting both parties' wishes in terms of specifics, what can be seen, heard, or felt rather than sharing attitudes or generalities. Once specifics are agreed-upon, decide who will do what, how often, when, and where. Consider if verbal or nonverbal reminders are needed. Discuss any exceptions to the plan that both parties will understand and accept in order to avoid disappointments. Make a specific appointment time in the future to assess the plan's effectiveness or if/what modifications are necessary to better meet both parties' needs and goals.
The Self-Changing Skill	Implement changes to implement personal agreements or objectives and to change behaviors positively	Utilize Discussion-Negotiation and Problem-Solution Skills with another to change one's own behavior(s). Expressive and Empathic Skills gain the other's active support, offer reminders about the desired behavioral change(s) and show appreciation for the help. Avoid becoming defensive or making excuses when the agreed-upon reminders are offered. Lack of progress in the self-changing process requires setting more realistic goals.
The Helping-Others Change Skill	Assist others in making changes in their attitudes, feelings, or behaviors in order to implement interpersonal agreements and objectives	Incorporate Discussion-Negotiation and Problem-Solution Skills with another person in order to change his or her behaviors by having a discussion specifying a firm agreement for change. The nature and circumstances of the agreed-upon reminders are discussed and viewed as helpful behaviors rather than criticism. Use Expressive Skills for positive reinforcement to encourage the other to work toward making the desired behavior change(s). Frustration or disappointment also can be described through Expressive Skills. Failure to change requires constructive reevaluation of the goal.

Continued on next page

Table 9.1. An Overview of Relationship Enhancement (RE) Skills *continued*

RE Skill	Goals	Guidelines
The Facilitation (Teaching) Skill	Monitor the self and others to ensure each RE Skill is applied most effectively	Participate in the RE Training process by using the skills daily and listening carefully to self/other. If necessary, modify the response of self/other by incorporating the most skilled RE statements while adhering to RE Goals and Guidelines. Consistently use modeling, reinforcement, and demonstration.
The Generalization Skill	Practice during RE training and continue to train to incorporate RE Skills regularly and consciously into daily life	Learn by practicing RE Skills in a variety of places and situations to test, and to strengthen RE Skills. Regard mistakes as natural stepping stones to eventual mastery. Use reminders at home or at work to remember to practice the skills and to incorporate goal setting and implementation to enrich relationships. Anticipate situations in which the skills can be employed and review each day the times and places the skills were or could have been used.
The Maintenance Skill	Apply all of the RE skills after the training sessions have ended by continuing to employ the skills as a routine part of the communication process	Continue to appreciate the benefits of employing RE Skills, to persist in planning and rehearsing the skills, to ask others to help monitor skills, and to review and to implement the skills habitually.

The Connections among Interpersonal Communication Concepts and RE

In the 1960s, with the launch of Watzlawick, Beavin, and Jackson's (1967) seminal book, *Pragmatics of human communication: A study of interaction patterns and paradoxes* (see Morreale & Backlund, 2002), concepts, such as "sensitivity training, conscious raising, axioms/pragmatics, uncertainty reduction, rule theory, and relational communication," were introduced and influenced the study and practice of interpersonal communication (see, specifically, Webb & Thompson Hays, 2002, p. 211; see also Berger, 2005).

Throughout the 1970s, communication professionals began publishing interpersonal communication research articles and textbooks. This literature focused on topics that included constructing an interpersonal communication inventory (Bienvenu, 1971), sharing approaches to interpersonal communication instruction (see, for example, McCroskey, Larson, & Knapp, 1971; Phillips & Metzger, 1976; Pearce, 1977; Stewart & D'Angelo, 1975) and examining factors affecting this instruction (Bochner & Yerby, 1977). Interpersonal communication theory (Cushman & Florence, 1974) and interpersonal communication conflict (Fitzpatrick, & Winke, 1979; Steinfatt, Seibold, & Frye, 1974) became driving features of interpersonal communication research at that time. Additionally, scholars examined reasons to engage in interpersonal communication study (Ilardo, 1972) and the effectiveness of popular magazines' advice about communicating interpersonally (Kidd, 1975).

During this time, two key theoretical concepts, rhetorical sensitivity and communication competence, were also studied. These concepts intensified the focus on interpersonal communication research. Rhetorical sensitivity affects social cohesion and facilitates successful interaction through effective persuasion (Hart & Burke, 1972). Rhetorically sensitive communicators exhibit knowledge of and display appropriate oral communication behaviors that reflect thoughtfulness and understanding toward others. They communicate appropriate personality and style and select the role that adapts best to the situation. Based on the situation, rhetorically sensitive communicators select and adjust what to say when speaking and understand when to remain silent (Hart, Eadie, & Carlson, 1975). Hart et al. (1975) concluded that rhetorical sensitivity comprises both the speaker's attitudes and those observable verbal and nonverbal behaviors he or she exhibits that create "reciprocity" while communicating (Hart & Burke, 1972).

Communication competence, which is grounded in sociolinguistics, initially focused on using speech to meet the social demands of a particular group of people or community (Hymes, 1972). In the late 1970s, scholars began to consider communication competence's function in the discipline and define it. Over the years, communication scholars have focused on communication competence's cognitive and behavioral components. For example, Wiemann and Backlund (1980) focused on the importance of knowledge or cognition but also emphasized the significance of behaviors or ability and skills (e.g., Weimann, 1977). Duran and Spitzberg (1995) added a cognitive component to communication competence and described "planning, presence, modeling, reflection, and consequence cognitions" (p.

270). Scholars also have considered the effects of the communicator's motivation (see Canary & MacGregor Istley, 2008; Spitzberg, 2006).

Mino (2012) has connected rhetorical sensitivity with communication competence. She concluded that rhetorically sensitive communicators bring specific attitudes to communication situations that constructively inform behaviors during relational interactions. Thus, rhetorical sensitivity results in more successful communication outcomes. Based on these positive communication outcomes, rhetorical sensitivity can be perceived as intrinsic to the study and practice of communication competence, and communication competence can be considered as essential to understanding the behavioral skills that comprise rhetorical sensitivity.

Taken as a whole and following the progression of thought reflected in the literature, both rhetorical sensitivity and communication competence comprise *attitude*, having the *motivation* to become a competent communicator, *cognition,* learning the appropriate speaking and listening *behaviors* that are applied within a variety of situational contexts, *skills* that are demonstrated and necessary to interact with and adapt to others in those contexts effectively, and *reflection,* assessing whether or not the communication choices made within the context were successful or need to be modified in order to maximize future communication effectiveness in a similar context.

Despite the need for individuals to learn effective behaviors through the use of skills, interpersonal communication study traditionally has focused on disseminating "research findings and theories" (Mortensen, 2007, p. 401) rather than promoting learning the interpersonal skills that exhibit effective communication behaviors (for an exception, see Frey & White, 2012). Similarly, Mino (2012) has observed that the behavioral components of rhetorical sensitivity are ambiguous and operationalizing communication competence has not been articulated definitively (see also Berger, 2005). Moreover, scholars have not given adequate attention to positive communication. Berger (2005), who has provided a comprehensive review of communication theories, has pointed to this void in the interpersonal communication literature. Although scholarship has been devoted to negativity, such as those communication theories that develops aspects of uncertainty and deception, interactive communication and conveying emotional support have not been studied enough. In order to increase the research related to positive communication, Berger (2005) believes interpersonal communication scholars need to focus their research on emotional management and emotion's effect on goal-directed communication.

More recently, interpersonal communication study may be shifting focus. As Mortensen (2007) has noted, unlike a traditional approach to interpersonal communication education of sharing research findings, "increasingly interpersonal communication texts are taking an interdisciplinary approach by incorporating philosophy, exercises, and ethics geared toward personal growth and awareness" (p. 401). Mino (2012) has defined the RE Approach as a valuable one when instructional objectives include teaching students to apply directly the behavioral skills that are components of rhetorical sensitivity and/or communication competence, such as listening effectively, sharing viewpoints successfully, helping the self or the other change his or her perspective or behavior positively, discussing and/or negotiating productively, or discovering the most constructive solutions for interpersonal conflicts.

In particular, this movement toward personal growth and awareness is especially fruitful for practitioners and scholars of positive communication. Because communication educators have been expanding interpersonal communication studies by including the academic work of colleagues in other disciplines, those interdisciplinary approaches that complement interpersonal theory and advance communication research in the areas of positive communication, and especially those approaches that improve individuals' health and wellness, are most beneficial to communication professionals who study these constructs.

The RE approach is a valuable means by which to assist interpersonal communication educators operationalize the components of sensitive, competent, and healthy interpersonal communication in action. Consequently, connecting the communication components of rhetorical sensitivity, communication competence, and the RE Approach, as Mino (2012) has suggested, comprise an interdisciplinary instructional approach that can result in "communication enrichment." It offers a communication context in which participants can communicate positively (Socha & Pitts, 2012) through communication competence (Mizco, 2012), teaches healthy communication (Guerney, 1977), and operationalizes communication excellence through the virtues of gentleness, generosity, courage, justice, and compassion (see, specifically, Mirival, 2012).

Origins and Applications of RE within Interpersonal Communication Instruction

During his tenure at Penn State, Guerney consistently offered a graduate course that focused on the RE Approach. Students who completed the RE class; who received additional RE Training through independent studies; and who accumulated significant course credit hours were given the opportunity to train couples who sought, through Guerney's RE Training Program, a skills-based approach to achieve relational goals. At Penn State, students who met these requirements and received superior ratings from their supervisors and Dr. Guerney could become certified through the National Institute of Relationship Enhancement (NIRE)[1] as a RE Program Leader and/or a Supervisor of RE Program Leaders. Human Development and Family Studies (HDFS) professionals and practitioners of psychology and counseling view RE certification as an endorsement of one's expertise in RE Training (NIRE). These professionals most often receive RE Certification because they understand the value of the RE Approach for their clients and want to incorporate the approach into their professional repertoire.

In 1988, this author, who was an assistant professor of Speech Communication (currently Communication Arts & Sciences) at Penn State DuBois campus and extensively studied the RE Approach with Dr. Guerney, developed, proposed, and received university approval to teach a 15 week, 3 credit undergraduate class, *Personal and Interpersonal Skills*, for Penn State's IFS (currently HDFS) Department. The course became one requirement selection for the department's majors and these majors enrolled in the course. Since that time, this class has been offered at Penn State DuBois and/or Penn State University Park campuses.[2] Based on her work in RE, in 1990, the author became a RE Program Leader and a Supervisor of RE Program Leaders.

Over 20 years, as the communication discipline has evolved, so has this class. Communication research and the principles of the RE Approach have been consistently integrated. This integration insures the class remains current when sharing with students the importance and successful outcomes of learning interpersonal communication and effectively applying interpersonal communication skills.

The *Personal and Interpersonal Skills* (HDFS 216) course content specifically focuses on individual student's communication experiences. In addition to HDFS students, students with diverse majors, such as business, science, and engineering enroll in the course. Course content is designed to directly relate to individual student's experiences, needs, and goals while learning each RE skill. The 20 students who enroll in the course participate in a highly interactive and personalized instructional environment designed to improve the individual's communication skills (see Frey & White, 2012). Each student also provides a final self-assessment paper that addresses his or her level of commitment, quality of skills development, and perceived learning outcomes throughout the RE training process. Therefore, the course is unique in its design and execution.

An Overview of RE Instruction

Because the RE Approach clearly conveys a means by which to help individuals learn, practice, and apply the skills that express their attitudes, feelings, ideas, thoughts, or needs to others both successfully and positively, applying RE Skills has the potential to empower individuals to control and to change their lives significantly (see, for example, Guernsey, 1977, 1982). However, in order for this change to occur, the individual's attitude about learning and applying the skills is a crucial component of the training process. Particularly, those individuals who want to study RE commit to engage, and engage as participants, in conscious, effortful, and collaborative attempts to understand fully and strive to master what they agree to learn and practice (Guerney, 1977, 1989).

The RE Approach also "deliberately seeks and directly instigates changes in the rules, organizational patterns, and interpersonal interactions existing [between or among] individuals" by introducing a new set of attitudes and skills that can be applied in a variety of interpersonal contexts (Guerney, 1990, p.117). These attitudes and skills alter the ways that individuals typically speak with and listen to others. Specifically, participants are taught to express themselves truthfully, while avoiding accusations, overgeneralizations, and ambiguity; to recognize the sentiments, desires, and motivations of themselves and others; and to respond to others with understanding, consideration, and acceptance (Guerney, 1977).

Learning and applying RE Skills can present participants with risks and challenges. Specifically, participants learn that they risk failure in order to help them perform well (Guerney, 1990). It is through their mistakes and errors that they become skilled at monitoring their communication by routinely assessing and correcting their speaking and listening behaviors.

Moreover, altering familiar behaviors is a challenging task. However, as participants learn to adjust their typical communication patterns and experience more positive reactions from others, they work harder to master RE Skills. Participants also discover as their communication skill level improves, others' interactive behaviors can be affected positively. That is, those who observe or interact with participants when they consistently demonstrate skillful communication learn, over time, to model these behaviors (Guerney, 1985).

In all, the positive outcomes associated with applying the RE Approach can result in or increase well-being (see, for example, Seligman, 2002,

2011).The satisfaction and psychological comfort that arise out of positive relational interactions are part of gaining the optimal experiences (see Csikszentmihalyi, 1990) that the RE Approach teaches and encourages.

The Basics of RE Exercises

Learning and applying RE Skills typically occur as a cumulative process over a term or semester but can be scheduled or employed at the instructor's discretion based on his or her pedagogical goals (see Mino, 2012). First, reading, one at a time, each RE goal and guideline is assigned. Each skill is discussed and related to current communication theory. Next, each skill is demonstrated in turn, immediately after which an exercise related to it is described. Each exercise directly pertains to the participants' daily interpersonal encounters, their specific interpersonal communication goals, and is used to simulate their past or current relationship experiences.

By personalizing the exercises, participants are more eager to understand how each of the RE skills function separately and as a whole and are more willing to practice and to apply them. Because of the nature of the *Personal and Interpersonal Skills* course, creating a safe environment in which to learn and to apply all of the RE Skills through collaborative instruction is essential (see Frey & White, 2012). Therefore, the instructor must demonstrate sensitive, competent, and positive communication behaviors. Additionally, there are no tests or quizzes. Grading is based solely on the instructor's evaluation of the participant's cumulative RE skill level at the end of the training process.

Exercises are designed to help the participant focus on and assess his or her typical interpersonal communication patterns and to emphasize that using RE Skills results in more constructive, positive, and healthier ways of communicating. Exercises are assigned as homework. Subsequently, in the *Personal and Interpersonal Skills* course, they are shared during the training sessions in order to provide multiple personal examples for participants. Exercises include Empathic, Expressive, and Skills Generalization Logs, goal planning and implementation, and role plays. Exercises determine the degree of comprehension related to each RE skill individually and as a whole. In addition, these exercises are used to evaluate skill levels at the onset of training and to monitor the extent of improvement throughout the training process.

Empathic and Expressive Logs recount interpersonal interactions. Empathic Skills are practiced first to emphasize listening's crucial role in the communication process (see Bodie, 2012). Each of these logs emphasize that each skill can be used during any interpersonal encounter. Thus, these logs share the person with whom, the time, and place the skill was used; indicate the purpose served when employing either skill; report the other person's statement or nonverbal cue that prompted the use of the skill; indicate the approximate number of additional skilled statements; and generate discussion concerning the positive, negative, or neutral interpersonal outcomes to emphasize for the participants and help them consider how skilled or unskilled communication behaviors can and do affect interpersonal outcomes.

Skills Generalization Logs indicate if participants can identify which specific skill (Expressive, Empathic, or Facilitation) they used. These logs not only recount with whom, where, when, and how effectively the participants used their skills but also report participants' positive or negative feeling(s) when communicating and if any feelings, in particular, prevented them from using an RE skill or from using it well. While reviewing the logs, the instructor invites discussion from all participants concerning the level of skill demonstrated and evaluates how effectively each skill was used.

Goal planning and implementation accommodate each participant's need or desire to make personal changes or to change another person's attitudes, feelings, or behaviors. For goal planning, participants design at least two specific goals, rank their order based on degree of difficulty, begin with their easiest goal in order to improve their skills before tackling the more difficult one(s), and engage in facilitation using what the participant believes will be and might be said when they carry out their goals. Planning allows participants to prepare for the best and the worst case scenarios.

Specifically, when planning a goal, the participants provide their responses on a Goal Implementation Form in a specific order. These responses follow, (a) Name the other involved and his or her relationship to you, (b) share a clear and specific expressive statement of the desired goal, (c) provide a statement or statements expressing the positive things the speaker thinks about the relationship and the positive things he or she believes the other thinks about him or her, (d) express the problem or lack of fulfillment in terms of the speakers' conflicts, "On the one hand..., but on the other hand...," (e) provide expressive statements about the speaker's views and/or emotions created by the problem, (f) share expressive statements about the implications for the speaker's self-concept if he or she does not receive a genuine attempt at cooperation from the other, (g) expressively share the speaker's interpersonal message by sharing the goal, "I would really appreciate it if_____" and how the speaker would feel if this request was met, h) express the potential effect(s) on the other's self-concept and emotions by providing the other's possible statement after the worst reaction to the speaker's request for a behavior change, (i) empathically respond to other's worst reaction and describe for the other his or her worst reaction and gain mutual understanding (j) provide the effect(s) on the other's self-concept and emotions after the potential most probable reaction to the speaker's request for a behavior change, (k) share the speaker's empathic response to the other's most probable reaction to gain mutual understanding, (l) expressively state the other's probable desire concerning the speaker's behavior or what the other might want from the speaker to do generally, before, or after the other's new behavior(s), (m) expressively state what the other might directly or indirectly say requesting the speaker to change his or her behavior(s), (n) share the speaker's empathic responses to the other's request for a behavioral change, (o) expressively describe what the other will most likely agree to do, and (p) expressively overview the agreed upon proposal that will meet both the speaker's and the other's needs.

Participants use goal implementation to apply Self-Changing and/or Helping-Others Change Skills. Each of these skills involves changing attitudes, feelings, or behaviors. Self-Changing Skills are directed to the person the participant wants to help him or her accomplish personal goals, such as "I want my roommate to help me to exercise at least two days a week." Using Helping-Others Change Skills are employed with the person who the participant wants to change. For example, "I want my roommate to clean up his dishes after each meal." Participants' goals are presented during class sessions. When they believe they are ready to use the skills effectively and before the conclusion of the training process, participants implement and report on the final outcome of each goal by reviewing how well they followed their goal planning and the RE Skills guidelines, if they were correct when anticipating the other's reactions, and if some or all of the specific behavior desired from the other during the goal implementation process were agreed upon.

In order to enable participants to practice consistently their Discussion-Negotiation, Problem-Conflict Resolution, and Facilitation Skills, based on situations with which the participant are familiar, role plays, involving two participants are used to simulate conversational turn-taking and problem-solving. Role plays are presented during several class sessions and also are assigned as homework. During class sessions, one or more role plays, involving two participants or one role play where participants take turns acting as expresser (speaker) and empathic responder (listener) are presented and evaluated immediately. Role plays assigned as homework are recorded (through audiotape) by the participants and presented in class with transcripts. These role plays include employing Discussion-Negotiation

Skills during a six-minute conversation and focus on applying Problem-Conflict Resolution Skills to solve a minor problem (10 minutes) and a major problem (15 minutes). In each case, Facilitation Skills also are used by the participants while recording the role play.

Transcripts are employed to help participants gain additional practice with their Facilitation Skills. By editing their own transcripts, the participants are provided with the additional opportunity to make any other changes that were not made through facilitation while they recorded the role plays. As a result, the participants' role play content reflects their most skillful communication efforts. In all, the transcript's editorial changes indicate the participants' level of skill facilitating their communication, identify the skills they need to improve, and share their best work during the training sessions. The instructor and other participants use any additional Facilitation Skills required while listening to the recorded role play and reading the corrected transcript. Based on the recordings and the transcripts, participants also receive extensive written evaluations from the instructor that focus on their communication strengths and weaknesses.

At the conclusion of a successful RE Training process, participants achieve the following goals: (a) recognizes the significance of mastering RE Skills; (b) appreciates the value of applying the skills in his or her daily life; (c) realizes that communicating positively with others is an ongoing learning process; (d) recognizes the importance of revisiting concepts and exercises; (e) applies the RE concepts as a routine part of the communication process.

Conclusion

The Relationship Enhancement (RE) Approach teaches ways to communicate with others most effectively and positively through its focus on shared conversation, skillful conflict resolution, productive self- and other-changing techniques, and, in all, shares a clear application method for enriching relationships. After committing to learn, consistently practice, and maintain RE skills beyond the instructional setting by employing them regularly, individuals can continue to benefit from RE Skills throughout their lifetimes. Above all, when emphasized by the communication discipline as an valid and effective approach, RE not only holds significant potential for positive communication scholars and educators in terms of contributing to individual awareness, personal growth, and wellness but also this approach presents numerous pedagogical and research possibilities for communication study and practice in general.

Notes

1. The National Institute of Relationship Enhancement (NIRE, www.nire.org) provides information about and offers programs related to RE Skills and skills training and provides its "Program Leader Directory" to help individuals locate certified RE professionals around the country to assist educators and those who seek communication skills training. This description of the RE Approach is derived from the author's RE Training and experience and the RE literature. The goals, guidelines, and exercises related to each skill are based on an overview of each skill shared by Guerney (1989) and the detailed descriptions and application Mino (2012) shares during her RE course and other RE Training activities.

2. Mino (1994) shared an initial version of the course with her Pennsylvania colleagues.

References

Accordino, M. P., & Guerney, B. J., Jr. (1993). Effects of Relationship Enhancement on community residential rehabilitation staff and clients. *Psychosocial Rehabilitation Journal, 17*, 131–144.

Avery, A. W., & Thiessen, J. D. (1982). Communication skills training for divorcees. *Journal of Counseling Psychology, 1*, 203–205.

Berger, C. (2005). Interpersonal communication: Theoretical perspectives, future prospects. *Journal of Communication, 55*, 415–447.

Bienvenu, M. J., Sr. (1971). An interpersonal communication inventory. *Journal of Communication, 21*, 381–388.

Bochner, A., & Yerby, J. (1977). Factors affecting instruction in interpersonal communication. *Communication Education, 26*, 91–103.

Bodie, G. D. (2012). Listening as positive communication. In T. J. Socha & M. J. Pitts (Eds.), *The positive side of communication* (pp. 109–126). New York: Peter Lang.

Canary, D., & MacGregor Istley, M. (2008). Differences that make a difference in assessing student communication competence. *Communication Education, 57*, 41–63.

Csikszentmihalyi, M. (1990). *Flow: The psychology of optimal experience*. New York: Harper Perennial.

Cushman, D. P., & Florence, B. (1974). The development of interpersonal communication theory. *Communication Quarterly, 22*, 11–16.

Duran, R. L., & Spitzberg, B. H. (1995). Toward the development and validation of a measure of cognitive communication competence. *Communication Quarterly, 43*, 259–275.

Eubanks, H. L. (1952). Teaching speech for human relationships. *Speech Teacher, 1*, 9–13.

Frey, L. R., & White, A. (2012). Promoting personal, interpersonal, and group growth through positive experiential encounter communication pedagogy. In T. J. Socha & M. J. Pitts (Eds.), *The positive side of communication* (pp. 297–312). New York: Peter Lang.

Fitzpatrick, M. A., & Winke, J. (1979). You always hurt the one you love: Strategies and tactics in interpersonal communication conflict. *Communication Quarterly, 27*, 3–11.

Gibin, P., Sprenkle, D. H., & Sheehan, R. (1985). Enrichment outcome research: A meta-analysis of premarital, marital, and family interventions. *Journal of Marital and Family Therapy, 11*, 257–271.

Ginsberg, B. G. (2004). *Relationship Enhancement family therapy.* Doylestown, PA: Relationship Enhancement Press.

Guerney, B. G., Jr. (1977). *Relationship Enhancement: Skills training programs for therapy, problem prevention, and enrichment.* San Francisco, CA: Jossey Bass.

Guerney, B. G., Jr. (1982). Relationship Enhancement. In E. K. Marshall & P. D. Kurtz (Eds.), *Interpersonal helping skills* (pp. 482–518). San Francisco, CA: Jossey Bass.

Guerney, B. G., Jr. (1984). Relationship Enhancement Therapy and training. In D. Larson (Ed.), *Teaching psychological skills: Models for giving psychology away* (pp. 99–134). Beverly Hills, CA: Sage.

Guerney, B. G., Jr. (1985). The medical vs. the educational model as a base for family therapy research. In L. L. Andreozzi & R. F. Levant (Eds.), *Integrating research and clinical practice* (pp. 71–79) . Rockville, MD: Aspen Systems Corporation.

Guerney, B. G., Jr. (1989). *Relationship Enhancement manual.* State College, PA: IDEALS.

Guerney, B. G., Jr. (1990). Creating therapy and growth inducing systems: Personal mooring, landmarks and guiding stars. In F. W. Kaslow (Ed.), *Voices in family psychology* (pp. 114–138). Beverly Hills, CA: Sage.

Guerney, B. G., Jr., Guerney, L., & Sebes, J. M. (1984). Promoting family wellness through the educational system. In R. D. Mace (Ed.), *Preventing in family services: Family wellness* (pp. 214–230). Beverly Hills, CA: Sage.

Guerney, B. G., Jr., & Jordon, L. (1980). Children of divorce—A community support group. *Journal of Divorce, 2,* 283–293.

Guerney, B. G., Jr., Waldo, M., & Firestone, L. (1987). Wife-battering: A theoretical construct and case report. *The American Journal of Family Therapy, 15,* 34–43.

Hart, R. P., & Burke, D. M. (1972). Communication and social interaction. *Communication Monographs, 39,* 75–91.

Hart, R. P., Eadie, W., & Carlson, R. (1975). Rhetorical sensitivity and communication competency, 1–43. Paper presented at the annual meeting of the Speech Communication Association. Retrieved at the Educational Research Information Center (ERIC), www.eric.ed.gov.

Hymes, D.M. (1972). On communication competence. In J. B. Pride & J. Holmes (Eds.), *Sociolinguistics* (pp. 269–294). New York: Penguin Books.

Ilardo, J. A. (1972). Why interpersonal communication? *The Speech Teacher, 21,* 1–6.

Jesse, R., & Guerney, B. G., Jr. (1981). A comparison of Gestalt and Relationship Enhancement treatments with married couples. *The American Journal of Family Therapy, 9,* 31–41

Kidd, V. (1975). Happily ever after and other relationship styles: Advice on interpersonal communication in popular magazines. *The Quarterly Journal of Speech, 61,* 31–39.

Matter, M., McAllister, W., & Guerney, B. J., Jr. (1984). Relationship enhancement for the recovering couple: Working with the intangible. *Focus on Family and Chemical Dependency, 7,* 21–40.

McCroskey, J. C., Larson, C., & Knapp, M. L. (1971). *An introduction to interpersonal communication.* Englewood Cliffs, NJ: Prentice–Hall.

Miczo, N. (2012). Reflective conversation as a foundation for communication virtue. In T. J. Socha & M. J. Pitts (Eds.), *The positive side of communication* (pp. 73–90). New York: Peter Lang.

Mino, M. (1994). Using Relationship Enhancement (RE) for teaching a course in interpersonal communication. *Pennsylvania Speech Communication Annual, 50,* 18–33.

Mino, M. (2012). Clarifying communication competencies through an interdisciplinary approach to communication pedagogy. *Journal of the Association of Communication Administration, 31,* 14–28.

Mirivel, J. C. (2012). Communication excellence: Embodying virtues in interpersonal communication. In T. J. Socha & M. J. Pitts (Eds.), *The positive side of communication* (pp. 57–72). New York: Peter Lang.

Morreale, S. P., & Backlund, P. M. (2002).Communication curricula: History, recommendations, resources. *Communication Education, 51,* 2–18.

Mortenson, S. T. (2007). Raising the Question #7 should we teach personal transformation as a part of interpersonal communication? If so, how is it done? *Communication Education, 56,* 401–408.

Pearce, W. B. (1977).Teaching interpersonal communication as a humane science: A comparative analysis. *Communication Education, 26,* 104–112.

Phillips, G. M., & Metzger, N. (1976). *Intimate Communication.* Boston, MA: Allyn and Bacon.

Rapport, A. F. (1976). Conjugal Relationship Enhancement Program. In D. H. Olsen (Ed.), *Treating relationships* (pp. 41–66). Lake Mills, IA: Graphic-Publishing.

Seligman, M. E. P. (2002). *Authentic happiness.* New York: Free Press.

Seligman, M. E. P. (2011). *Flourish: A visionary new understanding of happiness and well-being.* New York: Free Press.

Scuka, R. F. (2005). *Relationship Enhancement Therapy: Healing through deep empathy and intimate dialogue.* New York: Routledge.

Snyder, M., & Guerney, B. J., Jr. (1993). Brief couple/family therapy: The Relationship Enhancement Approach. In R. A. Wells & V. J. Granetti (Eds.), *Casebook of brief psychotherapies* (pp. 32–48). New York: Plenum Press.

Socha, T. J., & Pitts, M. J. (2012). Toward a conceptual foundation of positive communication. In T. J. Socha & M. J. Pitts (Eds.), *The positive side of communication* (pp. 1–18). New York: Peter Lang.

Spitzberg, B. H. (2006). Preliminary development of a model and measure of computer-mediated communication (CMC) competence. *Journal of Computer Mediated Communication, 11,* 629–666.

Spitzberg, B. H., & Cupach, W. R. (1989). *Handbook of interpersonal competence research.* New York: Springer.

Steinfatt, T. M., Seibold, D. R., & Frye, J. K. (1974). Communication in game simulated conflicts: Two experiments. *Speech Monographs, 41,* 24–35.

Stewart, J., & D'Angelo, G. (1975*). Together: Communication interpersonally.* Reading, MA: Addison-Wesley.

Waldo, M. (1988). Relationship Enhancement counseling groups for wife abusers. *Journal of Mental Health Counseling, 10,* 37–45.

Waldo, M. (1989). Primary prevention in university residence halls: Paraprofessional-led Relationship Enhancement groups for college roommates. *Journal of Mental Health Consoling, 67,* 465–471.

Waldo, M., & Guerney, B. J., Jr. (1983). Marital Relationship Enhancement Therapy in the treatment of alcoholism. *Journal of Marital and Family Therapy, 9,* 321–323.

Waldo, M., & Harman, M. J. (1993). Relationship Enhancement Therapy with borderline personality. *The Family Journal, 9,* 25–30.

Watzlawick, P., Beavin, J. H., & Jackson, D. D. (1967). *Pragmatics of human communication: A study of interaction patterns and paradoxes.* New York: Norton.
Webb, L. M., & Thompson Hays, M. E. (2002). Do popular collegiate textbooks in interpersonal communication reflect a common theory base? A telling content analysis. *Communication Education, 51,* 210–224.
Wiemann, J. M. (1977). Explication and test of a model of communication competence. *Human Communication Research, 3,* 195–213.
Wiemann, J. M., & Backlund, P. (1980). Current theory and research in communication competence. *Review of Educational Research, 50,* 185–199.

• CHAPTER TEN •

Positive Communication, Coaching, and Relational Health/Wellness

Jean DeHart
Appalachian State University

This chapter examines conceptual connections between the study of positive communication, life coaching, and relational wellness, arguing that "coaching" is a process that connects work in positive psychology and communication in ways that can enhance the health of relationships and the well-being of individuals. Specifically, this chapter examines nine points of connection between coaching, communication, health, and relationships. The chapter is informed by relevant academic literature but also by the author's perspective as a communication teacher-scholar who holds certifications in professional empowerment coaching.

Relationships, Health, and Wellness

The state of our many relationships can greatly affect our health and well-being; arguably these effects can be second to only our physical health. Be it relationships with a spouse, significant other in a dating relationship, roommate, colleague, parent, child, or any kind of friendship, relationships impact the quality of our daily lives and our well-being. Richardson (1998) explained: "The relationships you share with loved ones are the most important ingredient of a high-quality life. They shape who you are and add meaning to your life" (p. 39). Biswas-Diener and Dean (2007) concurred: "Whether complaining about a boss, looking for an inspiring collaborator, or trying to balance work with family life, social concerns are a large part of everyone's life" (p. 76). Indeed, Cline (2011) argued that everyday types of intepersonal communication play an important role in our health and well-being. Others have argued for the importance of "enacted social support," described by Goldsmith (2004) as "what individuals say and do to help one another" (p. 13).

Communication processes can be challenged in various ways that include specific events or by general tensions in a relationship. The well-being of important relationships is threatened by commonly recognized stressors, including marriage or marital breakdown, illness, bereavement, arguments, workload, roles (Jones & Bright, 2001; Holmes & Rahe, 1967), and physical distance of the two individuals (Guildner 1996) and Lyndon (1997). Other interpersonally focused stressors include a feeling of not being appreciated or not being a priority in someone's life, a feeling of inadequacy, a feeling that the other person does not value communication, concern that a partner is interacting more with other confidants (Duck, 1985), or a feeling by an individual that he or she is contributing much to a relationship to the detriment of his or her own personal aspirations.

In spite of the best intentions of partners to strive to create healthy relationship, cultural factors can interfere (e.g., see Jones & Bright, 2001 for a discussion of the effect of cultural factors on stress). Biswas-Diener and Dean (2007) explained that "one of the most toxic aspects of materialistic values, psychologically speaking, is that monetary, luxury, and work goals can steal time and attention away from other worthwhile pursuits, such as nurturing relationships" (p. 77).

Taken together, these stressors have detrimental effects on relational health. A number of studies have contributed "empirical evidence that stressors can significantly decrease relationship quality and stability" (Koranyi & Klaus, 2012, p. 180). Both positive psychologists and communication scholars note that maintaining high quality relationships provides substantial benefits to our health and wellness. Research has suggested that the one quality which happy people have in common is close trusting relationships, and further, healthy family relationships combat negative psychological effects of socio-economic factors such as poverty (Biswas-Diener & Dean, 2007). Bisiker (2001) evaluated the role of relationship quality in determining happiness and self-esteem, noting that negative feelings might stand in the way of happiness for people who are not at ease with their current relationships. He found that when individuals feel content in their relationships, they "can deal with the rejections of life far more easily, and will go out and push [themselves] more in [their] working life" (p. 9). Healthy relationships play an important role in achieving life-work balance, increasing both productivity and well-being. Realizing that happier people tend to be more productive in a work environment, have better performance evaluations, be seen as better citizens, live longer, and have more close and casual friends, Biswas-Diener and Dean (2007) explained that social relationships "offer a sense of security, opportunities for growth, and even promote physical health" (p. 17). Similarly, Baxter's (2006) work on relational dialectics examined the ways in which family relationships impact our health. Pecchioni and Keeley (2011) also provided a review of research on how affection exchange in relationships affects health.

Traditional Sources of Support

When individuals are in happy, supportive relationships or have support when they face stressors, their health and well-being are enhanced (e.g., see Gable, Gonzaga, & Strachman 2006). But, to whom do individuals turn when they lack supportive relationships or when a relationship that is normally supportive becomes tense? Traditional sources of social support include a partner, child, parent, friend, counselor/therapist, minister, supervisor or co-worker (Antonia, Abramis, & Caplan, 1985). Each of these sources of support offer benefits, but also have limitations. With relationship issues, for example, the stress or concern may be about a relationship with the person to whom one would normally turn for solace, advice, or counsel. The person with stress may think that the close relationship someone has with another will result in confidential information being shared, and thus not feel comfortable. An employee may feel uncomfortable talking with a colleague about a marriage issue or about an uncomfortable relationship with another colleague or supervisor. Partners may talk about issues, but at times, individuals may feel lonely and uncomfortable disclosing to each other. Likewise, a child might seek support from a parent, but not when the issue is about the parent. Friends often do not have a detached perspective or the skills to help someone overcome the difficulties he or she faces. Perhaps they are too attached to their friend to remain impartial, or they may have their own agenda. Ducaaese (2006) synthesized this idea by saying that friends are "hampered by too many different strings and misconceptions to be able to provide objective honest reflections to their own friends" (p. 6). He illustrated his point with the example of a close friend who might discourage someone from relocating because of the desire to have that friend remain "close" although physically distant. He noted that the friend might "have a strong incentive to either discourage the recognition of the truth, that their friend might want to move, or would lobby against the move in favor of keeping the friendship" (p. 6). Leatham and Duck (1990) noted that friends might not have the interpersonal communication competence or might not be willing or able to provide needed types of support.

Counseling or therapeutic discourse may occur with a trusted mentor or licensed professional. Professional counseling has benefitted many people but may not always be an optimal solution for creating healthy relationships.

Individuals may be in relationships that although are not ideal nor very satisfying, may not be deemed "dysfunctional enough" to warrant the time and expense of professional counseling. Such partners may be embarrassed by a perceived stigma of therapy or have fears about changes in a relationship. So, they instead continue existing in unhappy situations. Rusbult's (1998) investment scale model explains that people might maintain relationships because of important and consequential resources attached to the relationship and/or because of the quality of alternatives to the relationship. Social exchange theory contends that we seek the least costly, best option for a relationship—the one with more rewards (Thibault & Kelley, 1959). Griffiths and Campbell (2008) contend that there are similarities between coaching and counseling and suggest that the disciplines work together. Richardson (1998) argued, "there is a growing need for more than what therapy provides. In therapy, clients may talk about the changes they'd like to make in their lives, but the 'how to' and the resources are often missing" (p. 2). According to Seligman (2011):

> the takeaway lesson from positive psychology is that positive mental health is not just the absence of mental illness. It is all too commonplace not to be mentally ill but to be stuck and languishing in life. Positive mental health is a presence; the presence of positive emotion, the presence of good relationships, and the presence of accomplishment. Being in a state of mental health is not merely being disorder free; rather it is the presence of flourishing. (p. 183)

Relationships can provide support, but as Cohen and Wills (1985) noted, one high-quality relationship can provide more effective support than multiple casual relationships. Communication research has studied and advocated the importance of social support, but has not quite yet addressed the many elements of what might the thought of as a network of communication support delivery (e.g., see Macgeorge, Feng, Wilkum, & Doherty, 2012; McCullough & Burleson, 2012).

Empowerment Coaching

Since the 1990s individuals with relationship stresses have had an option of turning to a professional life or empowerment coach.[1] Coaching provides different advantages to the enhancement of personal and relational well-being than what traditional counseling or friends can offer. Noting the varied definitions and applications of coaching, Grant (2005) explained that

> the core constructs of professional coaching include a helping, collaborative and egalitarian rather than authoritarian relationship between coach and client; a focus

on finding solutions in preference to analyzing problems; the assumption that clients are from a population without significant levels of psychopathology or emotional distress; an emphasis on collaborative goal-setting; and the recognition that although the coach needs expertise in facilitating learning through coaching, the coach does not necessarily need a high degree of personal experience in the client's chosen area of learning. (p. 2)

When these core constructs are operationalized, coaching becomes an empowering, interactive process that involves questions and answers and results in helping clients determine and achieve their goals. As Bisiker (2001) noted, the life-coach works "with only one agenda, the support and personal success of you and your ideas" (p. 9).

Biswas-Diener and Dean (2007) suggested that the field of positive psychology "shows tremendous potential as a natural interface with the profession of coaching" (p. 5). Life coaches' philosophies are closely aligned with positive psychology, in the focus on what is right and good in someone's life. Coaching is consistent with Seligman's (2011) depiction of the elements of well-being, as coaching relies on the use of positive emotions, positive energy, and positive action (see, for example, Richardson, and IPEC). While helping individuals determine their strengths and dreams and work toward achieving those, a coach does not assume that the client is deficient or that anyone is to blame. Coaching takes a positive approach in focusing on what is right with the individual—assuming that individuals are okay the way they are—but the coach will help them move forward to where they experience greater personal and relational satisfaction. Coaching is practical and goal oriented, examining roadblocks that might prevent progress, but maintaining a focus on the future the client wants to create. For example, a coach would not encourage someone to stay in a relationship or to leave a relationship, but would rely on the perception of the client. The idea is that clients are capable of determining and achieving what they truly want in life.[2] Coach Cheryl Richardson (1998) wrote:

> Coaching is not about processing your emotional history or diagnosing and treating mental health issues. Coaching is action oriented, with a focus on a client's current life and plans for the future; although therapy deals with a client's current life, the focus is usually on the past and the healing of emotional wounds. (p. 2)

Coaching provides a practical way to implement positive psychology's focus on well-being. Discussing how positive psychology differs from traditional approaches, Seligman (2002) indicated that a negative mood results in a focus on what is wrong and how to be rid of that, as opposed to a positive mood that leads individuals to creativity, tolerance, and constructive thinking

(p. 38). Positive psychology focuses on what is right with the person—as does coaching. As coaches examine behavior, they ask questions such as "What has worked well for you in the past?" and tap into a positive emotion the client felt in the past. The coach then brings forth that feeling to the future. If someone believes a current relationship with a loved one or colleague is not working well, then the question would be about when the relationship did work well. If an individual has chosen to be in a relationship, there is likely a period of time when it worked well. Helping the individual tap into that is not just a means to discover what went wrong, but a way to make the individual feel the emotion that they experienced when things were good. Through a focus on strengths, coaching helps individuals tap into positive energy and emotions in order to achieve their goals.

Conceptually, "coaching" can be associated with many disciplines seeking to enhance individuals' and groups' well-being. For example, coaching is included as academic study at some universities (including Georgetown and Harvard) with at least seven offering coaching degrees (Grant & Cavanagh, 2011). Coaching, however, does not have an academic home per se, but rather is embraced by a number of disciplines, although surprisingly, communication has not been one of them. As Grant (2005) indicated, "Professional coaching can be considered an emerging cross-disciplinary occupation, its primary purpose being to enhance well-being, improve performance and facilitate individual and organizational change" (p. 1). Grant (2005) identified the behavioral sciences, business and economic science, adult education, and philosophy as academic areas that have the "best current knowledge directly related to the research and practice of executive, workplace and life coaching" (p. 7). Grant and Cavanagh (2011) further noted:

> Coaching is ideally placed to be a point of connection between disparate areas of research. The knowledge base of coaching remains an open question, and coaches can and do utilize multiple theories and models drawn from traditional psychology, positive psychology, and wider fields of endeavor such as management, medicine, biology, sociology, complexity and systems research, spirituality, education, and philosophy. (p. 304)

What is omitted in their assessment is the role of communication. Certainly communication could play an important role in this interdisciplinary work. The challenge will be understanding and a willingness to have the interdisciplinary approach.

There are many potential connections between communication and the different types of empowerment coaching. For relational communication, "life coaching" is especially relevant, as it focuses on the enhancement of personal life processes many of which are intertwined with communication. As a discipline, communication does examine aspects of communication processes that will improve the health and well-being of relationships, but has also neglected to link this work to larger frameworks such as life coaching. Yet, both life coaching and communication studies would clearly benefit by learning how to improve our networks of enacted social support and relational well-being.

Coaching provides a means for tailoring communication research to enhance relational and individual well-being. Life coaching utilizes principles of communication and links the principles of positive psychology and communication in a way that can be used to enhance the health and well-being of relationships; coaching provides a conceptual means to blend them together.

Positive psychology provides some of the theory and background for life coaching and coaching provides practical dimensions to further the aims of positive psychology, in particular improved health and wellness practices. A review of positive psychology literature reveals many works about coaching, but the concept appears virtually absent from communication literature about relational health and well-being.

Observing the irony that coaching helps others achieve their potential, but has not realized its own potential, Biswas-Diener and Dean (2007) suggested that coaching ground itself more in science. They acknowledged that the coaching field has been paying more attention to the benefits of science with the International Coach Federation (ICF) (http://www.coach federation.org/) sponsoring annual research symposia of the applications of coaching research, but stressed the need for more research and suggested that interfacing with positive psychology will help develop the coaching profession. They indicated that the foundation of positive psychology is based on scientific studies that include broad samples and can be replicated. They believed this research could provide insight into how to provide effective services for the widest range of people by looking at individual differences, the timing of interventions, and including surprising, counterintuitive results (such as a focus on strengths and the positive being more effective than a focus on weakness and problems). Biswas-Diener and Dean (2007) warned against becoming too scientific, noting: "There is an art to coaching, often seen in the spontaneity, playfulness, and use of intuition common to coaching sessions. We do not suggest here that systematic science ought to replace this art, nor do we argue in favor of cookie cutter interventions" (p. 22). Communication research seems well-suited to be able to contribute to the scientific base of coaching as well as its integration into larger frameworks. As life coaching is somewhat new, it remains for communication scholars to begin to examine its potential and to consider including it in interpersonal communication instruction (e.g., a review of interpersonal communication textbooks reveals no mention of "coaching").

Communication can certainly help to inform the concept of "coaching" and specifically to develop a positive communication-based coaching approach that brings together the many elements we study disparately. In addition, using theories of positive psychology, the professional expertise in coaching, and communication research and practice, communication can inform coaching and coaching can be a means for communication scholars to further disseminate their work and increase its impact on positive communication.

Coaching provides a practical, positive approach to relationship enhancement, but it is very broad. For example, the Institute for Professional Excellence in Coaching (IPEC) (http://www.ipeccoaching.com/) offers a coach training manual that lists eleven core competencies, 69 subparts, and 47 skill sets. Williams and Thomas (2005) provide 51 "life lessons" for coaches to use with clients. Moreover, McMahon and Archer (2010) compiled 101 coaching strategies and techniques. From among these various lists of skills and potential benefits coaching can bring to enhancing well-being, nine points of conceptual connection are spotlighted below. This list is not intended to be exhaustive, rather it is intended to illustrate the potential types of conceptual connections that might be fruitful to pursue in further communication research and education pertaining to coaching. These nine points of connection were derived from a review of coach training materials, coaching websites, newsletters as well as personal experience. They are intended to start a conversation between positive communication and professional coaching.

Points of Connection between Communication and Coaching

Goal Setting

One area inherent in the nature of coaching is goal setting and follow-through. Coaching helps individuals achieve their goals and enhance well-being through helping individuals identify goals and outcomes, using identity of strength and building self-efficacy to enhance motivation, develop and modify action plans and discover resources and monitoring and evaluating progress (Grant & Cavanagh, 2011). Positive psychology and communication researchers have stressed the importance and prevalence of goals in our lives. Biswas-Diener and Dean (2007) identified goals as being useful because "they create meaning for our lives, they provide us with a gauge for achievement, and they help us to structure our time and prioritize our activities" (p. 64). Communication research is prolific in the area of goals—especially with identifying and obtaining goals. Researchers contend that interpersonal communication is goal-directed (Dillard, 1993) and that individuals strive to achieve self-presentational, relational, and instrumental goals (Canary & Cody, 1994). Coaching helps further both of these areas by providing a focus on helping individuals determine their goals and reach them. Communication scholars create categorizations of the types of goals individuals typically seek to attain and then analyze how they go about achieving them. A coaching approach could help communication scholars widen their reach beyond the classroom, for example, to increase individuals' communication competencies in their everyday lives. What is unique in coaching is that the client determines the goals and how to achieve them, without expectation of meeting a particular category of goal. The feeling of empowerment that comes when one is actually working toward what he or she wants to achieve leads to more peace and well-being.

Coaching relies on SMART goals—specific, measurable, attainable, realistic, and time specific (IPEC, 2006) Through appropriate questions, a coach helps individuals put foundations under their dreams. Sometimes individuals want to do too much at the beginning. Getting a damaged work relationship or a thirty-year marriage back to the level of camaraderie or joy it used to have in a week or two is likely unrealistic. A life coach can help rein in the enthusiasm to a practical approach that will be more likely to be sustainable.

Communication research can inform coaching by examining how the goals individuals select fit in different categories and maybe looking at techniques that might be effective with the different types of goals. Coaching provides a practical means for helping communication research reach a wider audience and have a greater impact. Coaching helps individuals achieve relational goals; relationships play an important role in achieving life-work balance.

As Seligman (2002) noted, "people want more than just to correct their weaknesses. They want lives imbued with meaning, and not just to fidget until they die" (p. ix). Coaching gives meaning to lives—helps individuals set and achieve goals, so that they feel like they are accomplishing something, thus enhancing their mental well-being. Communication research has focused on identifying types of goals and looking at influences on goal achievement (e.g., see Trenholm & Jensen, 2013), but could benefit from more study of coaching's approach to trusting that the individual to determine his or her own goals.

Accountability

Coaching removes blame and focuses on accomplishment. By having accountability through working with a coach, the client makes weekly progress toward a goal by completing assignments that are constructed with the coach and client working together. If an individual does not want to do something, he or she is responsible for that choice. Because of the agreed upon relationship with the coach, clients typically accept and respond to probing questions about assignments. If a significant other, however, tries to hold them accountable, they may feel nagged. If a boss tries to hold them accountable, they may feel micro-managed. The result of working with a coach is empowerment.

Without the guidance of a coach, difficult interactions may be delayed. One college roommate, for instance, may plan to talk to the other about their tense relationship—but keep putting it off because the time "isn't right." The tension from the relationship will likely result in stress that continues to be carried around within the person. A coach can help the client determine when he or she will have the conversation—even getting a commitment to which hour of which day. The specific nature of the task increases the chance that it will be accomplished, as compared to someone just saying they will do it that week.

The accountability stage is where coaching taps into the action component of emotions. Consider a woman who is unhappy with her husband and views him as a unsupportive, but doesn't want to leave him. A coach might ask, "Why would you choose to stay with someone who is a unsupportive?" This will result in the individual having to decide if her husband really is unsupportive and if so how? When faced with the idea that if she labels him unsupportive, she is making a choice of staying with an unsupportive person, and cognitive dissonance may prompt her to reflect on this uncomfortable choice. Perhaps that will result in a change of language or a change in action. This could be informed by Gottman's (1999) distinction between complaint about a specific behavior to criticism that includes blame. Gottman indicates that criticism is one of the predictors of divorce. Without taking responsibility for one's actions, this could lead to contempt—a disgust with the other. Gottman notes, "Couples who are contemptuous of each other are more likely to suffer from infectious illnesses (colds, flu, and so on) than other people" (p. 31). When people think they have no option but to stay in a situation, they are able to play the victim. Once a person can no longer be the victim, he or she has to decide whether to remain in that situation. If the person makes a conscious choice to remain, then the tendency to blame the other or circumstances for making them stay is lessened. This is where social exchange theory could come into play—give the coach some ideas/techniques to include.

Well-Being of the Whole Person

Life coaching uses a holistic approach toward clients (Grant 2005). Coaches understand that the reason clients initially seek coaching may not be the most important issues they face or the ones that are most pressing in their lives. If a person seeks coaching to discuss his or her lackluster marriage, she or he may initially want to focus on the spouse's communication patterns. Through coaching, a client may discover that he or she is contributing to the unhealthy communication with the spouse because, perhaps, she or he is grieving over the fact that their children are about ready to go to college and as well as contemplating his/her own mortality. By coming to a coach to work on one issue, the possibility is opened up that the coach will tap into other areas that are affecting the relationship. Coaches use a number of tools, such as a wheel of life (IPEC, 2006) which is divided into eight areas, including health, intimate and social relationships, and personal development; or Clean Sweep (Bisiker, 2001), that looks at one hundred questions divided in the areas of physical environment, well-being, money, and relationships, to look at the whole individual. This allows coaches to gain insight into the client's perception of him or herself in a number of areas—including relationships, physical health, and financial health. By focusing on the whole person, coaching boosts esteem in a way that is based on real accomplishment.

Coaching tends to view well-being as a byproduct of the individual determining and achieving his or her own goals. Work-life balance is a focus for many coaches (e.g., see Nison-Witt, 2008). The challenge of achieving work/life balance can be illustrated by the concept of flow (Seligman, 2002). Flow (Csikszentmihalyi, 1990) involves engagement in an activity or sense of presence in the moment without feeling distractions or split in areas. Seligman explained that work contains many of the conditions of flow, including clear goals and guidelines, frequent feedback about how things are going, and an environment with minimized distractions. He noted, "people often feel more engaged at work than they do at home" (p. 175). Socha and Pitts (2012) identified areas in interpersonal settings where flow might occur, such as a reunion of old friends, a honeymoon for newlyweds, or loved ones intently listening in difficult situations. Coaching is a missing link to connect the theory of flow to individuals' everyday communication lives. Coaching emphasizes the concept of "centering" (IPEC, 2012) and being in the moment between coach and client. These techniques could be applied in everyday communication settings. To be able to create flow as a norm in relational interaction would be a wonderful idea for flow and connection.

Coaching helps people to feel connected at home, by aiding them in focus, structure, and goal-orientation. Coaches allow clients to discover what balance they want, without imposing societal expectations. The freedom to make choices that one's overall approach to life without being segmented into individual decisions allows an individual to focus on overall well-being. To find ways to improve home relationships with life-work balance would be a tremendous contribution.

Part of an individuals' overall well-being could include, for example, refraining from aggressive communication and understanding how to participate in episodes of conflict in ways that do not negatively affect health and well-being (e.g., see Resick et al., 1981, for a discussion of the negative physical effects of mismanaging conflict). Such an approach could be especially useful with serial arguing—those that recur, are focused on a particular issue, and consist of linked episodes (Malis & Roloff, 2006). Serial arguing has been associated with negative effects on relational quality (Malis & Roloff, 2006) and well-being of the individuals in the relationship (Roloff & Johnson, 2002). Likewise, if individuals perceive higher resolvability in a serial argument, this is negatively related to self-reported stress (Malis & Roloff, 2006). These arguments often utilize criticism and sarcasm (Resick et al., 1981) similar to Gottman's interactional negatives in relationships (mentioned earlier). The coping mechanisms used to more positively manage conflict include selective ignoring, resignation—a passive response without attempts at resolution, and optimistic comparisons (Malis & Roloff, 2006). Making optimistic comparisons has also been shown to decrease relational harm, while others (e.g., repeated confrontation) have been found to increase relational harm. (Malis & Roloff, 2006). As Schneider, Konijn, Righetti, and Rusbult (2011) noted, "to the extent that individuals find it difficult to trust their partners, they experience enhanced anxiety and depression and lower physical health. As such, an unhappy relationship may literally be unhealthy" (p. 675). Examining the overall well-being of individuals helps improve the overall health of the relationship itself.

Reframing

The ability to reframe and to see things from another perspective helps individuals understand others. Coaches help individuals create closeness in their relationships by having them practice the concept of reframing—looking at alternate ways of seeing things. As an uninvested third party, the coach can help the individual explore other interpretations—to see, perhaps, how their relationship partner came to the opinion he or she expressed and why that person might have had a different interpretation. Often we resist giving validity to another view if we are ego-involved in the relationship or feel embarrassed, hurt, or devalued by someone's comment. Coaching utilizes exercises that require clients to entertain for a short while the idea that the other's view is reasonable, perhaps leading to more closeness in the relationship due to understanding why someone may interpret things in a certain way. If a person is hurting emotionally and withdraws from communication, a partner can attempt to understand that the partner may see that as rejection, the connection in that relationship may improve. This can also be used to practice positive thoughts about someone. Research in interpersonal relationships has found that an "idealized construction" of a partner in a close relationship resulted in greater satisfaction. The satisfaction was magnified when both partners practiced this (Murray, Holmes, & Griffin, 2004). Trenholm and Jensen (2013) discuss reframing as a way of turning a conflict into a collaboration instead of a competition. Reframing that leads to understanding may also lead to forgiveness and decreased resentment. Seligman (2002) made this connection to physical well-being—"Physical health, particularly in cardiovascular terms, is likely better in those who forgive than those who do not. And when it is followed by reconciliation, forgiving can vastly improve your relations with the person forgiven" (p. 77).

Identification of Values and Priorities

A focus on, and striving for, values and virtues spans across cultures and throughout time. Positive psychology research (Seligman, 2002) has identified six virtues comprised of 24 character strengths that span time and culture. These virtues are: wisdom and knowledge, courage, love and humanity, justice, temperance, and spirituality and transcendence. These and other values undergird our daily lives. If we have cognitive dissonance or conflicting values with how we live our lives, we will have stress. A coach leads the client to in-depth thought about values. Contending that often we do not focus on our values because we are so busy living our daily lives,

Bisiker (2001) noted "many decisions in life are based on the immediate urgency of what is going on around us. Once coaching helps individuals identify their values, they are able to decide clearly which things will be fulfilling for them and which will not" (p. 115). It is not uncommon to see couples in a conflict over how important they are to each other. Coaches use value clarification exercises to help the individuals reflect on their values and see if the way they are practicing those values is how they would like to live. Ducaaese (2006) explained that this mirroring of values (without judgment) helps clients "use their newly discovered understandings of themselves to achieve their coachable goals on their terms and to the fullest" (paragraph 5). The result of improved clarification of values and a life aligned to value priorities is more peace of mind and likely, less physical stress.

Validation

One of the most common yearnings humans have is the desire to feel that they are okay—that they are accepted. Maslow (1970) emphasized the importance of the desires for belonging and esteem, by explaining that these needs must be met before we are motivated to satisfy the need of self-actualization. This ties in to our needs of inclusion and affection—the desire to be with others and the desire to express affection to others and have affection expressed to us (Schutz, 1952). We may long to hear words like "It's normal to feel that way." Whether we are middle school students who struggle with peer comments, mid-career supervisors who wonder about our supervisory styles, or stay at home parents who wonder if our parenting styles will traumatize our children, we have a desire to know that we are okay. Failure to feel validated signals a deficiency in social support, which will then negatively impact our relationships with those from whom we desire validation. Coaching provides a practical method for increasing achievement of the needs identified by academic scholars, providing a safe place for improvement, while starting with the premise that who we are is acceptable. Based on the premise of validation and expression of positive support, coaching emphasizes avoidance of judgment on disclosures by clients. The focus is on positive affirmation and empathy—not on wrong or right. Coaching relies on the use of questions and perception checking to reach understanding. This positive affirmation helps the client's well-being. Gottman (1999) includes validating emotions as a specific instruction for having a "stress-reducing conversation." Once an individual feels validated, he or she is more ready to move to the point of action, and to move on to fulfilling other needs.

Listening

A coach is trained to focus on the client and to fully listen to the individual (also see Bodie, 2012). Many people do not feel like they have someone who will really listen to them without judging them or worrying too much about them. A single parent may not want to burden a child with issues, but may have no one close to talk with about concerns. A CEO may feel uncomfortable talking to anyone in the business, and may not want to spend time with a significant other discussing the stresses of work—or may not want to talk at work about issues at home, due to concerns about this information being revealed to others. Coaches are trained to listen on multiple levels (IPEC, 2006). The highest level of listening is intuitive listening—where coaches listen "between the lines" to discover new meanings. They listen for feelings, energy level, and tone of voice. These messages may provide helpful clues to determining how much stress an individual is having from a particular situation, even if the individual has tried to suppress those feelings in order to "cope" with everyday life. Communication literature is ripe with research on listening (see Bodie, 2012). We teach listening in classes in public speaking, interpersonal communication, group communication, and so on. Communication could help inform coaching about research in listening—perhaps even reaching some agreed upon types or definitions of listening. Coaching could benefit from utilizing listening categories such as the person-oriented, content-oriented, action-oriented, and time-oriented developed by Watson, Barker, and Weaver (1985). Trenholm and Jensen (2013) discuss the importance of listening in conflict situations. The focus in coaching is more on listening to clients instead of helping clients know how to listen. Research in communication could help coaching have more in depth extensions of listening by relating more to how to help others with listening.

Celebrating and Encouraging

We all can use a cheerleader for our lives! Coaching provides someone who celebrates accomplishments with individuals, expresses happiness for them, and encourages them as they take action. Communication research has begun to recognize the concept of celebratory communication as an important part of supportive communication (e.g., see Vangelisti, 2009; McCullough & Burleson, 2012). The celebrating and encouraging behaviors are important in happy situations and in difficult ones. As Seligman noted, "The positive emotions of confidence, hope, and trust, for example, serve us best not when life is easy, but when life is difficult" (p. xi). A coach serves the role of sounding board, an individual who is there to cheerlead and to champion and to be trustworthy. By demonstrating positive emotions for clients, the coach helps the clients incorporate those emotions in their own lives. Coaching focuses on the future—to bring someone to a point of thinking about what can be achieved, regardless of the past. As Seligman (2002) stated, "To the extent that you believe that the past determines the future, you will tend to allow yourself to be a passive vessel that does not actively change its course" (p. 66). The remedy he gave to dwelling on the past was to have experiences that would bring about positive emotions, as these "cause negative emotion to dissipate rapidly" (p. xii). Coaching creates an atmosphere of positive emotion through encouragement and celebrating of accomplishments along the way. This function of coaching focuses on recognizing strengths, a central component of both life coaching and positive psychology. One interesting aspect is that a partner's perceived celebratory support was associated with enhanced quality of the relationship (Gable et al., 2006). One recent communication study found that the degree of sophistication of a celebratory support message made a difference in the way that message was received (McCullough & Burleson). This is the sort of communication research that could help coaches as they work with clients.

Positive Language

Coaching emphasizes positive language that focuses attention on potential (Socha, 2009). Coaches and clients replace the expressions "should" or "have to" with "want to" or "choose to." In coaching, there are no "problems." There are "opportunities" or "challenges." This style of language encourages the individuals to take responsibility and see the world in a more positive fashion. If we call something a problem, there is a paralyzing mood that sets in—perhaps a depression or hopelessness and the inability to act. Coaching concentrates on creating anabolic (positive) energy instead of catabolic (negative) energy. This helps people actually put into focus what they would like to have happen, instead of focusing on the dreaded aspect. Coaching helps clients identify what they want and to articulate these wishes, thus reducing the amount of passive/aggressive behavior in a relationship. Coaching relies on positive language—so the positive impact is in the process as well as in the outcome. Coaches use language that is empowering but that also requires responsibility from the individual. Sample coaching questions are: "What are you doing to contribute to the negativity in the relationship?" "What can you do to make your place of employment better?" "Why are you allowing yourself to remain angry?" Coaching gets to the heart of the matter—asking the tough questions with a spin that suggests the client makes positive choices for his or her life. Although it may seem counterintuitive that a more positive language focus would help alleviate dire situations more than a "hard-hitting" negative approach, the focus on positive language gives the energy to overcome the inertia and to make accomplishments. This is similar to scientific areas, such as light and heat measurements, which are done with reference to the amount of light or heat present, instead of to the negative of dark or cold (Wright, 1998). Coaching could be informed by understanding of concepts such as linguistic determinism, the idea that language determines how we interpret the world (Sapir & Whorf, 1956). Coaches could begin to help clients see the impact of their language on others. This is an area where communication and coaching can inform each other in a way to positively impact relationships. Although communication research includes areas such as politeness and positive face (Devito, 2013) and owning your thoughts and feelings (Devito, 2013), communication analysis of language often contains a heavy focus on the negative: impacts of stereotypes, euphemistic language, biased language, equivocation, abstracts and meaning (e.g., see O'Hair & Wiemann, 2012), language and domination and lying. Coaching could benefit from an understanding of code switching, which Bourhis (1985) notes can be useful in managing defensiveness.

Future Impact of Coaching

Life coaching is a fairly new phenomenon that has the potential to positively impact relationships. Included among the many types of coaches are wellness coaches, performance coaches, spiritual coaches, and career coaches. Coaching is a popular topic in television shows and print media, and is frequently used in fields as diverse as real estate, religion, and health care. Calling coaching a management trend that has changed organizations, Stewart and Cash (2006) reported that coaching is replacing discipline as the model for improving work in the corporate setting. The potential for coaching to have a major impact on relationships in the workplace is high. Biswas-Diener and Dean (2007) noted, "It is possible to coach clients through the process of meeting and connecting with coworkers, identifying those who offer a good social fit, and tending to the relationship in ways that will be beneficial to both parties" (pp. 77–78). Coaching is a good fit for improving the well-being of interpersonal relationships in a variety of settings from home life to the corporate arena.

Communication as a field of study has the opportunity to (1) develop a communication coaching model, (2) inform the practice of coaching through independent research and through collaboration with fields such as positive psychology, and (3) augment the findings of communication in personal relationships with insights from studies of coaching.

As positive psychology developed within an academic area that traditionally focused on what was wrong rather than what was right, positive communication (including the concept of communication coaching) must also develop within a discipline that includes a focus on both the dark and bright sides. While affirming their view of the importance of the study of the dark side of communication, Spitzberg and Cupach (2012) reasoned that "a legitimate science will account for the fact that humans and their relationships are inherently both good and bad, positive and negative." Looking at both aspects of a relationship should not mean only focusing on the "good" as it relates to the "bad." To focus on what is good and what helps us achieve healthy relationships is as important as understanding why we have unhealthy relationships. Otherwise, we just know that things are bad—but may lack the understanding of how to make it better. Starting with a few that we first discover the negative also may result in lesser satisfaction with our relationships even if we "improve" them. Improvement may be based on the idea that something was wrong, and we are finally doing better—as opposed to starting with a situation that is viewed as basically okay and improving that situation to where it is viewed as wonderful.

In spite of the evidence that other disciplines and schools have embraced coaching there are still reasons that communication might be slow to embrace it. Part of the problem may lie in the label "life coaching" that suggests that it is an over-reaching, pop culture trend —seeking to quick fix all things. Agreeing that some areas of coaching "address clearly substantive issues" Grant and Cavanagh (2011) noted, "some coaching applications seem trivial or even farcical" (p. 295). Referring to Seligman (2002) noting that coaching's reach was "almost without limits, with life coaches offering to coach you in arranging your closet, fighting dark thoughts, or organizing your memories in a scrap book! From such a perspective, it is hard to see that such activities bear the hallmark of a genuine helping profession." Comments such as those by Grant and Cavanagh reflect an assumption that scholars instead of individuals know what works best to improve someone's life. However, such an approach neglects to consider what would make a positive impact on an individual's well-being and the well-being of a relationship. Arranging a closet, for example, might represent the value of needing to feel in control, and/or a misplaced desire to improve a relationship for an individual with hoarding tendencies, and/or impediments that are hampering an individual's self-esteem and physical well-being. Organizing memories in a scrapbook might be a way to feel a connectedness in a relationship that is lacking connection. This is where coaching can help the academic areas, by providing an alternative perspective from the typical academic top down approach (assuming scholars know what is best). Coaching brings to us the idea that the individual knows what is best— empowering the individual.

Coaching relies on the notion that the client is responsible for his or her success, which requires work. As we sometimes want a quick fix with diet or exercise, will we want quick fixes with relationships? Areas where communication scholars could be helpful include investigating how coaching will work if applied to individuals who few life more negatively. Because it has been a matter of self-selection, positive individuals tend to come to coaching. Biswas-Diener and Dean (2007) explained, "Coaching is a wake-up call, challenging folks to tap their inner abundance. Because of this natural leaning toward positivity, growth, and optimism coaching has attracted practitioners who value service work and clients who are achievement oriented" (p. 2). Those who have a negative, pessimistic view would not tend to believe that coaching would be helpful to them, so they would not go to coaching. If one wanted to wallow in a depressed state, one would not select to interact with someone in a process that required them to move forward. Seligman (2007) argued that pessimists believe the cause of their frustration is personal as well as permanent and pervasive. They assume it is their fault and that it will undermine everything, whereas optimists see setbacks as temporary, surmountable, and not always their fault. This person would not believe in themselves to be coached. To be a major part of society will require getting the pessimists to convert to at least temporarily optimistic behavior.

Although the International Coach Federation provides guidance, it does not have regulatory authority over coaches. Coaching does not yet have agreed upon standards of training, so approaches to coaching can vary greatly (see Grant & Cavanagh, 2011; Sherman & Freas, 2004; Seligman, 2007). Seligman even refers to the ICF as "self-appointed" and talks about how most coaches are not even accredited through ICF. Without regulation, any self-proclaimed "coach" may represent the profession in a way that does not reflect the values and guidelines of the ICF. There has been a call for "well-grounded and commonly accepted standards of accreditation" (Grant & Cavanagh, 2011). In particular, communication could help to provide research that would lead to better, consistent standards.

Grant and Cavanagh (2011) expressed a belief that coaching "has a vital role to play in defining the research agenda and in assisting researchers in understanding the dynamics of positive human change" (p. 302) and called for more studies to measure the impact of coaching on goal attainment and challenged positive psychology researchers to help "elucidate the boundary between coaching and therapy" (p. 303); a boundary they see as complex and not best defined in terms of either/or. As research can help coaching, Grant and Cavanagh also argued that coaching provides "a valuable methodology for assessing the utility and adequacy" of positive psychology theories (p. 304). The same could be said for communication. Coaching could be practical in helping us see our theories—move beyond standard populations.

Coaching represents a practical fusion of communication and positive psychology research. Likewise, coaching aids communication by providing a setting to deliver to people what we have found in research and the tenets that we value. What a valuable opportunity to reach a population beyond what we would reach just on the university campus. The work of coaches could inform communication scholars. As ones who struggle to find populations beyond the classroom, coaching could supply that. Through their interactions with clients, coaches may be able to help identify areas for further study in communication and coaching.

This chapter has attempted to connect communication scholars, positive psychologists, and coaching to begin a positive dialogue about how these areas can work together to enhance relational health and well-being.

Notes

1. The term "life coach" is often used to refer to personal coaching, as contrasted with "executive coaching." Some people use "life coaching" as the general descriptor. "Empowerment coaching" is the broader term for coaching.
2. Coaches and therapists/counselors sometimes work together for the benefit of the client. A good coach will recognize if the client has a block to making progress that would best be treated by a therapist. An effective counselor or therapist will recognize when a client has progressed to the point of really benefiting more from coaching than therapy.

References

Antonia, A., Abramis, D. J., & Caplan, R. D. (1985). Effects of different sources of social support and social conflict on emotional well-being. *Basic and Applied Social Psychology, 6*(2), 111–129.

Baxter, L. (2006). Relational dialectics theory: Multivocal dialogues of family communication. In D. O. Braithwaite & L. A. Baxter (Eds.), *Engaging theories in family communication: Multiple perspectives* (pp. 130–145). Thousand Oaks, CA: Sage.

Bisiker, R. (2001). *Unlock your personal potential: A self-coaching workbook.* Naperville, IL: Sourcebooks.

Biswas-Diener, R., & Dean, B. (2007). *Positive psychology coaching: Putting the science of happiness to work for your clients.* Hoboken, NJ: John Wiley & Sons.

Bourhis, R. Y. (1985). The sequential nature of language choice in cross-cultural communication. In R. L. Street Jr. & J. N. Cappella (Eds.), *Sequence and pattern in communicative behavior* (pp. 120–141). London: Arnold.

Canary, D. J., & Cody, M. J. (1994). *Interpersonal communication: A goals-based approach.* New York: St. Martin's Press.

Cline, R. J. W. (2011). Everyday interpersonal communication and health. In R. Thompson, R. Parrott, & J. Nussbaum (Eds.), *The Routledge handbook of health communication* (2nd ed.) (pp. 377–396). New York: Routledge.

Cohen, S., & Wills, T. A., (1985). Stress, social support, and the buffering hypothesis. *Psychological Bulletin, 98,* 310–357.

Devito, J. A. (2012). *The interpersonal communication book* (13th ed.). Boston: Pearson Education.

Duck, S. W. (1985). How to lose friends without influencing people. In M. E. Roloff & G. R. Millers (Eds.), *Interpersonal processes: New directions in communication research* (pp. 278–298). Newbury Park, CA: Sage.

Dillard, J. P. (1993). A goal-driven model of interpersonal influence. In J. P. Dillard (Ed.) *Seeking compliance: The production of interpersonal influence messages* (pp. 41–56). Scottsdale, AZ: Gorsuch, Scarisbrick.

Ducaaese, B. (2006). Life coaching has arrived! Retrieved from http://findyourcoach.blogharbor.com/blog/_archives/2006/3/23/1837129.html.[and see http://www.coachfederation.org]

Gable, S. L., Gonzaga, G. C., & Strachman, A. (2006). Will you be there for me when things go right? Supportive responses to positive event disclosures. *Journal of Personality and Social Psychology, 91*(5), 904–917.

Grant, A. M. (2005). What is evidence-based executive, workplace and life coaching? In M. Cavanagh, A. M. Grant, & T. Kemp (Eds.), *Evidence-based coaching* (Vol. 1) (pp. 1 – 12). Bowen Hills: Australian Academic Press.

Grant, A. M., & Cavanagh, M. J. (2011). Coaching and positive psychology. In K. Sheldon, B. Todd, B. Kashdan, & M. F. Steger (Eds.), *Designing positive psychology: Taking stock and moving forward* (pp. 293–312). Oxford, UK: Oxford University Press.

Griffiths, K., & Campbell, M. A. (2008). Semantics or substance? Preliminary evidence in the debate between life coaching and counseling. *Coaching: An International Journal of Theory, Research and Practice, 1*(2), 164–175.

Goldsmith, D. (2004). *Communicating social support.* Cambridge, UK: Cambridge University Press.

Guldner, G. T. (1996). Long-distance romantic relationships: Prevalence and separation-related symptoms in college students. *Journal of College Student Development, 37,* 289–296.

Holmes, T., & Rahe, R. H. (1967). The social readjustment rating scale. *Journal of Psychosomatic Research, 11,* 213–218.

Honeycut, J. M. (2008). Imagined interaction theory: Mental representations of interpersonal communication. In L. A. Baxter & D. O. Braithwaite (Eds.), *Engaging theories in interpersonal communication: Multiple perspectives* (pp. 77–87). Thousand Oaks, CA: Sage.

Institute for Professional Empowerment Coaching (IPEC). (2006). *IPEC coach training manual.* Shrewsbury, NJ: IPEC.

Jones, F., & Bright, J. (2001). *Stress, myth, theory, and research.* Harlow, UK: Pearson Education Limited.

Leathan, G., & Duck, S. (1990). Conversations with friends and the dynamics of social support. In S. Duck (Ed.), *Personal relationships and social support* (pp. 1–29). London: Sage.

Malis, R. S., & Roloff, M. E. (2006). Features of serial arguing and coping strategies: Links with stress and well-being. In R. M. Dailey & B. A. Le Poire (Eds.), *Applied interpersonal communication matters: Family, health, & community relations* (pp. 39–65). New York: Peter Lang.

Maslow, A. (1970). *Motivation and personality*. New York: Harper & Row.

McCullough, J. D., & Burleson, B. (2012). Celebratory support: Messages that enhance the effects of positive experience. In T. Socha & M. Pitts (Eds.), *The positive side of interpersonal communication* (pp. 229–248). New York: Peter Lang.

McMahon, G. & Archer, A. (2010). *101 coaching strategies and techniques*. London: Routledge.

Murray, S. L., Holmes, J. G., & Griffin, D. W. (2004). The benefits of positive illusions: Idealization and the construction of satisfaction in close relationships. In H. T. Reis & C. E. Rusbult (Eds.), *Close relationships* (pp. 317–338). New York: Taylor & Francis.

Nison-Witt, C. (2008, Jan–March) A coaching approach for work/life balance. *Business & Economic Review*, 8–11.

O'Hair, D., & Wiemann, M. (2012). *Real communication: An introduction* (2 ed.). Boston: Bedford/St. Martin's.

Pecchioni, L. L., & Keeley, M. P. (2011). Insights about health from family communication theories. In T. L. Thompson, R. Parrott, & J. F. Nussbaum (Eds.), *The Routledge handbook of health communication* (2nd ed.) (pp. 363–376). New York: Routledge.

Resick, P. A., Barr, P. K., Sweet, J. M., Keiffer, D. M., Ruby, N. L., & Spiegel, D. K. (1981). Perceived and actual discriminators or conflict from accord in marital communication. *American Journal of Family Therapy, 9*, 58–68.

Richardson, C. (1998). *Take time for your life*. New York: Broadway Books.

Roloff, M. E., & Johnson, K. L. (2002). Serial arguing over the relational life course: Antecedents and consequences. In A. L. Vangelisti, H. T. Reis, & M. A. Fitzpatrick (Eds.), *Stability and change in relationships* (pp. 107–128). Cambridge, UK: Cambridge University Press.

Sapir, E., & Whorf, B. L. (1956). The relation of habitual thought and behavior to language. In J. B. Carroll (Ed.), *Language, thought, and reality: Selected writings of Benjamin Lee Whorf* (pp. 134–159). Cambridge, MA: MIT Press.

Schneider, I. K., Konijn, E. A., Righetti, F., & Rusbult, C. E. (2011). A healthy dose of trust: The relationship between interpersonal trust and health. *Personal Relationships, 18*, 668–676.

Schutz, W. C. (1958). *FIRO: A three-dimensional theory of interpersonal behavior*. New York: Holt, Rinehart & Winston.

Seligman, M. E. P. (2002). *Authentic happiness: Using the new positive psychology to realize your potential for lasting fulfillment*. New York: Free Press.

Seligman, M. E. P. (2007). Coaching and positive psychology. *Australian Psychologist, 42*(4), 266–267.

Seligman, M. E. P. (2011). *Flourish: A visionary new understanding of happiness and well-being*. New York: Free Press.

Sherman, S., & Freas, A. (2004). The wild west of executive coaching. *Harvard Business Review, 82*(11), 82–90.

Socha, T. J. (2009). Family as agency of potential: Towards a positive model of applied family communication theory and research. In L. Frey & K. Cissna (Eds.), *Routledge handbook of applied communication* (pp. 309–330). New York: Routledge.

Spitzberg, B., & Cupach, W. (2012). The power of the dark side. In T. Socha & M. Pitts (Eds.), *The positive side of interpersonal communication* (pp. 313–322). New York: Peter Lang.

Stewart, C. J., & Cash, W. B. (2006). *Interviewing principles and practices* (11th ed.). New York: McGraw-Hill.

Thibaut, J. W., & Kelley, H. H. (1959). *The social psychology of groups*. New York: Wiley.

Trenholm, S., & Jensen, A. (2013). *Interpersonal communication*. New York: Oxford University Press.

Vangelisti, A. L. (2009). Challenges in conceptualizing social support. *Journal of Social and Personal Relationships, 26*(1), 39–51.

Watson K. W., Barker, L. L., & Weaver, J. B. (1995). The listening styles profile (LSP-16): Development and validation of an instrument to assess four listening styles. *International Journal of Listening, 9*, 1–13.

Williams, P., & Thomas, L. J. (2005). *Total life coaching*. New York: W. W. Norton.

Wright, K. (1998). *Breaking the rules: Removing the obstacles to effortless high performance*. Boise, ID: CPM Publishing.

• CHAPTER ELEVEN •

Final Conversations: Positive Communication at the End of Life

Maureen Keeley
Texas State University

Paula Baldwin
George Mason University

"Should you shield the canyons from the windstorms, you would never see the beauty of their carvings."

—Kübler-Ross (1999, p. 11)

Kübler-Ross uses a "windstorm and canyon carving" metaphor to describe her work with individuals at the end of life. The metaphor highlights the fact that while most people want to protect themselves and others from the pain associated with the dying process; doing so is pointless; death comes to the ones they love whether or not they are a part of the journey. Denying, avoiding, or refusing to participate in the end of life journey with their dying loved one serves only to temporarily block the pain and grief that comes with death (McQuellon & Cowan, 2000). Further, this denial prevents adults and children alike from an opportunity to prepare for the death; as well as denies them an opportunity for growth and lessons about life (Kübler-Ross, 1999). The end-of-life journey resulting from a terminal illness or old age, as opposed to a sudden, unexpected, or accidental death, can be gentler, more fulfilling, and poignant for both those dying and the survivors through communication and participation (Keeley & Yingling, 2007; Kübler-Ross, 1999).

If people are truly honest about the death process, there are two choices when dealing with the death of a loved one: First, people can continue to feed their fear, to see only the skewed, negative view of communication at the end of life, and ultimately, be forced to face their grief alone after their loved one has died. Or second, people can accept the truth about death; that it is a natural and important phase of life that comes with tremendous potential for positive communication with the dying loved one and ultimately personal growth. This choice is a direct result of the influence that hospice and palliative care has had on people concerning their views about the end of life. Hospice was introduced to the United States during the late sixties and early seventies (National Hospice and Palliative Care Organization [NHPCO], 2012) and has generated hope for a peaceful death through the empowerment of the dying, family involvement, and compassionate end of life care (Foster, 2007; Kübler-Ross, 1997; NHPCO, 2012). This change in perspective about the end of life has given the opportunity for many people to experience final conversations and to that end demonstrate how these conversations exemplify *positive communication* within their relationships.

Positive communication at the end of life may seem, on the surface, to be oxymoronic in nature. But people that have this perspective only do so because these individuals are looking at death itself, at the loss of their loved one (hereafter referred to as the Dying) and all of its negative connotations, instead of recognizing the gift of time that accompanies the end of life journey. Through the awareness that hospice and palliative care organizations have created and the work that they do in communities throughout the United States, people are realizing that every person has the right to die pain-free and with dignity (NHPCO, 2012). Family members' roles at the end of life are also acknowledged and supported through hospice and palliative care programs (NHPCO, 2012). Family members are given care, assistance, and help through hospice programs. While this period in people's lives is challenging and difficult, the surviving loved ones (hereafter referred to as the Living) are also given an opportunity to slow down their busy lives to truly focus on the Dying, to concentrate on their relationship with the Dying, and to grow and learn about life in ways that can only be learned in the shadow of death (Keeley, 2007). The Dying are given the opportunity to complete their lives on their own terms and in the best of circumstances, surrounded by their loved ones (Kübler-Ross, 1997).

The Gift of Time

The advancements of palliative medicine in recent decades have helped offset the trend in America to prolong life through medical and technological advancements. While these medical advancements have the potential to prolong life and postpone death for a time (Pitts, 2011), they also have the potential to dehumanize individuals and prolong the agony associated with death (Costello, 2006). Consequently, hospice and palliative medicine has provided increased awareness and choice regarding how individuals choose to face their impending death (Aiken, 2001). The Dying can now negotiate what they want their final months, weeks, and days to look like (Doyle, 1994). Choosing to die under hospice care is a return to a more natural and traditional death when considering the human lifespan (Pitts, 2011). Family members are becoming more involved in the care giving out of financial necessity, family obligation, and a desire to give the Dying a peaceful death (Aiken, 2001; Callanan & Kelley, 1992; Lynn & Harrold, 1999). Some surprising positive outcomes are the sharing of treasured moments at the end of life (Keeley, 2007), witnessing the end to a life well lived (McQuellon & Cowan, 2000), and an honoring of the individual (Foster, 2007).

This gift of time, while often exhausting and heartrending, is also precious, inspiring, and perhaps offers some of the most meaningful weeks of the family members' lives. People do not usually forget this time spent together. The gift of time means that there is a window of opportunity to exchange messages that may not have occurred without the warning of an impending death (Keeley & Yingling, 2007). Loved ones are endeavoring to share a *good* goodbye to give the Dying a peaceful closure, and for their own welfare as well. This closure often occurs in the context of a final conversation. We define final conversations (FCs) as all interactions, verbal and nonverbal, that individuals have with the dying loved one between the point of a terminal diagnosis and the moment of death. Final conversations may involve only one conversation, but they can also be, and often are, a series of conversations (Keeley, 2007).

Final conversations offer the opportunity for uplifting, insightful, and empowering communication that leave people feeling positive about their relationships with the Dying (Keeley & Yingling, 2007); provide comfort as individuals cope with their grief (Aiken, 2001); and often present encouraging directions for the Living to go on after the Dying are gone (Keeley, 2007). Final conversations as described here emerge as perfect reflections of Socha's (2006) explanation of positive communication, in that FCs nourish relationships, facilitate positive subjective states (such as comfort), and enhance the development of positive character traits. Final conversations do not remove the grief that accompanies death, but participating in FCs shifts the focus from the process of dying to the living that occurs at the end of life. For instance, Ellen (adult) highlights this important shift in focus when she stated: "we weren't just getting out the crying towels waiting for him to die. It was what we could do to be with him while we still had him." Time spent together when faced with *terminal time* is almost always a precious gift and often becomes the catalyst for the FCs. Therefore, the authors argue that FCs are often the personification of positive communication and usually result in positive outcomes for the Living, as well as the Dying.

Achieving Positive Outcomes

Positive communication shines the focus of attention on the potential, constructive outcomes that communication can have in people's lives (Socha, 2005). Two types of communication present at the end of life that increase well-being include authentic communication and social support. Authentic communication focuses on direct and sincere self-expression (Rosenberg, 2003). Social support refers to communication that reduces uncertainty, thereby enhancing a perception of personal control in one's life experiences (Albrecht & Adelman, 1987). Both authentic communication and social support are mutually beneficial for the participants at the end of life and each are elaborated upon for greater clarification.

Authentic communication highlights what is important to the person and the situation; revealing what is honest and real (Rosenberg, 2003). Furthermore, this type of communication is thought to inspire compassion, empathy, and action in others (Rosenberg, 2003). Particularly at the end of life, authentic conversations have the power to enhance how people deal pragmatically with death and can enlighten and deepen the meaning of life for those dying and their loved ones (McQuellon & Cowan, 2000). Rosenberg (2003) believes that when people communicate from the heart they become more fully conscious of their words and actions. At the end of life, Levine (1984) suggests the clarity that comes with impending death reveals the importance of relationships and love. The circumstances surrounding the dying process encourage open and honest communication; as well as provide the time and impetus for individuals to truly reveal themselves to those closest to them (Keeley & Yingling, 2007; Kübler-Ross, 1997). Levine (1984) argues that at the end of life, the dying are forced to let go of everything (i.e., health, careers, hobbies, possessions, and identities) and that because of the decline of their physical bodies, the only thing remaining is love. Consequently, at the end of life, there is an urgency to pay attention to the present moment and an opportunity to cultivate connection with others. By engaging in positive, compassionate, and authentic communication, there is less time and energy wasted on judging, analyzing, complaining and comparing situations, resulting in more positive outcomes (Rosenberg, 2003) and fulfilling FCs (Keeley, 2007). Authentic communication could also lead to more social support communication because individuals' needs are often revealed during the honest interactions (Rosenberg, 2003).

Social support communication increases people's feeling of well-being by providing people the time and opportunity to make sense of the situation concerning serious life events such as a terminal illness or impending death (Keeley, 1996). Changes in health and life circumstances often increase individuals' doubts and insecurities; thus supportive acts are vital for reducing uncertainty for the participants concerning their own self perceptions, their end of life circumstances, and their relationships (Keeley, 1996). Communication at the end of life is filled with moments of social support through routine acts of service, the exchange of messages of love, and messages affirming individuals' identities (Keeley & Yingling, 2007). Both the Dying and the Living benefit from these shared moments because each participate in the giving and receiving of social support; ultimately leading to increased feelings of social well-being (Diener & Biswas-Diener, 2008). The emotional well-being of both the Living and the Dying is enhanced at the end of life through these acts of positive communication.

In this chapter, we hope to illustrate the potential benefits of actively engaging in FCs. Accordingly, in this chapter, we make the case that FCs provide positive communicative outcomes for individuals dealing with death and bereavement. We demonstrate support for this with FCs examples from the first author's program of research that has occurred over the past decade: *Adult's Final Conversations, Phase I* (Keeley, 2007), and the FCs examples from the authors' most recent expansion of that original program of research, *Children's Final Conversations, Phase II* (Keeley & Baldwin, 2012). Both studies utilized retrospective interviews and qualitative analysis.

Positive Communication through Confirmation, Acceptance, and Permission

Three outcomes of FCs reflecting the affirming qualities of positive communication are confirmation, acceptance, and permission. At the end of life, windows of opportunities present themselves for the enactment of positive communication by confirming love, coming to terms with the loss of a loved one, and giving the Living permission to go living in healthy and positive ways.

Confirmation

We define confirmation as the validation and the bolstering of the individual and relationship. Confirming messages indicate how much people value each other (Floyd, 2009) and are considered an important way to increase the amount of positivity in relationships (Montgomery, 1988). In light of the impending loss of their loved one; the Living desire and value confirmation as an outcome of these FCs. Relationships with loved ones are not always smooth, and are often marked by differing levels of closeness and intimacy; mutual understanding, recognition, and acceptance; as well as differing levels of interaction and daily activity. FCs that most often brought a feeling of confirmation for the Living centered on messages of love, identity, and everyday communication.

Messages of love served to validate and strengthen the relationship bonds between the Living and the Dying (Keeley, 2007). Whether love was expressed directly or indirectly, the recipients felt the love profoundly. For instance, Jayne's (child, age 12) bond with her mother was affirmed by knowing that not only was there a shared love, but that her mother took care to show Jayne that love:

> I loved my mom and she loved me and it really just showed that she really didn't want to leave. It makes me really happy.... My mom really thought about it so much and made it real for me, not just a couple of words in my head...real and tangible. (Jayne, age 12)

In contrast, Lori (adult) who had a strained relationship with her mother all of her life says of her mother:

> Just before she died she could barely speak ... somehow she got out, "I love you." It took her about five minutes to do it. But it meant so much to me. It was the first time that she'd said it in so long. It was the first time that I think she ever meant it.

In the end, Lori and her mother were able to overcome their history of difficult interactions and find a positive, emotional resolution.

Messages pertaining to identity underscore the fact that the Dying are often important authority figures for the Living. The opinion of beloved members of the family often provide invaluable points of support, insight, and even positive criticism for the Living, that will be greatly missed after the Dying are gone. For instance, Claire (adult), who was insecure and struggling to establish her own identity in her own right, shared a message her beloved uncle Matthew told her during one of their FCs:

I glad you're talking to me about these things. Because, nobody is going to be as blunt with you as I am. And I hope that you remember what I have to tell you. Because I am the only one that can leave you with this." And he said, "You have your whole life to live. Look at me! I don't have the rest of my life. And if I can leave you with any of these things...to find happiness in life, and not to spend so much time worrying ... I don't think you even have any idea how beautiful you are.

Even in adulthood, the Living still desire validation by the Dying. Laura (adult) shared her aunt's perception of her life as a college professor and community activist: "It was nice to see how she saw me through her eyes. She was very, very proud of all the education that I had received....It was nice to be seen in those ways."

Everyday communication is a third type of message that provides confirmation of both the person and the relationship at the end of life (Keeley, 2007; Keeley & Baldwin, 2012). Everyday communication in relationships includes both small talk and routine interactions, underscores the importance of one another, and confirms one another's commitment to each other (Canary & Stafford, 1994). Spending time together—making the ordinary extraordinary in the moment—demonstrates the significance of the relationship for adults and children, as well as the Living and Dying (Wood & Duck, 2006). *Tuesdays with Morrie* (Albom, 1997), the popular book and movie about the relationship between a former teacher and student, also highlights the importance of time spent together for the Dying at the end of life. Even at the end of life, it is important to continue living life with one another, to continue sharing and co-creating a relationship with one another through everyday communication for a continued sense of well-being (Keeley, 2007).

Some messages of confirmation come through the use of laughter and humor that are important aspects of everyday, healthy living. Participants recalled a lot of laughter and positive emotions during the FCs. Ellen (adult) described her relationship with her dying husband, Michael, as one in which they shared a lot of laughter, which continued until his death. Another participant, Laurie (adult), also noted, that "we all talked and about family times and things we remember. It was actually very happy [with] some laughter at times." Laughing and sharing in the ordinary moments of life is an important confirmation of love and life for both the Dying and the Living.

In the interviews with children, the topic of laughter came up frequently. Many children talked about, not just the frequency of laughter, but about the importance of laughter as well during their everyday conversations. Maya (child, age 14), whose grandmother died, shared: "We [talked] about really random stuff, because it really made her laugh and like even up until the very last day...she had high spirits...[these moments were important] because it makes you feel comfortable and happy, being safe." All of the everyday communication messages highlighted the importance of continuing to live in as much the same way as possible with the Dying up until the very end.

Ultimately, FCs' messages of love, identity, and everyday messages led to a sense of confirmation and were perceived by the Living and the Dying as positive (Keeley & Yingling, 2007) because they led to an increased sense of connection and to a strengthening of their relationship at the end of life (Marrone, 1999). In addition, the fact that these three types of messages at the end of life were clearly dyadic, interactive, and unfolding throughout the shared end of life experience, highlight the mutual benefit, and shared sense of well-being that comes from both giving and receiving acts of positive communication (Diener & Biswas-Diener, 2008).

Acceptance

We define acceptance as that point in time when the Living recognize that the death of their loved one is going to occur and that there is a sense of readiness and acquiescence to the inevitability of the situation for a variety of reasons. At the end of life, acceptance frequently comes from three ways: (1) a sense of completion in the relationship; (2) as a result of a shared spiritual connection that assures the Living that they will remain connected with the Dying when s/he is gone; and/or (3) recognition that the Dying is in pain and needs to let go of this life.

When there is nothing left to be said and after going through so much during the death journey, acceptance is a gift. Ellen's (adult) husband died and she was adamant about the need for accepting his inevitable death without feeling regret. She says:

> I guess what I'm trying to say is that we should all live as if we all know we're terminal. Because we all are terminal...I've completed my relationship with him. I didn't walk away thinking, aaugh, I should have said, I didn't say, I could have said, I wanted to say. There wasn't anything that we didn't really say. And in the final analysis, the most important, the absolutely most important things were all said. Because the person who is left doesn't get stuck holding a bunch of untied knots. It's complete.

For some of the Living, they reached a point of acceptance because they realized that they will still have a spiritual connection with the Dying; perhaps that they would meet again in heaven. For instance, although Lucia (adult) grieved the loss of her mother, she came to understand that their relationship could transcend the physical limitation of her mother's death: "I learned that I don't have to let go of that spiritual connection [with my mother]. I don't need to suffer." Similarly, Matthew's (child, age 8) dad died leaving behind nine children, and they all shared a similar story with us by telling us: [my dad] "said that no matter what we'll still be a family and that he's gonna be preparing a house up there [in heaven] for us to live in." These messages of spiritual and religious beliefs helped people of faith accept that it was God's will, God's time and God's decision; and in due course, that they would meet again when they joined them in heaven.

Sisters Nancy and Maryjo (adults) shared with us a spiritual experience they had with their mother while she was in a coma; the experience consisted of her shaking hands and talking with people who they perceived to be on the other side and of her receiving Holy Communion at the end of the gathering. The experience they described went on for seven hours as they sat by her bedside observing. When asked what this interaction meant to them they stated: "there was no doubt in our mind that she was crossing over to heaven." They felt that what they had witnessed was a "gift," that they had experienced a "very positive experience," and that they were "grateful and appreciative" of their FCs. Acceptance is a natural outcome if you believe that the Living and the Dying will meet once again someday in heaven or if you believe that the Dying can still somehow be present in your life from the *other side*. For instance, Katie (child, age 13), recalled her FCs with her father telling her: "Don't be sad when I'm gone. Just be happy that I'm in a better place and I'm still watching over you, so you're never really alone."

Individuals also discovered acceptance when they realized that the Dying was ready to go; and in some cases, hanging on to the Dying was causing them more stress, discomfort, and even pain. For example, Patti (adult) talked about her final conversation with her father, Joe. "He told us he was ready to die. He said, 'I have lived a whole life. There's nothing else that I would like to do except spend more time with you. But just know that I'm a happy man.'" In the same way, when Katie (child, age 13) was asked what advice she would give other children in the same situation, she said, "I would tell them you can be sad about it, but don't be wishing they were still here because if they were hurting like this and you were in that pain, you probably would want to be taken too." Ally (child, age 14) whose mother died from cancer, stressed the importance of acceptance and positive communication in this way: "Just um to like make them know that they'll probably be going to a better place than they were on Earth and that like since my mom, she had cancer, that she'll be released of all her pain and she'll feel 10 times better than she did here. Just to reassure them of that, that it'll be ok." It is often a relief to finally see a loved one that has been suffering, to finally be released from the pain (Kübler-Ross, 1999).

Permission

Permission is the act of giving consent or authorization. Permission is very important and perhaps an overlooked aspect of positive communication at the end of life because it empowers the Living to do something, such as (1) to feel strong emotions and then to move forward; (2) to be happy again; or (3) to give permission to the Dying to let go of the pain and to cross over.

The Living are the first to admit that there are a lot of negative emotions associated with the death of their loved one including fear, anger, and sadness. The Living that had FCs gave credit to those FCs at the end of life for helping them to learn how to cope with these powerful emotions. Case in point, Victoria (adult) clearly stated this outcome when she said:

> I was really beginning to get scared. And I remember…I was in the living room of our house, and I went back in the bedroom where he was…and for some reason I looked at him and I just got really scared, he was gonnna die. And I screamed at him, "You, you can't die. I can't live without you." And I remember that he was still strong enough, he grabbed me be the shoulders, and flung me around *and just* right in my face, were these really gleaming ice blue eyes and said "Yes, you can. Yes you can if you have to. And you will do it well."

Not everyone was as fortunate as Victoria; her husband, Kerry, was remarkable in his ability to accept and face death head-on, which in the end helped her to do likewise. This part of their story, however, is a beautiful portrayal of the fact that these three primary negative emotions, fear, anger, and sadness, are often present during the death journey. Victoria and Kerry's story, however, is a testament that FCs have the potential for healing, for increased self-awareness and growth, and for the ability to look at the good that came out of the experience. Those that have gone through the death of a loved one will never deny the ugliness and the negative emotions that shadow death; but the important thing to remember is that through final conversations, the potential for positive outcomes is possible and indeed probable.

Many of the Living also felt they were given permission to be happy again, to go on to lead a full life without the Dying. For example, some of the Living felt they had permission to love again. Wives that were given permission by their dying husbands to marry again found happiness, new love, and moved on without guilt. For example, Sondra's (adult) husband encouraged her to remarry. He said, "I want you to remarry," which was a further testament of his love for her. Sondra felt like her FCs with her husband helped her move on with her life in a positive manner.

Final Conversations can provide direction to loved ones for moving forward in life; this was especially true for children. For Dana (adult) who was 12 when her father died, her FCs with her father were both affirming and prescriptive: "He told me how wonderful I was, and that he wanted me to continue living life. . . ." Similarly, Jayne's (child, age 12) mother told her:

> "I know it's going to be hard on you, but it's ok to move on. It's ok for you to have other mother figures. You need to be shared with the world." She really cared about me. She wasn't selfish with me which I appreciated.

At times, permission comes from the Living through their consent to the Dying, that it is okay to let go of the pain and to leave them behind in life. Grace's (adult) first husband died of a heart attack on Christmas Day. She recalls "that moment, he looked at me...I looked in his eyes and I could tell that he was dying. . . I realized that I had to let him go. I said to him, 'It's all right if you have to go.' I gave him permission." Grace's second husband, Steve, also died from heart disease. Her FCs with Steve focused on his needs:

> If you can't breathe, just let go. Just let go. And it won't hurt. You have my permission. You can go. I'll be lonely without you and I love you, but don't fight it. Just let it happen....I kept telling him that I loved him....I told him he was beloved by everyone that knew him and that it had been my privilege to be his wife. And that I was so happy that we had that wonderful time together.

Grace was truly a remarkable woman to have been able to walk with both of her husbands on their death journeys. If you read between the lines, you can also see where she learned the lesson of permission with her first husband and in return, gave it more easily and quickly with her second husband.

Conclusion

Communication at the end of life often occurs in the shadow of sorrow, heartache and anguish. With closer examination, however, FCs offer a unique opportunity to generate psychological and relational health and wellness. Final conversations with dying loved ones are filled with powerful, inspiring, and positive messages that are remembered by those who go on living for years and decades after their loved one is gone. Final conversations present the Living with at least three positive outcomes that include confirmation, acceptance, and permission. Confirmation reaffirms to both the

Living and the Dying that they are loved and that their relationships are important. Love can never be taken away, not even by death. Acceptance comes from the realization that death is inevitable and highlights the importance of closure and completion for everyone. Permission is often overlooked and perhaps even dismissed in this age of independence; yet, permission at the end of life should be a reminder that everyone from time to time needs a nudge to move forward. Experiencing lessons of confirmation, acceptance, and permission through FCs also teaches people how to have engage in FCs the next time; because, while it may not get easier to have FCs, with experience, people get better participating in them.

Final conversations are a pragmatic tool to help people survive and endure under adverse conditions that are typical of the end of life journey. More importantly, FCs result in powerful experiences with positive outcomes for both the Living and the Dying. Seligman and Csikszentmihalyi (2000) view positive psychology as comprised of subjective emotions that represent the past, present, and future. Specifically, when individuals can recall their past experiences with a sense of well-being, contentment, and satisfaction; feel a sense of flow and happiness in the present; and experience a sense of hope and optimism for the future; then they are the beneficiaries of positive points of view. Based on the Living's stories, FCs are an important type of positive communication because they deal with issues pertaining to contentment with the past insomuch as the Living believe they have helped their loved one to have a good death; and they also recognize that they are satisfied with their FCs and the resulting positive outcomes.

The circumstances of the dying process, force the Living and the Dying to live in the moment and share authentic communication through their FCs, thereby truly experiencing the flow and happiness that comes with full awareness of the importance of that moment in time. In addition, individuals develop an appreciation for both the living and the dying process (Pitts, 2011). Lastly, hope for the future is created at the end of life because FCs often results in an increase in individuals' ability to talk about death across the lifespan with family and friends (Pitts, 2011). Through the participation in FCs, people have experience and knowledge to share with others and potentially create positive expectations about the end-of-life journey.

Socha (2005) suggests that communication scholars "continue to develop both the bright sides as well as the dark sides of communication inquiry" (p. 42). This is particularly salient in the end-of-life context because much of what is focused upon is the dark side of death; yet anyone who has experienced a final conversation, has familiarity with hospice, or has had the privilege to serve the Dying, understands that much of the communication that occurs at the end of life is illuminating and bright. Implementing this mind-set can help individuals move towards a better understanding of the role and importance of positive communication when faced with life's challenges, such as the passing of a loved one.

References

Aiken, L. A. (2001). *Dying, death, and bereavement.* Mahwah, NJ: Lawrence Erlbaum.

Albom, M. (1997). *Tuesdays with Morrie.* New York: Doubleday.

Albrecht, T. L., & Adelman, M. B. (1987). *Communicating social support.* Newbury Park, CA: Sage.

Callanan, M., & Kelley, P. (1992). *Final gifts: Understanding the special awareness, needs, and communications of the dying.* New York: Bantam Books.

Canary, D. J., & Stafford, L. (1994). Maintaining relational characteristics through communication strategies and routines. In D. J. Canary & L. Stafford (Eds.), *Communication and relational maintenance*, (pp. 3–22). New York: Academic Press.

Costello, J. (2006). Dying well: Nurses' "experiences of good and bad" deaths in hospital. *Journal of Advanced Nursing, 54,* 594–601.

Diener, E., & Biswas-Diener, R. (2008). *Happiness: Unlocking the mysteries of psychological wealth.* Malden, MA: Blackwell Publishing.

Doyle, D. (1994). *Caring for a dying relative: A guide for families.* Oxford, UK: Oxford University Press.

Floyd, K. (2009). *Interpersonal communication: The whole story.* Boston: McGraw Hill.

Foster, E. (2007). *Communicating at the end of life: Finding magic in the mundane.* Mahwah, NJ: Lawrence Erlbaum.

Keeley, M. P. (2007). 'Turning toward death together': The functions of messages during final conversations in close relationships. *Journal of Social and Personal Relationships, 24,* 225–253.

Keeley, M. P. (1996). Social support and breast cancer: Why do we talk and who do we talk to? In R. Parrott & C. Condit (Eds.), *Evaluating women's health messages* (pp. 293–306). Beverly Hills, CA: Sage.

Keeley, M. P., & Baldwin, P. (2012). Final conversations, phase II: Children and everyday communication, *Journal of Loss and Trauma,* 376 – 387.

Keeley, M. P., & Yingling, J. (2007). *Final conversations: Helping the living and the dying talk to each other.* Acton, MA: VanderWyk & Burnham.

Kübler-Ross, E. (1997). *Living with death and dying.* New York: Simon & Schuster.

Kübler-Ross, E. (1999). *The tunnel and the light.* New York: Marlowe and Company.

Levine, S. (1984). *Meetings at the edge: Dialogues with the grieving, and the dying, and the healing and the healed.* New York: Doubleday.

Lynn, J., & Harrold, J. (1999). *Handbook for mortals: Guidance for people facing serious illness.* Oxford, UK: OxfordUniversity Press.

Marrone, R. (1999). Dying, mourning, and spirituality: A psychological perspective. *Death Studies, 23,* 495–519.

McQuellon, R. P., & Cowan, M. A. (2000). Turning toward death together: Conversation in mortal time. *American Journal of Hospice and Palliative Care, 17,* 312–318.

Montgomery, B. M. (1988). Quality communication in personal relationships. In S. W. Duck (Ed.), *Handbook of personal relationships* (pp. 343–366). New York: John Wiley.

Morse, J. M. (2000). Determining sample size. *Qualitative Health Research, 10*, 3–5.
National Hospice and Palliative Care Organization. (2012). History of hospice care. Retrieved from http://www.nhpco.org/i4a/pages/index.cfm?pageid=3285.
Pitts, M. (2011). Dancing with the spirit: Communicating family norms for positive end-of-life transition. In M. Miller-Day (Ed.), *Family communication, connections, and health transitions: Going through this together* (pp. 377–404). New York: Peter Lang.
Rosenberg, M. (2003). *Nonviolent communication: A language of life*. Encinitas, CA: Puddle Dancer Press.
Seligman, M. E. P., & Csikszentmihalyi, M. (2000). Positive psychology: An introduction. *American Psychologist, 55*, 5–14.
Socha, T. J. (2005). Towards a positive ontology of communication theorizing: Lessons from Pollyanna. *Conference Proceedings—National Communication Association Hope Faculty Development Institute*, 37–45. Retrieved from EBSCO*host*.
Socha, T. J. (2006). Orchestrating and directing domestic potential through communication: Towards a positive reframing of "discipline." In L. Turner & R. West (Eds.), *Family communication: A reference for theory and research* (pp. 219–236). Thousand Oaks, CA: Sage.
Wood, J. T., & Duck, S. (2006). *Composing relationships: Communication in everyday life*. Belmont, CA: Wadsworth.

Section Three
Positive Communication and Healthy Organizations and Institutions

• CHAPTER TWELVE •

Affirming Communication within the Healthcare Organization: Validating Strength through Talk in Trauma Medicine

Theodore A. Avtgis
Ashland University

Andrew S. Rancer
University of Akron

Sherry G. Ford
University of Montevallo

Evidence of the power of positivity and positive expression continues to emerge in the communication literature (e.g., see Socha & Pitts, 2012). This pro-social form of communication, until only recently, has been overshadowed by a field that has been primarily focused on the more anti-social elements of human expression and human relationships (Cupach & Spitzberg, 1994; Kinney & Pörhölä, 2009). With hundreds of studies focusing on problematic features of communication such as apprehension and aggression, it is a natural progression that we, as a field, take another cue from our colleagues in psychology and begin, with earnest, to investigate the important and powerful impact of communication that is considered "well" alongside that which is regarded as pathological. One challenge to such study is the conceptualization of outcomes that would be logical as a result of positive communication expression with another challenge being how to effectively assess such positive communicative practices. It is the goal of this chapter to present a long standing organizational communication theory, the Theory of Independent Mindedness (Infante, 1987c), as one that, as a cornerstone, requires positive communication for employee wellness. We will also demonstrate the successful application of this theory to a rural emergency trauma medical network and provide empirical evidence of the impact that positive communication expression has on members of the medical team via increased patient safety.

Positive Expression in Workplace Approaches

It has been well documented across several social scientific disciplines that employee well-being is in the best interest of the employer (Harter, Schmidt, & Keyes, 2003). One of the known contributors to an employee's sense of well-being is a person's capacity to communicate effectively (Grawitch, Gottschaulk, & Munz, 2006). The era of co-dependence and collaborative work teams has been thrust upon us by both technological and scientific advances over the last several decades. Most, if not all, professions require communication within a team context in order to ensure organizational efficiency and effectiveness. As such, the investigation of human dynamics involved in teamwork and the interpersonal relationships within those teams is fast becoming a central focus of organizational research (Wilson, Dejoy, Vandenberg, Richardson, & McGrath, 2004).

Perhaps one of the most comprehensive frameworks for understanding teamwork, and the impact positive expression has on team functioning, was developed in response to human error and its role in aviation crashes. More specifically, Crew Resource Management (CRM) is an industrial training approach that highlights the impact that team-related behaviors and attitudes have on safety and performance (Helmreich & Foushee, 1993). The underlying assumption of CRM is that there are certain communication and coordination behaviors characteristic of high-stakes environments (e.g., medical teams) and that these behaviors are identifiable, teachable, and applicable. These identified behaviors are assumed to be unstandardized and only become protocol through established training mechanisms, redundancy, and reinforcement (Morey et al. 2002). Early incarnations of CRM training focused on increasing the participant's self- and other-awareness and promoting recognition of one's own emotional state on group dynamics (Vandermark, 1991). These are established factors for productive and meaningful communication (Metts & Wood, 2008).

Following the lead of these initial efforts within the aviation industry, other industries in high-stakes contexts followed suit. By high-stakes contexts we are referring to industries where team work and team performance is required for success, and failure often results in a loss of life or other catastrophic consequences. Such contexts include fire services, nuclear plant operations, oil drilling, merchant marines, and a host of other industries that have utilized CRM to enhance team performance (O'Connor et al., 2008). Few contexts are more appropriate for developing teamwork via approaches such as CRM than specialty areas of healthcare and medicine. Areas such as anesthesiology, emergency medicine, and nursing can all benefit from the integration of CRM principles. For these safety-critical contexts, incidents of failure can be attributed to failures in communication and operational leadership; two of the human factors vital in professional performance (Hunt & Callaghan, 2008).

While much of the research in the United States attributes negative patient outcomes to poor communication (Awad et al., 2005), studies from other countries also implicate deficiencies in inter-professional collaboration as contributing to adverse events (Haller et al., 2008; Hewett, Watson, Gallois, Ward, & Leggett, 2009). Specific failures include poor communication during patient-care transfer, conflict among healthcare team members, and failure to develop contingency protocols for potential complications (Despins, 2009; Polack & Avtgis, 2011). In a comprehensive effort to curtail the communication-related threats to patient safety, the Joint Commission on Accreditation of Healthcare Organizations formally recommended the inclusion of team training that fosters interdisciplinary collaboration in any comprehensive plan for patient safety (Musson & Helmreich, 2004). Thus, the application of CRM principles and training in healthcare have become commonplace. The design and implementation of of such programs can take a variety of forms with focus on improving communication among various team members. For example, some approaches prioritize standardized preoperative briefing and dialogs for creating a shared understanding (Awad et al., 2005). Although these types of training are important, it is when they are specifically focused on teamwork principles and performance that they can be of greatest use (Chakraborti, Boonyasai, Wright, & Kern, 2008).

While CRM has been shown to be a viable approach to team-building in high-stakes professions, effective team-building is but a microcosm of a larger system. As such, efforts need to be set within a larger management perspective in order to have lasting systemic effect. We believe that there is a larger cultural temperament that allows mechanisms such as CRM and other positive communication practices to flourish. One such temperament setting approach is that of the Theory of Independent Mindedness.

Theory of Independent Mindedness

The Theory of Independent Mindedness (TIM) was born out of the unique societal and economic conditions that emerged in the United States during the 1980s (Infante, 1987c). That is, American business and management practices generally sought solutions to an uninspired workforce by importing management strategies from collectivist cultures. This theory is designed for organizations primarily from low-context and individualistic cultures such as the United States, as an organization's success is inherently linked to "the cultural values of organizational members and the larger culture within which they operate" (Hinner, 2007, p. 183). Management strategies that were being implemented in eastern countries such as Japan and Korea were seen as the mechanism from which superior goods and services were being imported into the U.S. As such, management techniques that were developed and practiced in collectivist cultures were being imported and implemented in a wanton fashion in hopes of gaining an edge over international competition. The main drawback from adopting the management strategies which were so successful and effective in Japan and Korea were based on the cultural patterns and practices of these nations, not the management strategy itself. By importing only the techniques and approaches without accounting for the cultural practices and behaviors required to make such an approach successful, often resulted in failure. For example, the concept of lifetime employment is one that is common in Japanese culture with some data showing as much as 20% of employees in government and large corporations engaging in such employment (Kato, 2001). Yet, the notion of lifetime employment is a concept that does not exist, if it ever did, in contemporary American society. Observing such inconsistencies between management approach and cultural framework, Infante (1987a, 1987b, 1987c) advanced a theory that is exclusively communicative in nature, corporatist in nature, and designed to be effective in low-context and more individualistic cultures.

The Theory of Independent Mindedness (TIM) assumes that organizational productivity, satisfaction, and commitment are directly linked to relational dynamics and the communication-trait profiles that exist between and among organizational members. TIM assumes that the degree to which the larger cultural values are practiced and/or are present within a specific organizational culture, the more the worker will be able to exhibit more culturally congruent behaviors within the workplace resulting in a more satisfying organizational experience (Avtgis & Rancer, 2007). Infante (1987c) believed that American cultural values of freedom of expression, individualism, and individual performance should also be present in the specific organization within which people work. Not only should these values be present but should be fostered in employee training development programs (Avtgis & Chory, 2010). It is argued that such congruity in practices and behaviors should be extended into relational expression as well. More specifically, organizational relationships should possess the same type of relational expectancies (e.g., open expression of ideas, validation of face, positiveness) found in non-work relationships. This is not to dismiss the notion that in U.S. society, organizations have clear status and power differences which account for much of the "stylized" interaction patterns that underlie organizational relationships (Avtgis & Rancer, 2007). For example, a superior can walk into a subordinate's office, often without knocking, and ask for a ride home. This would not be normative behavior for a subordinate to engage in with a superior, unless the nature of the relationship permitted it.

Three of Hofstede's (1984) cultural dimensions are quite relevant here. Hofstede's (1984) theory argues that organizations are bound by culture and offers four work-related cultural dimensions. The first dimension, *Power-Distance*, argues that organizations differ regarding power inequality between superiors and subordinates. High power distance organizations have clear power and status differences between organizational members which influence the amount and type of interaction between superiors and subordinates. Subordinates from these types of organizations recognize that they have less power and consequently less input into organizational decision-making. In high power distance organizations, decision-making is more autocratic. The second dimension, *Uncertainty Avoidance*, refers to employee's tolerance of ambiguity (Wu, 2006). In high uncertainty avoidance organizations, there are more written rules and regulations and there is less tolerance for change. The third dimension is *Individualism-Collectivism*. This dimension refers to "how people value themselves and their groups/organizations" (Wu, 2006, p. 34). Cultures, and consequently organizations within those cultures, differ regarding the focus on the individual versus the group. Employees in high individualistic organizations place greater emphasis on their individual values, achievements and rights. Thus, the tenets of Hofstede's cultural dimensions theory clearly relate to the applicability and acceptance of the theory of independent mindedness. Organizations high in power distance, high in uncertainty avoidance, and high on collectivism would likely not adopt the tenets of independent mindedness.

The TIM requires that employees be involved in organizational decision making based on the application of U.S. values such as freedom of speech and the necessity of freedom of expression. Such a degree of involvement assumes that there is an exchange of ideas between two or more organizational members. However, simply engaging in decision making is not enough to bring about a state of independent mindedness. In order for any employee to feel validated and valued, there must be a perception that there is an opportunity to openly dissent regarding policy and procedures without fear of negative retribution or unjust retaliation on behalf of the supervisor or organization. Such a degree of employee voice brings about a dialectical exchange in which all parties are functioning from a place of strength and self-determination (Gorden & Infante, 1987; Kassing, 1997). Given there are many confounding variables associated with dissent within an organization, how can a person truly feel self-determined, valued, and affirmed in the face of obvious power and status differences that exist in contemporary organizations? According to Infante (1987a), although capitalist societies readily acknowledge overt differences in power and status between organizational members in order to function, when there is an open exchange of ideas between people of different power and status levels, the perception of such barriers diminish and thus, move all organizational members toward self-determination. Such a process allows for the use of the traditional organizational hierarchy which is the hallmark of many top global corporations, yet allow employees at all levels to feel as if they have a voice and that this voice is being validated in determining organizational processes.

Elements of the TIM

TIM diverges from the more scientific management based approaches that advocate the use of unilateral power. Instead, TIM assumes a more mindful and critically aware communication exchange between all members of the organization (Ewing, 1982; Infante & Gorden, 1987). Independent mindedness is displayed in human behavior by the presence of three communication predispositions that are manifest in employee communicative expression. These communication predispositions are *argumentativeness* (Infante & Rancer, 1982), *verbal aggressiveness* (Infante & Wigley, 1986), and *communicator style* (Norton, 1978). This tripartite of communication predispositions can be conceptualized as communication tendencies that are generally considered pro-social (i.e., argumentativeness) or anti-social (i.e., verbal aggressiveness) in nature by the way that they are mediated by their expression (i.e., communicator style).

On the positive side, the argumentativeness trait is defined as a predisposition for people in communication situations to advocate positions on controversial issues while simultaneously refuting the positions others take on controversial issues (Infante & Rancer, 1982). Argumentativeness is considered a subset of assertiveness in which both are considered to be "healthy" as they allow for the expression of basic human needs in ways that research has shown to be constructive and non-threatening (Infante & Rancer, 1996; Rancer & Avtgis, 2006). More specifically, research indicates that within organizations, increased levels of argumentativeness have been linked to increased levels of subordinate relational and job satisfaction (Infante & Gorden, 1985), increased use of constructive dissenting messages (Kassing & Avtgis, 1999), solution-oriented conflict strategies (Martin, Anderson, & Sirimangkala, 1997), and higher levels of perceived organizational justice (Gorden & Infante, 1987).

On the dark side, verbal aggressiveness is considered a subset of hostility and defined as a predisposition to attack a person's self-concept, instead of, or in addition to the positions that they take on controversial issues (Infante & Wigley, 1986). In fact, one of the central effects of verbal aggression use is the psychological pain inflicted on the victims. In juxtaposition to argumentativeness, research findings indicate the destructive nature of verbal aggressiveness in all sectors and types of work (see Avtgis & Chory, 2010). Specific findings indicate that subordinates who perceive their supervisors as being high in verbal aggressiveness report lower levels of social justice and satisfaction (Infante & Gorden, 1987), greater negative affect toward the supervisor (Infante, Anderson, Martin, Herington, & Kim, 1993), utilize more ineffective strategies for expressing dissent (Kassing & Avtgis, 1999), and view the supervisor as being inattentive and unfriendly (Infante & Gorden, 1989).

Communicator style plays a vital role as it serves to accentuate the impact of communication content in either pro- or antisocial ways. That is, whether someone is defending a position on a controversial issue in a contentious fashion, or whether they are attacking a person's self-concept in a contentious fashion, the outcome may very well be the same; destructive. The communicator style construct is considered a trait in that it reflects "the way one verbally and paraverbally interacts to signal how literal meaning should be taken, interpreted, filtered, or understood" (Norton, 1978, p. 99). Communicative signaling is cross-contextual and becomes part of an individual's "communication signature." Norton (1978) identified nine different dimensions or styles of communication consisting of *friendly* (e.g., affiliative, non-threatening, and increase intimacy), *relaxed* (e.g., free of anxiety or arousal), *animated* (e.g., using both physical and other nonverbal behavior), *dramatic* (e.g., exaggerating information), *contentious* (e.g., antagonistic and confrontational), *dominant* (e.g., creating or maintaining control of a situation), *open* (e.g., extroverted and spontaneous), *precise* (e.g., accurateness and correctness), *attentive* (e.g., showing interest and involvement in a conversation), and *impression leaving* (e.g., others remember you based on your interaction style). Collectively, these nine dimensions comprise a person's communicator image or the degree to which a person is seen as a competent and effective communicator (Avtgis & Rancer, 2007). Particular combinations contribute to communicator images that are positive and validating to the self and other while other combinations contribute to communicator images that are negative and invalidating to the self and other. The affirming communicator style is based on the concepts of affirmation, validation, and positivity.

Affirming Communication Expression

The concept of affirming communication expression, as used within organizations, can be considered a "best practices" approach in that it assumes organizational communication should be that which supports the face of both communicants (e.g., superior and subordinate) while simultaneously creating a climate that is less aggressive and more productive (Avtgis, Polack, & Martin, 2010; Infante & Gorden, 1989). That is, a best practices approach would require all organizational members to be respected and valued by the organization as well as by people within the organizational structure (see, for example, Mirivel, 2012). Affirming communication would allow "individuals to engage in an aggressive form of communication such as arguing and realize positive rather than negative outcomes" (Infante & Gorden, 1989, p. 83). What specific communication behaviors constitute an affirming communicator style? A person who demonstrates a highly relaxed, friendly, and attentive style would encompass such positive expression. Research suggests that individuals who are high in argumentativeness, low in verbal aggressiveness, and who communicate with an affirming communicator style enjoy more favorable perceptions are perceived as more effective in communication situations where disagreement is present (see, for example, Edge & Williams, 1994; Infante, Rancer, & Jordan, 1996; Jordan-Jackson, Lin, Rancer, & Infante, 2008; Rancer, Jordan-Jackson, & Infante, 2003).

Enhancing Organizational Relationships through Training

Both superiors and subordinates would benefit greatly from training designed to enhance the ability to argue and foster argumentativeness, minimize the use of verbal aggression and reduce verbal aggressiveness, and develop an affirming communicator style. The adoption of this profile should result in more satisfactory and rewarding organizational relationships as well as positively impact organizational decision-making. Other research programs focusing on similar traits such as empathy and assertiveness have had direct impact on fiscal as well as relational outcomes for the organization (Seibold, Kudsi, & Rude, 1993). To date, no comprehensive training efforts have been constructed to develop superiors and subordinates toward greater independent-mindedness. However, Infante (1988) developed the Inventional System that attempts to increase a person's ability to formulate or invent arguments. This system of invention is broad enough to be effective regardless of the nature of the conflict and can be effective in a myriad of interpersonal and organizational communication situations. These conflict situations can include those involving policy issues (e.g., a new objective reward/promotion system should be implemented), value issues (e.g., employees who are more dedicated should be given preferential treatment), and factual issues (e.g., using temporary workers will save the company thousands in benefit costs).

The Inventional System (Infante, 1988) is based on a series of questions that address both main issues as well as sub-issues that aid a person in the development of argument generation. Table 12.1 presents the Inventional System.

Table 12.1. The Inventional System

Major Issues and Sub-Issues

1. **Problem**
    a. What is the problem that exists?
    b. What is the specific harm from the problem?
    c. How widespread is the problem?

2. **Blame**
    a. Who or what is to blame for the problem?
    b. Is the person or system at fault for the problem?
    c. Should the status quo be changed?

3. **Solution**
    a. What course(s) of action will reduce or eliminate the problem?
    b. Which solution would best solve or reduce the problem?

4. **Consequences**
    a. What good outcomes will result from adopting the new solution?
    b. What bad outcomes will result from adopting the new solution?

(Adapted from Infante, 1988)

Although this system is focused on skill enhancement, several studies have shown that training in the Inventional System (as well as other argument training programs) bring about longitudinal changes in trait argumentativeness and trait verbal aggressiveness and thus lend support for several components of TIM (Rancer, Avtgis, Kosberg, & Whitecap, 2000; Rancer, Whitecap, Kosberg, & Avtgis, 1997). Anderson, Schultz, and Courtney-Staley (1987) investigated the impact that argumentation training has on assertiveness focusing on the three assumptions of (a) effective conflict management assumes that a person is willing to engage in a conflict situation, (b) cognitive knowledge about arguing and conflict is needed in order to change negative stereotypes about arguing and conflict, and (c) when perception has been altered by knowing how to effectively argue, persuasion and theories of argumentation can be taught. The three hour training consisted of lecture, discussion, and small group role play. Utilizing a non-equivalent pre-test/post-test experimental design, Anderson et al. (1987) found that women showed the greatest amount of change from the training. Therefore, this particular curriculum was determined to be effective in increasing the argumentativeness of women in the workplace (Schultz & Anderson, 1984).

It is a main contention of the TIM model that if a state of independent-mindedness is to be achieved for all employees (i.e., increased trait argumentativeness, lower verbal aggressiveness, and an affirming communicator style) organizations must foster, through coaching, training, and organizational development efforts, this type of employee enhancement programming.

Implementing Positive Communication in the Extra-Hospital Environment

Two studies illustrate the application of positive communication and the profound impact that such training can have on a healthcare system (Kappel, Rossi, Polack, Avtgis, & Martin, 2011; Rossi, Polack, Avgis, Kappel, & Martin, 2009). Rossi et al. sought to investigate communication barriers and failures that routinely occur between members of medical teams in trauma medicine. The focus on the application of affirming communication on trauma medical teams in the inter-hospital transfer becomes greatly important in light of the limited resources available for process improvement and the fact that most of those resources are being dedicated to intra-hospital processes. As a result of limited resources and the allocation of these resources, there has been a general neglect to the extra-hospital processes involved in patient care. One such neglected area is the inter-hospital processes and the associated communication practices.

To investigate this, Rossi et al. (2009) assessed personnel throughout a state-wide trauma medical system consisting of physicians, nurses, registrars, and allied medical personnel from both definitive care facilities (i.e., facilities equipped with the qualified staff and technology to address all types of traumatic injury) as well as lower-level facilities (i.e., facilities equipped with personnel and technology that have a much more limited capacity to treat significant trauma injuries). Personnel answered open ended questions about the communication problems they believe exist within their trauma system network with a specific focus on the decision-making processes regarding trauma patient transfer (i.e., problems associated with outgoing transfer and incoming transfer). The findings indicated that medical personnel regularly felt unappreciated, condescended to, and dismissed when communicating with members of the definitive care facilities. On the other hand, medical personnel at the definitive care facilities reported great levels of frustration and incompetent of communication (e.g., wasted time with unimportant or redundant information) when interacting with medical team members from lower-level facilities. These data exposed the lack of quality and meaningful communication that is necessary for medical teams to effectively perform over long periods of time involving hundreds of patients annually. Such a high-stakes environment is ripe for improvement in effectively circumventing mistakes that result in adverse and/or sentinel events.

Based on these data, an affirming communication intervention was developed as a way to assess whether the mindful practice of positive communication will influence the process of trauma patient transferability status (Kappel et al., 2011). The training was partnered with the Rural Trauma Team Development Course (RTTDC). The RTTDC is a daylong training of advanced trauma treatment and protocol. The training was employed in a sub-sample of trauma centers throughout the state of West Virginia. More specifically, twenty-one of the thirty-two designated trauma facilities in West Virginia participated (that represents approximately 62% of all acute care facilities throughout the state). This resulted in the tracking of 302 trauma patient cases from which trauma transfer times were derived. The times for transfer of trauma patients were used as a metric to compare efficiency/performance rates of each trauma facility.

Utilizing a quasi-experimental design, Kappel et al. (2011) assigned each facility into one of three conditions: personnel who received additional trauma medical training and one hour of affirming communication training ($n = 36$ patients); personnel who received additional trauma medical training only ($n = 117$ patients); and personnel who receive no training ($n = 191$ patients). The transfer process was divided into five stages historically known for bottlenecking the transfer process: time of arrival to the facility to the decision to transfer; time from the decision to transfer to the time to find an accepting facility; time from decision to transfer to the time the transferring squad arrives; the number of receiving facilities contacted; and the number of transferring squads contacted.

The results of this effort concretize the notion that affirming communication is indeed a form of positive expression that has profound systemic effects. Overall, the results were most fruitful in that the group receiving the medical trauma training and affirming communication training had an average reduction of 37 minutes in wait time when compared to the control group and a 19 minute reduction when compared to the RTTDC-only trained group. The group that received medical and communication training also realized a 36 minute reduction in the time it took for the transfer squad to arrive when compared to the medical training only and control groups (the RTTDC-only training group improved by only ten minutes over the control group).

These findings are indicative of several significant implications for the role that positive communication and related positive communication theories (CRM and the larger theory of TIM). These results indicate that given the unlimited variables that exist during an extra-hospital processes that include great variation in trauma, triage, and treatment, we cannot conclude that positive communication training is the exclusive causal factor for the reduction in trauma patient transfer time. Avtgis et al. (2010) argue,

> destructive patterns have clearly been identified as a major problem in the transfer process. By improving these interactions, there stands a greater probability that the inter-hospital transfer process will not be hindered by relational and communication difficulties among and between team members…affirming communication can enhance at best, and keep from hampering at the least, inter-hospital transfer processes. (p. 289)

General Conclusions of Affirming Communication in the Practice of Healthcare

This chapter has sought to illuminate the power that positive expression and closely related communication constructs have on organizational outcomes in general, and healthcare outcomes in particular. While we seek to discover new positive communication strategies on this quest to investigate the good of communication, we ought not to forget about those constructs and theories that have long been utilized yet never cast as positive communication approaches. In this case, theories like TIM that recognize the importance of cultural values and that work toward the improvement of the human condition are not necessarily leading us to avoid possible disaster or negative consequence. Instead, reinterpretation indicates approaches that move us forward toward the communicative betterment of people can have an "added value" component where mistakes and disrespect begin to dissipate.

References

Anderson, J., Schultz, B., & Coutney-Staley, C. (1987). Training in argumentativeness: New hope for nonassertive women. *Women's Studies in Communication, 10,* 58–66.

Avtgis, T. A., & Chory, R. M. (2010). The dark side of organizational life: Aggressive expression in the workplace. In T. A. Avtgis & A. S. Rancer (Eds.), *Arguments, aggression, and conflict: New directions in theory and research* (pp. 285–304). New York: Routledge.

Avtgis, T. A., Polack, E. P., & Martin, M. M. (2010). Improve the communication, decrease the distance: The investigation into problematic communication and delays in interhospital transfer of rural trauma patients. *Communication Education, 59,* 282–293.

Avtgis, T. A., & Rancer, A. S. (2007). The theory of independent-mindedness: An organizational theory for individualistic cultures. In M. B. Hinner (Ed.), *Freiberger beitrage zur interkulturellen und wirtschaftskommunikation. The role of communication in business transactions and relationships* (pp. 187–201). Frankfurt, Germany: Peter Lang.

Awad, S. S., Fagan, S. P., Bellows, C., Albo, D., Green-Rashad, B., De La Garza, M., & Berger, D. H. (2005). Bridging the communication gap in the operating room with medical team training. *American Journal of Surgery, 190,* 770–774.

Chakraborti, C., Boonyasai, R. T., Wright, S. M., & Kern, D. E. (2008). A systematic review of teamwork training interventions of medical student and resident education. *Journal of General Internal Medicine, 23,* 846–853.

Cupach, W. R., & Spitzberg, B. H. (Eds.). (1994). *The dark side of interpersonal communication.* Hillsdale, NJ: Lawrence Erlbaum.

Despins, L. A. (2009). Patient safety and collaboration of the intensive care unit team. *Critical Care Nurse, 29,* 85–92.

Edge, H. A., & Williams, M. L. (1994). Affirming communicator style of superior and subordinate use of upward influence tactics: An analysis of non-managerial and managerial employees. *Communication Research Reports, 11,* 201–208.

Ewing, D. (1982). *Do it my way or you're fired: Employee rights and the changing role of management perspectives.* New York: John Wiley & Sons.

Gorden, W. I., & Infante, D. A. (1987). Employee rights: Context argumentativeness, verbal aggressiveness, and career satisfaction. In C. A. B. Osigweg (Ed.), *Communicating employee responsibilities and rights* (pp. 149–163). Westport, CT: Quorum.

Grawitch, M. J., Gottschalk, M., & Munz, D. C. (2006). The path to a healthy workplace: A critical review linking healthy workplace practices, employee well-being, and organizational improvements. *Consulting Psychology Journal: Practice and Research, 58,* 129–147.

Haller, G., Morales, M., Pfister, R., Garnerin, P., Chipp, P., Guillemot, V., & Kern, C. (2008). Improving interprofessional teamwork in obstetrics: A crew resource management based training programme. *Journal of Interprofessional Care, 22,* 545–548.

Harter, J. K., Schmidt, F. L., & Keyes, C. L. M. (2003). Well-being in the workplace and its relationship to business outcomes: A review of the Gallup studies. In C. L. M. Keyes & J. Haidt (Eds.), *Flourishing: Positive psychology and the life well-lived.* Washington, DC: APA.

Helmreich, R. L., & Foushee, H. C. (1993). Why crew resource management: Empirical and theoretical bases of human factors training in aviation. In E. L. Wiener, B. G. Kanki, & R. L. Helmreich (Eds.), *Cockpit resource management*. San Diego, CA: Academic Press.

Hinner, M. B. (2007). Introduction to the theory of independent-mindedness: An organizational theory for individualistic cultures. In M. B. Hinner (Ed.), *Freiberger beitrage zur interkulturellen und wirtschaftskammunikation. The role of communication in business transactions and relationships* (pp. 183–184). Frankfurt, Germany: Peter Lang.

Hewett, D. G., Watson, B. M., Gallois, C., Ward, M., & Leggett, B. A. (2009) Intergroup communication between hospital doctors: Implications for quality of patient care. *Social Science and Medicine, 69*(12), 1732–1740.

Hofstede, G. (1984). *Culture's consequences: International differences in work-related values*. Newbury Park, CA: Sage.

Infante, D. A. (1987a). *Argumentativeness in superior-subordinate communication: An essential condition for organizational productivity*. Paper presented at the American Forensic Summer Conference of the Speech Communication Association, Alta, UT.

Infante, D. A. (1987b). Superior and subordinate profiles: Implications for independent-mindedness and upward effectiveness. *Central States Speech Journal, 38,* 73–80.

Infante, D. A. (1987c). *An independent-mindedness model of organizational productivity: The role of communication education*. Paper presented at the annual meeting of the Eastern Communication Association, Syracuse, NY.

Infante, D. A. (1988). *Arguing constructively*. Prospect Heights, IL: Waveland Press.

Infante, D. A., Anderson, C. M., Martin, M. M., Herington, A. D., & Kim, J. (1993). Subordinates' satisfaction and perceptions of superiors' compliance-gaining tactics, argumentativeness, verbal aggressiveness, and style. *Management Communication Quarterly, 6,* 307–326.

Infante, D. A., & Gorden, W. I. (1985). Superiors' argumentativeness and verbal aggressiveness as predictors of subordinates' satisfaction. *Human Communication Research, 12,* 117–125.

Infante, D. A., & Gorden, W. I. (1987). Superior and subordinate communication profiles: Implications for independent-mindedness and upward effectiveness. *Central States Speech Journal, 38,* 73–80.

Infante, D. A., & Gorden, W. I. (1989). Argumentativeness and affirming communicator style as predictors of satisfaction/dissatisfaction with subordinates. *Communication Quarterly, 37,* 81–90.

Infante, D. A., & Rancer, A. S. (1982). A conceptualization and measure of argumentativeness. *Journal of Personality Assessment, 46,* 72–80.

Infante, D. A., & Rancer, A. S. (1996). Argumentativeness and verbal aggressiveness: A review of recent theory and research. In B. Burleson (Ed.), *Communication Yearbook* (Vol. 19, pp. 319–351). Thousand Oakes, CA: Sage.

Infante, D. A., Rancer, A. S., & Jordan, F. F. (1996). Affirming and non-affirming style, dyad sex, and the perception of argumentation and verbal aggression in an interpersonal dispute. *Human Communication Research, 22,* 315–334.

Infante, D. A., & Wigley, C. J. (1986). Verbal aggressiveness: An interpersonal model and measure. *Communication Monographs, 53,* 61–69.

Jordan-Jackson, F.F., Lin, Y., Rancer, A.S., & Infante, D.A. (2008). Perceptions of males and females use of aggressive affirming and non-affirming messages in an interpersonal dispute: You've come a long way baby? *Western Journal of Communication, 72,* 239–258.

Kappel, D. A., Rossi, D. C., Polack, E. P., Avtgis, T. A., & Martin, M. M. (2011). Does the RTTDC (rural trauma training team delivery course) shorten the interval from trauma patient arrival to decision to transfer? *Journal of Trauma, 70,* 315–319.

Kassing, J.W.(1997). Articulating, antagonizing, and displacing: A model of employee dissent. *Communication Studies, 48,* 311–330.

Kassing, J. W., & Avtgis, T. A. (1999). Examining the relationship between organizational dissent and aggressive communication. *Management Communication Quarterly, 13,* 100–115.

Kato, T. (2001). The end of lifetime employment in Japan?: Evidence from the national surveys and field research. *Journal of Japanese and International Economies, 15,* 489–514.

Kinney, T. A., & Pörhölä, M. (Eds.). (2009). *Anti and pro-social communication: Theories, methods, and applications.* New York: Peter Lang.

Martin, M. M., Anderson, C. M., & Sirimangkala, P. (1997, April). *The relationship between use of organizational conflict strategies with socio-communicative style and aggressive communication traits.* Paper presented at the annual meeting of the Eastern Communication Association, Baltimore, MD.

Metts, S., & Wood, B. (2008). Interpersonal emotional competence. In M. T. Motley (Eds.), *Studies in applied interpersonal communication* (pp. 267–285). Thousand Oaks, CA: Sage.

Mirivel, J. C. (2012). Communication excellence: Embodying virtues in interpersonal communication. In T. J. Socha & M. Pitts (Eds.), *The positive side of interpersonal communication* (pp. 57–72). New York: Peter Lang.

Morey, J. C., Simon, R. R., Jay, G. D., Wears, R. L., Salisbury, M. M., Dukes, K. A., & Berns, S. D. (2002). Error reduction and performance improvement in the emergency department through formal teamwork training: Evaluation results of the MEDTEAMS project. *Health Services Research, 37,* 1553–1581.

Musson, D. M., & Helmreich, R. L. (2004). Team training and resource management in healthcare: Current issues and future directions. *Harvard Health Policy Review, 5,* 25–35.

Norton, R. (1978). Foundation of a communicator style construct. *Human Communication Research, 4,* 99–112.

O'Connor, P., Campbell, J., Newson, J., Melton, J., Salas, E., & Wilson, K. A. (2008). Crew resource management training effectiveness: A meta-analysis and some critical needs. *International Journal of Aviation Psychology, 18,* 353–368.

Polack, E. P., & Avtgis, T. A. (2011). *Medical communication: Defining the discipline.* Dubuque, IA: Kendall Hunt.

Rancer, A. S., & Avtgis, T. A. (2006). *Argumentative and aggressive communication: Theory, research, and application.* Thousand Oaks, CA: Sage.

Rancer, A. S., Avtgis, T. A., Kosberg, R. L., & Whitecap, V. G. (2000). A longitudinal assessment of trait argumentativeness and verbal aggressiveness between seventh and eighth grades. *Communication Education, 49,* 114–119.

Rancer, A. S., Jordan-Jackson, F. F., & Infante, D. A. (2003). Observers' perceptions of an interpersonal dispute as a function of mode of presentation. *Communication Reports, 16,* 35–46.

Rancer, A. S., Whitecap, V. G., Kosberg, R. L., & Avtgis, T. A. (1997). Training in argumentativeness: Testing the efficacy of a communication training program to increase argumentativeness and argumentative behavior in adolescents. *Communication Education, 46,* 273–286.

Rossi, D., Polack, E. P., Avtgis, T. A., Kappel, D., & Martin, M. M. (2009). It's not about being nice: It's about being a better doctor: The investigation into problematic communication and delays in trauma patient transfer. *Medical Encounter, 23,* 5–6.

Schultz, B., & Anderson, J. (1984). Training in the management of conflict: A communication theory perspective. *Small Group Behavior, 15,* 333–348.

Seibold, D. R., Kudsi, S., & Rude, M. (1993). Does communication training make a difference?: Evidence for the effectiveness of a presentational skills program. *Journal of Applied Communication Research, 21,* 111–131.

Socha, T. J., & Pitts, M. (Eds.). (2012). *The positive side of interpersonal communication.* New York: Peter Lang.

Wilson, M. G., Dejoy, D. M., Vandenberg, R. J., Richardson, H. A., & McGrath, A. L. (2004). Work characteristics and employee health and well-being: Test of a model of healthy work organization. *Journal of Occupational and Organizational Psychology, 77,* 565–588.

Wright, K. B., Banas, J. A., Bessarabova, E., & Bernard, D. R. (2010). A communication competence model approach to examining healthcare social support, stress, and job burnout. *Health Communication, 25,* 375–382.

Wu, M. Y. (2006). Hofstede's cultural dimensions 30 years later: A study of Taiwan and the United States. *Intercultural Communication Studies, 15,* 33–42.

• CHAPTER THIRTEEN •

Positive Communication and Organizational Crisis: Can CEOs Look on the Bright Side?

Sandra L. French
Radford University

The prevalent disease-based model of psychology focuses on problematic and abnormal mental processes, seeking cures for diagnosed conditions. This model largely uses what most people would call "healthy" mental states and processes as a contrast to the "diseased" states laid out in the latest edition of the *Diagnostic and Statistical Manual of Mental Disorders* (2000) (the title of which clearly indicates the prevailing perspective). Moreover, this focus on disorders does not take into account or examine the mental development, processes or practices of fulfilled, thriving individuals. The positive psychology movement seeks to rectify this by studying strength and virtue (Seligman & Csikszentmihalyi, 2000). Peterson and Seligman (founder of the positive psychology movement) developed a manual of *Character Strengths and Virtues* (Peterson & Seligman, 2004) specifically as a "positive" counterpart to the *Diagnostic and Statistical Manual of Mental Disorders* (DSM). By calling for psychological research that focuses on "knowledge of what makes life worth living" (Seligman & Csikszentmihalyi, 2000, p. 5), the positive psychology movement has produced myriad articles, handbooks, and edited volumes investigating the "conditions, and processes that contribute to the flourishing or optimal functioning of people, groups, and institutions" (Gable & Haidt, 2005, p. 103). While positive psychology focuses on positive emotions, positive relationships, and positive institutions, this chapter focuses on how positive psychology benefits institutions, specifically, business organizations. In this chapter, I examine the role positive communication plays in cultivating healthy employees, which in turn fosters healthy organizations, starting with CEOs as organizational exemplars. I argue that the ability of organizations to withstand negative events, in particular, organizational crises, is bolstered by CEOs who demonstrate positive organizational behaviors and who seek to cultivate these behaviors in their employees. First, I examine briefly the history of positive psychology's contributions to organizational scholarship. Second, relevant positive organizational behaviors, including the "core four" of self-efficacy, hope, optimism, and resiliency, are explored. Third, a discussion of CEOs and "traditional" versus emerging methods of crisis communication are discussed. Finally, the chapter ends with an exploration of new directions of crisis communication research that a positive psychology perspective offers.

Positive Psychology Goes to Work

A new paradigm, born out of the positive psychology movement, has arisen in relation to studying organizations. Although it has many names, including applied positive psychology, appreciative inquiry, positive organizational scholarship (POS), and positive organizational behavior (POB), all include a shift in perspective from a "disease" based, weakness, and problem-solving model as the most suitable approach to improved organizational performance, to one in which positive resources are identified and investigated (Linley, Harrington, & Garcea, 2010). Rather than establishing a dichotomy of health and productivity, positive psychology purports that "health is an essential underpinning for sustained productivity and the long-term well-being" of organizations (Quick & Macik-Frey, 2007, p. 25). In other words, healthy organizations are comprised of healthy individuals, and investments in creating healthy employees assist organizations in the goal of maintaining healthy, productive organizations. In particular, two distinct subsets of this type of research (sometimes used interchangeably) warrant further investigation: positive organizational scholarship and positive organizational behavior.

Positive organizational scholarship is a marriage of positive psychology and organizational studies. POS seeks to understand how to cultivate excellence in organizations by unlocking individuals' potential. By cultivating understanding of workplace conditions that foster positive behavior, POS seeks to improve overall organizational performance and well-being. Specifically, through an investigation of "positive deviance," POS attempts to explain and generate environments where individuals and organizations can flourish ("The Essence of Positive Organizational Scholarship," n.d.). Positive deviance explores the ways in which individuals use and develop strengths leading to exceptional performance at both the individual and organizational levels (Linley et al., 2010). Positive deviance involves stepping outside the organizational norms in positive ways. "Studying and focusing on such concepts as strengths, resiliency, healing, and restoration is for the purpose of cultivating extraordinary individual and organizational performance" (Mroz & Quinn, 2010). Thus, a key component of positive deviance is its simultaneous focus on cultivating individual, group, and organizational results. In investigating extraordinary performance, POS focuses on the macro or institutional levels of analysis (Yousef & Luthans, 2007) rather than looking solely at individual organizational actors, however, the overall benefit at both the individual and organizational levels is the creation of healthier, more productive workplaces.

A similar line of organizational research, positive organizational behavior, is defined by Luthans (2003), as "the study and application of positively oriented human resource strengths and psychological capacities that can be measured, developed, and effectively managed for performance improvement in today's workplace" (p. 179). POB capacities are those that can be measured and developed (Luthans, 2002). POB also tends to focus more on individuals, or micro levels of analysis, and is designed to link behaviors to positive workplace performance. Thus, in order to be considered part of the POB literature, a research approach must investigate the psychological resource capacities of individuals that are "state" like, rather than "trait" like (Youssef & Luthans, 2007). This means that the individual behaviors studied are grounded in theory/research, situation-dependent, and open to change, development, and training. POB tends to focus on four core capacities: self-efficacy, hope, optimism, and resiliency (Donaldson & Ko, 2010; Luthans, Avey, Avolio, Norman, & Combs, 2006). By focusing on measurable criteria that directly contribute to workplace performance improvement, POB scholarship moves beyond the idea of personal development as an end in itself, and seeks rather to demonstrate how developing these core capacities can directly impact workplace performance. Further, Youssef and Luthans (2007) argue that a POB approach and its emphasis on measurable "state-like" capacities more readily lends itself to empirical study, and to the fast pace of changes experienced in the contemporary workforce, than POS.

While there is still debate on whether these positive psychological capacities are "traits" or "states" or, as Luthans argues, "state-like," it is clear that trait characteristics, such as intelligence, can be effectively empirically evaluated by test-retest correlations (Conley, 1984). Citing research from Luthans, Avolio, Avey, and Norman (2007), Youssef and Luthans (2007) contend that there is less, although still significant, test-retest correlations for state-like positive psychological resource capacities. Thus we can best think of "state-like" positive psychological capacities as those that are open to development and training, and more likely to be influenced by changing organizational factors, while our "traits" are likely developed over our life span. Additionally, POS character strengths and virtues can be ends in themselves, rather than requiring a direct impact on organizational outcomes. Given these distinctions, this chapter focuses on the POB state-like psychological capacities of self-efficacy, hope, optimism, and resiliency outlined by Youssef and Luthans (2007). Since crisis situations are usually time-dependent, involving drastic organizational change and chaos, it is more likely that the positive capacities exhibited during crises are related to psychological "states" rather than "traits." To begin, we need to clearly define our four core capacities, beginning with self-efficacy.

Self-efficacy

With roots in Bandura's theory of social cognitive processing, self-efficacy has been found to be a positive psychology capacity that can be developed in the workplace through the experience of an employee of "mastering" various tasks, with an eye to increasing the level of task complexity (Luthans et al., 2006, p. 14). Bandura (1986) defines self-efficacy as "people's judgments of their capabilities to organize and execute courses of action required to attain designated types of performances" (p. 391). Bandura conceptualizes self-efficacy in three dimensions: magnitude, strength, and generality. Magnitude refers to a person's belief regarding the level of task difficulty they feel they can attain. Strength refers to the conviction one has regarding magnitude and is gauged from strong to weak. Generality is the degree to which one's expectations can be generalized across various situations (Gist, 1987). Within the POB literature, the concept of self-efficacy, or confidence, is defined by Stajkovic and Luthans (1998) as "an individual's convictions (or confidence) about his or her abilities to mobilize the motivation, cognitive resources, and courses of action needed to successfully execute a specific task within a given context" (p. 66). In their 1998 meta-analysis, they examined 114 previous studies and determined that there is a positive, significant correlation between self-efficacy and performance outcomes. Stajkovic and Luthans (1998) suggest that "employees who perceive low self-efficacy are likely to cease their efforts prematurely and fail at the task"

(p. 66). Combs and Luthans (2007) examined the role of self-efficacy in diversity training and concluded that a focus on self-efficacy increased the likelihood that employees would return to the workplace and promote diversity initiatives.

Hope

Snyder et al. (1991) define hope as a two-pronged cognitive construct, built from the aspects of "pathways" and "agency." Pathways reflect an individual's self-perception of their capability to secure a plausible route to their personal goals. The second aspect, agency, relates to an individual's motivation (and self-efficacy) to proceed toward goal achievement. Working in concert, these two components provide individuals with the means and motivation to achieve their personal goals. According to Peterson et al. (2009), "those lower in hope lack the ability to conceive of strategies to meet goals and to overcome obstacles and the motivation to pursue the strategies that lead to goal achievement" (p. 350). POB scholars argue that hope can be developed as an individual psychological capacity by challenging employees to reach for new or higher goals, assisting individuals in developing coping mechanisms and developing alternative pathways/alternative goals when routes to goal achievement are blocked (Luthans et al., 2006). According to Youssef and Luthans (2006), hope "allows blockages or problems to be perceived as challenges and learning opportunities" (p. 779).

Optimism

Optimism as a trait is the generalized expectation of an individual that good things will happen, despite potentially adverse circumstances (Carver & Scheier, 1999). Those possessing the trait of optimism tend to focus on the good. Optimism has been demonstrated to have a positive impact on work performance (Luthans et al., 2005). The optimist differs in their interpretation of positive and negative events from those low in this psychological resource. Seligman (1998) defines optimism as an "attributional style" that views positive events as permanent and negative events as temporary. Of particular interest to the communication scholar is that for Seligman, optimism is not simply viewed in these terms, but rather *explained*. Thus optimism is not only internal, but clearly measurable through individuals' communication.

Armstrong-Stassen and Schlosser (2008) examined the impact of optimism on organizational downsizing, demonstrating that optimism serves as a valuable resource during such stressful organizational situations.

Further, their research demonstrated that optimistic individuals were more likely to employ positive thinking and coping strategies. Their research suggests that generalized optimism positively predicts post-downsizing job performance. Armstrong-Stassen and Schlosser (2008) argue that high-optimism individuals are needed in today's turbulent work environment. Developing optimistic employees can contribute to a healthier work environment more able to cope with the sudden and oftentimes dramatic changes facing today's organizations.

Resiliency

Defining resiliency as "the capacity to modify responses to changing situational demands, especially frustrating or stressful encounters," Tugade and Frederickson (2004, p. 322) argue that one's ability to use positive emotions results in finding positive meaning in negative circumstances. As a result, resilient individuals tend to rebound more quickly from negative situations. In addition to the notion of "rebounding," resilience also allows for individual learning and growth in the midst of personal and organizational setbacks. Since resiliency is reactive, rather than proactive, the development of resiliency in individuals could be important in today's quickly changing work environments.

Positive Psychology and Organizational Crises

The positive psychological capacities of self-efficacy hope, optimism, and resiliency seem particularly necessary during times of organizational crises. Since no organization is immune to crises, the ability of an organization and its employees to utilize positive psychological capacities in times of organizational chaos seems a fruitful avenue of study. It is theorized here that cultivation of these positive psychological capacities prior to organizational crises can help organizations move past the shock and narrow-thinking that often accompanies crisis situations and more quickly engage in creative and positive crisis resolution. By weaving together traditional communication approaches to organizational crisis and positive psychology research, this chapter offers a new approach to crisis management with a long-term goal of not merely "surviving" an organizational crisis, but long-term "thriving" of individual employees and organizations.

Organizational crises, defined as "specific, unexpected and non-routine events or series of events that create high levels of uncertainty and threaten or are perceived to threaten an organizations' high priority goals" (Seeger, Sellnow, & Ulmer, 1998, p. 233) have been the focus of a significant and growing body of literature. Research has been conducted on the importance of constructing and revisiting crisis communication plans (Katz, 1987), the importance of preparing organizational executives to handle media (Seeger, 2006), how to apologize to organizational stakeholders (Ware & Linkungel, 1973) and strategies for repairing tarnished organizational images (Benoit, 1995). The bulk of crisis communication research focuses on problems and failures: what organizations have done badly, how crises have been poorly handled, and what public relations mistakes corporations have made (Small, 1991; Ulmer & Sellnow, 2000). Thus, crisis communication literature is stuck in its own version of a "disease" model, expending most research resources examining organizational deficits rather than organizational strengths.

However, research has been conducted that suggests a reframing of the dominant mode of thinking is in order. For example, according to Dutton and Jackson (1987), the ability of decision makers to cognitively process complex organizational issues such as crises is directly impacted by whether they fame the crisis as a threat or opportunity. Research conducted by Milliken (1990) demonstrates that framing issues as opportunities allows decision makers to feel more in control and less uncertain than when framing issues as threats. Ulmer et al. (2011) developed a crisis communication theory called the Discourse of Renewal that focuses on opportunities for growth that naturally occur during times of organizational crisis. Their theory calls for an organization's leaders to "exemplify communication that models optimism and commitment to actions that can resolve the crisis" (Ulmer et al., 2011, p. 213). During times of organizational crisis, the media and organizational stakeholders often focus on the role of the CEO. Seeger and Ulmer (2001) contend that during a crisis, the CEO is usually the designated spokesperson and "may also establish the moral tone for the crisis response" (p. 369). It is often the CEO who is expected to face the media, establish the facts of the crisis, make important judgment calls, and defend those decisions to stakeholders and company boards (Modzelewski, 1990). The media has increased its focus on CEOs in the last thirty years, prominently featuring them in news stories and books as celebrities in their own right (Useem, 2001; Zachary, 1997).

Scholar and business consultant Leslie Gaines-Ross studies the relationship between CEOs, their personal reputations, and their companies' success. Coining the term "CEO Capital," Gaines-Ross' book of the same name cites a 1998 poll of the general public indicating that a CEO's reputation accounted for 48 percent of a company's reputation. Gaines-Ross argues: "The CEO must come to terms with the idea of being the ultimate spokesperson for the organization, the embodiment of the brand, and the official storyteller who knits together the company's past, present, and future" (p. 39). Park and Berger (2004) argue that CEOs are the public face of a company, particularly during organizational crises, and as such warrant particular attention as the subject of crisis research.

Following in the "disease" based tradition, much crisis literature examines the mistakes made by CEOs during organizational crises and the resulting negative impacts. For example, former Exxon CEO Lawrence Rawl is often excoriated for his handling of the *Valdez* oil spill, in particular for his failure to publicize his personal trip to the spill site (Mozelewski, 1990) and his attempt to avoid responsibility by blaming Captain Joseph Hazelwood (Small, 1991). In examining the speeches of Philip Morris' CEO during the 1990s, researchers illustrate how the tobacco company subtly changed its message strategy away from health concerns and toward philanthropy in an attempt to be more widely perceived as socially responsible (de Fatima, Oliveira, & Murphy, 2009).

More recently, BP executive Tony Hayward was rebuked by public relations professionals and the general public alike in regard to the 2010 oil spill of the United States gulf coast. Hayward sent BP's public reputation into a tailspin when visiting Venice, Louisiana to survey damage and issue an apology, in which he stated: "The first thing to say is I'm sorry," he told reporters. "We're sorry for the massive disruption it's caused their lives. There's no one who wants this over more than I do. I would like my life back" ("BP Chief to Gulf Residents" 2010). It is apparent that negative exemplars demonstrating what not to do such as these are a key focus of crisis communication research.

However, within the crisis communication literature, a handful of positive, "exemplary" crisis responses from CEOs have been studied and applauded, such as the response of Tylenol's James Burke to the cyanide tampering that killed seven people in 1982, which *Fortune* magazine described as "the gold standard in crisis control" (Yang & Levenson, 2007). According to Seeger and Ulmer, two additional models of effective crisis management are CEO of Malden Mills' Aaron Feuerstein's response to the 1995 factory fire, where Feurerstein gained national recognition for the extraordinary devotion he demonstrated to his factory workers in Massachusetts after his textile manufacturing plant burned down, continuing to pay for both employee salaries and benefits during the rebuilding process, (Seeger & Ulmer, 2001; Ulmer, 2001) and Milt Cole's similar response to Cole Hardwoods' 1998 fire (Seeger & Ulmer, 2001). Cole's lumber mill burned for over six days, and was described as the largest fire in Indiana history, yet while the lumber mills were still burning, Cole announced he would continue paying employee salaries and benefits while the mill was being rebuilt. Seeger and Ulmer applaud these CEOs for their "virtuous" responses to their respective organizational tragedies. These exemplary cases involve a leader, usually a CEO, responding quickly and ethically to an organizational crisis. Both these CEOs exhibit what POS would call "positive deviance." In each of the crises, it would not have been unreasonable for either CEO to simply cash in the insurance and leave their places of business. However, both Feuerstein and Cole went "against the norm" in a positive way, rebuilding their businesses and inspiring their employees, and Cole Hardwoods went on to achieve record profits after their rebuilding efforts. The virtues of compassion, integrity, and altruism are seen in these cases to have positively impacted organizational commitment and performance.

By combining the insights gained from positive exemplars in crisis communication research with the offerings of positive organizational behavior (POB) literature, we gain a picture of CEO psychological capacities that are more likely to lead to positive outcomes during organizational crises. By examining whether or not CEOs can and should adopt a positive communicative framework during times of crisis, I hope to illuminate the intersections of crisis communication and the power of positive communication, expanding current thinking on effective organizational crisis management strategies.

Positive Psychology and CEOs

Although several studies have sought to link aspects of positive psychology to improved organizational life, to date, no research has been done focusing specifically on the role positive psychological capacities may play in crisis management. Nevertheless, there are a handful of studies that have explored the relationship between CEO performance and positive psychology which offer us a place to begin this investigation. Brockner and James (2008) investigate when executives view organizational crises as opportunities, stating "crises have the potential to be a catalyst for positive organizational change" (p. 95). Focusing on when executives transition from framing a crisis as a threat versus an opportunity, Brockner and James argue that in a crisis, decision makers tend to tighten control and rely on traditional ways of thinking in an attempt to reduce uncertainty. They propose that executives who are willing to engage in reflection and learning are more inclined to view organizational crises as opportunities to enact positive change.

Several scholars have sought to establish a connection between positive psychological capacities and the theory of transformational leadership. Bass' (1998) research on transformational leadership outlines four essential dimensions: charisma, inspirational motivation, intellectual stimulation and individualized consideration. Given the emphasis in transformational leadership on developing followers as full human beings, intuitively this connection appears warranted. Peterson, Walumbwa, Byron, and Myrowitz (2009) investigated the relationship between CEO positive psychological traits and transformational leadership, applying these transformational leadership dimensions to examine how the psychological resources of hope, optimism, and resiliency foster organizational change and inspire followers in both start-ups and more established firms.

Their research illustrates that CEOs rated as more hopeful, optimistic, and resilient are also rated (both in self-ratings and the ratings of their followers) as engaging in more transformational leadership behaviors. Further their research establishes a relationship between the positive psychological capacities of hope, optimism, and resiliency, and transformational leadership behaviors. Thus leaders' positive psychological capacities indirectly impacted organizational performance, with their transformational leadership behaviors, serving as a mediating factor. Of particular importance here is their finding that transformational leadership had a greater impact in start-up firms than established organizations. This is consistent with the argument of Bass, Avolio, Jung, and Berson (2003) that transformational leadership is more effective in chaotic, complex, or otherwise dynamic environments. Our few positive exemplars of CEOs in crisis situations, such as Feuerstein and Cole, are perhaps drawing on positive psychological capacities in order to enhance (and in terms of crises, restore and/or maintain) organizational performance. In order to examine the potential for positive psychology to enrich the crisis communication plans implemented (most often by CEOs) during times of organizational crisis, we turn now to the positive exemplar of CEO Aaron Feuerstein for insight.

The Case of Malden Mills

Henry Feuerstein founded Malden Mills, in Malden, Massachusetts in 1906 under the name Malden Knitting. Originally a textile manufacturing facility, Malden produced knitted clothing items such as sweaters and bathing suits ("The Many Lives of Malden Mills," n.d.). In 1956, the company, then led by Henry's grandson Aaron, moved to Lawrence, Massachusetts.

Following a 1981 declaration of bankruptcy, the Feuerstein family called for Aaron's removal from his position as Mill president. Aaron resisted, instead restructuring the mill, creating Polartec and Polarfleece, an apparel fabric developed from recycled plastic ("About Polartec," 2012). Clothing manufacturers including L.L. Bean, Land's End, and Patagonia, purchased Polartec, a synthetic, extremely warm, and lightweight material, in large quantities, for use in winter clothing and accessories. By 1995, Polartec sales were approximately $200 million, and the Mill and its four divisions employed roughly 3,100 workers. Feuerstein's operation was one of the few U.S. textile companies that did not move its operations overseas to secure less expensive labor. It looked as though Aaron had breathed new life into the family business.

Then, in December 1995, just two weeks before the Christmas holiday, Malden Mills experienced a devastating fire that left three key buildings of his eight-building complex in ruins, totaling over 600,000 square feet, and resulted in injuries to 36 workers (Goldberg, 1997). What makes this fire and type of organizational crisis—later deemed an "industrial accident"—unique is a combination of several factors. First, Malden Mills garnered deep loyalty from its employees as it was one of only a handful of textile manufacturers who had not moved operations overseas to trim labor expenses. As an example of their loyalty, although the mill workers were unionized, the mill had never experienced a strike. Feurerstein's employees are some of the highest paid in the textile industry. Second, the small New England town of Lawrence where the mill was located was dependent on the mill for economic survival. As of 2001, Lawrence was rated the 23rd poorest community in the country (Mcgrory, 2001). The Feuerstein family was well established in the community and had a reputation for fairness and generosity. "The community loves him very much and it's not hype and it's not the upper class, it's the people," said Julio Fernandez, a Malden Mills machine operator (Goldberg, 1997). Third, the mill was privately held by the family, and as such, was not beholden to a group of stakeholders. All these factors together helped set the stage for Aaron Feuerstein's extraordinarily positive and resilient response to the fire.

Fire insurance payments for the mill were expected to be in excess of $300 million, and many feared the then 69-year-old CEO would either take the money and retire, or finally succumb to outside pressures and move the mill operation overseas. Instead, upon learning of the fire and rushing to the mill, Feuerstein gathered his workers in a local high school gymnasium and said that the workers would all be kept on at full pay for the next 30 days (at a cost of over $13 million) and that they would even receive a Christmas bonus. He also continued providing their health insurance for another 30 days (Freedland, 1996). He also stated that the mill would definitely rebuild and seek to put all its employees back to work as soon as possible.

In September of 1997, 21 months after a fire rated the worst in Massachusetts in a century devastated the mill, Feuerstein dedicated a new $130 million factory having rehired almost all of his workers (Goldberg, 1997).

Speaking in 2000 at a seminar entitled "Money, Morality and the Marketplace," and reflecting upon the fire, Feuerstein said, "Before I got there, while I was there and afterwards, I was only thinking in terms of how to create a bigger business and restore my people to employment. That's all that was in my head" (Pasternak, 2000). Clearly even Feuerstein's initial reaction to the fire was to see it as an opportunity, rather than a threat. By 1 a.m. that morning, when it was clear the fire would consume most, if not all, of the factory buildings, Feuerstein said, "No, I'll not weep," repeating a favorite line from Shakespeare's *King Lear*. "We have to think creatively. There will be a Malden Mills tomorrow" (Butterfield, 1996).

The positive impact Feuerstein on not only his employees and the local community, but also on the national consciousness is hard to ignore. Feuerstein's actions were covered by both local and national media. He received 12 honorary degrees and he estimates that he received as many as 10,000 letters of support, many with cash or checks for the workers (Butterfield, 1996). Feuerstein was hailed as a public icon of corporate responsibility; even President Clinton sent his congratulations on the mill's reopening. The fire at Malden Mills has been covered by the media, featured in a *Harvard Business Review* case study, and studied by public relations professionals, but to date has not been examined for the insights positive psychology brings to this incredible story.

It is clear that Feuerstein had several of the key positive psychological capacities. Had he not had the confidence (self-efficacy) in himself to rebuild, the story could have ended that awful December night. Feuerstein possessed both optimism and resilience, which allowed the mill to weather the setbacks that inevitably accompanied the rebuilding. As Youssef and Luthans (2006) suggest, hope is necessary to overcome obstacles, without which Feurestein might never have chosen to rebuild, opting instead for an easy retirement. It seems intuitive in retrospect to argue that examination of any successfully navigated organizational crisis would contain evidence of positive psychological capacities, but more research must be conducted to see if such case study observations can be empirically supported.

Directions for Future Research

While the time-sensitive and pressurized nature of organizational crises would make it difficult to do in real-time, there may be real benefit to using the recognized scales for measuring a CEOs levels of the main POB constructs of hope, optimism, and resiliency. One potentially fruitful avenue of future research would be to use the PsyCap measurement instrument to gauge these capacities in current CEOs. From their POB perspective, Luthans, Youssef and Avolio (2006) have developed a measure of psychological capital, referred to as PsyCap. PsyCap is an attempt to determine the positive psychological capacities of an individual across four dimensions: self-efficacy, hope, optimism, and resiliency. By using the PsyCap questionnaire, or PCQ, seeks to gauge the four core positive psychological capacities by six items with a resulting total score that indicates an individual's level of PsyCap. A meta-analysis of using 51 independent samples with a total of 12,567 employees reveals significant positive relationships between PsyCap and positive employee attitudes and behaviors, as well as several performance measures (Avey, Reichard, Luthans, & Mhatre, 2011). By gauging the level of these psychological capacities in CEOs (and possibly their employees) prior to the occurrence of an organizational crisis, we may be able to better assess the likelihood that an organizational crisis will be treated as an opportunity for growth and flourishing, rather than treated as a threat to be contained and minimized.

References

About Polartec. (2012). *Polartec*. Retrieved from http://www.polartec.com/about/

Armstrong-Stassen, M. A., & Schlosser, F. (2008). Taking a positive approach to organizational downsizing. *Canadian Journal of Administrative Sciences, 25*, 93–106.

Avey, J. B., Reichard, R. J., Luthans, F., & Mhatre, K. H. (2011). Meta-analysis of the impact of positive psychological capital on employee attitudes, behaviors, and performance. *Human Resource Development Quarterly, 22*, 127–152.

Bass, B. (1998). The ethics of transformational leadership. In J. Ciulla (Ed.), *Ethics: The heart of leadership* (pp. 169–192). Westport, CT: Praeger.

Bass, B. M., Avolio, B. J., Jung, D. I., & Berson, Y. (2003). Predicting unit performance by assessing transformational and transactional leadership. *Journal of Applied Psychology, 88*, 207–218.

Benoit, W. L. (1997). Image restoration discourse and crisis communication. *Public Relations Review, 23*, 177–186.

BP chief to Gulf residents: 'I'm sorry.' (2010, May 30). Retrieved from http://articles.cnn.com/2010-05-30/us/gulf.oil.spill_1_oil-spill-heavy-oil-dudley?_s=PM:US

Brockner, J., & James, E. H. (2008). Toward an understanding of when executives see crisis as opportunity. *The Journal of Applied Behavioral Science, 44*, 94–115.

Butterfield, B. (1996, September 8). What flames could not destroy: Faith, loyalty inspire mill owner to rebuild from ashes and rubble. *The Boston Globe*, p. A1.

Carver, C. S., & Scheier, M. F. (1999). Optimism. In C. R. Snyder (Ed.), *Coping: The psychology of what works* (pp. 182–204). New York: Oxford University Press.

Conley, J. J. (1984). The hierarchy of consistency: A review and model of longitudinal findings on adult individual differences in intelligence, personality, and self-opinion. *Personality and Individual Differences, 5*, 11–25.

de Fatima Oliveira, M., & Murphy, P. (2009). The leader as the face of a crisis: Philip Morris' CEO's speeches during the 1990s. *Journal of Public Relations Research, 21*(4), 361–380.

Diagnostic and Statistical Manual of Mental Disorders (2000). Washington, DC: American Psychological Association.

Donaldson, S. I., & Ko, I. (2010). Positive organizational psychology, behavior, and scholarship: A review of the emerging literature and evidence base. *The Journal of Positive Psychology, 5*, 177–191.

Dutton, J. E., & Jackson, S. (1987). Categorizing strategic issues: Links to organizational action. *Academy of Management Review, 12*, 76–90.

The essence of positive organizational scholarship: Unlocking the generative capabilities in human communities. (n.d.). Retrieved from Center for Positive Organizational Scholarship Web site: http://www.bus.umich.edu/Positive/Center-for-POS/What-is-POS.htm

Freedland, J. (1996, March 25). Caring tycoon hailed as US stakeholder hero. *The Guardian*, p. 9.

Gable, S. L., & Haidt, J. (2005). What (and why) is positive psychology? *Review of General Psychology, 9*, 103–110.

Gaines-Ross, L. (2003). *CEO capital: A guide to building CEO reputation and company success*. New York: Wiley.

Goldberg, C. (1997, September 16). A promise is kept: Mill reopens. *The New York Times*, p. A14.

Katz, A. R. (1987). Ten steps to complete crisis planning. *Public Relations Journal, 43*, 46–47.

Linley, P. A., Harrington, S., & Garcea, N. (2010). Finding the positive in the world of work. In P. A. Linley, S. Harrington, & N. Garcea (Eds.), *Oxford handbook of positive psychology and work* (pp. 3–9). New York: Oxford University Press.

Luthans, F. (2002). The need for and meaning of positive organizational behavior. *Journal of Organizational Behavior, 23*(6), 695–706.

Luthans, F. (2003). Positive organizational behavior (POB): Implications for leadership and HR development and motivation. In R. M. Steers, L. W. Porter, & G. A. Begley (Eds.), *Motivation and leadership at work* (pp. 187–195). New York: McGraw-Hill/Irwin.

Luthans, F., Avey, J., Avolio, B. J., Norman, S. M., & Combs, G. M. (2006). Psychological capital development: Toward a micro-intervention. *Journal of Organizational Behavior, 27*, 387–393.

The many lives of Malden Mills. (n.d.). *Boston.com*. Retrieved from http://www.boston.com/business/gallery/maldenmillshistory?pg=5

Mcgrory, M. (2001, December 20). A CEO who lives by what's right. *The Washington Post*, p. A3.

Milliken, F. J. (1990). Perceiving and interpreting environmental change: An examination of college administrators' interpretation of changing demographics. *Academy of Management Journal, 33*, 42–63.

Modzelewski, J. (1990). "What would I do?" CEOs consider corporate crises. *Public Relations Quarterly, 35*, 12–14.

Mroz, D., & Quinn, S. (2010). Positive organizational scholarship leaps into the world of work. In P. A. Linley, S. Harrington, & N. Garcea (Eds.), *Oxford handbook of positive psychology and work* (pp. 251–264). New York: Oxford University Press.

Park, D., & Berger, B. K. (2004). The presentation of CEOs in the press, 1990–2000: Increasing salience, positive valence, and a focus on competency and personal dimensions of image. *Journal of Public Relations Research, 16*, 93–125.

Pasternak, J. (2000, September 20). When his past went up in flames, he redesigned his future. *National Post*, p. C09.

Peterson, C., & Seligman, M. E. P. (2004). *Character strengths and virtues: A handbook and classification*. New York: Oxford University Press.

Peterson, S. J., Walumbwa, F. O., Byron, K., & Myrowitz, J. (2009). CEO positive psychological traits, transformational leadership, and firm performance in high-technology start-up and established firms. *Journal of Management, 35*, 348–368.

Quick, J. C., & Macik-Frey, M. (2007). Healthy, productive work: Positive strength through communication competence and interpersonal interdependence. In D. L. Nelson & C. L. Cooper (Eds.), *Positive organizational behavior* (pp. 3–8). Thousand Oaks, CA: Sage.

Seeger, M. W. (2006). Best practices in crisis communication: An expert panel process. *Journal of Applied Communication Research, 34*, 232–244.

Seeger, M. W., Sellnow, T. L., & Ulmer, R. R. (1998). Communication, organization, and crisis. In M. E. Roloff (Ed.), *Communication yearbook:* Vol. 21 (pp. 231–275). Thousand Oaks, CA: Sage.

Seligman, M. E. P., & Csikszentmihalyi, M. (2000). Positive psychology: An introduction. *American Psychologist 55*, 5–14.

Small, W. (1991). Exxon Valdez: How to spend billions and still get a black eye. *Public Relations Review, 17*, 9–26.

Snyder, C. R., Harris, C., Anderson, J. R., Holleran, S. A., Irving, L. M., Sigmon, S. T. . . & Hareney, P. (1991). The will and the ways: Development and validation of an individual differences measure of hope. *Journal of Personality and Social Psychology, 60*, 570–585.

Stajkovic, A., & Luthans, F. (1998). Social cognitive theory and self-efficacy: Going beyond traditional motivational and behavioral approaches. *Organizational Dynamics, 26*, 62–74.

Tugade, M. M., & Fredrickson, B. L. (2004). Resilient individuals use positive emotions to bounce back from negative emotional experiences. *Journal of Personality and Social Psychology, 86*, 320–333.

Useem, J. (2001, February 19). Most admired: Who is this man? *Fortune, 143*(4), 97–101.

Ware, B. L., & Linkungel, W. A. (1973). They spoke in defense of themselves: On the generic criticism of apologia. *Quarterly Journal of Speech, 59*, 273–283.

Wright, T. A. (2003). Positive organizational behavior: An idea whose time has truly come. *Journal of Organizational Behavior, 24*, 437–442.

Yang, J. L., & Levenson, E. (2007, May 28). Getting a handle on a scandal. *Fortune, 155*(10), 20.

Youssef, C. M., & Luthans, F. (2007). Positive organizational behavior in the workplace: The impact of hope, optimism, and resilience. *Journal of Management, 33*, 774–800.

Zachary, G. P. (1997, September 3). Faces of the '90s: CEOs are stars now, but why? And would Alfred Sloan approve? *The Wall Street Journal*, p. A1.

• CHAPTER FOURTEEN •

Communication Joy: Print Journalists and the Experience of Flow

Janet Fulton
University of Newcastle, Australia

Flow has been identified as a positive experience that leads to happiness and well-being (Csikszentmihalyi, 1997) with well-being recognized as a core feature of positive psychology (Donaldson, Csikszentmihalyi, & Nakamura, 2011). Experiencing flow in the workplace has been identified as enhancing employees' job satisfaction (Ko & Donaldson, 2011) leading to fulfillment in their work but there have also been a number of studies demonstrating how productivity in a workplace can improve if employees experience flow in their work process (Csikszentmihalyi, 2004; Demerouti, 2006; Nielsen & Cleal, 2010). Ko and Donaldson (2011) suggest that if a workplace provides support and resources to its employees, there is a higher likelihood of an increase in flow, which has "the potential for improving employee job satisfaction, motivation, and job performance" (p. 149), thus improving productivity in the workplace. This chapter applies these ideas to print journalism and discusses how the provision of structures in a workplace, or institution to connect the term to positive psychology, provides journalists with a work environment that supports them during their creative process, and when journalists learn these structures and use them a state of flow may be achieved.

Seligman contends that the institutions of "democracy, strong family, and free press" (2002, p, xiii) are crucial for the well-being of individuals, institutions and communities. If Seligman's contention is correct, it is timely to examine the institution of the press and how it can support the well-being of its employees. Burke and Matthiesen (2004) examined the experience of flow among Norwegian journalists and this chapter discusses these ideas in relation to the domain of print journalism in Australia.

With all the gloomy predictions about the demise of print journalism, it is encouraging to discover that there is positive motivation within print journalists' work practices: there are journalists who love what they do. In Australian print journalism, there is, in a relative sense, little financial reward for the majority of journalists (Solly, Isbister, & Birtles, 2007). The industry is considered to be in turmoil (MEAA, 2008). New technology and media platforms are eroding traditional journalistic values. Its practitioners are accused of sensationalism and celebrity-driven reporting, and journalism regularly lists among the least trusted professions (Roy Morgan Research, 2009). Gardner, Csikszentmihalyi, and Damon (2001), writing from a North American perspective, claim that journalism is a profession in crisis:

> many practitioners feel that it is difficult to honor the precepts of the domain, their field is wracked by tension, the stakeholders are threatening the core values and the principal roles, and the future may well hold even worse tidings. (p. 35)

With such a negative work environment in these national contexts, the question can be asked: What motivates journalists to continue to do what they do?

This chapter contends that Mihaly Csikszentmihalyi's concept of *flow* (1991), where individuals are so absorbed in what they are doing that they lose track of time, is experienced by journalists. It can be argued that flow, and the feeling it generates, is one of the motivations that encourage journalists to produce creative work within the challenges of journalism. However, the chapter will also demonstrate that flow does not occur in a vacuum, but is experienced when a journalist, as an active agent, learns and interacts with the structures of the system of print journalism to produce texts. While it would seem that the structures journalists must interact with to produce their work could stifle enjoyment, this chapter contends that learning and internalizing these very structures means journalists' practices become intuitive or automatic, enabling a journalist to enter a state of flow. These structures include the rules and procedures of the domain of print journalism and the publication a journalist works for, as well as the preferences of a social field and the support this social field provides to journalists. By learning these structures, journalists increase their skill level to meet the challenges of producing creative texts. A journalist experiencing flow (during writing) can contribute to a positive communication experience for both the journalist and the audience as well as a positive work environment.

The information used in this chapter is derived from a larger research project that examined how print journalists in Australia produce, or create, their work by interacting with cultural, social and individual structures. The project used semi-structured interviews, observation, document and artifact analysis, and secondary sources to gather data. The data analyzed are from interviews conducted in 2007/2008 with 36 newspaper and magazine journalists and editors from a range of Australian publications and the observation of three newsrooms that took place in 2009/2010. One of the outcomes of the research was how the social and cultural structures provided by the domain of journalism as well as the journalists' workplaces enabled these journalists to produce creative outcomes but also enabled them to enter a state of flow.

According to Csikszentmihalyi (1997), creativity occurs when an individual learns from a domain of knowledge, produces a variation to that knowledge, and presents it to a social field that verifies that the variation is novel and appropriate. Moreover, Csikszentmihalyi (2003) states that motivation is one of the factors an individual needs to possess in order to produce a creative contribution. In what follows, the systems model developed by Csikszentmihalyi is explained and applied to the domain of print journalism including an account of the "structures" of the system of print journalism. This is followed by a brief discussion on motivation in the context of creativity research as well as an introduction to flow and how flow applies in a journalistic context. Finally, there are examples of flow in print journalism drawn from the data collected during the research, examples of how the cultural, individual and social structures of print journalism can enable a journalist to enter a flow state, and a discussion of how organizations can provide an environment where journalists are able to enter a state of flow and thus increase their well-being and enjoyment in their work.

Creativity

Csikszentmihalyi (1997) argues that creativity can be found when three elements in a system interact: a *domain* of knowledge (the cultural structure), an *individual* who understands and uses that knowledge to produce a novel change, and a *field* (the social structure) that understands the domain and uses that knowledge to judge the individual's contribution as novel and appropriate. The contribution is then included in the domain for other individuals to draw on in their own practice. All three elements, person, field, and domain, are equally important in producing creativity.

One of Western culture's creativity myths is that an individual must have freedom to be able to produce novel products and structures are seen to limit, or constrain, creativity (Sawyer, 2006). However, research has discounted this contention and found that structures can also enable creative practice (Giddens, 1984; Wolff, 1993). Journalism researcher Herbert Gans (1980) claimed that if journalists learn the structures inherent in journalism they can write without needing to consciously think about what is required; they are able to concentrate on the core activity, that is, doing journalism. Each of the three elements in the systems model provides structures that enable a journalist to "do without thinking." Gans' claims can also be applied at a micro-level with an organization's structures consisting of both cultural and social elements that need to be learnt by journalists but Gans' claims can also be applied in any work environment: an individual is more likely to work at an optimal level if the workplace's structures are known.

The domain is the cultural structure of the system and includes the knowledge, rules, conventions, techniques, guides, and procedures an individual interacts with in producing a creative contribution and these structures must be learned before a variation can be made. As Sawyer (2006) explains,

> creativity researchers think of the domain as a kind of creativity language. Of course, you have to learn a language before you can talk; it's impossible to communicate without sharing a language. In the same way, it's impossible to create anything without the shared conventions of a domain. (p. 137)

The creativity language of print journalism includes, for example, rules that govern how a story is written (language, style, and length); formal State laws such as defamation; guidelines such as ethical obligations; ideological principles such as truth in reporting; and, procedures such as knowing a publication's requirements on how to submit a story. The domain also includes "all of the created products that have been accepted by the field in the past" (Sawyer, 2006, p. 125). It is the understanding of these structures of the domain and, on a micro-level, the familiarity with the expectations of the organization that enables journalists to create their work.

The field is the social structure of the system and is constituted by what have been called the *gatekeepers* (Csikszentmihalyi, 1997) to the domain. It is the field's role to recognize and accept valuable contributions. The field can be thought of as all the people who can affect the decision as to what contributions are to be included in the domain (e.g., other journalists, editors, deputy editors, sub-editors, chiefs-of-staff, media owners, and the audience). The individual must learn "the criteria of selection, the preferences of the field" (Csikszentmihalyi, 1997, p. 47) to work effectively with that field. The support and resources that the field of journalism provides in the work environment includes the following: "The field is a source for stories, other journalists are used as sounding boards, senior members of the field are mentors and teachers, management provides training courses, there is an awards system and a journalist's work is edited before publication" (Fulton, 2011, p. 5).

The other element in the system is the individual who is the producer of a variation. Csikszentmihalyi (1997) contends that it is an individual's background and personal qualities that provide the structures to assist in production as well as the individual's ability to internalize the rules of the domain and expectations of the field. Influences such as family structure, education, social class, cultural background, and work experience all contribute to an individual's ability for creative action as do talent, genetic predisposition, cognitive structures, and personality traits. Interaction with the domain and field of journalism also means these individual structures are constantly changing. Hirst and Patching (2005) provided an apt summary of the individual structures a journalist brings to the system when they wrote:

> Each day, in the newsroom, or out on a job, every news worker carries with them, as items in their 'tool-kit', a set of emotional and intellectual attitudes towards sources, their audience, and the news they report. This emotional and intellectual tool-kit has been gathered since early childhood—it's how they see the world, and will vary from journalist to journalist depending on their family background, their upbringing, their education, their friends, the area and environment in which they grew up, etc. (p. 29)

Motivation

A number of researchers agree that motivation is a vital factor in creativity (Csikszentmihalyi, 1997; Evans & Deehan, 1988; Sternberg, 2003). Early research on the role of motivation and creativity seemed to conclude that intrinsic motivation (i.e., "the motivation to engage in some activity primarily for its own sake"), and not extrinsic motivation (i.e., "the motivation to engage in some activity primarily in order to achieve some external goal"), promoted creativity (Amabile & Tighe, 1993, p. 15). Amabile and Tighe concluded initially that extrinsic motivation hindered creativity and found five inhibitors to a creative outcome: reward, evaluation, surveillance, time constraints, and competition. Notably, journalism is an industry that is based on extrinsic rewards: journalists work for money; the audience and other members of the field evaluate their work; their work process is subject to scrutiny throughout the production process; there are tight deadlines; and, they work in a highly competitive environment in both workplace relations and industry expectations. Yet, journalists produce articles on a regular, if not daily, basis.

In recognition of these and similar problems, later studies by Amabile and others (Collins & Amabile, 2003; Dacey & Lennon, 1998; Eisenberger & Shanock, 2003) recognized that both could motivate a creative producer. A further observation is that if an activity is intrinsically *rewarding*, this is what provides the motivation to produce (Csikszentmihalyi & Csikszentmihalyi, 1988). Martindale (1989) provided the following reflection: "Indeed, if intrinsic rewards alone were important to creative people, it would be difficult to explain why scientists would bother to publish their findings and why artists would exhibit and sell their paintings" (p. 224).

Flow

The challenge in reaching a consensus about motivation led Csikszentmihalyi (1991, 1997, 1988) to suggest that the motivation to continue doing something is generated because an individual experiences *flow*, when a person is so involved in what they are doing that time seems to fly, and the feeling flow generates motivates a person to continue with an activity.

Csikszentmihalyi's (1993) early research into happiness set out to discover why people continued to pursue an activity when fame and money were not the prime motivation and he discovered it was because of the feeling of enjoyment that came from engaging with the activity. He called this feeling *flow,* or "autotelic experience" (1988, p. 29). When flow is experienced, "there is the rush of well-being, of satisfaction that comes when the poem is completed or the theorem is proved" (Csikszentmihalyi, 1997, p. 123) or, in a journalistic context, the satisfaction in producing a well-written article. Csikszentmihalyi (1991) describes flow as:

> a sense that one's skills are adequate to cope with the challenges at hand, in a goal directed, rule-bound action system that provides clear clues as to how well one is performing. Concentration is so intense that there is no attention left over to think about anything irrelevant, or to worry about problems. Self-consciousness disappears, and the sense of time becomes distorted. An activity that produces such experiences is so gratifying that people are willing to do it for its own sake, with little concern for what they will get out of it, even when it is difficult, or dangerous. (p. 71)

Flow occurs when the level of challenge of a task is equal to the level of a practitioner's skill. If the skill level increases, typically through practice, boredom will set in and to return to the state of flow, the individual must look for greater challenges. Alternatively, if the challenges increase, the individual will feel anxious and must improve skill levels to enter the flow channel.

To apply these ideas to journalism, it can be seen that if a journalist learns the "skills" that are provided by the system, that is, knowledge from the domain and field, and works at a level that is commensurate with those skills, a journalist could feasibly enter the flow channel. But, a journalist must also continue to find challenges within the work environment or risk boredom. On the other hand, when a journalist is expected to write without adequate knowledge of the expectations of the field or domain, anxiety will most likely occur and this distraction may lead to a less optimum outcome.

Like any employee of an organization, not all journalistic endeavors are positive; as positive psychologist Christopher Peterson (2006) states, "everyone's life has peaks and valleys and positive psychology does not deny the valleys" (p. 4) and it is possible for journalists to be overwhelmed by the rules of the domain and the expectations of the field and perceive them as constraints rather than enablers, which can lead to work that is less than satisfactory. Amabile and Tighe (1993) label this process *satisficing*. By this term they mean, "Ceasing engagement in a task prior to achievement of the ultimate goal ... doing the task 'well enough' by simply giving a response that is satisfactory, sufficient to meet demands or requirements" (p. 20). Thus, certain conditions in the workplace, such as unclear goals, limited feedback, challenges that do not match employees' skills, a lack of autonomy, and rigid time constraints, can be an obstacle to achieving a flow state and result in a less than satisfactory outcome (Csikszentmihalyi, 2004).

In order to understand the process of flow in journalists' work practices and how the publications these journalists work for enable or constrain the possibility of flow in the workplace, the respondents in this research were asked what motivated them to continue writing and their answers are discussed briefly in the next section. However, another question was: 'Have you ever been so involved in writing that you lose track of time?' In other words, had the journalists in this study ever experienced flow? The following section applies Csikszentmihalyi's proposals about flow to journalists and their workplaces, that is, newsrooms and magazine editorial offices, and provides examples of how a journalist, as active agent, can use the structures of the system of print journalism to assist in achieving flow, thus providing a feeling of well-being and satisfaction in the work process. It is important to keep in mind, however, that many of the following examples and explanations can also be applied in workplaces other than newsrooms.

Flow in the Workplace

When practitioners love their work, they are highly likely to be motivated to produce a creative outcome (Collins & Amabile, 2003). Responses from within this journalistic sample indicated that the respondents loved their work: "passionate about writing," "really enjoy writing," "it's fun," "it's exciting," "I love doing it," and "I love the challenge." Most of the sample in this study loves their work with J17[1] saying: "I don't think you'll find many journalists who don't really love being a journalist. It's one of those things that people really fall in love with as a profession." When journalists in this cohort were asked about what motivates them to continue working as journalists, responses varied from wanting to tell peoples' stories to getting a "buzz" out of talking to people to a love of the English language. But the largest response to that question was how much they loved to write. J8, for example, said he loved to write and loved public affairs and so the journalism profession suited him. Researcher and journalist David Conley (2006) described journalism as, "one of the greatest professions on earth, so good at times that being paid to do it seems like a bonus" (p. 435), a sentiment agreed with by J15:

> I would have to say that there have been times where I've been in a situation where I have been so exhilarated and enjoyed it so much, I've had to stop and think, 'Gee, I'm being paid for this!'

While a love of the process of journalism can provide motivation to continue working and assists in enabling a journalist to reach a state of enjoyment, there were also direct references within the data that indicated that journalists can lose track of time and enter a flow state:

> most weeks at some stage I'll look up and go, 'Christ it's three o'clock and I haven't had lunch yet'. Most weeks at some point I'll go, 'Oh my God, I've got to go to the loo [toilet] *right now* or I'm going to wet my knickers' [underpants]. And somehow in the last hour and a half I haven't noticed that fact but now it's gotten to the point where I've reeeeally got to go to the loo. (J6)

J15 described his writing process and it fittingly sums up the feeling of flow and the satisfaction it can provide:

> It [writing] is hard but yes I do [love it]. I think everyone does this when they're creating, in a creative mode, you struggle up this slope of research and preparation and planning and you start writing and you're still climbing. And you reach a plateau where you're in a different world and time is stretched and compressed, but it's hard. It's not pleasant being up there all the time because you're fighting chaos;

you're trying to bring this order and it's very difficult. And you finish it and come down off the plateau and three weeks later I read the published article and I think, 'God, did I write that! That's amazing! How did I write that?'

J15's description demonstrates how important experience, preparation, and knowledge are in the production of a story and when other responses about losing track of time are analyzed, it is also possible to recognize the structures that journalists interact with, thus providing evidence of the importance of knowing and understanding the traditions and conventions of the domain and the requirements of the field. For example, when J17 was asked whether she had ever become so absorbed in a story that she lost track of time, her initial response was, "not often. I mean, I find writing really painful; I find it excruciating." However, she did continue by saying:

> There's the anxiety and fear about the deadline and at some point the anxiety grows greater than the desire to procrastinate. Or the fear, or the actual horror, of writing and that's when I start writing—when that fear is big enough. And actually, what the weird thing is, when I'm actually really immersed in it then time does go past. And sometimes the days seem interminable when you just don't want to write the story and I'm always saying to myself, 'If you would just do it the time would fly by!' And it's funny I can, I'll often, not often but if I'm writing well, I'll look up at the clock on the screen and three hours have passed and I don't remember it. I had a lovely deputy editor here, she's now back in England, and she used to call it being in the zone.

When the theory of flow was explained to J17, that is, if the level of preparation and the level of experience are equal a state of flow can be achieved, she described how the theory applied to her work processes: "Isn't that interesting? And that would probably explain why it doesn't happen all the time because of course there are variations in my levels of preparation or stress levels or whatever." J17's comments about her knowledge preparation and individual preparation place her experiences firmly within the premise underlying this chapter: interacting with and working within the structures of the systems model can lead to a flow experience.

J17's earlier reference to being "in the zone" also indicates a flow state as this phrase has been used to describe autotelic experience, particularly in sports (see, for example, Houge Mackenzie, Hodge, & Boyes, 2011). Its use is typical of the way journalists working in the observed newsrooms in this study described the feeling of flow. When questioned, one newsroom journalist said she went into a "zone" to block out noise. This enabled her to write an article quickly. A junior reporter (cadet) in one of the observed newsrooms said she found it "very hard work" to write when she first started in the newsroom but she had learnt to "zone out," a comment agreed with by another journalist involved in the conversation. The cadet's experience illustrates that an increase in knowledge both about her work processes and the workplace has led to a more optimal outcome. Observations in the three newsrooms showed that journalists often wrote in a newsroom that had ringing telephones, chatting journalists, phone interviews happening, and, in the smaller newsrooms, a public that regularly visited. The journalists observed in these situations did not seem to hear the noise. These observations revealed that journalists showed concentration when they were writing a story or thinking about what to write, but were able to quickly bring their attention back if required such as if their phone rang or their name was called. If their attention was not needed, for example when the journalist at the next desk was talking, they could still concentrate on their own work.

In line with the thesis put forward in this chapter, it is also possible to find indications within the data gathered that clearly show how the three elements in the systems model—the domain, the individual, and the field—provide structures that enable a journalist to create and the opportunity to enter the flow channel. J20 summarized this idea in regards to journalism when he made the comment that working within parameters is an important part of the creative process, but they can also lead to a flow experience:

> It [flow] is, briefly, an intensely creative process. I mean you're working within limited, defined parameters and with certain materials but it is, nonetheless, very intense and once you achieve that mental state, it's a good state, because it means you're coming up with stuff.

To apply J20's ideas in a practical sense, one of the "parameters" of the domain is the deadline. According to Amabile (1993), time constraints are one of the five extrinsic motivators that should inhibit productivity and it has been argued that deadlines are one of the largest constraints a journalist must contend with (Machin & Niblock, 2006; Sheridan Burns, 2001; Tiffen, 2006). On saying this, though, others have recognized that some journalists actually thrive under deadlines (Meunier, 2004) and use the deadline as an enabling factor. As E3 noted, "You have to be ever mindful of the deadline, keep your editor informed of progress, but in pressure situations the zone is the only place to be."

Research into creativity and an organization's effect on an individual has found a complicated relationship between deadlines and creativity because an individual's traits also need to be included in any examination (Hennessey & Amabile, 2010, p. 583). Therefore, it is also possible to find evidence of how an individual's "structures" or personal characteristics and background, can lead to a flow state for journalists. A Norwegian study investigating journalists and flow (Burke & Matthiesen, 2004) discovered that older journalists who had worked for longer in, and had more experience with, the industry were more likely to experience flow. Similar results were seemingly found within this study with journalists stating that as they gained more experience within the domain, their writing and work processes improved.

> I think it's the whole confidence thing. I think when you feel confident, and I feel a lot more confident now than I did probably even two or three years ago. Because you just feel like you have a kind of right to write the stories you want to. And you've got the experience and the expertise and so you don't second guess yourself; you don't think, 'Oh, is this the right way?' (J17)

However, others have argued that any individual may achieve a flow state if provided with work conditions such as clear goals, immediate feedback and a balance between skills and challenges (Csikszentmihalyi, 2004; Nakamura & Csikszentmihalyi, 2005). Burke and Mathieson (2004) failed to recognize the fundamental premise behind flow: flow occurs if the level of skill and the level of challenge are equal. In other words, a less experienced journalist may experience flow if members of the field allocate stories that are commensurate with the junior reporter's skill level. This contention was evident during newsroom observations. The earlier example of the newsroom cadet getting into "the zone" illustrates that even at a junior level, positive outcomes can occur if the field (for example, positions such as editor, news editor and chief-of-staff) recognizes a journalist's skill level and assigns articles accordingly.

The nature of journalism and the expectations of the field means that the two other conditions noted earlier, clear goals and immediate feedback, are also observable. For example, deadlines provide a clear goal for journalists, as do the expectations of an audience, a part of the field. The audience also provides feedback via letters, emails, and comments on news sites. At a more immediate level, journalists are given feedback by workmates including other journalists and senior staff. Focusing on the newsroom observations reported here, the editor in the second newsroom, as a senior member of the field, gave clear instructions to the editorial staff on the direction of the week's publication. The editor was involved in each section of the newspaper and was observed talking to journalists about their stories, issuing instructions on how to improve stories, accepting/rejecting suggestions regarding pictures and story ideas, and encouraging staff on what they had written. In addition, throughout each journalist's work process, senior editorial staff approached the journalists to provide feedback on the progress of their news stories.

Conclusion

The observations and interviews reported in this chapter demonstrate that despite the challenges that print journalists in Australia (and perhaps worldwide) are facing, it is still possible for journalists to enjoy the creative process of producing journalism and increase their sense of well-being and one of the motivations could be the enjoyment of entering a flow state. The data also demonstrated how the structures that journalists learn and interact with can enable a journalist to enter a flow state, leading to a more enjoyable experience in the workplace. These structures are provided in a broad context by the domain and field of journalism but, on a more immediate level, the institution a journalist works for also provides them. In a similar fashion to Ko and Stewart's (2011) contention, flow in the work environment can be enhanced if an organization provides the support and resources an employee requires.

As Seligman (2002) notes, the press, or journalism, is one of the institutions that should be examined to understand how institutions can enable well-being and happiness in its employees. What this chapter has illustrated is that it is possible to recognize the structures that are provided by the system of journalism and the organization a journalist works for and it is also possible to recognize how these structures can enable journalists to enter a state of flow. In other words, if journalists have knowledge of the rules, conventions, techniques, guides and procedures of the domain, understand the preferences of the field, and are aware of their own "tool-kit" (Hirst & Patching, 2005, p. 29), a state of flow could be achieved. Journalists' knowledge of these structures can support and enable creative production and provide the opportunity for a journalist to enter a flow state, thus providing a positive work experience.

However, what needs to be pointed out here is that these same ideas can be applied to any workplace. If an institution provides the organizational and social structures, and the employees learn and use these structures in their work practice, a flow state can be achieved. This can lead to an increase in job satisfaction and well-being for the employees but also to increased productivity in the workplace as well as an increase in the well-being of individuals, institutions, and communities.

Notes

1   Anonymity was a requirement of the research so each journalist was allocated a number (J1, J2, J3, etc.) as was each editor (E1, E2, E3, etc.). Each newsroom observed was also allocated a non-identifiable number (NR1, NR2, and NR3). Any information used from secondary data is attributed as it is on the public record.

References

Amabile, T., & Tighe, E. (1993). Questions of creativity. In J. Brockman (Ed.), *Creativity: The reality club 4* (pp. 7–28). New York: Simon and Schuster.

Burke, R., & Matthiesen, S. (2004). Correlates of flow at work among Norwegian journalists. *Journal of Transnational Management, 10*(2), 249–258.

Collins, M. A., & Amabile, T. M. (2003). Motivation and creativity. In R. J. Sternberg (Ed.), *Handbook of creativity* (pp. 297–312). Cambridge, UK: Cambridge University Press.

Conley, D. P., & Lamble, S. (2006). *The daily miracle: An introduction to journalism* (3rd ed.). Melbourne, Australia: Oxford University Press.

Csikszentmihalyi, M. (1991). *Flow: The psychology of optimal experience* (1st ed.). New York: Harper Collins.

Csikszentmihalyi, M. (1993). Activity and happiness: towards a science of occupation. *Journal of Occupational Science, 1*(1), 38–42.

Csikszentmihalyi, M. (1997). *Creativity: Flow and the psychology of discovery and invention* (1st ed.). New York: HarperCollins.

Csikszentmihalyi, M. (2003). Implications of a systems perspective for the study of creativity. In R. Sternberg (Ed.), *Handbook of creativity* (pp. 313–335). Cambridge, UK: Cambridge University Press.

Csikszentmihalyi, M. (2004). *Good business: Leadership, flow and the making of meaning*. London: Coronet.

Csikszentmihalyi, M., & Csikszentmihalyi, I. S. (1988). *Optimal experience: Psychological studies of flow in consciousness*. Cambridge, UK: Cambridge University Press.

Dacey, J. S., & Lennon, K. (1998). *Understanding creativity: The interplay of biological, psychological, and social factors* (1st ed.). San Francisco: Jossey-Bass.

Demerouti, E. (2006). Job characteristics, flow, and performance: The moderating role of conscientiousness. *Journal of Occupational Health Psychology, 11*(3), 266–280.

Donaldson, S. I., Csikszentmihalyi, M., & Nakamura, J. (2011). *Applied positive psychology: improving everyday life, health, schools, work, and society*. Hoboken, NJ: Taylor & Francis.

Eisenberger, R., & Shanock, L. (2003). Rewards, intrinsic motivation and creativity: A case study of conceptual and methodological isolation. *Creativity Research Journal, 15*(2 & 3), 121–130.

Evans, P., & Deehan, G. (1988). *The keys to creativity*. London: Grafton.

Fulton, J. (2011). Print journalism and the creative process: Examining the interplay between journalists and the social organisation of journalism. *Altitude: An E-journal of Emerging Humanities Work, 9*, 1–15.

Gans, H. J. (1980). *Deciding what's news*. New York: Vintage Books.

Gardner, H., Csikszentmihalyi, M., & Damon, W. (2001). *Good work: When excellence and ethics meet*. New York: Basic Books.

Giddens, A. (1984). *The constitution of society: Outline of the theory of structuration*. Berkeley: University of California Press.

Hennessey, B., & Amabile, T. M. (2010). Creativity. *Annual Review of Psychology, 61*(1), 569–598.

Hirst, M., & Patching, R. (2005). *Journalism ethics: Arguments and cases*. South Melbourne, Australia: Oxford University Press.

Houge Mackenzie, S., Hodge, K., & Boyes, M. (2011). Expanding the flow model in adventure activities: A reversal theory perspective. *Journal of Leisure Research, 43*(4), 519–544.

Ko, I., & Donaldson, S. I. (2011). Applied positive organizational psychology: The state of the science and practice. In S. I. Donaldson, M. Csikszentmihalyi, & J. Nakamura (Eds.), *Applied positive psychology: Improving everyday life, health, schools, work, and society* (pp. 137–154). Hoboken, NJ: Taylor & Francis.

Machin, D., & Niblock, S. (2006). *News production: Theory and practice*. London: Routledge.

Martindale, C. (1989). Personality, situation, and creativity. In C. R. Reynolds, E. P. Torrance, R. R. Ronning, & J. A. Glover (Eds.), *Handbook of creativity* (pp. 211–232). New York: Plenum Press.

MEAA. (2008). Life in the clickstream: The future of journalism. Retrieved from http://www.alliance.org.au/documents/foj_report_final.pdf

Meunier, J. (2004). *News writing as a schema-driven process: A proposed model*. Paper presented at the annual meeting of the International Communication Association, New Orleans, LA.

Nakamura, J., & Csikszentmihalyi, M. (2005). The concept of flow. In C. Snyder & S. J. Lopez (Eds.), *Handbook of positive psychology* (pp. 89–105). New York: Oxford University Press.

Nielsen, K., & Cleal, B. (2010). Predicting flow at work: Investigating the activities and job characteristics that predict flow states at work. *Journal of Occupational Health Psychology, 15*(2), 180–190.

Peterson, C. (2006). *A primer in positive psychology*. New York: Oxford University Press.

Roy Morgan Research. (2009). Image of 23/29 professions declines in 2009: Nurses most ethical—15 years in a row; advertisers hit new low of only 6%. Despite global financial crisis-bank managers unchanged at 33%. Retrieved from http://www.roymorgan.com/news/polls/2009/4387/

Sawyer, R. K. (2006). *Explaining creativity: The science of human innovation*. Oxford, UK: Oxford University Press.

Seligman, M. (2002). *Authentic happiness: Using the new positive psychology to realize your potential for lasting fulfillment*. Milsons Point: Random House Australia.

Sheridan Burns, L. (2001). Comfort or curse? In S. Tapsall & C. Varley (Eds.), *Journalism: Theory in practice* (pp. 23–39). South Melbourne, Australia: Oxford University Press.

Solly, R., Isbister, H., & Birtles, B. (2007). *Journalism: Jobs that make news*. Ultimo, N.S.W.: Career FAQs.

Sternberg, R. J. (2003). *Wisdom, intelligence, and creativity synthesized*. Cambridge, UK: Cambridge University Press.

Tiffen, R. (2006). Political economy and news. In S. Cunningham & G. Turner (Eds.), *The media and communications in Australia* (pp. 28–42). Crows Nest, Australia: Allen & Unwin.

Wolff, J. (1993). *The social production of art* (2nd ed.). London: Macmillan.

CHAPTER FIFTEEN

Happy Classrooms = Happier Students: Making the Case for Positive Communication in Education

Jenny Tatsak
Walsh College

Hollie D. Petit
Estes Park, Colorado

Perhaps in no institution or organization are the concepts of positive psychology and positive communication more salient than in the world of education. As a nation, Americans struggle with the perceived decline in both the quality of education and the performance of American students. Positive communication strategies offer the potential to address some of the root causes of this concern, while also contributing to the development of healthier and happier citizens.

First we explain how the pursuit of academic benchmarks such as grades or degrees is analogous to the pursuit of money in society at large. Research illustrates why this approach is both short-sighted and unsatisfying. We then argue that by applying principles of positive psychology in the educational environment and focusing on the process rather than the outcome, both teaching and student achievement can be enhanced. Finally, we review some specific positive psychology strategies and how they may be integrated into college communication studies curricula.

The Pursuit of Benchmarks

The United States is the epitome of an individualistic culture, and Americans are the epitome of a single-minded quest for personal achievement.

Americans strive for achievements, often in the form of outcome goals, success, money, prestige, and power because they are believed to bring happiness as the ultimate destination. These achievements, referred to as "benchmarks" throughout this chapter, are typically used in primary education as a point of comparison against which to measure a student's progress. At all stages of our education, and life in general, we understand success based on the aforementioned benchmarks of achievement. Despite the pervasiveness of our cultural mindset, benchmarks do not usually create sustainable happiness. Because of hedonic adaption, or the tendency of humans to "rapidly and inevitably adapt to good things by taking them for granted" (Seligman, 2002, p. 49), benchmarks produce only temporary happiness before becoming the norm. Yet individuals continue to seek enduring happiness only to find "the pursuit of goals that are intrinsic, authentic, approach-oriented, harmonious, activity-based, and flexible will deliver more happiness than the pursuit of goals that are extrinsic, inauthentic, avoidance-oriented, conflicting, circumstance-based, or rigid" (Lyubomirski, 2007, p. 215).

One of the most common benchmarks in American society is educational achievement such as earning a college degree. Although there are many reasons why students pursue a degree (urged by parents, friends, society, and educators; a belief it will lead to a good job and financial stability), earning a degree primarily for the benchmark or to reach other benchmarks (e.g., position, money, status) sends the message that college is about earning a degree rather than gaining an education. Educators, parents, and society in general encourage students to finish school and get good grades, so they can get a good job, make a good wage, and have all the good things that life has to offer. The implied message is happiness is in the distant future and "too often, the best years of our lives are spent getting ready to be happy" (Gotz, 1995, pp. 14–15). This approach emphasizes the destination (external product) over the journey (internal process) and happiness as the *reward* for attainment rather than a *cause* of it.

Lyubomirsky, King, and Diener (2005), in a cross-sectional analysis of literature about happiness, provide compelling evidence that happiness, or "the frequent experience of positive emotions" (p. 820), likely increases a person's potential for success in work, relationships, and health. This is not to say that happiness is the single cause of success, or that those who are happy are devoid of negative affect, but that happy individuals display a propensity toward success. For educators, this simply means that a focus on happiness, rather than benchmarks, could lead to success, and also that happiness is not dependent on the level of success one reaches in life.

If happiness should be encouraged in higher education, it is important to explain what it is and where it is most commonly found. Researchers frequently relate happiness to positive emotion. Gotz (1995) suggests that "happiness often means temperament; that is, a disposition to be cheerful, and, generally, to be unmoved or greatly disturbed by reverses of fortune. It also connotes mood, or frame of mind, as when we say we are 'feeling happy,' or 'feeling good'" (p. 3). Lyubomirsky (2007) refers to happiness as the "experience of joy, contentment, or positive well-being, combined with a sense that one's life is good, meaningful, and worthwhile" (p. 32). Peterson (2006) explains what is most likely to bring about an improved state of happiness:

> First, demographic factors like age, gender, ethnicity, education, and income....are all associated with happiness but at low levels.... Second, among the more-robust determinants of happiness are social or interpersonal factors—number of friends, marriage, extraversion, and gratitude....[Also] religiousness, leisure activities, and employment (although not income per se). . . .Third, several personality traits—optimism, extraversion, conscientiousness, self-esteem, internal locus of control (believing that you have control over what happens to you)—have moderate to strong correlations with avowed happiness, as do low scores on neuroticism. (pp. 93–94)

Notably, those aspects that bring a great degree of happiness are within an individual's sphere of control. While biology plays a role in an individual's happiness level, individual choice has proven highly significant as well (Lyubomirsky, 2007; Seligman, 2002). Additionally, numerous academic journals and popular books (e.g., *The How of Happiness* by Lyubomirski, *Positivity* by Fredrickson, *Authentic Happiness* by Seligman), provide philosophies and tools to help readers become happier people. With increased research and scholarly acceptance of positive psychology, integration of these principles into college curricula is not only feasible, but potentially engaging and enjoyable as well.

Communication programs in higher education are well positioned to integrate methods to increase happiness, positivity, and optimism into their programs because of their focus on relationships and messages. While the critical components of happiness studies appear to be a close match to communication, a review of scholarly literature shows very little research on happiness, or even positive psychology, as it relates to communication pedagogy. Consequently, we will use communication literature, in concert with seminal happiness and positive psychology research, to better understand how educational institutions are structured to promote the achievement of benchmarks, which do not lead to permanent happiness.

Then, we will explain specific strategies college educators can employ to encourage greater student happiness, or the experience of frequent positive emotion, in the classroom and beyond.

Unhappy Classrooms

There is a propensity for educators, as well as students, to look to the future for the rewards for their efforts; however, the rewards are elusive and fleeting. This way of thinking creates a habit of overlooking the potential for happiness that exists in the present moment. The hurried pace among many on campus, expressing a range of emotions from stress to panic, suggests that students are not savoring, or maximizing their "awareness of pleasure" and making a "deliberate attempt to make it last" (Peterson, 2006, p. 69). "When goals facilitate the enjoyment of our present experience, they indirectly lead to an increase in our levels of well-being each step of the way, as opposed to a temporary spike that comes with the attainment of a goal" (Ben-Shahar, 2007, pp. 70–71). Withholding happiness, until *some day* when a particular benchmark is achieved, creates a habit of postponing happiness.

Nowhere is this delayed gratification more apparent than in attitudes toward wealth and money. Ben-Shahar (2007) points out that students are misdirected about their educational pursuits; students are told that the "purpose of going to school is to get good grades so that he can secure his future. He is *not* told that he should be happy ... or that learning can be ... fun" (p. 16). Security is often equated with money. However, research shows that "rich people are, on average, only slightly happier than poor people" (Seligman, 2002, p. 49). Myers and Diener (1996) explain, "People have not become happier over time as their cultures have become more affluent. Even though Americans earn twice as much in today's dollars as they did in 1957, the proportion of those telling surveyors from the National Opinion Research Center that they are 'very happy' has declined from 35 to 29 percent" (p. 70).

Csikszentmihalyi (1999) explains why money does not bring happiness: (1) "Money raises expectations"; therefore, the bar of achievement gets set higher. (2) As a person achieves some benchmark, he or she compares the accomplishment to those who have the most; by comparison, the achievement seems small. (3) Money alone does not ensure happiness. Other factors typically bring happiness, "such as a satisfying family life, having intimate friends, having time to reflect and pursue diverse interests" (p. 823).

With an emphasis on benchmarks rather than an appreciation for learning, a student's education becomes a chore rather than a privilege. Ben-Shahar (2007) suggests that students often look at education as work, and the social bias against work—the belief that it is difficult and a necessary evil—sets up a standard that it should be disliked. The objective of going to college becomes earning a degree rather than learning, life enhancement, and enriching experiences like positive emotion and flow. This pattern can continue when reaching further benchmarks, like jobs, which can minimize future happiness.

Through the process of adaptation, the excitement that accompanies an achievement or acquisition dissipates and is replaced by a sense of normalcy. Like a child with a new toy, the novelty wears out. Despite the goal attained or the positive experience created, individuals typically return to the happiness set point that is normal for them. Lyubomirsky (2007) defines set point as the "characteristic potential for happiness throughout our lives" (p. 57), which is largely biologically determined. Many continue striving to reach a permanent elevated condition, but through misguided efforts find themselves on the hedonic treadmill. Seligman (2002) explains:

> As you accumulate more material possessions and accomplishments, your expectations rise. The deeds and things you worked so hard for no longer make you happy; you need to get something even better to boost your level of happiness into the upper reaches of its set range. But once you get the next possession or achievement, you adapt to it as well, and so on. (p. 49)

In a fashion similar to substance addiction, benchmarks often leave individuals unfulfilled and in need of increasing higher highs.

Education, Benchmarks, and Emotions

Historically, learning models privileged a cognitive perspective that do not account for the propensity and impact of emotions on the model. With the growth of attribution theory, and later achievement goal theory, the cognitive model of learning persisted (Schutz & Lanehart, 2002). However, Allen, Witt, and Wheeless (2006) studied the often unexplored relationship between emotions and cognition. They found an indirect relationship between emotions and cognitive processes with higher teacher immediacy to cause increased cognitive learning (Allen et al., 2006). Those students believed the teacher cared were more likely to learn.

Linnenbrink and Pintrich (2002) too recognized the impact of emotions and studied the links between the achievement goals emphasized and affect in the classroom. Their study was conceived and based on their observations:

> In particular, because perceptions of the classroom environment are thought to influence personal goal adoption, students in mastery-oriented classrooms should experience emotions such as happiness and elation as well as relief. In contrast,

students in performance-oriented classrooms may at times experience some positive affect such as happiness but also will be likely to experience negative affect such as anxiety, sadness, and anger. (p. 73)

The findings confirmed their observations. While some experienced elation as an effect of superior performance of a task, over time, performance-oriented students studied were less likely to be satisfied with their progression toward goals (Linnenbrink & Pintrich, 2002). Consequently, these students developed more negative feelings about school in general (Linnenbrink & Pintrich, 2002). While these emotions are fluid and complex, as evidenced in how they change from the positive emotions of perceived success in task performance to the negative emotions of performance-oriented students, we cannot deny that education is a landmine for emotions.

Individuals come to understand how to act, specifically, which emotions are preferred, based on our observations of others (Shutz & DeCuir, 2002). These comparisons are further situated within a social-historical context from a lifetime of observations (Shutz & DeCuir, 2002). Furthermore, the educational system encourages heightened comparisons based on high-stakes benchmarks of success, such as grades, retention rates, diplomas, and degrees. As a result of these comparisons, individuals regulate their performance and relentlessly pursue benchmarks based on their understanding of preferred achievements (Shutz & DeCuir, 2002).

This mind-set of evaluating success in terms of institutional benchmarks or in comparison to others may leave the student, and the educational system as a whole, dependent on the fear of failure and unrealistic comparisons, to motivate action. The strategic rhetoric of education serves to perpetuate existing power structures (Fassett & Warren, 2004). These strategic rhetorics are evident in the taken-for-granted labels used to identify students, and in turn, shape understanding. Fassett and Warren (2005) compare "at risk" to perceptions of race and gender which "becomes sedimented, normalized, and taken for granted. Our discipline's reification of this term only secures it as a hegemonic norm, recreating students' limitations even as we seek to assist them" (p. 253). The eventual result of this educational concentration on the negative with a higher propensity for stress, is that the individual begin to exhibit "battle-stations mode of thinking: the order of the day is to focus on what is wrong and then eliminate it" (Seligman, 2002, p. 39).

Although the flaws in our current educational system are pronounced in its embrace of the negative, educators have the power to enact the type of change that will profoundly impact education and transform the student. Emotions give individuals the drive to act and these emotions serve as motivators (Ben-Shahar, 2007). Educators can encourage positive thought and the expression of positive emotions to show students the path toward a happy life.

A Positive Classroom Is a Happy Classroom

Formal schooling usually involves learning *practical* skills to perform particular tasks effectively; this allows students to become effective in future jobs and productive citizens in society. Although practical skills are important, very little attention is given to *life* skills—learning to live a complete and happy life. For example, emotional intelligence, defined as the *"ability to monitor one's own and others' feelings and emotions, to discriminate among them and to use this information to guide one's thinking and actions"* (Salovey & Mayer, 1989 – 90, p. 189), is an important quality for not only landing a job, but being successful once in that position, but this skill is rarely emphasized. Furthermore, the emotional intelligence necessary for fruitful personal relationships is not often taught despite being an indicator of sustaining happiness. Like the value of emotional intelligence, knowing how to cultivate happiness within the self is a valuable life, health, and relational skill. Most people are not instructed how to be happy; they are left to figure it out on their own.

Encouraging happiness in the classroom, specifically in the form of positive emotion, has clear advantages. "Positive mood produces broader attention, more creative thinking, and more holistic thinking. This is in contrast to negative mood, which produces narrowed attention, more critical thinking, and more analytic thinking" (Seligman, 2011, p. 80). While negative or critical thinking is needed in some situations, Seligman (2011) argues that schools promote too much negative thinking and not enough positive. This is particularly true in higher education, where critical thinking is often a rubric in virtually every course development strategy and evaluation; unfortunately, evaluations of happiness, positive emotion, and well-being are not typical considerations.

Witt, Wheeless, and Allen (2004), in a meta-analysis of 81 studies of instructor verbal and non-verbal immediacy found that a student's emotional response to the content, instructor and learning environment impacts the quality and quantity of the information retained in the course. Enthusiastic teachers, those who engage the student and are positive about the learning environment are perceived favorably (Allen et al., 2006). These students believe an engaging and enthusiastic teacher cares about them; therefore, they are motivated to actively participate in the learning process (Allen et al., 2004). Most significant for instructors is the findings that confirmed an increased likelihood that this motivated student, engaged in the learning process because of the instructor's positive traits, has a greater likelihood to utilize the behaviors learned and to enroll in a similar course (Allen et al., 2004). Consequently, instructors have the potential to have a lasting impact on their students' perception of the learning process as well as the learning environment. Furthermore, communication instructors can positively impact their students' communication competency, by modeling enthusiastic and engaged communication, to have produced sustaining change.

Strategies for Encouraging Happiness in the Classroom

In the remainder of this chapter, we offer specific strategies that communication educators can employ to encourage greater happiness within college students. These strategies, like most happiness and positivity based strategies are oriented around thinking. Thinking, in turn, affects emotions (Beck, 1979); therefore, the pathway to positive emotions is through positive thoughts. The benefit of positive thoughts and emotions is that they are self-fulfilling, meaning that thoughts produce expectations, which evoke responses that confirm those expectations (Griffin, 2009). In brief, what a person expects often becomes their experience.

If a student or teacher thinks about a course as difficult, boring, stressful, or meaningless, via self-fulfilling prophecy, the experience will follow their expectation. Teachers have may have a positive or negative influence on students' self-fulfilling prophecies and level of academic achievement (Madon & Jussim, 1997). To promote productive thinking and enhance academic achievement, educators might explore how they can employ positive expectations in their teaching.

Educators can provide the much needed positive encouragement, exposure to new possibilities, and methods for moving up the scale of happiness. It may sound cliché to hear sayings like "Happiness is not something that happens to people but something that they make happen" (Csikszentmihalyi, 1999, p. 824), but a little encouragement does help. Similarly,

> The potential for happiness may be all around us, but if it goes unnoticed—if our focus is elsewhere and we fail to perceive it—we risk losing it. To turn a possibility into a reality, we first need to realize that the possibility exists. (Ben-Shahar, 2007, p. 107)

Simple methods of increasing happiness, positive emotion, optimism, and well-being abound in various positive psychology sources. These include: engagement/flow (Csikszentmihalyi, 1990, 1997), using strengths and virtues

(Seligman, 2002), savoring (Peterson, 2006), exercising (Lyubomirski, 2007), journaling, appreciating/gratitude (Lyubomirski, 2007), cultivating optimism (Lyubomirski, 2007; Seligman, 1998), disputing negative thinking (Beck, 1979; Fredrickson, 2009; Seligman, 1998), engaging in intrinsically rewarding goals (Lyubomirski, 2007), creating high-quality connections/relationships (Fredrickson, 2009), among many others. None of these methods are based on achieving something or reaching some benchmark; they are rewarding in themselves and require very little to do, yet they heed healthy results.

Of all these focus areas of positive psychology, two are particularly well suited for application within a communication classroom setting: 1) flow and engagement and 2) cultivating optimism. We will first explain each category briefly and then explain its potential uses in particular communication courses.

Flow and Engagement

Perhaps the most important way to promote happiness in the classrooms is to teach the process of *flow*. As a skill, as well as a way of perceiving activities, flow holds the potential to increase enjoyment in the classroom. Additionally, this skill can carry into a career, hobbies, relationships, etc. Teaching students to engage in flow could prevent students' perceptions that education is boring or too much like work, and could potentially creating an appreciation for learning through total engagement. Csikszentmihalyi (1990) maintains that the best moments in life are not those of passivity and relaxation, but rather those in which a person's "body or mind is stretched to its limits in a voluntary effort to accomplish something difficult and worthwhile" (p. 3). Flow is achieved through effectively balancing skills and challenge (Lyubomirski, 2007). Rather than viewing a challenge as a grueling task toward a destination, challenge can be envisioned as a meaningful process toward self-learning and growth. Csikszentmihalyi's (1990) explains that people experience such total engagement and absorption in an activity for mere purpose of doing it. Unlike the attempt to achieve benchmarks, which is destination oriented, flow is about being fully engaged in the present moment.

The concept of flow contradicts traditional notions of happiness, which is often characterized as leisurely and pleasure filled. Flow often requires a great deal of concentration and effort. "Usually, the more difficult a mental task, the harder it is to concentrate on it. But when a person likes what he does and is motivated to do it, focusing the mind becomes effortless even when the objective difficulties are great" (Csikszentmihalyi, 1997, p. 27). Flow is felt most strongly while mastering a new task, mainly because it is both stimulating and demanding (Lyubomirsky, 2007); and it dissipates as an activity becomes less challenging.

In addition to increasing personal fulfillment in the educational process, Seligman, Ernst, Gillham, Reivich, and Linkins (2009) suggest that flow strategies increase happiness: "Flow only occurs when you deploy your highest strengths and talents to meet the challenges that come your way, and it is clear that flow facilitates learning" (p. 296).

To integrate more flow into the classroom, educators must select teaching methods that challenge students and provide students with novel experiences. In Csikszentmihalyi's (1990) studies show commonalities among the flow experience: "It provided a sense of discovery, a creative feeling of transporting the person into a new reality. It pushed the person to higher levels of performance, and led to previously undreamed-of states of consciousness" (p. 74). In many ways, models of service-learning are designed to produce more flow, and thus more discovery and learning. Service-learning is "various pedagogies that link community service and academic study so that each strengthens the other" (Isaacson, Dorries, & Brown, 2001, p. 2). Contrasted with the typical college classroom, where a student gets lectured to and maybe has a brief bit of interaction, service-learning allows students to literally engage with the subject material rather than just hearing or reading about it. "Service-learning offers the chance to enter new situations and stretch our capabilities. Performing service gives you an opportunity to reflect on yourself as a person and respond to life's challenges" (Isaacson et al., 2001, p. 8). Rather than analyzing hypothetical problems and devising hypothetical solutions, which can seem contrived and meaningless, giving students the opportunity, freedom, and responsibility to manage real problems and solutions encourages students to rise to the challenge. By approaching a problem both theoretically, through research, and practically, through real-life experience, students are challenged in ways that classroom education cannot provide alone.

In addition to increasing the opportunity for flow experiences, service-learning and civic engagement promote creative thinking, building connections with others, and positive emotions through helping others. Service-learning promotes personal growth; this type of growth is consistent with the predictors of happiness suggested by Peterson (2006), including social and interpersonal factors, as well as personality traits.

Cultivating Optimism

Communication instructors can reduce the anxiety that plagues students by changing the language of evaluation. All assignments, including speeches written work, can benefit from multiple evaluations—instructor and peers. Instead of using "evaluation" or "criticism" (albeit constructive), the instructor can use "opportunities for improvement" to describe this critical component of the learning process. A simple change in the language, used to describe evaluations, minimizes the negative connotations associated with both the giving and receiving of feedback.

Similarly, the fear associated with most college's public speaking requirement can be reduced on day one with a positive change in the language used to describe the public speaking process. Instructors should stress daily that everyone is "in the same boat." Both students and instructors have to stand in front of the class and give presentations. Instead of emphasizing the anxiety associated with public speaking, the instructor can point out that the class is a rare opportunity to practice public speaking skills where others are also developing these same skills. The instructor can solidify this common ground by sharing experiences with public speaking and discussing mistakes, lessons learned, and fears experienced. The instructor cannot discuss nervousness and problem areas they still encounter despite experience and know-how. The sharing of common experiences, even vulnerabilities, takes what was perceived negatively and turns it into a positive opportunity for connection with classmates and the instructor.

By simply changing the topic of particular assignments, the effects can change. Focusing an assignment on something positive and be fun, engaging, and educational.

> Teachers of rhetoric have changed their speaking assignments from "Give a speech about a time you made a fool out of yourself" to "Give a speech about when you were of value to others." Student preparation for these speeches takes less time, they speak more enthusiastically, and listening students do not fidget as much during the positive speeches. (Seligman, 2011, p. 90)

Above all else, the instructor should communicate positive emotions. Enthusiasm is contagious. As Allen et al. (2006) explained, students who perceive their teacher as excited about the content are more eager to learn. Likewise, students who believe the teacher cares are also more motivated to learn (Allen et al., 2006). Communication instructors, prepared with the knowledge of the complexities of audience analysis, are able to convey our interest and enthusiasm, for learning and the individual student, in our delivery of course content. Ultimately, our communication instruction, and model of communication best practices, will empower our students to effectively communicate in the classroom and throughout life.

The Side Effect of Happiness for Our Classrooms

The benefits of positivity are many. Since cognitions control health to a great degree, it is easy to understand why positive people are healthier than negative people. Optimists have better health than pessimists (Rasmussen, Scheier, & Greenhouse, 2009; Seligman, 1998); they suffer fewer infectious diseases (Seligman, 1998). An individual's immune system even works better when they are positive (Seligman, 1998).Therefore, it would be in an educator's best interest to learn how to cultivate more optimism, or positive thinking, within themselves and within their students. Very generally, "Optimistic people tend to interpret their troubles as transient, controllable, and specific to one situation. Pessimistic people, in contrast, believe that their troubles last forever, undermine everything they do, and are uncontrollable" (Seligman, 2002, pp. 9 – 10).

If one would like to change their thinking orientation from negative to positive, a wealth of information exists in the field of positive psychology. One method, for example, involves distracting or disputing negative thoughts when one encounters them (Seligman, 1998). Optimism is not just about thinking positive thoughts though; it is about framing negative events in a positive light: "Changing the destructive things you say to yourself when you experience the setbacks that life deals all of us is the central skill of optimism" (Seligman, 1998, p. 15). Handling setbacks in this manner build resiliency, another characteristic of optimistic people. These ideas should sound familiar to communication scholars, as these ideas have been highlighted in many basic communication books that introduce *intra*personal communication. Self-talk is a common subject in intrapersonal communication, human communication, and public speaking courses. Perhaps it is a topic that should be discussed and utilized more often, given its significance.

The expression of positive emotions has the potential to show students the way to greater meaning than our current system that privileges punishment. Positive emotions can motivate a student to achieve and to persevere even in the most daunting of situations. "A positive mood... buoys people into a way of thinking that is creative, tolerant, constructive, generous, undefensive and lateral. This way of thinking aims to detect not what is wrong, but what is right" (Seligman, 2002, p. 39). Instead of focusing on how we failed, educators must encourage positive thought and emotional expressions to emphasize successes. Educators have the potential to change thought to "produce optimal functioning, not just within the present, pleasant moment, but over the long-term as well" (Fredrickson, 2005, p. 217). This change is the path to a happy life in which students can derive pleasure and meaning from the learning process instead of solely the reward of a goal such as a grade.

Conclusion

Educational institutions have traditionally promoted the achievement of benchmarks as the measurement of success, this structure and focus negatively impacts the student with fleeting and unattainable power and money without the appreciation and application of the transformative learning process. Instead, we recommend the application of the principles and practices of positive communication to transform education. Such a revision of the time-honored and taken-for-granted educational system will inspire an appreciation for learning and the emotions that create sustainable happiness.

References

Allen, M., Witt, P. L., & Wheeless, L. W. (2006). The role of teacher immediacy as a motivational factor in student learning: Using meta-analysis to test a causal model. *Communication Education, 55*(1), 21–31.

Beck, A. T. (1979). *Cognitive therapy and the emotional disorders.* New York: Meridian.

Ben-Shahar, T. (2007). *Happier: Learn the secrets to daily joy and lasting fulfillment.* New York: McGraw Hill.

Csikszentmihalyi, M. (1990). *Flow: The psychology of optimal experience.* New York: Harper Collins.

Csikszentmihalyi, M. (1997). *Finding flow: The psychology of engagement with everyday life.* New York: Basic.

Csikszentmihalyi, M. (1999). If we are so rich, why aren't we happy? *American Psychologist, 54*(10), 821–827.

Fassett, D. L., & Warren, J. T. (2004). "You get pushed back": The strategic rhetoric of educational success and failure in higher education. *Communication Education, 53*(1), 21–39.

Fassett, D. L., & Warren, J. T. (2005). The strategic rhetoric of an "at risk" educational identity: Interviewing Jane. *Communication and Critical/Cultural Studies, 2*(3), 238–256.

Fredrickson, B. L. (2009). *The broaden-and-build theory of positive emotions.* In F. A. Huppert, N. Baylis, & B. Keverne (Eds.), The science of well-being (pp. 217–238). New York: Oxford University Press.

Fredrickson, B. L. (2009). *Positivity.* New York: Crown.

Gotz, I. L. (1995). *Conceptions of happiness.* Lanham, MD: University Press of America.

Griffin, E. (2009). *Communication, communication, communication* (7th ed.). Boston: McGraw-Hill.

Isaacson, R., Dorries, B., & Brown, K. (2001). *Service learning in communication studies: A handbook.* Toronto, Canada: Wadsworth.

Linnenbrink, E. A., & Pintrich, P. R. (2002). Achievement goal theory and affect: An asymmetrical bidirectional model. *Educational Psychologist, 37*(2), 69–78.

Lyubomirsky, S. (2007). *The how of happiness: A new approach to getting the life you want.* New York: Penguin.

Lyubomirsky, S., King, L., & Diener, E. (2005). The benefits of frequent positive affect: Does happiness lead to success? *Psychological Bulletin, 131*(6), 803–855.

Madon, S., & Jussim, L. (1997). In search of the powerful self-fulfilling prophecy. *Journal of Personality and Social Psychology, 72*(4), 791–809.

Myers, D. G., & Diener, E. (1996, May). The pursuit of happiness. *Scientific America,* 54–56.

Peterson, C. (2006). *A primer in positive psychology.* New York: Oxford University Press.

Rasmussen, H. N., Scheier, M., & Greenhouse, J. B. (2009). Optimism and physical health: A meta-analytic review. *Annals of Behavioral Medicine, 37*(3), 239–256.

Salovey, P., & Mayer, J. D. (1989–90). Emotional intelligence. *Imagination, Cognition, and Personality, 9*(3), 185–211.

Schutz, P. A., & Lanehart, S. L. (2002). Introduction: Emotions in education. *Educational Psychologist, 37*(2), 67–68.

Seligman, M. E. P. (1998). *Learned optimism: How to change your mind and your life.* New York: Pocket Books.

Seligman, M. (2002). *Authentic happiness: Using the new positive psychology to realize your potential for lasting fulfillment.* New York: The Free Press.

Seligman, M. E. P. (2011). *Flourish.* New York: Simon & Schuster.

Seligman, M. E. P., Ernst, R. M., Gillham, J., Reivich, K., & Linkins, M. (2009). Positive education: Positive psychology and classroom interventions. *Oxford Review of Education, 35*(3), 293–311.

Shutz, P. A., & DeCuir, J. T. (2002). Inquiry on emotions in education. *Educational Psychologist, 37*(2), 125–134.

Witt, P. L., Wheeless, L. R., & Allen, M. (2004). A meta-analytic review of the relationship between teacher immediacy and student learning. *Communication Monographs, 71*(2), 184–207.

• CHAPTER SIXTEEN •

Positive Organizations for Older Adults in Community Settings

Linda M. Johnston
Siegel Institute for Leadership, Ethics, and Character

Deanna F. Womack
Kennesaw State University

As the Baby Boomer generation ages, retires, and increasingly depends on the health delivery system, different elements of the system (e.g., governmental, community-based, for-profit, etc.) focus their attention on best practices to provide quality services to meet this growing demand. As adults live longer lives, more of them will require assistance with the activities of daily living or nursing care. Increasingly, institutions such as assisted living residences or nursing homes provide these services. Nursing homes are federally regulated institutions that have been available for the elderly for more than thirty years. For the majority of residents, Medicaid covers the costs of a nursing home. In comparison, assisted living residences are a newer phenomenon and are state regulated. They provide services including assistance with activities of daily living, meals, taking medications, activities, transportation, and incontinence care. Typically, living costs are separated from the costs of care, at different levels and types of assistance.

As people age and their needs surpass what their families can meet, many older adults will relocate to one of these residential facilities and, in the process, give up some degree of independence. Not surprisingly, many older adults resist this move. Positive communication has the potential to increase residents' eudemonic happiness (see Pitts & Socha, chapter 1) and enrich their lives throughout this transition.

While this chapter focuses on Positive Institutions, the third of the three pillars of positive psychology, one cannot discuss communication characteristics of positive organizations without also considering Positive

Experiences and Positive Individual Traits. Although it is beyond the scope of this chapter to review the positive organizations research (cf. Linley, Harrington, & Garcea, 2010), we relate communication scholarship to characteristics of positive organizations and positive organizational behavior (Muse, Harris, Giles, & Field, 2008).

The majority of the positive organization literature focuses on the individual-level worker and leader variables like authentic leadership (Avolio, Griffith, Wernsing, & Walumbwa, 2010), transformative cooperation (Sekerka & Fredrickson, 2010), psychological capital (Youssef & Luthans, 2010), and positive emotions (Higgs, 2010). Furthermore, some research indicates characteristics like employee engagement lead to positive outcomes for the organization, its stakeholders, and the community. Engaged employees are more emotionally involved in their work and therefore put forth a greater amount of effort than other employees (Soldati, 2007). This effort to "go the extra mile" benefits the organization and the broader community, as evidenced by the fact that organizations with higher levels of employee engagement are more profitable (Towers Perrin, 2005) and have better sales performance and customer satisfaction (Harter et al., 2003; Harter et al., 2002). So positive organizations benefit stakeholders like elders who "live inside" community residences. If those places of residence truly empowered workers and created abundance, both the organization and the residents' lives would be enriched, as Ulrich (2010) emphasized. Residents may experience personal development and growth, eudemonic happiness, and even better health outcomes.

The Approach of This Study

With the goal of enriching the lives of older adults and the organizations that serve them, we proposed an evidence-based approach to positive communication for older adults in nursing homes and assisted living facilities based on in-depth interviews with staff, families, and residents of these facilities. In order to conduct the research, the authors contacted heads of agencies and programs working with older adults; these contacts all possessed extensive knowledge and experience with nursing homes and assisted living facilities in northwest Georgia. After compiling a list of facilities identified by the group of experts as being facilities that do a good job of communicating with older adults, the authors contacted the facilities and conducted these in-depth interviews. The interview questions were from an Appreciative Inquiry approach; that is, all questions were framed in a positive manner. "What do you do at this facility to promote positive communication?" "How do you select staff who demonstrate positive individual traits?" Nine additional nursing home and assisted living facility personnel were recruited during a training session conducted by the authors; they represented assisted living facilities and county and regional services organizations for older adults. The interviews lasted between thirty minutes and one hour, and were audiotaped for further analysis. The authors interviewed twenty-four individuals representing eleven facilities, including five assisted living facilities, one nursing home, and one facility with both assisted living and nursing home residents. These interviewees included nurses, nursing assistants, other staff, as well as family members and residents. Included in these numbers are three residents and three family members from the facilities and representatives of three government senior services organizations.

As the literature did not provide a set of pre-existing categories to describe best practices in communication with older adults, the authors asked open-ended questions and identified common themes from the interviews using a thematic analysis approach.

Older Adults' Communication Experiences

The research most often frames effective communication in contrast to ineffective practices. While effective communication corrects problems, it does not necessarily create individual benefits or "abundant organizations" (Ulrich, 2010). This is especially true of the literature on older adults, which reflects a "deficit model" (Seligman & Csikszentmihalyi, 2000), identifying communication that demeans and infantilizes older persons.

Early research indicated that age-related differences impair the physical communicative abilities of older adults. As adults age, they may experience reductions in capacity to sense, process, and store information (e.g., Case, 1970, as cited in Liebermann et al., 1988; Pascual-Leone, 1970; Weiss, 1982). For example, Lieberman, Rigo, and Campaign (1988) found that older adults were less successful in decoding nonverbal behaviors than younger adults. Rosenthal (1979) concluded that increased distraction and fatigue and decreased concentration accounted for poorer decoding abilities. Brink and Stones (2007) found that hearing impairment affected communication, that impaired communication negatively affected mood, and lower mood reduced social interaction of residents in complex continuing-care facilities. Brink and Stones (2007) suggested that hearing aids or alternative techniques could improve residents' communication and thus their quality of life.

As the previous studies indicate, much of the research on older adults is grounded in the communication predicament of aging model (Ryan, Giles, Bartolucci, & Henwood, 1986) that identifies communication deficits. This research explores negative age stereotypes and media portrayals (Harwood & Giles, 1992; Robinson, Skill, & Turner, 2004) or negative interpersonal communication with older adults (Hummert & Ryan, 2001). Harwood (2007) summarizes the research on age identity and communication from the perspective of social identity theory (Taifel & Turner, 1986). Both young and old people hold negative stereotypes of aging (Kite, Stockdale, Whitley, & Johnson, 2005), and these ageist attitudes are reflected in negative communication practices.

To illustrate, communication accommodation theory (Shepard, Giles, & LePoire, 2001) explains the effect of adapting communication in conversation with others and mirroring others' behaviors like speech patterns ("You say tomato and I respond by saying tomato, too, instead of tomahto"). Communication accommodation proposes an optimal level of accommodation that involves adjusting to mirror others' communication, but not so much as to be offensive. When speaking to older adults, young people with ageist stereotypes (Coupland, Coupland, Giles, & Henwood, 1988) often over accommodate, for example, by adjusting to elders' perceived special communication needs by using patronizing language ("baby talk" or elderspeak) (Hummert & Ryan, 2001). When they encounter adults with ageing cues such as gray hair or vocal quality (Harwood & Williams, 1998), younger speakers modify their normal patterns to simplify vocabulary, exaggerating pitch variations, speaking more slowly, or over-clarifying (Kemper, Finter-Urczyk, Ferrell, Harden, & Billington, 1998; Ryan et al., 1986). Hummert and Shaner (1994) identify patronizing speech as inherent in negative stereotypes of older adults. Elderspeak has negative effects on older adults' identity, self-esteem, and even communication skills (Ryan, Hamilton, & Kwong See, 1994).

In addition, researchers have found that ageism itself results in decreased frequency and amount as well as quality of communication. For example, grandchildren who perceived grandparents' health to be impaired decreased personal communication with the grandparents (Soliz & Harwood, 2006). Schroeder's (1986) case study of four individuals confirmed that restricted visiting hours and locations may also reduce communication when adults transition from independent living to residential communities.

Hoping to improve communication, researchers have also studied the quality of communication between caregivers and older adults. Research indicates that communication needs of families and patients may go unmet. Teeri, Leino-Kilpi, and Valimaki (2006) found that communication interactions between caregivers and residents as well as between caregivers and residents' families involved problematic behaviors including indifference, insufficient information, and lack of respect for patients' self-determination. The primary behaviors consisted either of offensive or derogatory treatment (e.g., staff members' rude or derogatory behavior, nurses' indifference, etc.) or lack of respect for patients' self-determination (e.g., staff's unwillingness to listen to or respond to requests and lack of information provided to residents or their relatives). Nurses reported communicating more information than patients and families reported receiving, a further indication of unmet needs. Teeri et al.'s research also identified caregivers' "lack of respectful touching," a nonverbal communication behavior (2006, p. 123). Overall, residents experienced lack of respect, poor treatment, and failure to meet their needs. Research also shows that members of minority groups appear to receive even lower quality communication than other residents. In a study involving audiotape-recorded conversations between caregivers and residents of a long-term care facility in Canada, Jones and Jones (1986) found that commands comprised the primary form of conversation (compared to sentences and questions). A large number of residents' questions remained unanswered, and staff were least likely to respond to "ethnic" females. Jones and Jones (1986) recommended in-service training in residents' cultural needs to increase effective communication. This research is important because long-term care facilities increasingly reflect the racial and ethnic diversity of the general population, and minorities experience less effective communication than do older adults from majority groups.

Reports of the effectiveness of training programs to improve communication between health care providers and older adults comprise another trend in the communication literature. For example, Intrieri, Kelly, Brown, and Castilla (1993) trained third-year medical school students in three aspects of communication: techniques to compensate for patients' sensory losses; interviewing techniques, such as using open-ended questions and clarifying statements; and methods to manage difficult patients. After the training, participating medical students were more skillful at interviewing than non-participants. Although results of geriatric training programs in medical schools and universities have been mixed, multimodal training programs combining instruction and exercises with clinical experiences (e.g., Makoul & Curry, 2007) and programs focusing on medical interviewing (Birenbaum, Aronson, & Seiffer, 1979; Sachs, McPherson, & Donnerberg, 1985) have improved medical students' knowledge and attitudes. Intrieri et al.'s (1993) results confirm previous findings (Kelly, 1982) that multimodal training programs including interpersonal skills training can be effective in improving the quality of medical students' interactions with older adults.

The body of research on physician-patient communication also demonstrates connections between effective communication and patients' physiological well-being. Negative physician attitudes may compromise medical care and may prompt the aging to avoid using the medical system (Intrieri et al., 1993). Furthermore, patients may also avoid interacting with the medical system if they do not believe caregivers maintain confidentiality. In a study at a large medical clinic, Paulsel, Richmond, McCroskey, and Cayanus (2005) found that patients believed physicians, nurses, and staff whose communication behaviors included nonverbal immediacy, assertiveness, responsiveness, competence, and caring were more likely to respect patient confidentiality. Franklin, Ternestedt, and Nordenfelt note: "Care focusing on and aiming to promote an elderly person's identity and dignity demands interest and a desire to know the person" (2006, p. 144). This observation supports the importance of caregivers' effective communication with nursing home residents, as does Sloane et al.'s (2003) recommendation that assisted living and nursing home staff provide communication support to patients nearing death.

Contrast these experiences above with those of residents in a living facility that is also an abundant organization (Ulrich, 2010). Making one's home in such an organization can provide support, happiness, and generally increase residents' resources of hope, optimism, resiliency, and efficacy, creating psychological capital (Luthans, Youssef, & Avolio, 2007) to allow them to adapt successfully (Freund & Baltes, 2002) to the changes associated with aging. Frederickson (2003) supports the idea that a ratio of three positive emotions for every negative emotion is a minimum requirement for increasing individual well-being. Thus, emerging research indicates that positive organizations and communication have the potential to enhance residents' lives by improving both physical and psychological well-being.

Positive Communication

With his communication model of successful aging, Nussbaum (1985) began the trend of exploring positive communication. Older adults with more frequent communication interactions and who perceived themselves to be closer to family and friends experienced greater life satisfaction. Nussbaum found the primary determinant of closeness with family was location, that is, whether the older adult lived at home or in a retirement village. Elders who were optimistic, enthusiastic, and believed they had accomplished their life goals felt closest to friends and family, and those who perceived themselves to be close to family and friends aged more successfully than those who were distant. Thus, communication helps older adults sustain relationships that promote successful aging and contribute to happiness.

Following this trend and to counter the communication predicament of ageing model, Ryan, Meredith, MacLean, and Orange (1995) developed the communication enhancement of ageing model to show how the negative communication spiral associated with ageism can be reversed. Using this model, communicators who assess older adults' needs individually rather than through stereotyping are more likely to accommodate appropriately, and thus empower elders and improve interpersonal communication (Nussbaum, Pitts, Huber, Raup Krieger, & Ohs, 2005).

Although not yet fully tested in the context of aging, Wiemann's (1977) six-dimensional model of competence incorporates both attitudinal and behavioral variables. Older adults judge others as competent communicators if they display at least one of the following effective communication behaviors: (1) affiliation/support (e.g., being open to and supportive of messages from others as indicated by behaviors such as proximity, eye contact, nodding, duration of speaking time); (2) social relaxation (e.g., posture, speech rate, and nonfluencies); (3) empathy (e.g., perceived active listening, reciprocating nonverbal immediacy cues, and verbal responses indicating understanding); (4) behavioral flexibility (indicated by particular speech choices and verbal immediacy cues); and (5) interaction management (e.g., sustaining a smooth conversation by avoiding interruptions and long pauses and interchanging speaker turns) (Downs, Smith, Chatham, & Boyle, 1986). In addition to the limited research on the characteristics of effective communication with older adults, Ryan, Kennaley, Pratt, and Shomovich, (2000) found that high-quality communication can aid in well-being of aging adults dependent on others for their care.

Finally, we explore two effective practices as examples related to caring for older adults. Hickman, Newton, Halcomb, Chang, and Davidson (2007) conducted content analysis to identify common themes in twenty-six studies published between 1985 and 2006 that reported controlled trials of interventions to benefit older adults in acute care settings. Hickman et al. (2007) distilled the research into four types of best practice interventions, including "enhanced communication between care providers across the care continuum" between members of a multidisciplinary medical team and between patients and team members (p. 113). The authors further identified a common theme that communication could improve patient outcomes. The best communication practices reported in these studies were: (1) identifying and communicating risk factors; (2) implementing individualized treatments and nursing plans to promote patient independence; and (3) planning and delivering care designed to meet patients' individual needs. Levy-Storms et al. (2011) conducted focus groups on the meaning and experiences of care from the perspectives of both the nursing home aides and residents. Their research supports the conclusion that individualized care, a concept consistent with the communication enhancement of ageing model (Ryan et al., 1995) can improve both psychological and physical well-being.

While these two studies highlight the importance of communication, they emphasize communication as information sharing and exchange between team members. Therefore, new trends in studying positive communication in health and wellness, and in identifying characteristics that create abundant organizations indicate that positive organizations can benefit workers, residents, other organizational stakeholders, and the broader community (Peterson, Stephens, Park, Lee, & Seligman, 2010). There is a need for research that focuses on the interpersonal and organizational communication characteristics of abundant organizations (Ulrich, 2010).

Best Practices in Residential Settings for Older Adults

The Best Practices that emerged from the data analysis were related to four categories associated with positive organizations. Many of these reflect elements of Youssef and Luthans' (2010) integrated model of positive individual and organizational traits.

First, Youssef and Luthans (2010) identified organizational antecedents associated with high organizational performance related to efficiency and effectiveness. Two of these antecedents, organizational culture and structure, emerged from our data. Positive organizations tended to be supportive of residents, families, and staff. Best practices included providing extra administrative support for residents and families, including completing paperwork for private insurance plans to pay certified nursing assistants and setting up in-home care providers for residents. Consistent with Youssef and Luthans (2010) behavioral outcomes of positive citizenship, almost all employees mentioned the periodic resident evaluation meeting as an effective communication practice. Resident evaluation meetings ideally included staff representing many different organizational departments such as nursing, housekeeping, activities, food services, and administration, although the different departments represented differed from facility to facility. For example, one facility with more than two hundred beds, that included independent living residences as well as assisted living apartments, included the chaplain and the head of housekeeping, but not the activities coordinator, as part of the weekly evaluation meeting. Other, smaller, assisted living facilities included the activities coordinator but had no housekeeping supervisor or full-time chaplain. Other structural aspects of communication involved using a variety of media to communicate with residents and families: telephone (including families' cell phones), email, and newsletters introducing new residents to the group and highlighting upcoming events.

In a second theme from the positive organizations literature, Richardson and West (2010) note that high-performing teams collaborated to increase organizational performance and outcomes. The inputs in their model are: team attachment, positive relationships, clear but evolving team roles, appreciating diversity, and members being involved in team tasks. Teams were important because most living facilities in our sample held formal resident evaluation meetings involving all available family members, even those family members living out of state. Our effective teams often held staff-only planning meetings prior to the formal meetings with family. The staff brainstormed ways to achieve goals set for the resident and tried to anticipate the family's questions so that they could agree on a team response and therefore offer positive and well thought out recommendations. One administrator explained why planning meetings were important. She acknowledged that family members evaluated residents' capabilities differently from staff. The staff meeting resulted in a shared evaluation and goals for the resident. It was important for staff to share opinions and collaborate in deciding what to recommend to the family. That way, team members had already come to an agreement and were united in their understanding of the resident's needs and their shared recommendations to the family. One administrator we interviewed described a meeting to decide whether a resident who had been hospitalized could return to independent living with his wife or needed to move into nursing care, a change that would have separated him from their shared living quarters. She stressed that the health care team tried to help the family be realistic by honestly expressing concerns regarding transfers from his bed to a chair, for example. By creating a collaborative evaluation and plan before the meeting, the team members were better able to resist being persuaded by the family that the resident needed less support than the team had recommended. They were united in making and justifying their recommendations.

Several interviewees stressed the importance of positive team work that resulted in better inter-team cooperation and more effective team performance. High-performing teams are more likely to be innovative and provide social support to each other (Richardson & West, 2010) and, we believe, to the residents. In one example, the husband of a couple living together was taken to the hospital, but no one could locate the wife to inform her. One staff member knew the wife had her hair styled at a particular salon on a certain day and time every week. The resident services coordinator located the wife at the salon, drove her to the hospital, and remained at the hospital with her for a short time. Staff members mentioned that it was easy to recognize and work with representatives from other organizational units even if they did not know each other's names. Certified nursing assistants might recognize a physical therapist and know what department she represented, for example. Members of high-performing teams are thus able to work together for the greater good of the organization and its residents (Steger & Dik, 2010).

Many staff interviewees mentioned the importance of on-the-job training programs for new employees and periodic in-service training programs in areas such as teambuilding, ethics, and the Health Insurance Portability and Accountability Act (HIPAA) rules and regulations. These training programs were seen by the staff and families as keeping employees up to date on important changes in health policy but also as ways to best serve the residents. Steger and Dik (2010) "argue that meaningful work arises when people have ...an accurate understanding of the nature and expectations of their work environment and understand how to transact with their organizations to accomplish their work objectives" (p. 131). Training programs are necessary to help workers keep pace with rapidly changing health care laws and policies. Low employee turnover, another characteristic of abundant organizations (Ulrich, 2010), also strengthened team members' abilities to know and work with each other and thus to achieve transformative cooperation (Sekerka & Fredrickson, 2010). Two administrative-level interviewees provided an example of an especially effective orientation and training program at a continuing care retirement community that housed residents who lived independently, in assisted living, and in a nursing wing. A marketing director who had been employed at the facility for less than one year mentioned the full-day orientation program offered to all new employees, regardless of their positions in the organizational hierarchy. After the orientation day, employees were paired with experienced workers who volunteered to train new employees. Such workers find work meaningful because they can align their personal purposes with the organizational purpose and provide leadership to others (Steger & Dik, 2010). This organization encouraged workers who were interested to volunteer as trainers so that the new worker worked alongside an experienced worker to demonstrate the proper way to do tasks and procedures and to make the new employee feel welcome. This practice provided not only training but social support for the new worker and gratification to the experienced employee. It also mirrored the emphasis in the positive organizations literature on the importance of coaching in promoting "a flourishing workforce" (Grant & Spence, 2010, p. 175).

Organizational Culture

Another common theme we found in the interviews was organizational cultures that supported caring attitudes from the top to the bottom of the organization. This finding is also consistent with Youssef and Luthans' (2010) integrated model of positive individual and organizational traits. One worker at a church-sponsored facility mentioned that she viewed her job as a mission to care for others. Several interviewees mentioned that the staff— who are generally low paid— sincerely cared about the residents. The staff-members look at family pictures, get to know family members, and come to know the residents as individuals and as "somebody's grandmother." The interviewees from the continuing care retirement facility mentioned that they had had some residents living in different parts of the facility for as long as ten years. In this organization, residents often resided in independent living houses or apartments at first, then moved to assisted living, and finally to nursing home beds as the need arose for increased levels of care. One of the clear benefits of continuing care retirement facilities is that they support change and adjustment by providing residents continuity of caregivers and environment. This practice is in line with Higgs' (2010) research on the role of positive emotions in change, which indicates that positive emotions significantly affect well-being.

Supportive organizations and organizational culture benefit all members and stakeholders of the organization (Youssef & Luthans, 2010). The interviewee who described her recent orientation session also provided an interesting description of a supportive organizational culture. At the orientation luncheon, she noted that all employees were made to feel valuable and that they all contributed equally, regardless of their role, from housekeeping to skilled nursing care. All the new employees introduced themselves and described their jobs so that everyone at the luncheon understood the variety and importance of jobs performed at the facility. The human resources director shared information about her personal background, and this helped the others introduce themselves and develop personal relationships at the orientation. Managers showed an interest in employees as individuals with families and lives outside work, as well as employees. This organizational culture emphasized making everyone feel important, needed, and part of an emerging team. This same organization encouraged employees to know each other's personal situations (for example, the staff sent flowers and fruit baskets to each other and even visited on personal occasions such as a hospitalization and a death in the family) and as well as had an incentive program for workers to meet quality of care standards in their area (thus recognizing worker excellence and helping to retain employees). The value of these programs has also been noted in previous research. Hodges and Asplund's (2010) research established that strengthened development in the workplace facilitates personal growth and development. Rath (2007) reports that employees with supervisors who focused on their strengths are more than twice as likely to be engaged as those with supervisors who focused on their weaknesses. In addition, positive work environments are associated with employee engagement and retention (Harter & Blacksmith, 2010).

While the above examples represented the facilitation of communication across the facility, these traits were also common to many organizations within our sample. We should also note one especially effective practice for facilitating communication that was unique to a continuing care retirement community. Because residents lived in different buildings providing different levels of care but on the same multi-acre living community for a number of years, they became well known to staff members, who recognized them when they moved to new locations as their health care needs changed. This organization scheduled regular weekly opportunities which enabled assisted living residents to visit those in the nursing area. In this church-sponsored facility, residents at all levels of care attended church services together, so that they were truly members of the same community. The residents were encouraged and enabled to maintain contact with each other even as their medical needs change. Thus, the organization maintained continuity of relationships between residents and between residents and staff, supporting opportunities for communication and social support.

Communication Skills and Behaviors

Finally, we identified effective communication behaviors related to positive organizational cultures. The positive psychology and positive organizations literature stresses the development of authentic leadership and followership (Avolio, Griffith, Wernsing, & Walumbwa, 2010). Authentic leaders are self-aware and self-reflective. Because leaders provide feedback and rewards to followers, they significantly affect the followers' emotional states through communication, creating high-quality social environments (Staw, Sutton, & Pelled, 1994). Workers with positive moods experience positive emotions and thereby greater motivation, job and personal satisfaction, and productivity (Sekerka & Frederickson, 2010). Several interviewees emphasized the use of open and honest communication with residents and co-workers in order to create positive relationships and to better assist residents. Specific behaviors mentioned included always listening to information from other staff and other residents about a particular resident's needs. They mentioned that it was also important to respect the privacy and dignity of residents as when talking directly to both an Alzheimer's patient and her husband rather than addressing only the husband. Thus, workers' positive emotional states also enhance residents' psychological well-being. Furthermore, a positive organization atmosphere is characterized by forgiveness. This type of communication is consistent with Peterson, Stephens, Park, Lee, and Seligman's (2010) character strengths of curiosity, zest, hope, gratitude, and spirituality. One administrator suggested that staff should consider the background and context if a resident or family member communicates harshly. She said, "I don't take it personally if families or residents lash out at me. They're scared." The interviewee further stressed that employees should keep focused on the goals for that resident, not on specific behaviors at a particular time. These character strengths increased employees' resiliency in difficult times. Providing positive leadership by example through these more difficult times helped the residents adjust to these changes in their lives.

Discussion

This chapter has provided a preliminary analysis of the interviews with twenty-four staff, family, and residents. While this chapter focuses on positive institutions primarily, the positive experiences and positive individual traits are evident from the interviews. Perhaps the most helpful information to come from the interviews centers on effective organizational communication practices such as the types of orientation and training sessions conducted, the deliberate forms of communication such as regular evaluation meetings, and aspects of organizational culture that support positive and effective communication between the staff, residents, and family members. These positive organizations seem to work from a framework of abundance.

Some of the outcomes of this abundance approach to dealing with older adults have been demonstrated by staff in several ways: 1) through individual outcomes, especially in terms of the staff's commitment to organizational goals, and 2) through organizational goals, especially through employee well-being as it relates to retention, commitment to their work, and productivity on the job. The family members and residents we interviewed were well aware of the individual and organizational goals that produced these positive community encounters. They shared many examples that demonstrated how much they recognized and appreciated this positive approach. One daughter of a nursing home resident summed it up: "My Mom was at another home before this. You could tell this one was different when you walked in the door." She continued by explaining that people spoke to you when you first walked in the door, that they didn't seem rushed, they took the time to respond thoughtfully to questions, and that they seemed to care deeply about and take pride in where they worked. This one interview summed up the important combination of a positive institution, a positive experience, and positive individual traits, which in this vital grouping of qualities, demonstrated best practices in the communication with and care of older adults.

It is possible that training or self-selection of personnel prevents staff from adopting negative communication practices or that we only interviewed staff at well-recognized institutions. We did approach this study by focusing on well-recognized and recommended organizations and then asked staff, residents, and family members at these organizations what they were doing that was right or was working for them. The interviewees knew they worked or lived in (or had their family members in) quality places of care. They realized that positive communication was an integral part of that care approach. Thus, based on our research, we offer the following model of positive communication for older adults in residences that are also positive organizations.

Positive Organization Characteristics and Processes

First, positive organizations shared certain characteristics and processes (Youssef & Luthans, 2010). These abundant organizations provided additional administrative support for residents. Support came in the form of help in completing forms and reaching out to residents to bring them to vote, for example, rather than placing all the responsibility on the residents by simply making announcements and providing forms. Residents were encouraged to participate and given extra support in doing so. Another form of administrative support was the variety of media used to communicate with residents and families. Our positive organizations recognized frequent communication as important and facilitated it by using a variety of face-to-face, mediated interpersonal (e.g., telephone), and group and mass communication channels like newspapers for sharing public information with families and residents.

Periodic resident evaluation meetings with staff and family were another important characteristic. Often staff met separately prior to the meeting scheduled with families. Staff members at these meetings represented many organizational departments, not just nursing, to provide a comprehensive view of many facets of the resident's life.

High-performing teams characterized these organizations (Richardson & West, 2010). Team members collaborated, they appreciated each other's diverse roles, and they viewed tasks as team-related rather than individual work. Teams had outstanding inter-team cooperation and social support that resulted in effective performance and innovation. To create and maintain high-performing teams, positive organizations offered periodic in-service training programs not only for health care changes but also for teambuilding and ethics. They emphasized coaching by managers and team leaders (Grant & Spence, 2010). The low turnover (Ulrich, 2010) in these organizations strengthened team relationships and produced transformative cooperation (Sekerka & Fredrickson, 2010).

Supportive Communication Cultures

Our organizations' cultures supported caring attitudes not just between team members, but from top to bottom of the organization, thus increasing residents' experience of positive emotions that improve physical and psychological well-being (Higgs, 2010). These organizations emphasized making employees feel important, needed, and part of an emerging team. They encouraged familiarity with workers' personal lives, a practice that facilitates personal growth and development (Hodges & Asplund, 2010) and increases employee engagement (Rath, 2007) and retention (Harter & Blacksmith, 2010). Continuity of relationships between residents and between residents and staff further increases opportunities for communication and social support.

Employee Emotions and Attitudes

The positive structures and practices and supportive cultures resulted in authentic leadership and followership (Avolio, Griffith, Wernsing, & Walumbwa, 2010). Self-aware and self-reflective leaders act as coaches to followers and promote positive moods for employees. Leaders improved followers' emotional states through supportive communication, creating high-quality social environments (Staw, Sutton, & Pelled, 1994) that promote positive emotions and increase motivation, job and personal satisfaction, and productivity (Sekerka & Fredrickson, 2010). These organizations emphasized open and honest communication with residents and co-workers including listening carefully to each other and to residents and respecting residents' privacy and dignity. Employees focused on residents' goals and were forgiving of residents and each other. Thus, workers' positive emotional states enhanced residents' psychological well-being.

This model of positive organizational characteristics and processes, supportive communication cultures, and positive emotions and attitudes is a first step in identifying positive communication in organizations. Future research is needed to identify more characteristics like those from the positive organizational behavior literature. In addition to expanding the model, scholars should conduct research to further test the relationship between positive organizations and positive outcomes for organizations, workers, and other stakeholders. More specific communication characteristics and practices need to be identified and integrated with the existing literature on organizational abundance. Furthermore, the results of this research should be confirmed and extended to different types of organizations, especially those providing services for older adults.

References

Avolio, B. J., Griffith, J., Wernsing, T. S., & Walumbwa, F. O. (2010). What is authentic leadership development? In P. A. Linley, S. Harrington, & N. Garcea (Eds.), *Oxford handbook of positive psychology and work* (pp. 39–52). New York: Oxford University Press.

Birenbaum, A., Aronson, M., & Seiffer, S. (1979). Training medical students to appreciate the special problems of the elderly. *The Gerontologist, 19*, 575–579.

Brink, P., & Stones, M. (2007). Examination of the relationship among hearing impairment, linguistic communication, mood, and social engagement of residents in complex continuing-care facilities. *The Gerontologist, 47*, 633–641.

Coupland, N., Coupland, J., Giles, H., & Henwood, K. (1988). Accommodating the elderly: Invoking and extending a theory. *Language in Society, 17*, 1–41.

Downs, V. C., Smith, J., Chatham, A., & Boyle, A. (1986). Elderly perceptions of a competent communicator. *Communication Research Reports, 3*, 120–124.

Franklin, L. L., Ternestedt, B. M., & Nordenfelt, L. (2006). Views on dignity of elderly nursing home residents. *Nursing Ethics, 13*(2), 130–146.

Frederickson, B. L. (2003). The value of positive emotions. *American Scientist, 91*, 330–335.

Freund, A. M., & Baltes, P. B. (2002). Life-management strategies of selection, optimization, and compensation: Measurement by self-report and construct validity. *Journal of Personality and Social Psychology, 82*(4), 642–662.

Grant, A. M., & Spence, G. B. (2010). Using coaching and positive psychology to promote a flourishing workforce: A model of goal-striving and mental health. In P. A. Linley, S. Harrington, & N. Garcea (Eds.), *Oxford handbook of positive psychology and work* (pp. 173–188). New York: Oxford University Press.

Harter, J. K., & Blacksmith, N. (2010). Employee engagement and the psychology of joining, staying in, and leaving organizations. In P. A. Linley, S. Harrington, & N. Garcea (Eds.), *Oxford handbook of positive psychology and work* (pp. 121–130). New York: Oxford University Press.

Harter, J. K., Schmidt, F. L., & Hayes, T. L. (2002). Business-unit-level relationship between employee satisfaction, employee engagement, and business outcomes: A meta-analysis. *Journal of Applied Psychology, 87*, 268–279.

Harter, J. K., Schmidt, F. L., & Keyes, C. L .M. (2003). Well-being in the workplace and its relationship to business outcomes: A review of the Gallup studies. In C. L. M. Keyes & J. Haidt (Eds.), *Flourishing: Positive psychology and the life well-lived* (pp. 205–224). Washington, DC: American Psychological Association.

Harwood, J. (2007). *Understanding communication and aging: Developing knowledge and awareness.* Los Angeles: Sage.

Harwood, J., & Giles, H. (1992). "Don't make me laugh": Age representations in a humorous context. *Discourse & Society, 3*, 403–436.

Harwood, J., & Williams, A. (1998). Expectations for communication with positive and negative subtypes of older adults. *International Journal of Aging & Human Development, 47*, 11–33.

Hickman, L., Newton, P., Halcomb, E. J., Chang, E., & Davidson, P. (2007). Best practice interventions to improve the management of older people in acute care settings: A literature review. *Journal of Advanced Nursing, 60*(2), 113–126.

Higgs, M. (2010). Change and its leadership: The role of positive emotions. In P. A. Linley, S. Harrington, & N. Garcea (Eds.), *Oxford handbook of positive psychology and work* (pp. 67–80). New York: Oxford University Press.

Hodges, T. D., & Asplund, J. (2010). Strengths development in the workplace. In P. A. Linley, S. Harrington, & N. Garcea (Eds.), *Oxford handbook of positive psychology and work* (pp. 213–220). New York: Oxford University Press.

Hummert, M. L., & Ryan, E. B. (2001). Patronizing. In W. P. Robinson & H. Giles (Eds.), *The new handbook of language and social psychology* (pp. 253–270). Chichester, England: John Wiley.

Hummert, M. L., & Shaner, J. L. (1994). Patronizing speech to the elderly as a function of stereotyping. *Communication Studies, 45*, 145–158.

Intrieri, R. C., Kelly, J. A., Brown, M. M., & Castilla, C. (1993). Improving medical students' attitudes toward and skills with the elderly. *The Gerontologist, 33*, 373–378.

Jones, D.C., & Jones, G. M. M. van A. (1986). Communication patterns between nursing staff and the ethnic elderly in a long-term care facility. *Journal of Advanced Nursing, 11*, 265–272.

Kelly, J. A. (1982). *Social skills training: A practical guide for interventions.* New York: Springer Publishing.

Kemper, S., Finter-Urczyk, A., Ferrell, P., Harden, T., & Billington, C. (1998). Using elderspeak with older adults. *Discourse Processes, 25*, 55–73.

Kite, M. E., Stockdale, G. D., Whitley, B. E., & Johnson, B.T. (2005). Attitudes towards younger and older adults: An updated meta-analytic review. *Journal of Social Issues, 61*, 241–266.

Lieberman, D. A., Rigo, T. G., & Campain, R. F. (1988). Age-related differences in nonverbal coding ability. *Communication Quarterly, 36*, 290–297.

Levy-Storms, L., Claver, M., Gutierrez, V. F., & Curry, L. (2011). Individualized care in practice: Communication strategies of nursing aids and residents in nursing homes. *Journal of Applied Communication Research, 39*(3), 271–289.

Linley, P. A., Harrington, S., & Garcea, N. (2010). Finding the positive in the world of work. In P. A. Linley, S. Harrington, & N. Garcea (Eds.), *Oxford handbook of positive psychology and work* (pp. 39–52). New York: Oxford University Press.

Luthans, F., Youssef, C. M., & Avolio, B. J. (2007). *Psychological capital: Developing the human competitive edge*. New York: Oxford University Press.

Makoul, G., & Curry, R. H. (2007). The value of assessing and addressing communication skills. *Journal of the American Medical Association, 298*(9), 1057–1059.

Muse, L., Harris, S. G., Giles, W. F., & Feild, H. S. (2008). Work-life benefits and positive organizational behavior: Is there a connection? *Journal of Organizational Behavior, 29*, 171–192.

Nussbaum, J. F. (1985). Successful aging: A communication model. *Communication Quarterly, 33*, 262–269.

Nussbaum, J. F., Pitts, M. J.. Huber, F. N., Raup Krieger, J.L., & Ohs, J. E. (2005). Ageism and ageist language across the life span: Intimate relationships and non-intimate interactions. *Journal of Social Issues, 61*, 287–305.

Pascual-Leone, J. (1970). A mathematical model for the transition in Piaget's developmental stages. *Acta Psychologica, 32*, 301–345.

Paulsel, M. L., Richmond, V. P., McCroskey, J. C., & Cayanus, J. L. (2005). The relationships of perceived health professionals' communication traits and credibility with perceived patient confidentiality. *Communication Research Reports, 22*, 129–142.

Peterson, C., Stephens, J. P., Park, N., Lee, F., & Seligman, M. E. P. (2010). Strengths of character and work. In P. A. Linley, S. Harrington, & N. Garcea (Eds.), *Oxford handbook of positive psychology and work* (pp. 221–234). New York: Oxford University Press.

Rath, T. C. (2007). *StrengthsFinder 2.0*. New York: Gallup Press.

Richardson, J., & West, M. A. (2010). Dream teams: A positive psychology of team working. In P. A. Linley, S. Harrington, & N. Garcea (Eds.), *Oxford handbook of positive psychology and work* (pp. 235–250). New York: Oxford University Press.

Robinson, J. D., Skill, T., & Turner, J. W. (2004). Media usage patterns and portrayals of seniors. In J. F. Nussbaum & J. Coupland (Eds.), *Handbook of communication and aging research* (2nd ed.). Mahwah, NJ: Lawrence Erlbaum.

Rosenthal, R. (1979). *Skill in nonverbal communication: Individual differences*. Cambridge, MA: Oelgeschlager, Gunn, & Hain.

Ryan, E. B., Giles, H., Bartolucci, G., & Henwood, K. (1986). Psycholinguistic and social psychological components of communication by and with the elderly. *Language and Communication, 6*, 1–24.

Ryan, E. B., Hamilton, J. M., & Kwong See, S. R. (1994). Patronizing the old: How do younger and older adults respond to baby talk in the nursing home? *International Journal of Aging & Human Development, 39*, 21–32.

Ryan, E. B., Kennaley, D. E., Pratt, M. W., & Shumovich, M. A. (2000). Evaluations by staff, residents, and community seniors of patronizing speech in the nursing home: Impact of passive, assertive, or humorous responses. *Psychology and Aging, 15*, 272–285.

Ryan, E. B., Meredith, S. D., MacLean, M. J., & Orange, J. B. (1995). Changing the way we talk with elders: Promoting health using the communication enhancement model. *International Journal of Aging and Human Development, 41*, 87–105.

Sachs, L. A., McPherson, C., & Donnerberg, R. (1985). Influencing medical students' attitudes toward older adults: A curriculum proposal. *Gerontology and Geriatrics Education, 4*, 91–96.

Schroeder, A. B. (1986). *An analysis of the interaction patterns of the elderly: The deterioration of relationships*. Chicago, IL: Annual Meeting of the Speech Communication Association. (ERIC Document Reproduction Service No. ED278084).

Sekerka, L. E., & Fredrickson, B. L. (2010). Working positively toward transformative cooperation. In P. A. Linley, S. Harrington, & N. Garcea (Eds.), *Oxford handbook of positive psychology and work* (pp. 81–94). New York: Oxford University Press.

Seligman, M. E. P., & Csikszentmihalyi, M. (2000). Positive psychology: An introduction. *American Psychologist, 55*, 5–14.

Shepard, C., Giles, H., & LePoire, B. A. (2001). Communication accommodation theory. In W. P. Robinson & H. Giles (Eds.), *The new handbook of aging and social psychology* (pp. 33–56). Chichester, England: Wiley.

Sloane, P. D., Zimmerman, S., Hanson, L., Mitchell, C. M., Riedel-Leo, C., & Custis-Buie,V. (2003). End-of-life care in assisted living and related residential care settings: Comparison with nursing homes. *Journal of the American Geriatric Society, 51*, 1587–1594.

Soldati, P. (2007, March 8). Employee engagement: What exactly is it? *Management Issues*.

Soliz, J., & Harwood, J. (2006). Shared family identity, age salience, and intergroup contact: Investigation of the grandparent-grandchild relationship. *Communication Monographs, 73*, 87–107.

Staw, B. M., Sutton, R. I., & Pelled, H. (1994). Employee positive emotion and favorable outcomes at the workplace. *Organization Science, 5*, 51–72.

Steger, M. F., & Dik, B. J. (2010). Work as meaning: Individual and organizational benefits of engaging in meaningful work. In P. A. Linley, S. Harrington, & N. Garcea (Eds.), *Oxford handbook of positive psychology and work* (pp. 131–142). New York: Oxford University Press.

Tajfel, H., & Turner, J. C. (1986). The social identity theory of intergroup behavior. In S. Worchel & W. Austin (Eds.), *Psychology of intergroup relations* (pp. 7–24). Chicago: Nelson-Hall.

Teeri, S., Leino-Kilpi, H., & Valimaki, M. (2006). Long-term nursing care of elderly people: Identifying ethically problematic experiences among patients, relatives and nurses in Finland. *Nursing Ethics, 13*(2), 116–129.

Towers Perrin (2005, May). *Reconnecting with employees: Quantifying the value of engaging your workforce*. London, England: Towers Perrin.

Ulrich, D. (2010). Foreword: The abundant organization. In P. A. Linley, S. Harrington, & N. Garcea (Eds.), *Oxford handbook of positive psychology and work* (pp. xvii–xxi). New York: Oxford University Press.

Weiss, A. D. (1982). Auditory perception in relation to age. In *Human aging* (pp. 114–140). New York: Research & Education Association.

Wiemann, J. M. (1977). Explication and test of a model of communication competence. *Human Communication Research, 3*, 195–213.

Youssef, C. M., & Luthans, F. (2010). An integrated model of psychological capital in the workplace. In P. A. Linley, S. Harrington, & N. Garcea (Eds.), *Oxford handbook of positive psychology and work* (pp. 277–288). New York: Oxford University Press.

• CHAPTER SEVENTEEN •

Committed: Fostering Respect and Well-Being through Collaborative Theatrical Performance at Piedmont Regional Jail

Claire E. Deal
Hampden-Sydney College

This play that we put together over the past three months has really proved to me that I can accomplish anything that I really put effort into. I know what I gotta do now. I still got my job when I get home. Two, three, years from now I plan on being on the way to finish paying for my own house—on the way to getting my contractor's license—that's pretty much it. I want to own my own house and own my own business. I want to go in halves with my brother—'cause see he works in the same company. Probably be something with "Robert and Jonathan," something like that, or "R and J's," "J and R's," something like that.

— Robert Davis, *Committed* actor and former prisoner

Robert's expressed commitment to building a better life after incarceration may strike some readers as surprising, others as laudable, given the many challenges facing prisoners, prison staff, and the corrections system nationwide. Prisoners, whose incarceration separates them not only physically from home and family but also, as Kendig (1993) noted, emotionally from their sense of identity, may experience physical, psychological and emotional challenges during their incarceration. Prisoners' marginalized status coupled with other challenges during incarceration such as a lack of mental and physical stimulation, discrimination, and violence contribute to the challenges they face. For prison employees, charges of inadequate housing, mistreatment of prisoners, low pay, and long hours lead to decreased morale and frequent employee turnover. Building and maintaining a healthy institution in the face of so many challenges is difficult, at best.

Compounding the challenge is the fact that media tend to focus on what is going wrong with the "prison-industrial" complex rather than on what is going right. Many positive experiences occur behind the steel doors and razor wire fences; university communication faculty have long facilitated programming that benefits prisoners, employees, and the institution itself.

Although these teacher-activists readily acknowledge the ongoing challenges of working in such sites, they argue that the benefits—for college students, prisoners, and, in many cases, jails or prisons—significantly overshadow the costs. Prison Communication, Activism, Research, and Education (PCARE; 2007) highlighted several programs, including a debate program that pairs University of Georgia college students with prisoners at Lee Arrendale State Prison. Temple University's Inside-Out program offers students, prisoners, and community members the opportunity to take courses together, allowing participants to "talk, think, problem-solve, and act across profound social barriers as equals" (PCARE, p. 412). University of Michigan's Prison Creative Arts Project facilitates dance, poetry, and art workshops linking students and prisoners. A related project linked undergraduate writing majors with a group of maximum-security prisoners at the Penitentiary of New Mexico, creating an educational partnership that could be replicated in other settings as well (Lockard & Rankins-Roberston, 2011). When these creative products are shared publicly, citizens may view prisoners and institutions in a more favorable light than is typical (PCARE, p. 413), challenging sterotypical thinking and contributing to the well-being of the institution.

In this chapter I examine the role of positive communication in improving the lives of prisoners while building rapport between prisoners and staff, ultimately contributing to the institution's health overall. Specifically, I examine how engaging in a theater project allowed prisoner-actors to identify and enhance their core strengths and values, to nurture self-awareness and self-confidence, and to experience what Csikszentmihaly (1990) describes as "flow." The prisoner-actors' experience reflected Seligman's (2002) assertion that "the positive emotions [such as] confidence, hope, and trust…serve us best not when life is easy, but when life is difficult" (p. xiii). Similarly, Kobau et al. (2011) assert that "[p]ositive individual traits…such as creativity, bravery, kindness, perseverance, and optimism…when cultivated, can increase resiliency, buffer against psychological disorder and other adversities, and promote mental health" (p. 3).

This performance project was completed in the fall semester of 2006; a service-learning project, it linked students from Hampden-Sydney College (HSC), a small liberal arts college for men located in rural Virginia, with prisoners at Piedmont Regional Jail (PRJ), a facility located seven miles from the college campus. Together, under my direction, students and prisoners created a play drawn from the life stories of all participants. While the project provided both groups of actors with significant challenges and successes, I focus in this chapter on the positive outcomes afforded the prisoners and, by extension, the institution itself.

The prisoners housed in PRJ come from Prince Edward County, VA, and four other surrounding counties and are representative of the region's citizenry: 62.8% white and 35.8% African American, with 18.3% of families living below the poverty line (U.S. Census Bureau, 2007). The prisoner participants were selected from men who expressed interest in an acting course that I offered at the jail. Three men chose to participate and each prisoner-actor received permission to travel outside the jail (with an officer) for dress rehearsals and performances. Hampden-Sydney's student population is largely homogeneous: all-male, overwhelmingly white, affluent, politically conservative, heterosexual, and Southern-born. Each of the four student-actors identified as such. They were enrolled in a theater course at HSC taught by my colleague, Professor Shirley Kagan. I facilitated the service-learning portion of the class—the collaborative creation of a theater of testimony performance—which began in early October 2006.

The actors and I spent significant time together during the next three months, engaging in both structured and informal discussions, acting exercises, script development, rehearsals, and performance. Student–actors and prisoner–actors participated equally in all facets of the production. An important component of the project was frequent reflection on both the process itself as well as the project's impact on individuals. As such, all participants engaged in both guided and informal conversation during the rehearsal period and the HSC students were required to post a blog after each rehearsal. I interviewed each of the prisoner-actors after the final performance. Reflecting on their experiences led to numerous positive outcomes for participants: they identified their core strengths and values, recognized their personal accomplishments, articulated future goals, and acknowledged one another's contributions. The sections that follow are organized chronologically, reflecting the various stages of the project: script development, rehearsal, and performance. Throughout the chapter, I demonstrate the influence that positive communication behaviors and strategies had on the prisoner-actors, PRJ staff, and audience members and argue that these outcomes ultimately contributed to the institution's overall health.

Behind the Scenes: Positive Communication in Script Development and Rehearsal

Theater of testimony refers to performance genre in which the script is developed primarily from persons' oral narratives, although scripts also may include excerpts from primary documents such as letters, journal entries, and court transcripts. Mann (1997), Smith (1993, 1994, 2011), and Kaufman and Members of Tectonic Theater Project (2001, 2011) have produced numerous works in this genre that challenge cultural assumptions and stereotypes. For example, Kaufman and Members of Tectonic Theatre Project's *The Laramie Project*, a play about the murder of college student Matthew Shepard, provided a multidimensional portrayal of the circumstances surrounding Shepard's death and Laramie citizens' attitudes about homosexuality. Drawn from court documents and interviews, the play exposed the marginalized status of people who are gay and the tragic effects of homophobia. Stereotypes marginalize prisoners, as well; hence, creating a performance piece based on the prisoners' narratives had the potential of challenging stereotypes. Providing the prisoner-actors the opportunity to tell their own stories on stage—stories not about their incarceration but about family, interests, work, friendships, and life goals—offered an opportunity to challenge negative stereotypes and replace those with positive images of prisoners as individuals, not simply as persons defined by their crimes. In the following section, I discuss both script development and rehearsal, noting how providing prisoners the opportunity to give voice to their life experiences enhanced their well-being.

Developing the Performance Script

The prisoner-actors, student-actors, and I developed the script collaboratively, drawing on material obtained from large group discussions, acting exercises, and one-on-one interviews that I conducted with each participant. These stories comprised the script. I began with the question, "What do you, as a HSC student or prisoner, want people on the outside to know about you and your experiences in college or in jail?" I also asked participants to tell me about important turning points in their lives, encouraging them to search for what Ulmer (1989) referred to as the "punctum or sting of memory" (p. 209) to recreate those experiences. The HSC students and I painstakingly transcribed the hours of interviews and then I selected stories that both reflected interesting similarities among the men's experiences and added dramatic interest to the script. Later, the group read aloud the draft and suggested changes that we incorporated in the final script. The most poignant moments of the performance centered on these life stories of student-actors and prisoner-actors. The public performance of *Committed* served to dispel misconceptions that actors and audience members held about prisoners and students alike. While both groups of participants benefited from the project, my focus centers on the positive experiences of the prisoner-actors.

During their interviews, the prisoner-actors were animated and engaged, speaking with enthusiasm, emboldened and pleased at the opportunity to talk about something other than the details of their criminal past and current incarceration. Numerous scholars point to the positive effects of constructing and performing personal narrative; that is, shaping and sharing stories about oneself. Some of the benefits include representing a deeply held and sometimes guarded "truth" (Frazier, 2011), working through traumatic events (Spry, 1998), generating analyses of "complex structures of cultural power" (Hantzis, 1998, p. 206), ending the "silence and invisibility of isolation" (Kendig, 1993, p. 198), and "reflecting upon and discovering meaning in experience" (Kendig, 1993, p. 197). Recalling memories of life on the outside—such as happy times spent with loved ones, rewarding experiences at school or work, and recollections of leisure activities and hobbies—enabled prisoner-actors to recognize their self-worth and to articulate core strengths and virtues. Retelling these experiences was both gratifying and satisfying for participants. Seligman (2002), a leading scholar of the Positive Psychology movement, noted that when people exercise strengths and virtues in everyday life their lives are "imbued with authenticity" (p. 9). For an incarcerated person, although daily life in the institution may not provide many opportunities to engage those strengths and virtues, the remembrance of times when it was possible can be empowering. Eric, a prisoner-actor, describes his love for playing chess, demonstrating his curiosity and determination:

> I play chess a lot to relax. I learned to play chess, believe it or not, here [in jail]—almost seven or eight years ago. I got locked up when I was about 21 and I always wanted to learn how to play chess. They always told me it was a smart man's game. I said well, "I'm gonna see can I learn how to play." After I learned [and was released], one of my cousins came home and me and him started playing. Is it a smart man's game? I don't know – but it's easy after you just learn how to move the

pieces. It came to me—just natural to me, I guess. I love it so much, my wife, she bought me a board for the house, and I have one I keep in my car so [after I'm released again] if I go anywhere and somebody wants to play I can.

Recalling interactions with loved ones led to mixed emotions among participants: a longing to be with the loved one, comfort in the knowledge of the loved one's support, and desire to reconnect with the loved one upon release. Tim, a prisoner-actor, shared his emotions about his family, particularly his daughter:

My little daughter, I know she misses me. I was in here when my little daughter was born. I stayed like six months after she was born, then I got out. The first time I held her I was like—I couldn't believe she was mine! Then, I got locked up again—then, she grew up on me! She in school, she get A's and B's, so I don't think she goin' do bad. I call her on the phone—she tell me this, tell me that about school, this and that. I'm goin' have to look out for her cause I know it's—being in the situation I do—it's goin' be a hard time out there.

Reflecting on the choices that led to incarceration had the potential, too, of encouraging the prisoner to move forward. Eric, a prisoner-actor, reflected on his actions, past, present, and future:

Right now I'm in 'twixt and tween' on anything so I'm trying to hold [myself together]. I just keep prayin, and my spirits is real good. I mean, I'm like "hey, you know, this is already done, so there's not no sense in me looking back thisaway, let's keep on going forward." You're gonna face more challenges every day. So this right here, I look at it like this—it's just a little stepping stone, you know what I'm saying? It's just up to me—it's not up to nobody else but me. I leave it up to me to try to do the best I can do.

Speaking about prior accomplishments in school or the workforce encouraged the prison-actors, nurturing their self-confidence and resolve to build a better life upon release. For example, Robert spoke with pride about his skill in masonry work:

I went to VoTech school in Russburg and took the masonry class—I was supposed to done it for two years but I only attended it for one year since I dropped out in 10th grade after my mom died. I learned some things, but I didn't learn as much as I did on the job. You get on jobs and it's a totally different story. Layin' brick, I can start with nothing and end up with a house, really. Start from nothin'—from trash and end up with something that looks like, you know [real professional]. In Lynchburg, I can probably, every two or three miles, I can point out something I built. Actually, in Lynchburg on Ward's road, we done a Sonic [restaurant]—and that was on the news! It was so *hot* that summer the News actually came to the job and showed us laying brick. That was pretty cool.

The six weeks that group members spent in script development and rehearsal instilled a collective sense of purpose. The play the actors created, titled *Committed*, was a theatrical collage—monologues and scenes moved back and forth in time, voices overlapped, and stories were interwoven to highlight both the differences and the often striking similarities among the student-actors' and prisoner-actors' experiences. In one scene, for example, prisoner-actor Robert and student-actor Greg discussed the shared satisfaction they derived from hard work, Robert as a brick layer and Greg as an Emergency Medical Technician. Stories of students' and prisoners' teenage "bad boy" experiences highlighted the short-lived thrill of risk-taking and the serious consequences of those actions.

The most interesting and ultimately empowering narratives reflected the men's childhood influences, adolescent adventures, adult setbacks and successes, and aspirations for the future. Several of the prisoner-actors' narratives centered on a recurring theme. For example, Robert talked often of his connection with younger brother Jonathan, a bond that steadied him during his incarceration and on which he built his hope for the future. Eric returned often to stories of long days spent with his grandmother and the skills and life lessons she taught him. Her influence was reflected in Eric's upbeat attitude about his incarceration, describing it as "a stepping stone" to a better situation upon his release. Tim's stories about his daughter reflected his great love for her, a love that he explained encouraged him to turn his life around so that he could provide for her after his release.

The Rehearsal Process

With a workable text, the actors enthusiastically launched into rehearsal. The students and prisoners met as a group once a week at the jail and, more often, in individual coaching sessions with me both at the jail with the prisoners and at the college with the students. The process had its inevitable challenges, but on the whole, the actors maintained their commitment to the project—running lines together, writing biographies for the program, and suggesting further script edits. Over time, the students and prisoners formed a true ensemble, encouraging one another, laughing with (and sometimes at) one another in rehearsal, talking about their interests, and joking around. For the prisoner-actors, the opportunity to work toward a common goal with fellow prisoners away from the cell block (we rehearsed in a small out building on the prison grounds, and later, in town at the performance venue), provided the opportunity for new friendships: As Tim, a prisoner-actor, explained, "Like I said, I didn't really know Rob but when we started coming together with this play thing, that's when I really started to know Rob."

Engaging in the play production process was a challenging experience for both prisoner-actors and student-actors. We focused on the successes of the process rather than the setbacks, seeking a proactive, rather than a reactive approach to dealing with the challenges. Borrowing from the principles of positive psychology (Cornum, Matthews, & Seligman, 2011), I encouraged actors to demonstrate their resilience by committing to the process for "the long haul"—and they delivered! Memorizing lines, for example, proved to be particularly difficult for some. Robert, however, one of the prisoner-actors, was the first person "off book." The other actors complimented him on this accomplishment, and asked him how he was able to learn his lines so quickly. He responded that he had made a commitment to the group, and he knew he "couldn't let any one of you down." When I pointed out the strength of his commitment and what that said about him as a person, he nodded, and seemed pleased. On opening night, he sent me a letter that said, in part, "Doing this play has shown me that I have come a long way since I've been locked up. It makes me feel absolutely confident about returning to the streets."

Eric struggled with both reading and memorization. To address his challenges, I condensed the number of lines he had to learn and scheduled some extra one-on-one rehearsals with him. To my delight, and his, Greg, a student, volunteered to work with him on the days I needed to work with others. Greg's action demonstrated to Eric that he was a valuable member of the group and that Greg wanted to help him succeed, a gesture that both encouraged and pleased Eric.

Simply spending time together engaged in a common goal led to many benefits for the ensemble members, as noted above. So, too, did engaging in the physical, mental, and emotional act of theatrical rehearsal. Actors participated in a variety of performance activities including voice and body exercises, character development, and scene staging, each of which offered participants the opportunity to learn new things and to enhance physical and psychological growth and well-being.

An important aspect of our project was the stipulation that participants would portray fellow members of the performance ensemble. That meant that each prisoner would play the role of one of the students; students, in turn, would portray prisoners. Embodying the role of a fellow actor provided the opportunity, as prisoner-actor Tim explained, "to walk in another man's shoes." I modeled my directing approach after Stucky's (2002) everyday life performance (ELP) and Smith's (1993, 1994, 2011) character development techniques, both of which encourage the actor to find the character's identity in the nuances of the character's movement and voice. Stucky's conversational approach, whereby the actor tries to emulate a character's speech, breathing, and mannerisms in exacting detail, worked well for Chase, a student-actor, in his portrayal of Robert. Chase did an excellent job of uncovering the nuances of Robert's character, portraying him with strength and dignity, and capturing his physical and vocal characteristics so well that his performance evoked the feeling that he was "dreaming, dancing, breathing with another…performing an other" (Stucky, 2002, p. 139). In other words, in Chase's performance, he represented Robert so accurately that he seemed to mirror Robert's every move.

Numerous scholars (Denzin, 2003; Jenkins, 1998; Madison, 1998, 2005; Pelias, 1999; Schweitzer, Levin, Ball, & Macdonald, 2011) point to the value of performance as a "way of knowing"—an active, hands-on method on learning that allows performers to acquire knowledge that they may not gain through more conventional means such as reading or listening to lectures. The rehearsal process allowed actors to experience two phenomena: First, a growing awareness, empathy, and respect for the person he portrayed on stage, and, second, with the detachment that resulted from watching a fellow actor tell his own story, a greater awareness of himself and his circumstances.

Embodiment and Empathy

Pineau (1998) explains that playing the role of another allows performers to challenge stereotypical thinking about others:

> Every time that we ask [actors] to perform across gender, ethnic, or generational lines we have the opportunity to unpack their resistance to the unfamiliar, their stereotypic assumptions about how others move through the world, as well as to confront their own habituated responses and experiences. (p.133)

Eric, who performed the role of Evan, a student, explained what he learned through performance. When I asked, "Do you feel that you can relate to Evan any better now, after having portrayed him on stage?" Eric replied:

> A little bit. [I saw that] he went through some things with his mom, his father, the divorce, so to me, it was like he had a pretty rough childhood coming up. It seemed like to me he respected his mom cause she was a hard-working woman, but he also don't respect her cause she wasn't always there for him, you know, to help him through certain things, so I learned that from performing him. So, that was touching, knowing that he done went through that, you know.

Playwright and actor Smith (1993) also points to the potential of embodied performance to enhance the actor's capacity for empathy. Smith is well known and respected for her theater or testimony productions in which she portrays dozens of diverse characters based on her interviews with people across the United States, playing across race, sex, socioeconomic status, and age, embodying their physical movements and vocal patterns. In the preface to *Fires in the Mirror*, Smith suggests that such embodiment can lead to a clearer understanding of people different than oneself. Smith describes the impetus of her artistic approach: "If we were to inhabit the speech pattern of another, and walk in the speech of another, we could find the individuality of the other and experience that individuality viscerally....Learning about the other by being the other requires the use of all aspects of memory, the memory of the body, mind, and heart, as well as the words" (p. xxvii). The ability to empathize allows actors the potential for positive growth as they transcend stereotypes associated with the other as they connect viscerally with others' thoughts and emotions.

For example, HSC student Chase noticed something about Robert that he later incorporated in the production when he portrayed Robert:

> Robert clutched a letter throughout today's meeting and as his eyes focused upon it frequently it seemed as though his thoughts were too. A great deal of the strength these guys have undoubtedly comes from support from friends and family, otherwise [incarceration] would be almost unbearable in my opinion.

When I asked Chase to describe embodying Robert on stage, he said: "By saying Robert's words on stage, I was able to see the impact that his experience has had not only on him but what his experience can make others realize."

Both Eric's and Chase's experiences support Jenkins (1998) assertion that embodied performance allows actors to "connect with the emotions of the performed other" (p. 271). Chase also reflects Stucky's (2002) view that the act of performance "uncovers nuances we cannot fully express, evokes things unique, personal, and intimate," while also allowing actors to develop "felt knowledge," or "a kind of insight unique to the performer" (pp. 137–138). Theater's potential to engender understanding between group members strengthened the relationships among all the actors, and enriched the experience for all.

Personal Narrative Performance and Self-Awareness

Performance leads to knowledge in other ways, as well. Often, when people see their own stories performed, they see their own situations anew. For example, Didion (2007) described watching Vanessa Redgrave portray herself in the one-woman show about Didion's life. When Redgrave said Didion's words during a rehearsal, Didion observed, "There it was: Vanessa Redgrave was standing on a stage in an empty theater and she was telling me a story I was hearing for the first time" (Didion, p.7). Similarly, Eric shared his insights about Evan's performance, when I asked, "When Evan was playing you and said some of the things you said in your interview about your grandmother's illness, how did it make you feel?" Eric replied:

> Every time he would repeat that...I could feel the same emotions that I felt when I told it. That's why it, I don't know what the word is for it, overwhelmed me, saddened me, 'cause I was like, it was me. I was already feeling it as he was saying it, so it was kind of crazy.

In this instance, the power of the Evan's embodiment helped Eric to reconnect to his earlier experience. Robert, too, was able to step outside of the performance and find insight into his situation: "Watching Chase portray me got me started thinking about my brother and what I'm going to do when I get out. It just took my mind somewhere totally different than where I was, sitting on stage."

Through the collaborative acts of script development and embodied performance in rehearsal, prisoners and students experienced numerous positive outcomes. First, the actors' work resulted in a compelling theater of testimony performance that centered on their life experiences. Second, the challenges of acting encouraged actors to work hard, both individually and collectively, to succeed. Third, the success that followed the effort led to affirmation and encouragement, enhancing participants' self-confidence. Fourth, through embodied performance as both performer and viewer, participants learned much about themselves and others. Finally, their collaboration forged a strong sense of community, a community based on mutual respect of one another as individuals, not simply as "students" or "prisoners."

Utopia in Performance: Flow and Institutional Well-Being

After a 6-week rehearsal period, it was time to perform the show for the community. We presented the show at Farmville's former Robert R. Moton High School (now a museum). In 1951 students at the all-Black school led a strike to protest inadequate conditions. The act culminated in Prince Edward County's inclusion in the groundbreaking *Brown v. Board of Education*. Performing at the museum, with its didactic banners and historic photographs, added an important dimension to the performance, forcing spectators to contemplate African-Americans' struggles for equality in education. Even after 50 years, the legacy of that time remains, no doubt influencing the life chances and stories of some of the prisoner-actors. We used portable platforms to fashion a stage in the former cafeteria; we arranged audience seating on three sides, creating an intimate environment for the production. Set pieces and props were kept to a minimum: stools, a small table, and a few hand props (e.g., a chess board, beer bottles, brick mason's trowel, and a backpack). Performers wore jeans and T-shirts in shades of gray and blue.

After weeks of collaboration, opening night finally arrived with a full house. The audience was comprised of people from a cross-section of the community, including members of the Museum board; jail staff and administrators; prisoner-actors' and student-actors' family members; local residents; and students and employees from HSC and Longwood University. As the lights dimmed and the actors entered the playing space, I felt a tremendous amount of pride at what they had accomplished. When the lights brightened, the actors, seated on stools, tentatively began, quickly gaining confidence as the opening scene unfolded. Evan soon began his portrayal of Eric, who worked as a cook in the jail's kitchen. Evan captured Eric's physical presence and deep booming voice with precision, using Eric's own words to describe his memories of canning vegetables with his grandmother. As Evan performed, Eric gazed across the stage at him earnestly, smiling when Evan got to a favorite part, "My grandma always say, 'stock up—you never know when something going to happen!' She got so much food on her shelves ain't nothing going to be left in the stores!" When the audience laughed, Eric beamed as if to say, "That is *my* story."

Each of the actors, in turn, rose to the challenge with intense concentration, and, in so doing, experienced the optimal experience described by Csikszentmihalyi (1990) as "flow":

> a sense that one's skills are adequate to cope with the challenges at hand....Concentration is so intense that there is no attention left over to think about anything irrelevant, or to worry about problems. Self-consciousness disappears, and the sense of time becomes distorted. (p. 71)

The final scene, a series of overlapping lines about the men's aspirations for the future, brought the audience to their feet. This time, the men spoke their own words, in their own voices. The prisoner-actors' conviction to forge a new life after their release rang true; the student-actors' goals for the future were ripe with youthful anticipation. The sense of pride, especially from the prisoner-actors at the audience's appreciation, was palpable. For an hour, at least, the men were not identified by their crime; they were identified by their humanity.

The transcendent moment that we, as a community of actors and audience members, experienced in that makeshift theater space was what Dolan (2005) describes as "utopian performatives," those

> small but profound moments in which performance calls the attention of the audience in a way that lifts everyone slightly above the present, into a hopeful feeling of what the world might be like if every moment of our lives were as emotionally voluminous, generous, aesthetically striking, and intersubjectively intense. (p. 5)

Post-Performance Reflections

I have argued that the prisoner-actors benefited in many ways from their participation in our project, but in what ways did the creation and performance of *Committed* impact Piedmont Regional Jail? For one, the positive experience of the actors and the staff members involved in the project had a ripple effect within the institution. Fellow prisoners who were not in the production interacted daily with the prisoner-actors, helping them memorize lines and asking about the production process. The performance process provided a diversion from the daily routine, even for those prisoners not directly involved in it. The staff members who accompanied the prisoner-actors to rehearsals saw the production process in its entirety, watching the prisoner-actors put in the long hours needed to mount a successful production. Numerous other staff members attended the production. Their experience enabled staff to view the prisoner-actors as individuals, hard working men committed to a task. Tim and Robert both shared that in the days following the performance, several officers at the jail had spoken to them for the first time—calling out, "Hey, actor, good job!"—and they both agreed that such acknowledgment was welcomed. Several PRJ administrators came to the production, noting how the performance raised awareness of positive experiences at the jail.

Tim recognized that the play had the potential to affect audience members' perceptions of prisoners: "A lot of them were thinking that don't nothing come out of jail toward being good but now they see—they still got good people in jail that's willing to change their life around." Eric, too, pointed out theater's potential to challenge stereotypes:

> When people see you wearing these type of clothes [indicating his jail jumpsuit], that stereotype is what they're [thinking] —"you know, well, he did something, you

know, real bad." But he might be in here for not paying child support or something 'cause he ain't got a job.

I was curious to learn about the audience's perceptions, and asked members to email me their thoughts. A faculty member from Longwood University wrote: "I enjoyed watching one prisoner's face, particularly, when he delivered a line that drew a laugh from the audience and then saw that pleasure reflected back to him." She continued, "I felt the connection at that moment, and I wondered how many times [he] had received that positive kind of feedback before in his life." For some audience members, the performance had significant meaning. One woman wrote, "it was a profound experience for me." She explained that she left the performance "feeling that I had been part of privileged information. This genre is an excellent vehicle for presenting cultural and life-experience diversity issues to students, faculty, and people, in general."

The production highlighted the ability of the college and the jail to work together in a manner that was mutually beneficial to both institutions. Several people noted the connection among the students and prisoners, including a jail employee who said, "It was very plain to see that they had worked together very well to compose this, and the swapping of roles was unbelievably good."

Healthy institutions, an important component of healthy communities, are fostered from the inside-out, emanating from the people living and working within them. Even in difficult circumstances, prisoners, given the opportunity to engage in positive experiences such as *Committed,* can improve their well-being by tapping into their core strengths and values in collaboration with others. As I have discussed, the enhanced self-awareness and self-confidence derived from the performance process led prisoner-actors to interact positively with fellow prisoners, staff, administrators, and—in performance—with audience members, contributing to the health and well-being of the institution overall.

References

Csikszentmihalyi, M. (1990). *Flow: The psychology of optimal experience.* New York: Harper and Row.
Cornum, R., Matthews, M. D., & Seligman, M. P. (2011). Building resilience in a challenging institutional context. *American Psychologist, 66,* 4–9.
Denzin, N. (2003). *Performance ethnography: Critical pedagogy and the politics of culture.* Thousand Oaks, CA: Sage Publications.
Didion, J. (2007, March 4). The year of hoping for stage magic. *The New York Times.* Sec. 2:1+.

Dolan, J. (2005). *Utopia in performance: Finding hope at the theater.* Ann Arbor, MI: University of Michigan Press.

Frazier, I. (2011). Life stories. *New Yorker, 87*(22), 21–22.

Hantzis, D. M. (1998). Reflections on "A dialogue with friends; 'performing' the 'other/self' OJA 1995." In S. J. Dailey (Ed.), *The future of performance studies: Visions and revisions* (pp. 203–206). Washington, DC: National Communication Association.

Jenkins, M. M. (1998). "Personal narratives changed my life: Can they foretell the future?" In S. J. Dailey (Ed.), *The future of performance studies: Visions and revisions* (pp. 264–271). Washington, DC: National Communication Association.

Kaufman, M. (2011). *33 Variations.* New York: Dramatists Play Service.

Kaufman, M., & Members of Tectonic Theater Project. (2001). *The Laramie Project.* New York: Vintage Books.

Kendig, D. G. (1993). Acting on conviction: Reclaiming the world and the self through performance. *Anthropological Quarterly, 66*(4), 197–202.

Kobau, R., Seligman, M., Peterson, C., Diener, E., Zack, M., Chapman, D., & Thompson, W. (2011). Mental health promotion in public health: Perspectives and strategies from positive psychology. *American Journal of Public Health, 101*(8), e1–e9.

Madison, D. (1998). Performance, personal narratives, and the politics of possibility. In S. J. Dailey (Ed.), *The future of performance studies: Visions and revisions* (pp. 276–286). Washington, DC: National Communication Association.

Madison, D. (2005). *Critical ethnography: Method, ethics, and performance.* Thousand Oaks, CA: Sage.

Mann, E. (1997). *Testimonies: Four plays.* New York: Theatre Communications Group.

PCARE. (2007). Fighting the prison–industrial complex: A call to communication and cultural studies scholars to change the world. *Communication and Critical/Cultural Studies, 4,* 402–420.

Pelias, R. J. (1999). *Writing performance: Poeticizing the researcher's body.* Carbondale: Southern Illinois University Press.

Pineau, E. L. (1998). Performance studies across the curriculum: Problems, possibilities, and projections. In S. J. Dailey (Ed.), *The future of performance studies: Visions and revisions* (pp. 128–135). Washington, DC: National Communication Association.

Schweitzer, M., Levin, L., Dee Ball, C., & Macdonald, M. (2011). Elephants in the classroom: A forum on performance pedagogy. *Canadian Theatre Review, 147,* 74–85.

Seligman, M. E. P. (2002). *Authentic happiness: Using the new positive psychology to realize your potential for lasting fulfillment.* New York: Free Press.

Smith, A. D. (1993). *Fires in the mirror: Crown Heights, Brooklyn, and other identities.* New York: Anchor Books/Doubleday.

Smith, A. D. (1994). *Twilight—Los Angeles, 1992: On the road: A search for American character.* New York: Doubleday.

Smith, A. D., & National Institutes of Health (2011). *Let me down easy.* Bethesda, MD: National Institutes of Health.

Spry, T. (1998). Performative autobiography: Presence and privacy. In S. J. Dailey (Ed.), *The future of performance studies: Visions and revisions* (pp. 254–263). Washington, DC: National Communication Association.

Stucky, N. (2002). Deep embodiment: The epistemology of natural performance. In N. Stucky & C. Wimmer (Eds.), *Teaching performance studies* (pp. 131–144). Carbondale: Southern Illinois University Press.

Stucky, N., & Wimmer, C. (Eds.). (2002). *Teaching performance studies*. Carbondale: Southern Illinois University Press.

Ulmer, G. L. (1989). *Teletheory: Grammatology in the age of video*. New York: Routledge.

U.S. Census Bureau. (2007). *State & county quickfacts: Prince Edward County, Virginia*. Retrieved from http://quickfacts.census.gov/qfd/states/51/51147.html

• CODA •

Apples and Positive Messages: Towards Healthy Communication Habits and Wellness

Thomas J. Socha
Old Dominion University

Margaret J. Pitts
University of Arizona

An apple a day keeps the doctor away. According to Hunter (2012) the first printed mention of this saying can be found in the February 1866 issue of the publication "Notes and Queries" where Hunter states the publication printed the proverb as: "Eat an apple on going to bed, and you'll keep the doctor from earning his bread." Since then science has unequivocally demonstrated the merits of apple-eating (among other things) in maintaining health and wellness, but is the field of communication ready to make a similar claim about messages? Perhaps we could offer a revision of the famous proverb: "Speak and hear positive messages before going to your beds, and you'll talk with the doctor about reducing your meds?" Or, perhaps more simply: "Positive talk at day and night will keep you feeling healthy and bright."

Although the field of communication may still have a long way to go before fully understanding the properties of messages as well as medical science understands the properties of apples, the chapters in this volume clearly make the case that communication research about positive messages in health and wellness is a significant, worthy, and necessary pursuit. And, as there are many kinds of apples, as well as other fruits and leafy green vegetables shown to promote health and wellness, the volume shows there are undoubtedly many kinds of messages and message episodes that have the potential to contribute to our individual, relational, and communal health and wellness. So, what's next?

What Are the Qualities of Messages that Promote and Diminish Health and Wellness?

Similar to physical health and wellness, it is safe to say that there are no single magic cures for all that ails us. As much as we would like to simplify our overall health and wellness to apple-eating, with regards to communication, there are simply too many hard- and soft-wired individual differences, far-ranging contexts, varied circumstances, differing purposes, divergent abilities, varied needs, and uniquely held communication values to adopt a one-size-fits-all approach to understanding communication, health, and wellness. Rather, we need to more closely examine positive communication as it occurs in everyday life in order to better understand the specific kinds and qualities of the array of messages that are likely to prompt positive states of mind, positive emotions, and increased awareness that can facilitate health, wellness, and healing.

The chapters in this volume collectively make an important contribution as they spotlight various kinds and qualities of messages that can have the potential to facilitate positive states including genuineness, empathic listening, esteem support, gratitude, humor, effectively responding to good news and triumphs, and more. Moreover, contributors to this volume do not naively engage positive communication, but rather apply positive communication in contested contexts where the norm has been to focus on problematics and challenges of communication instead of the opportunities and potential that positive communication can unveil (e.g., mental health, self-help, cancer management, end of life communication, communicating effectively during traumatic episodes, organizational crises, and even positive talk in prisons). Most importantly the chapters in this volume also begin offer data about how these processes may (or may not) work when used as interventions in overcoming obstacles, in healing, as well as in the development of positive communication habits supportive of wellness. Future work on positive communication in health and wellness should focus on expanding upon the topics contained in this volume.

What Communication Habits and Routines Promote and Diminish the Health and Wellness of Individuals and Organizations?

Duhigg's (2012) recent book on habits suggests that we spend a great deal of our everyday lives operating on autopilot—letting habits punctuated by occasional moments of awareness and strategic actions guide our behaviors.

Duhigg's book highlights various case studies that show how habits develop but also how commercial interests spend lots of time and money figuring out ways to make the purchase of their product an integral part of our habits. One case, for example, involved teeth brushing and Pepsodent toothpaste. After WWII, advertisers created a campaign to increase individuals' awareness of a cued negative state (film on teeth reduces attractiveness), showed people how to resolve this state (brush with Pepsodent accompanied by a snappy jingle), in order to have a white-teeth smile and appear more attractive. According to Duhigg, as the result of this advertising campaign, brushing teeth with Pepsodent went from an action that had a relatively low frequency of occurrence and was a relatively unknown product to become a necessary habit of good dental hygiene. Pepsodent maintained its status as a standard household product until later when Colgate came along with a toothpaste that had what consumers perceived was a stronger response to the negative cue of tooth film—foaming minty freshness (thus considerably lowering Pepsodent's market status).

According to Duhigg (2012) when habits kick in we don't stop to engage in conscious rational thought—we just simply notice a salient cue and then perform the linked behavior (e.g., automatically turning to the right when we enter grocery stores rather than to the left). And, it seems that there are lots of habits that shape our everyday lives, so much so that increasing awareness about our habits (a first step to changing them) is challenging.

If lots of habits shape everyday life it is safe to assume that communication habits are among them. But, what are these communication habits and, central to this volume, how can we make positive messages a habit or a part of the bedrock of positive communication wellness? For example, if the feeling of being genuinely "listened to" increases validation, self-efficacy, and contributes to a feeling of being loved and a closeness with others, then what kinds of communication behaviors lead to being listened to and how can these positive message behaviors become a habit?

We can, for example, make a habit of engaging in therapeutic episodes with a professional in order feel listened to (of course for a fee). We can make interactions with others (known and strangers) via computer technology a habit and seek solace in communicating with people through machines, or even directly with machine (robots) programmed to mirror what we say and even to offer compliments (Turkel, 2011). Or, we can of course seek out people with whom to form genuine friendships, that is people who really care about what we have to say, and then make it a habit to routinely engage in conversations with them. Of course we can also turn to family members in hopes of sharing in what could be a mutual habit of deep listening with positive regard (although admittedly this seems to be an ideal).

When the TV character Norm entered the fictional Boston Bar, "Cheers," to shouts of "Norm!" he (and us as viewers) could not help but feel validated and to habitually return (night after night) to "Cheers." The Yellow Pages list many professionals who will listen for a price, but do we have family and genuine friends who truly and fully want to listen to us? Those to whom we want to return night after night? And, to what extent do the people who make up our most meaningful social relationships engage in authentic and positive communication behaviors? If today we are spending lots of time presenting ourselves electronically on social networking sites, who is taking the time to read and listen—deeply? It seems a worthy pursuit to make positive communication a healthy habit. Positive communication behaviors, such as routine empathic listening and person-centered communication, should become habitual, like brushing teeth, a part of what might be called good communication hygiene—an empathic listening episode a day keeps loneliness at bay (e.g., see Seligman, 2011). More work is needed on understanding the development of communication habits and how we might create patterns and opportunities for the practice and habituation of positive messages that move beyond mere politeness or rote social exchanges.

How Can the Field of Communication Become a Greater Positive Force in Promoting the Health and Wellness of Individuals, Organizations, and Our Planet?

Edward O. Wilson's (2012) latest book examines sociality as a part of the biological development of humankind on planet Earth. Wilson points out that one significant factor which separates us from other life forms is that since our early beginnings humans have been gathering around fire pits to cook, and to share and compete for food—it seems other creatures can't cook. Through years of evolution, we have grown accustomed to gathering and sharing meals in conjoint spaces, and have created special social conventions that support cooperative food sharing (although competition for food clearly still exists). Rituals (habits) of communication during shared dining experiences have been a significant means by which we connect, reconnect, learn about each other, as well as share and receive cultural understandings, and nourish ourselves in presumed healthy ways, and much more (e.g., Blum-Kulka, 1997). Yet, we seem to be creating habits of eating alone, in shifts, accompanied by electronic devices (e.g., see Kaufmann, 2010, the fridge culture pp. 37–43)—habits that not only undermine and work against giving and receiving potential positive communicative benefits, but also create unhealthy physical outcomes including obesity (e.g., see Weber, 2009).

It would seem that as communication scholars work on the next phases of positive communication inquiry we not only seek to better understand the array of positive behaviors we have at our disposal, but that we also become advocates for the development of healthy communication habits, such as supporting daily communication at shared tables. Healthy communication campaigns could play off of Elizabeth Gilbert's (2006) wildly popular *New York Times* Best Seller, *Eat, Pray, Love*. We could encourage families to "Eat. Play. Talk." We could move toward a national "Time Out for Table Talk" day to encourage American families to engage positively with each other through communication at the dinner table. Society does not yet think to turn to the field of communication studies to assuage their problems and improve their health and quality of life; instead they turn to medical science, psychology, and other sources. But, if quality messages, like quality apples, are shown to make a difference in our health and wellness, people will want to know about the communication habits that can lead them to improved living and will turn to communication scholarship for that information.

Thus, communication scholarship should work to continue to better understand the role of messages in the positive outcomes of everyday life, as well as advocate for positive communication habits that can improve the quality of daily living for us all.

References

Blum-Kulka, S. (1997). *Dinner talk: Cultural patterns of sociability and socialization in family discourse*. Mahwah, NJ: Lawrence Erlbaum.

Duhigg, C. (2012). *The power of habit: Why we do what we do in life and business*. New York: Random House.

Gilbert, E. (2006). *Eat, pray, love: One woman's search for everything across Italy, India and Indonesia*. New York: Viking.

Hunter, A. (2012). Will an apple a day keep the doctor away? Retrieved July 10, 2012, from http://tlc.howstuffworks.com/family/an-apple-a-day.htm.

Kaufmann, J. C. (2010). *The meaning of cooking*. Cambridge, UK: Polity.

Seligman, M. E. P. (2011). *Flourish: A visionary new understanding of happiness and well-being*. New York: Free Press.

Turkel, S. (2011). *Alone together: Why we expect more from technology and less from each other*. New York: Basic Books.

Wilson, E. O. (2012). *The social conquest of earth*. New York: Liveright.

Weber, K. (Ed.). (2009). *Food, Inc: How industrial food is making us sicker, fatter, and poorer—And what to do about it. A participant's guide.* New York: Public Affairs and Participant Media.

Contributors

Editors-Authors

Margaret J. Pitts, Ph.D., Assistant Professor of Communication, University of Arizona. She actively researches "everyday" interpersonal communication across the lifespan, especially as it relates to identity, adjustment, and decision-making during significant life events (including health, well-being, and quality-of-life issues such as end-of-life discussions, successful aging, organ donation, and vaccination decisions). She teaches graduate and undergraduate courses in interpersonal and relational communication, health communication, nonverbal communication, intercultural communication, and communication research methods with an emphasis on qualitative communication research. Her research has been published in several international, interdisciplinary, boutique, and flagship journals such as the *Journal of Social Issues, Journal of Language and Social Psychology, Journal of Applied Communication Research, Health Communication, Communication and Medicine, International Journal of Intercultural Relations*, and *Qualitative Research*. She has been on the Executive Board of the International Association of Language and Social Psychology since 2006, from 2006 to 2010 she served as chair and co-chair of the Intergroup Communication Interest Group of the International Communication Association, and is presently the Vice-Chair Elect of the Communication and Aging Division of the National Communication Association.

Thomas J. Socha, Ph.D., University Professor, Professor of Communication, Graduate Program Director (MA Program in Lifespan & Digital Communication), Old Dominion University, Norfolk, Virginia. His areas of teaching and research include family communication, children's communication, lifespan communication, group communication, and positive communication. He has published six books, over thirty-seven articles and chapters, and presented almost sixty conference papers. He was the recipient of the National Communication Association's (NCA) Bernard J. Brommel Award for Outstanding Family Communication Scholarship, numerous teaching awards including the Robert L. Stern Award for Excellence in Teaching (Old Dominion University, College of Arts & Letters), and in recognition for excellence in advising was named the Old Dominion University's 2012

Advisor of the Year, received the National Academic Advising Association's (NACADA) Mid-Atlantic region's 2012 Outstanding Faculty Advisor Award, and is the recipient of a National Certificate of Merit for Outstanding Advising from NACADA (as a runner-up for the NACADA national advisor of the year award). He was the Founding Editor of the *Journal of Family Communication*, Past President of the Southern States Communication Association, and is the editor of the book series, *Lifespan Communication; Children, Families, and Aging* for Peter Lang International Publishers.

Authors

Kelly Albada, Ph.D., Associate Professor, Department of Communication, North Carolina State University. She teaches courses in Nonverbal Communication, Relational Communication, Communication Research Methods, and Media and Family. She received her doctorate from the University of Texas at Austin in 1997. Dr. Albada's research interests lie at the nexus of relational communication, media, and health. She has been interested in issues related to physical attractiveness, body image, pregnancy, and media for the last several years. Her research has appeared in *Communication Theory, Journal of Communication, Health Communication,* and *Journal of Broadcasting and Electronic Media.*

Chuck Aust, Ph.D., Professor, Department of Communication, Kennesaw State University. Aust also taught at Stillman College in Tuscaloosa, Alabama and the University of West Georgia in Carrollton. He also served as a family and children's services caseworker for 3 years and as a drug and alcohol education specialist for 2 years. Aust has published articles in *Journal of Personality and Social Psychology, Journalism & Mass Communication Quarterly, Journal of Broadcasting and Electronic Media,* and *Journal of Counseling and Values.* He published a chapter titled "Face-to-Face Communication Outside the Digital Realm to Foster Student Growth and Development" in *Teaching, Learning, and the Net Generation: Concepts and Tools for Reaching Digital Learners,* as well as "Factors in the Appeal of News" in *Communication and Emotion: Essays in Honor of Dolf Zillmann.* His areas of interest include media effects, media literacy, using media to grieve, and communication and positive psychology. Aust earned his Ph.D. in mass communication from the University of Alabama. His master's degree is in telecommunication from Indiana University. His bachelor's degree in psychology is from the University of Pittsburgh.

Theodore A. Avtigis, Ph.D., Professor and Chair, Department of Communication Studies, Ashland University. He is Editor-in-Chief of *Communication Research Reports* and has served on the editorial boards of *Communication Quarterly, Argumentation and Advocacy, Communication Research Reports, Human Communication, Journal of Intercultural Communication Research,* among others. Among several awards, he was recognized as one of the top twelve most productive scholars in the field of communication studies (1996–2001) and recipient of ECA's Past Presidents Award (2011) and Distinguished Research Fellow Award (2012). Avtgis has published articles in *Communication Education, Management Communication Quarterly, Communication Research Reports,* and *Journal of Intercultural Communication Research,* among others. He is co-author of seven books, including *Arguments, Aggression and Conflict: New Directions in Theory and Research* (2010). He is also co-founder of Medical Communication Specialists and recently named as a Centennial Scholar by the Eastern Communication Association.

Paula Baldwin, Ph.D., Post-Doctoral Fellow, Department of Community and Family Medicine, University of Missouri. She is a health communication scholar whose research centers on end-of-life and palliative care's interpersonal, instructional and organizational issues. For the last five years, she has worked with a national interdisciplinary research group focusing on end-of-life communication issues. Published in multiple international and national journals, Paula has also presented her work at regional, national, and international conferences. While finishing her doctoral degree, Paula was recognized both inside and outside her university for her academic achievements through multiple awards. George Mason University's Department of Communication honored Paula with an award for outstanding external research, the Outstanding Doctoral Student award, and several other awards for her service to the department through her graduate student leadership. In recognition of Paula's exceptional commitment to her academic scholarship, the College of Humanities and Social Sciences awarded her a Dissertation Completion Grant for her final semester. On a national level, Paula won an appointment as one of 15 Health Communication Doctoral Fellows through the

Kaiser Permanente's Cancer Communication Research Center and the National Cancer Institute. Paula was also chosen as one of 25 finalists for the National Cancer Institute's Cancer Prevention Fellowship.

Christine S. Davis, Ph.D., Associate Professor, Department of Communication Studies, University of North Carolina at Charlotte. Her research interests are in the intersection of family, health, and disability and in the ways in which liminality in health status affects identity. Prior to coming to UNCC, she was a researcher at the Louis de la Parte Florida Mental Health Institute (FMHI) at the University of South Florida, where she was involved in numerous projects that studied the communication processes involved in children's mental health services At the University of North Carolina at Charlotte, Dr. Davis is currently involved in several participatory community action projects: with researchers from UNCC's departments of Psychology and Political Science and from Carolinas Healthcare System, studying the role of communication and political action in the lives of patients with traumatic brain injury and their families; and with researchers from the University of South Florida and FMHI studying mental health literacy among caregivers of children with Severe Emotional Disturbances (SED) and social support among caregivers of children with SED. She is also conducting autoethnographic research on body image and aging. She teaches graduate and undergraduate courses in Health Communication, Communication and Aging, and Research Methods.

Claire E. Deal, Ph.D., Associate Professor of Rhetoric, Hampden-Sydney College. She received her Ph.D. in Cultural Studies from George Mason University, her M.F.A. in Directing from the University of North Carolina at Greensboro; her M.A. in English Education from Furman University; and her B.A. in Speech and Dramatic Art, English, and Psychology from Mercer University. In addition to teaching courses in both the Rhetoric Program and the Honors Program at Hampden-Sydney, she currently serves as the director of the Rhetoric Program and the director of the Ferguson Center for Public Speaking. While at Hampden-Sydney College, Dr. Deal has facilitated several service-learning programs and participated in a NEH Summer Institute focused on experiential learning.

Jean DeHart, Ph.D., Professor, Department of Communication, Appalachian State University. She is a Certified Empowerment Coach. Dr. DeHart has a Ph.D. in Speech Communication from The University of Georgia and is a graduate of the Institute for Professional Empowerment Coaching. She teaches courses in Interpersonal Communication, Political Communication, Persuasion, and Life Coaching.

Carla L. Fisher, Ph.D., Assistant Professor of Communication Studies, George Mason University. She is a former Pre-doctoral Fellow with the National Institute on Aging and received advanced post-doctoral training in health behavior theory with the National Cancer Institute. Prior to becoming part of Mason's Center for Health & Risk Communication, she was Coordinator of Research for the Family Communication Consortium at Arizona State University. Using a life-span perspective her research focuses on the centrality of family communication to health. Her primary research program on mother-daughter communication, breast cancer coping, and prevention has been honored with national research awards (www.motherdaughterbreastcancer.com), and she collaborates with leading medical institutions like Mayo Clinic and Memorial Sloan-Kettering Cancer Center. She has chaired the Communication & Aging Division at the National Communication Association and served on the editorial board of the *Journal of Family Communication.* Her research has appeared in books and journals like *Health Communication,* and she is currently writing a book about mothers and daughters coping with breast cancer.

Sherry G. Ford, Ph.D., Associate Professor of Communication Studies and Director of Honors Program, University of Montevallo. She has served in a variety of positions for the Southern States Communication Association and has presented her research at regional and national communication conferences.

Sandra L. French, Ph.D., Associate Professor, School of Communication, Radford University. Her research focuses on organizational discourse with a particular emphasis on CEO communications. She was recently nominated for her university's teaching award, the Donald N. Dedmon Teaching Excellence award for outstanding undergraduate teaching. She teaches Organizational Communication, Business and Professional Communication, Leadership, and Teamwork, among other classes.

Janet Fulton, Ph.D., Lecturer in Communication, School of Design, Communication and IT, University of Newcastle, Australia. Her doctoral research was an ethnographic study investigating the creative practices of print journalists in Australia. Using Mihaly Csikszentmihalyi's systems model of creativity, her research examines how cultural, social and individual influences affect how print journalists in Australia produce their work. Janet's research interests include creativity and cultural production, journalism, journalism education, and cultural production in the digital space.

Amanda Holmstrom, Ph.D., Assistant Professor, Department of Communication, Michigan State University. Her research centers on the contributions of social support interactions to indices of mental, physical, and relational health and well-being. She is particularly interested in the effects of esteem support on a variety of outcomes. Recently, her research has focused on esteem support interactions during the job search as well as at the end of life. Her work has been published in journals such as *Communication Monographs*, *Communication Research,* and *Sex Roles*. It has been honored with several Top Paper awards at national and international conferences, as well as the outstanding dissertation award from the interpersonal communication division of NCA.

Linda M. Johnston, Ph.D., Executive Director of the Siegel Institute for Leadership, Ethics, and Character and Associate Professor, Kennesaw State University. She has extensive international consulting and training experience as well as publications on conflict management. She has twenty years experience working in the public health field. Her dissertation work used narrative and discourse analysis to look at tobacco issues. Dr. Johnston contributed a chapter on "Narrative Analysis" to *Doing Research: Methods for Inquiry for Conflict Resolution* (Druckman, Ed.); this book received the 2006 outstanding book award from the International Association for Conflict Management (IACM). She also submitted a chapter on "Conflict Research" in *the International Encyclopedia of Peace*; this book was designated as "Book of the Year 2010" by the Council of the Conflict Research Society (CRS) and awarded the prize for Scholarly achievement by the Dayton Literary Peace Prize Committee.

Maureen Keeley, Ph.D., Professor, Communication Studies, Texas State University, San Marcos. She is the co-author of the three-time award-winning book of the year: *Final Conversations: Helping the Living and the Dying Talk to Each Other*. She has also published in numerous international and national academic journals. She conducts qualitative research with people about the communication that occurs during a time in their life when they are emotional and vulnerable. During times of distress, people need realistic and practical examples of productive and positive communication that gives a clear understanding about the importance of communication amongst loved ones during difficult periods in life. There is tremendous potential to build closer relationships, to repair broken relationships, to develop trust, and to learn about themselves, when they are faced with life-ending events.

John Mayo, M.A., L.M.H.C., Deputy Executive Director, Success 4 Kids & Families, Tampa, Florida. S4KF is a not-for-profit agency following system of care principles that provides community-based services to families of children with emotional disturbances. Mr. Mayo has been a Licensed Mental Health Counselor since 1982. He has held a variety of positions since graduating from Antioch University in 1980 with a master's degree in Developmental Clinical Psychology. Positions included Counseling Supervisor at the Adolescent Day Treatment Program at USF, Family Builders Therapist, Children's Clinical Case Manager, Case Review Committee Chairperson, Human Rights Advocacy Committee Member, Clinical Consultant to Department of Child and Family Studies at Florida Mental Health Institute – University of South Florida, Board of Directors–Federation of Families for Children's Mental Health, Chair Policy & Prevention Committees-Juvenile Justice Board 13th Judicial Circuit in Tampa, along with a private practice working with children and families.

Michelle Miller-Day, Ph.D., Professor, Department of Communication Studies, Chapman University. Her research centers on how communication in the family positively or negatively affects the health and well-being of its members. She examines interpersonal communication variables related to problem behavior such as substance abuse and suicide. Dr. Miller-Day is the author of four published books and has also published numerous articles in professional journals such as the *Journal of Family Communication* and *Journal of Applied Communication Research*. She has chaired the Family Communication and Applied Communication Divisions of the National

Communication Association and coordinated several community-based prevention projects (gang prevention, substance abuse prevention). As a co-PI she was recently awarded a 5-year, $3.2 million grant from the National Institute on Drug Abuse (National Institute of Health) to continue the Drug Resistance Strategies Project's work on adolescent drug prevention by examining how their federally recognized *keepin' it REAL* curriculum is adapted when used by rural middle schools in PA and OH.

Mary Mino, Ph.D., Associate Professor, Communication Arts and Sciences, Pennsylvania State University, DuBois. In 1980, while studying at Penn State with Gerald M. Phillips, Ph.D., she developed her Oral Interpretation Skills Training Approach for his Reticence Training Program. From 1987 to 1990, as a postdoctoral student, Dr. Mino studied with Bernard J. Guerney Jr., Ph.D., Penn State Professor Emeritus. In 1988, based on her study in RE, she designed for Penn State an undergraduate course, "Personal and Interpersonal Skills," a RE interpersonal communication course that, since 1989, she has taught at both at Penn State's DuBois and at University Park campuses. For over 20 years, she has been a certified Relationship Enhancement (RE) and Supervisor of Relationship Enhancement Program Leader and appears in the National Institute of Relationship Enhancement's Directory. She also teaches basic public speaking, small group, and gender communication courses. Over the years, she has been honored with several teaching and research awards. Since 1997, she has been an Eastern Communication Association Teaching Fellow. Her research interests focus primarily in the area of communication instruction. Her publications have appeared in *The Pennsylvania Scholar Series, The Pennsylvania Speech Communication Annual, Speech Communication Teacher, Basic Communication Course Annual, Communication Research Reports, Qualitative Research Reports in Communication, The International Journal of the Humanities,* and *Issues and Inquiry in College Learning and Teaching.*

Jessica Moore, Ph.D., Assistant Professor, College of Communication, Butler University. Dr. Moore's research explores the intersection of interpersonal relationships, new technology, and social influence. Her research has been published in several scholarly texts and journals, and she has received numerous honors for her dedication to undergraduate education. Dr. Moore is the Director of the Organizational Communication and Leadership program at

Butler University where she teaches courses in Communication Theory, Research Methods, and courses in her areas of expertise. She is a member of the National Communication Association and the International Association of Relationship Researchers.

Jon Nussbaum, Ph.D., Professor of Communication Arts and Sciences and Human Development and Family Studies, Pennsylvania State University. He is the Past President of the International Communication Association and the International Association of Language and Social Psychology, former editor of the *Journal of Communication*, a Fulbright Research Fellow in the UK (1991–1992), the B. Aubrey Fisher mentor award winner (2010), a Fellow of the International Communication Association, and a Fellow within the Adult Development and Aging Division of the American Psychological Association. Nussbaum has a well-established publication record (13 books and over 80 journal articles and book chapters) studying communication behaviors and patterns across the life span including research on family, friendship, and professional relationships with well and frail older adults. Three recent books are entitled *Brain Health and Optimal Engagement for Older Adults*; *Communication and Intimacy for Older Adults*; and the *Routledge Handbook of Health Communication*. His current research centers on quality health care for older adults, healthcare organizations and intimacy across the life span. He has served as major professor and has directed 34 dissertations.

Hollie Petit, Ph.D., Co-owner and Manager of Atlas Unlimited in Estes Park, Colorado. She taught for twelve years in higher education before leaving in 2010 to pursue other passions. She has presented at national and regional conferences, and has published articles and a book about communication and spirituality.

Beth Piecora, B.S., Family Specialist for Success 4 Kids & Families, Tampa Florida. She has a B.S. in Elementary Education from the University of South Florida and a B.S. in Advertising and Communications from the University of Florida. In 2008 she was certified as a Family Peer Specialist in the state of Florida.

Andrew Rancer, Ph.D., Professor, School of Communication, University of Akron. His research focuses primarily on the role of argumentative and aggressive communication and other personality traits across a wide range of contexts. His research has been published in *Communication Monographs, Human Communication Research, Communication Education, Communication Quarterly,* and *Communication Research Reports,* among others. He is the co-author of five books including *Arguments, Aggression, and Conflict: New Directions in Theory and Research* (2010, Routledge). He is the recipient of the Eastern Communication Association's Past President's Award (1989), Distinguished Research Fellow Award (1997), and was named as an ECA Centennial Scholar (2009).

Juliann Scholl, Ph.D., Associate Professor and Graduate Director, Communication Studies, Texas Tech University. Her research emphasizes health and crisis communication. Recent projects include the effects of humor in patient-provider interactions, crisis communication with local communities, and use of end-of-life care by West Texas Hispanics/Latinos. Dr. Scholl has published in such journals as *Health Communication, Journal of Applied Communication Research, Communication Quarterly, Communication Research Reports, Public Relations Review, International Electronic Journal of Health Education, Qualitative Health Research,* and *American Journal of Distance Education.* She also serves on the editorial board of *Communication Research Reports.* In addition to her research endeavors, Dr. Scholl teaches courses in organizational communication, particularly health communication, small group, leadership, and organizational communication.

Claire F. Sullivan, Ph.D., Associate Professor, Communication and Journalism, The University of Maine. Claire has been teaching and conducting research at the University of Maine for the past 17 years. She has published in the area of social support during stressful life events. Taking a gendered perspective, she has researched online support groups. Recently she has taken an interest in college health issues and sports communication.

Jenny Tatsak, Ph.D., Associate Professor, Communications, Walsh College. In addition to her presentations and top paper awards at national conferences, she has published and continues to conduct research in the areas of organizational communication and rhetoric, persuasive campaigns and teaching pedagogy. Her research and teaching is informed by her work as a communication consultant, specializing in general message construction, crisis communication, and media coaching.

Tessa Wimberley, B.A., Contracted Case Manager for Success 4 Kids and Families, Tampa, Florida. She is a recent graduate of the University of Tampa with her degree in Psychology and a Research Assistant for the Rothman Center for Pediatric Neuropsychiatry. As a prospective graduate student, her research interests currently include perfectionism, depression, anxiety, and family factors that contribute to psychopathology. She aspires to a primarily academic career with a focus on research and teaching.

Deanna F. Womack, Ph.D., Professor, Department of Communication, Kennesaw State University. Dr. Womack has published qualitative and quantitative research on interpersonal communication, conflict management, and intercultural communication. During her 28-year career as a university professor and administrator, she has also published two Harvard Business School case studies and conducted workshops on effective interpersonal communication and conflict management. She is co-author of an undergraduate communication theory textbook in its fourth edition.

Author Index

•A•

Abel, M. H., 53, 58
Abramis, D. J., 169, 186
Abramson, L. V., 136, 146
Accordino, M. P., 150, 164
Adamle, K., 57, 59
Adams, S., 69, 80
Adelman, M. B., 193, 202
Agnew, C. R., 188
Aiken, L. A., 192, 202
Al-Anon/Alateen, 83, 85, 87–88, 96
Albo, D., 219
Albom, M., 196, 202
Albrecht, T. L., 183, 202
Algoe, S. B., 35, 38
Allen, M., 256, 258–259, 262, 264–265
Alper, C. M., 38
Amabile, T. M., 243, 245, 247, 250
Amann, W., 7, 23, 25
Amateau, L. M., 32, 40
Anderson, C. M., 213, 220–221
Anderson, J. R., 213, 216, 222, 237
Anderson, P., 146
Andreozzi, L. L., 164
Annunziato, B., 32, 40
Antonia, A., 169, 186
Antonio, V., 186
Applegate, J. L., 43, 59
Archer, A., 74, 188
Ardern-Jones, A., 102, 112
Argyle, M., 118, 128
Armstrong-Stassen, M. A., 227–228
Arnett, J. J., 111
Arnett, N., 45, 58
Aron, A., 133, 146
Aronson, E., 58
Aronson, M., 270, 281

Asher, E. R., 34, 39, 124, 129
Aspinwall, L. G., 78–79
Asplund, J., 277, 280, 282
Aune, K. S., 6, 22
Austin, W., 284
Averill, J. R., 78–79
Avery, A. W., 150, 163
Avey, J. B., 225–226, 235–236
Aviram, A., 143, 146
Avolio, B. J., 225–226, 232, 235–236, 267, 271, 277, 280–281, 283
Avtgis, T. A., vi, 7, 16, 209–211, 213–214, 216, 218–219, 221–222
Awad, S. S., 209, 219
Ayers, S., 131

•B•

Babrow, A. S., 44, 58
Bachrach, C., 130
Backe, H., 36, 40
Backlund, P. M., 154, 165–166
Baesler, E. J., 7, 22
Baikie K., 121, 126, 128
Baldwin, P., vi, 5, 9, 15, 194, 196, 202
Baltes, P. B., 271, 281
Banas, J. A., 222
Banks, P., 100, 111
Barada, B., 106, 113
Barefoot, J. C., 38
Barker, L. L., 181, 189
Barr, P. K., 188
Bartolucci, G., 268, 283
Bass, B. M., 232, 235
Baucom, D. H., 121, 129, 132, 134–135, 146
Baum, A., 131
Baumeister, R., 118, 129
Bavelas, J. B., 54, 58

Baxter, L. A., 5, 13, 22, 76, 80, 169, 186–187
Baylis, N., 265
Bazzini, D., 125, 127, 129
Beall, S. K., 33, 41
Beardslee, C., 123, 129
Beavin, J. H., 153, 166
Beck, A. T., 259–260, 264
Beck, C. T., 44, 52, 55, 58
Begley, G. A., 236
Bellert, J. L., 43, 45, 50, 53, 58
Bellows, C., 219
Bennett, M. P., 36, 38
Benoit, W. L., 229, 235
Ben-Shahar, T., 255, 257, 259, 264
Berg, I. K., 73, 79
Berger, B. K., 230 237
Berger, C., 153, 155, 163
Berger, D. H., 219
Berk, L. S., 36, 38, 45, 58
Berkman, L. F., 31, 38, 118
Berlin, K. L., 101, 111
Berlyne, D. E., 47, 48, 52, 54, 58
Bernard, D. R., 222
Berns, S. D., 221
Berntson, G. G., 42
Berscheid, E., 118, 129
Berson, Y., 232, 235
Bessarabova, E., 222
Bienvenu, M. J., Sr., 154, 163
Billington, C., 269, 282
Birenbaum, A., 270, 280
Birtles, B., 239, 251
Bisiker, R., 168, 171, 177, 180, 186
Biswas-Diener, R., 9, 18–19, 23, 167–168, 17, 173, 175, 183, 185, 187, 194, 197, 202
Black, A., 54, 58
Blacksmith, N., 277, 280–281
Bloom, J. R., 41, 100, 111
Blumberg, C. J., 121, 131
Blum-Kulka, S., 304–305
Bochner, A., 154, 163,
Bodie, G. D., 6, 14, 22, 141, 146, 149, 159, 163, 181
Boes, M., 45, 62
Boonyasai, R. T., 209, 219
Booth-Butterfield, M., 36, 42, 44, 62, 128–129
Booth-Butterfield, S., 36, 42, 44, 62

Bosworth, H. B., 38,
Bourhis, R. Y., 183, 187
Bowlby, J., 133, 146
Boyer, B. A., 102, 111
Boyes, M., 246, 251
Boyle, A., 272, 281
Bradbury, T., 122, 129–130
Braithwaite, D. O., 186–187
Breen, W. E., 35, 40
Breslow, L., 31, 38
Bright, J., 168, 187
Brink, P., 268, 281
Brockman, J., 250
Brockner, J., 231, 235
Bronfenbrenner, U., 65, 79
Brown, J. D., 119–120, 126, 132
Brown, K., 261, 265
Brown, M. M., 270, 282
Brown, R., 36, 39
Brown, S. L., 31, 36
Brown, W. M., 31, 36
Brummett, B. H., 32, 38
Bryant, F. B., 8, 22, 125, 129
Bubel, D., 111
Buckman, E. S., 45–46, 58–59
Buehlman, K., 129,
Bureau of Labor Statistics, 143, 146
Burgoon, J. K., 54, 58
Burke, D. M., 154, 164
Burke, R., 239, 248, 250
Burleson, B. R., 5, 14, 24, 33, 40, 134–135, 137, 140–141, 146–147, 171, 182, 188, 220
Burns, G. W., 10, 19–20, 22–23, 25
Burns, L., 247, 251
Buss, D. M., 36, 38
Butterfield, B., 234–235
Buxman, K., 45, 52–53, 59.
Byron, K., 232, 237

•C•

Cacioppo, J. T., 42, 132
Cain, V., 130
Callanan, M., 192, 202
Calonico, J. M., 133, 146
Campain, R. F., 282
Campbell, J., 221
Campbell, M. A., 170, 187

Canada, A. L., 31, 39
Canary, D. J., 155, 163, 175, 187, 196, 202
Caplan, R. D., 169, 186
Caprariello, P.A., 131
Cardeña, I., 46, 59
Carels, R. A., 134–135, 146
Carlson, R., 154, 164
Carmichael, C. L., 131
Carrere, S., 123, 129
Carroll, J. B., 189
Carstensen, L. L., 125, 136
Carver, C. S., 34, 227, 235
Cash, W. B., 183, 189
Castilla, C., 270, 282
Catlin, G., 78–79
Cavanagh, M. J., 172, 175, 184–187
Cayanus, J. L., 128–129, 271, 283
Cernerud, L., 49, 59
Chakraborti, C., 209, 219
Chalmers, K., 101, 110–111
Chang, C., 46, 60
Chang, E., 272, 282
Chapman, D., 299
Chapple, A., 37–38
Chatham, A., 272, 281
Chiang, L., 57, 59
Chiang-Hanisko, L., 57, 59
Chipp, P., 219
Chon, K. K., 78–79
Chory, R. M., 211, 213, 219
Chovil, M., 54, 58
Chow, E., 31, 38
Christenfeld, N., 39
Cissna, K., 189
Ciulla, J., 235
Clapp-Channing, N. E., 38
Clare, D. D., 143, 149
Claver, M., 282
Cleal, B., 238, 251
Clements, P. J., 60
Cline, R. J. W., 11, 22, 167, 187
Coan, J., 129
Cobb, S., 30, 38
Cody, M. J., 175, 187
Cohen, C., 130
Cohen, M., 100–102, 110–111
Cohen, S., 30, 37–38, 170, 187
Collins, M. A., 243, 245, 250

Combs, G. M., 225, 227, 236
Condit, C., 202
Conley, D. P., 245, 250
Conley, J. J., 226, 236
Consedine, N. S., 31, 38
Cook, J. R., 72, 79–80
Coolsen, M. K., 131
Cooper, C. L., 237
Cooper, L. A., 53, 59
Coopman, S. J., 43, 59
Corbin, J., 103, 113
Cornum, R., 292, 298
Cornwell, J. C., 71, 75, 79
Costello, J., 192, 202
Coupland, J., 269, 281, 283
Coupland, N., 268, 281
Cousins, N., 36, 38, 45, 59
Coutney-Staley, C., 219
Cowan, M. A., 190, 192–193, 202
Coyne, J. C., 31, 38
Crawford, M., 53, 59
Crespin, T. R., 113
Crosnoe, R., 29, 42
Crowell, T., 53, 61
Crumpler, C. A., 35, 39
Csikszentmihalyi, I. S., 243, 250
Csikszentmihalyi, M., 10, 17, 21–22, 29, 41, 64, 71, 78–79, 81, 134, 145, 147, 159, 163, 177, 201, 203, 223, 237–244, 248, 250–251, 255, 259–260, 284, 286, 296, 298
Cunha, M. P. E., 16, 23
Cunningham, S., 250
Cupach, W. R., 131, 165, 184, 207, 219
Cupchik, G. C., 48, 55, 59–60
Curry, L., 282
Curry, R. H., 270, 283
Cushman, D. P., 154, 163
Custis-Buie,V., 284

•D•

D'Angelo, G., 154, 165
Dacey, J. S., 243, 250
Dailey, R. M., 188
Dailey, S. J., 299
Damon, W., 239, 250
Davidhizar, R., 45, 47, 59
Davidson, K., 47, 60
Davidson, P., 272, 282

Davidson, R. J., 34, 41
Davila, J., 130
Davis, C. S., 6, 7, 12, 66–67, 71, 75, 77, 79
Davis, C., 125, 129
Davis, M., 79
de Fatima Oliveira, M., 230, 236
De La Garza, M., 219
De Raeve, L., 99, 111
Deal, A. G., 79–80
Dean, B., 167, 171, 173, 175, 183, 185, 187
DeCuir, J. T., 257, 265
Dee Ball, C., 299
Deehan, G., 242, 250
Degner, L. F., 100, 111
Deiss, D. M., 4, 23
Dejoy, D. M., 208, 222
Delongis, A., 30, 39
Demerouti, E., 238, 250
Denzin, N., 293, 298
Derlega, V. J., 7, 22
DeShazer, S., 72, 79
Despins, L. A., 209, 219
Devito, J. A., 183, 187
Diamond, L. M., 124, 130
Didion, J., 294–295, 298
Diener, E., 4, 9, 18–19, 23–24, 118, 129, 167, 194, 197, 202, 253, 255, 265, 299
Dik, B. J., 275, 284
Dillard, J. P., 175, 187
DiMatteo, R., 43, 54, 60
Dinn, D., 44, 58
Doan, B. D., 99, 112
Dobbin, J. P., 45, 60
Doherty, E., 4, 24, 73, 80
Dolan, J., 297, 299
Dolderman, D., 130
Dollard, N., 66–67, 79
Donahue, P., 45, 60
Donaldson, S. I., 225, 236, 238, 250–251
Donnerberg, R., 270, 283
Doohan, E. M., 123, 129
Dorries, B., 261, 264
Dorsey, A. M., 22
Douvan, E., 118, 132
Dowd, E. T., 46, 61
Downs, V. C., 272, 281
Doyle, D., 192, 202
Doyle, W. J., 38

Drigotas, S., 124, 129
du Pré, A., 47–48, 52–54, 59, 82, 96
Ducaaese, B., 169, 180, 187
Duck, S. W., 13, 16, 23, 168–169, 187–188, 196, 202–203
Duckworth, A. L., 40, 59
Duhigg, C., 302–303, 305
Dukes, K. A., 221
Dull, V. T., 43, 60
Dunkel-Schetter, C., 30, 39
Dunst, C. J., 65–66, 71, 75, 79–80
Duran, R. L., 154, 163
Durrant, M., 65, 80
Dutton, J. D., 24
Dutton, J. E., 7, 13, 15–16, 23–24, 236, 239

•E•

Eadic, W., 154, 164
Eby, W. C., 58
Eden, D., 143, 146
Edge, H. A., 214, 219
Eeles, R., 102, 112
Eisenberger, N. I., 32, 39
Eisenberger, R., 243, 250
Ekman, P., 125, 130
Elashoff, R., 39
Ellis, R. A., 143, 146
Emmons, R. A., 21–23, 35, 39–40, 84, 96
Engel, G. L., 39
Erickson, B. A., 19, 23
Ernst, R. M., 261, 265
Ervin-Tripp, S. M., 36, 40
Eubanks, H. L., 148, 165
Evans, J. J., 46, 57, 59
Evans, P., 242, 250
Evy, W., 36, 38
Ewing, D., 212, 220

•F•

Fagan, S. P., 219
Fahey, J. L., 39.
Fanger, M. T., 72, 80
Farrell, D., 188
Fassett, D. L., 257, 264
Fawzy, F. I., 31, 39
Fawzy, N. W., 31, 39
Feild, H. S., 283

Feng, B., 4, 24, 73, 80, 170
Ferrell, P., 269, 282
Fincham, F. D., 122, 129
Finkel, E. J., 131
Finter-Urczyk, A., 269, 282
Firestone, L., 184
Fischer, L. R., 101, 111
Fisher, C. L., 4, 6, 13, 24, 101–102, 106, 112
Fiske, S., 129
Fitness, J., 118, 123, 129–131
Fitzpatrick, M. A., 154, 163, 188
Fleming, P., 35, 39
Fletcher, G. J. O., 118, 123, 129–131
Flora, J., 122, 131
Florence, B., 154, 163
Floyd, K., 4, 23, 112, 195, 202
Fobair, P., 100, 111
Folkman, S., 30, 39
Folwell, A., 53, 61
Fontanilla, I., 126, 131
Ford, D. E., 7, 16, 59
Foster, E., 191–192, 202
Foster, S. L., 46, 59
Foushee, H. C., 208, 220
Frankel, R. M., 43, 60
Franklin, L. L., 271, 281
Franzini, L. R., 45, 50, 52–53, 59
Frazier, I., 289, 299
Freas, A., 185, 189
Fredrickson, B. L., 98, 112, 237, 254, 260, 263–264, 267, 275, 280, 284
Freedland, J., 233, 236
Freud, S., 47, 59
Freund, A. M., 271, 281
Frey, L. R., 7, 23, 80, 89, 96, 155, 157, 159, 163, 189
Friedman, R. M., 79, 81
Friedman, S., 65, 79–80
Friesen, W. V., 125, 130
Frohs, J. J., 35, 40
Fry, W. F., 36, 39, 58
Frye, J. K., 154, 165
Fryers, T., 143, 146
Fulton, J., 7, 17, 242, 250
Furlong, R., 143, 146
Furst, D. E., 60

•G•

Gable, S. L, 2, 7, 13, 30, 32–35, 39, 41, 124–125, 129, 169, 182
Gadish, O., 125, 132
Gaines-Ross, L., 229, 236
Galef, B. G., 61
Galinsky, M. J., 82, 97
Gallois, C., 209, 220
Gans, H. J., 241, 250
Garcea, N., 7, 23–25, 224, 236, 276, 281–284
Gardner, H., 239, 250
Garnerin, P., 219
Gecas, V., 133, 146
George, A., 36, 39
Geraghty, J. 42
Gerin, W., 39
Gettings, P. E., 7, 25
Gibin, P., 150, 163
Giddens, A., 241, 250
Giger, J. N., 47, 59
Gilbert, D., 129
Gilbert, E., 305
Giles, H., 267–269, 281–284
Giles, W. F., 283
Gillett, R., 35, 42
Gillham, J., 261, 265
Ginsberg, B. G., 149, 164
Glaser, B. G., 103, 112
Glaser, R., 30, 32–33, 40–42, 120, 131
Glover, J. A., 251
Glynn, L. M., 39
Goffman, E., 52, 59
Gohm, C. L., 118, 129
Goldberg, C., 233–234, 236
Goldsmith, D. J., 137, 140, 146, 167, 187
Goldstein, J. H., 61–62
Gonzaga, G. C., 169, 187
Goodfriend, W., 119, 129
Goodman, N., 147
Gorden, W. I., 212–214, 219–220
Gordon, K. C., 121, 129, 132
Goscicka, M., 111
Goshen-Gottstein, E. R., 48, 52, 54, 59
Gottheil, E., 41
Gottlieb, B. H., 30, 38
Gottman, J. M., 127, 129, 176–178, 180
Gottschalk, M., 219

Gotz, I. L., 253–254, 264
Granetti, V. J., 165
Grant, A. M., 170, 172, 175, 177, 184–187, 281
Grant, J., 53, 61
Grawitch, M. J., 208, 219
Gray, R. E., 99, 112
Greene, J. O., 62
Greenhouse, J. B., 263, 265
Green-Rashad, B., 219
Greer, S., 98, 112
Gregg, M. E., 32, 41
Gressley, D., 53, 59
Griffin, D. W., 119, 130, 179, 188
Griffin, E., 259, 264
Griffin, T., 77, 80
Griffith, J., 170, 267, 277, 280–281
Griffiths, K., 187
Grigg, F., 123, 129
Grodin, D., 87, 96
Groopman, J., 73, 78, 80
Gruen, R. J., 30, 39
Guba, E. G., 69, 80
Guerney, B. G., Jr., 149–151, 156–158, 163
Guerrero, L. K., 145
Guillemot, V., 219
Guindon, M. H., 133, 146
Guldner, G. T., 187
Guthrie, D., 39
Gutierrez, V. F., 282

•H•

Haase, J., 106, 113
Haidt, J. D., 2, 7, 13, 23–24, 35, 38, 41, 219, 223, 236, 282
Halcomb, E. J., 272, 282
Haller, G., 209, 219
Hamilton, J. M., 269, 283
Hampes, W. P., 41, 45, 62
Hansdottir, I., 60
Hanson, L., 284
Hantzis, D. M., 289, 299
Harden, T., 269, 282
Hareney, P., 237
Harman, M. J., 150, 165
Harrington, S., 23–25, 224, 236, 267, 281–284
Harris, C., 237

Harris, J., 68, 80
Harris, S. G., 267, 283
Harrold, J., 192, 202
Hart, R. P., 155, 164
Harter, J. K., 208, 219, 267, 277, 280–282
Harter, S., 133, 146
Harwell, V. D., 111
Harwood, J., 269, 282, 284
Hayes, T. L., 282
Helgeson, V. S., 100–101, 110, 112
Helmreich, R. L., 208–209, 220–221
Hendrick, C., 130
Hennessey, B., 247, 250
Henwood, K., 268–269, 281, 283
Herington, A. D., 213, 220
Herth, K. A., 45, 52–53. 59
Hewett, D. G., 209, 220
Heyes, C. M., 61
Hickman, L., 272, 282
Hicks, A. M., 124, 130
Higgins, E. T., 41
Higgs, M., 267, 276, 280, 282
Hill, D. R., 41
Hilmert, C. J., 32, 39
Hinner, M. B., 210, 219–220
Hirst, M., 242, 249–250
Hodge, K., 246, 251
Hodges, T. D., 277, 280, 282
Hofstede, G., 211, 220, 222
Holleran, S. A., 237
Holmes, J. G., 119. 122–123, 126, 130–131, 164
Holmes, T., 168, 179, 187–188
Holmstrom, A. J., 5, 14, 134–135, 141, 143–144, 147
Holt-Lunstad J., 31, 39
Honeycut, J. M., 36, 39, 123, 130, 187
Hooven, C., 127, 129
Horowitz, S., 43, 58–59
Hosei, B., 106, 113
Houge Mackenzie, S., 244, 251
House, J. S., 29, 39
Houston, D. M., 54, 59
Hsiao, Y., 47, 60
Hsieh, C., 47, 60
Hubbard, R. W., 58
Huber, F. N., 272, 283
Hummert, M. L., 61, 269, 282

Hunt, A. H., 45, 52, 60, 209
Hunter, A., 301, 305
Huppert, F. A., 264
Huston, T. L., 120, 130
Hymes, D. M., 154, 164
Hyun, C. S., 39

•I•

Ilardo, J. A., 154, 164
Impett, E. A., 34, 39, 124, 129
Infante, D. A., 208, 210, 212–215, 218, 220–221
Intrieri, R. C., 270, 27, 282
Irving, L. M., 237
Isaacson, R., 261, 264
Isbister, H., 239, 251

•J•

Jackson, D. D., 153, 166
Jackson, S., 229, 236
Jacobs, S. R., 111
James, E. H., 231, 235
James, J. E., 32, 41
James, W., 136, 147
Jay, G. D., 221
Jenkins, M. M., 293–294, 299
Jennings, J. R., 32, 40
Jensen, A., 176, 179, 181, 189
Jesse, R., 149, 164
Jobe, J., 130
Johnson, B. T., 269, 282
Johnson, K. L., 178, 188
Johnson, M., 127, 130
Johnson, R. L., 159
Johnston, M., 7, 17, 100, 111
Jones, D. C., 270, 282
Jones, F., 168, 187
Jones, G. M., 270, 282
Jordan, F. F., 214, 220
Jordan-Jackson, F. F., 214, 220–221
Jordon, L., 150, 164
Joseph, S., 35, 42
Jourard, S. M., 32, 40
Jung, D. I., 232, 235
Jussim, L., 259, 265

•K•

Kahane, D. H., 99, 112
Kaiser, S., 16, 23
Kamarck, T. W., 32, 40
Kanki, B. G., 22
Kappel, D. A., 216–217, 221–222
Karney, B., 130
Kashdan, B., 187
Kashdan, T. B., 25, 36, 40
Kaslow, F. W., 164
Kassing, J. W., 212–213, 221
Kato, T., 210, 221
Katz, A. R., 229, 236
Katz, L. F., 127, 129
Katz-Leavy, J., 65, 80
Kaufman, M., 288, 299
Kaufmann, J. C., 304–305
Kearney, P. M., 77, 80
Keegan, A., 111
Keeley, M. P., 5, 9, 15, 169, 188, 190–197, 202
Keiffer, D. M., 186
Kellett, P. M., 6, 23
Kelley, D. L., 6, 14, 23
Kelley, H. H., 170, 189
Kelley, P., 192, 202
Kelly, J. A., 270, 282
Kelly, T. M., 78, 80
Kemp, T., 187
Kemper, S., 269, 282
Kendig, D. G., 285, 289, 299
Kenen, R., 102, 112
Kennaley, D. E., 272, 283
Kern, C., 219
Kern, D. E., 209, 219
Keverne, B., 264
Keyes, C. L. M., 23–24, 41, 208, 219, 282
Khan, S., 7, 23, 25
Kidd, V., 154, 164
Kiecolt-Glaser, J. K., 30, 32–33, 40–42, 120, 131
Kilmer, R. P., 72, 79, 80
Kilpatrick, S. D., 35, 40
Kim, J., 213, 220
Kim, Y. Y., 23
King, K. B., 134, 147
King, L., 4, 24

Kinney, T. A., 207, 221
Kirchner, J. L., 131
Kite, M. E., 269, 282
Kitzinger, C., 99, 109, 113
Knapp, M. L., 58, 154, 164
Knolls, M. L., 111
Ko, I., 225, 236, 238, 249, 251
Kobau, R., 287, 299
Kobres, M., 66–67, 79
Kock, M., 36, 40
Konijn, E. A., 189
Korani, N., 168, 188
Kosberg, R. L., 216, 221
Kowalski, K., 65, 80
Kramer, H. C., 41
Kreps, G. L., 6–7, 23, 44–45, 60
Kristjánsson, K., 46, 60
Kruglanski, A. W., 41
Krupat, E., 43, 49, 61
Kudsi, S., 215, 222
Kübler-Ross, E., 190, 193, 199, 202
Kuiper, N. A., 36, 40
Kulka, R. A., 118, 132
Kumashiro, M., 131
Kurtz, P. D., 164
Kurtzman, H., 130
Kutash, K., 79
Kwong See, S. R., 269, 283

•L•

Lambert, N. K., 45, 60
Lambert, R. B., 45, 60
Lamble, S., 250
Lamdan, R. M., 113
Lampert, M. D., 36, 40
Landis, K. R., 29, 39
Lanehart, S. L., 256, 265
Langston, C. A., 33, 34, 40, 125, 130
Larson, C., 164
Larson, D. B., 35, 40, 154, 164
Laurance, J., 133, 137
Laveman, L., 65, 80
Lawrence, E., 130
Layton, J. B., 30, 39
Lazarus, R. S., 30, 39, 136–138, 147
Leary, M. R., 146
Leary, M., 117, 129
Leathan, G., 188

Lee, J. W., 58, 273, 278
Lefcourt, H. M., 36, 40, 47, 60
Leggett, B. A., 209, 220
Leiber, D. B., 46, 60
Leino-Kilpi, H., 269, 284
Lengacher, C. A., 36, 38
Lennon, K., 243, 250
LePoire, B. A., 269, 284
Lepore, S. J., 32, 40
Levant, R. F., 164
Levenson, E., 230, 237
Levenson, R. W., 125, 130
Leventhal, H., 48, 55, 59, 60
Levin, L., 293, 299
Levine, S., 193, 202
Levinson, W., 43, 60
Levy-Storms, L., 273, 282
Lewis, J. E., 58
Liberton, C., 79
Lichtman, R. M., 100, 140, 147
Lieberman, D. A., 268, 282
Lieberman, M. D., 32, 39
Lin, Y., 214, 220
Lincoln, Y. S., 68, 80
Lindsey, G., 58
Lindzey, G., 129
Linkins, M., 261, 265
Linkungel, W. A., 229, 237
Linley, P. A., 7, 23–25, 35, 42, 224, 236, 267, 281–284
Linn, L. S., 43, 54, 60, 256
Linnenbrink, E. A., 256–257, 265
Lipchik, E., 77, 80
Litchman, R. R., 112
Liu, S., 47, 60
Lloyd, P. J., 46, 59
Lockard, J., 286, 299
Lolley, J., 7, 22
Lopes, M. P., 16, 23
Lopez, S. J., 29, 40, 96, 251
Lourie, I. S., 65, 80
Luthans, F., 17, 25, 225–227, 234–237, 267, 271, 273, 276, 279, 283–284
Lydon, J., 188
Lynn, J., 192, 202
Lytle, B. L., 38
Lyttle, J., 43, 60

•M•

Lyubomirsky, S., 4, 9, 24, 253–254, 256, 260–261, 265

Macdonald, M., 293, 299
Mace, R. D., 164
MacGeorge, E. L., 4, 24, 73, 80, 140, 147, 170
MacGregor Istley, M., 155, 163
Machin, D., 247, 251
Macik-Frey, M., 224, 237
MacLean, M. J., 283
Madison, D., 293, 299
Madon, S., 259, 265
Magai, C., 31, 38
Mainous II, A. G., 188
Makoul, G., 270, 283
Malcarne, V. L., 60
Malis, R. S., 178, 188
Maltby, J., 35, 42
Maniaci, M., 131
Mann, E., 288, 299
Manuck, S. B., 32, 40
Mark, D. B., 38
Markman, H. J., 127, 129–130
Marrone, R., 197, 202
Marsh, C., 54, 59
Marshall, E. K., 164
Marshall, R. J., 45, 60
Martin, M. M., 213–214, 216, 219, 220–222
Martin, R. A., 4, 36, 40, 45, 47
Martincin, P., 125, 129
Martindale, C., 243, 251
Martz, J. M., 188
Marziah, E., 45, 60
Maslow, A., 133, 147, 180, 188
Matter, M., 150, 164
Matthews, M. D., 292, 298
Matthiesen, S., 239, 248, 250
Mayer, J. D., 258, 265
Mayo, J., 6, 63, 66–67, 79, 313
McAllister, W., 150, 164
McCabe, C., 53, 60
McCroskey, J. C., 154, 164, 271, 283
McCullough, J. D., 4, 14, 24, 33, 35, 40, 170, 181–182, 188
McCullough, M. E., 35, 39–40
McDonald, L., 45, 60

McGhee, P. E., 61, 62
McGrath, A. L., 208, 222
Mcgrory, M., 233, 236
McGuire, L., 30, 40
McGuire, P. A., 46, 60
McKee, K. J., 54, 59
McMahon, G., 174, 188
McManus, C., 131
McPherson, C., 270, 283
McQuellon, R. P., 190, 192–193, 202
MEAA, 239, 251
Mead, G. H., 85, 96
Melton, J., 221
Meredith, S. D., 283
Merz, E. L., 45, 60
Metts, S., 208, 221
Metzger, N., 154, 165
Metzner, H. L., 39
Meunier, J., 247, 251
Meyer, J. C., 6, 24, 36, 40, 43–45, 48, 60–61
Mhatre, K. H., 235
Miczo, N., 6, 14, 24, 164
Middleton, A., 121, 130
Millar, M., 33, 41
Miller, G. R., 58, 187
Miller, K. I., 22
Miller, P. J., 120
Miller, R. S., 117, 120
Miller-Day, M., 4, 6, 24, 98, 101, 112, 203, 313
Milliken, F. J., 229, 236
Mills, D. E., 47, 60
Minden, P., 45, 47, 53, 55, 61
Mino, M., 5, 14, 148, 151, 155, 156, 159, 163–165, 314
Mirivel, J. C., 6, 14, 24, 141, 147, 149, 165, 214, 221
Mishra, A., 35, 40
Mitchell, C. M., 284
Modzelewski, J., 229, 236
Montez, J. K., 29, 37, 42
Montgomery, B. M., 76, 80, 195, 202
Moore, J. L., 5, 14, 33, 41, 117, 121, 130, 314
Morales, M., 219
Moran, C. C., 45, 61
Morey, J. C., 208, 221
Morman, F. T., 112

Morreale, S. P., 153, 165
Morris, T., 98, 112,
Morse, J. M., 203
Mortenson, S. T., 165
Motley, M. T., 221
Mott, D. W., 65, 80
Mroz, D., 225, 236
Müller–Seitz, G., 16, 23
Mullett, J., 54, 58
Mullooly, J. P., 43, 60
Munsell, E., 72, 80
Munz, D. C., 208, 219
Murphy, P., 230, 236
Murray, H. A., 47, 62
Murray, S. L., 119–120, 126, 130, 179, 188
Muse, L., 267, 283
Musson, D. M., 209, 221
Myers, D. G., 255, 265
Myrowitz, J., 232, 237

•N•

Nakamura, J., 238, 248, 250, 251
Napier, B. J., 36, 38, 58
National Institute for Mental Health, 130
Nebel, S., 4, 22
Nelson, D. L., 237, 284
Nesse, R. M., 38
Newman, C., 79
Newman, S., 131
Newson, J., 221
Newton, G. R., 46, 61
Newton, P., 272, 282
Niblock, S., 247, 251
Niehuis, S., 120, 130
Nielsen, K., 238, 251
Nison-Witt, C., 177, 188
Nordenfelt, L., 271, 281
Norman, S. M., 45, 225–226, 236
Norsen, L. H., 134, 147
Norton, R., 59, 166, 189, 212–213, 221
Norwood, K. M., 4, 22
Notarius, C. I., 127, 129
Nussbaum, J. F., 4, 6, 8, 24, 53, 55, 61, 98, 101, 112, 187–188, 271– 272, 283, 315

•O•

O'Connor, P., 209, 221

O'Hair, D., 183, 188
O'Heeron, R. C., 32, 41
Ohs, J. E., 272, 283
Oishi, S., 118, 129
Olsen, D. H., 165
Olsson, H., 36, 40, 49, 59
Orange, J. B., 272, 283
Osigweg, C. A. B., 219
Owen, W. F., 104, 112
Owens, T. J., 133, 147

•P•

Palmer, S. C., 31, 38–39
Park, C. L., 121, 130
Park, D., 229–230, 237
Park, N., 4, 18–19, 24, 64–65, 81, 273, 278, 283
Parks, A. C. 64, 65, 81
Parrott, R., 22, 187, 188, 202
Pascual-Leone, J., 268, 283
Pasternak, J., 234, 237
Patching, R., 242, 249–250
Paulsel, M. L., 271, 283
PCARE., 286, 299
Pearce, W. B., 154, 165
Pecchioni, L. L., 53, 61, 101, 112, 169, 188
Pelias, R. J., 293, 299
Pelled, H., 278, 280, 284
Pennebaker, J. W., 32–33, 41,120, 121–122, 126, 130–131
Perlman, D., 117, 120, 130
Peters-Golden, H., 100, 112
Peterson, C., 224, 237
Peterson, S. J., 227, 232, 237
Petrie, K. J., 126, 131
Pettingale, K. W., 98, 112
Pfister, R., 219
Phillips, G. M., 154, 165, 314
Pierce, T., 188
Pineau, E. L., 293, 299
Pintrich, P. R., 256–257, 265
Pirson, M., 7, 23, 25
Pitts, M. J., 1, 13, 22–25, 29, 40–41, 45, 58, 60– 62, 64, 75, 80–81,135, 146–147, 149, 150, 156, 163–165, 178, 188, 189, 192, 201, 203, 207, 221–222, 266, 272, 283, 302, 307
Polack, E. P., 209, 214, 216, 219, 221– 222

Pollack, S., 102, 111
Pörhölä, M., 207, 221
Porter, L. A., 134, 147
Porter, L. W., 236
Powe, N. R., 59
Powell, F. C., 43, 45, 62
Pratt, M. W., 272, 283
Pressey, L. C., 140, 147
Pride, J. B., 164
Prkachin, K. M., 47, 60
Provine, R. R., 48–49, 61
Pryor, J., 68, 80

•Q•

Quick, J. C., 224, 237
Quinn, S., 225, 236

•R•

Ragan, E. P., 127, 130
Ragan, S. L., 46, 48–49, 53–54, 61
Ragins, B. R., 13, 15–16, 23–24
Rahe, R. H., 168, 187
Rancer, A. S., 7, 16, 210–214, 216, 219–221
Rapport, A. F., 149, 165
Rashid, T., 64–65, 81
Rasmussen, H. N., 263, 265
Rath, T. C., 277, 280, 283
Raup Krieger, J. L., 272, 283
Ray, E. B., 58
Reczek, D., 29, 42
Reichard, R. J., 235
Reis, H. T, 30, 34, 39, 41, 118, 124–125, 129, 131, 134, 147, 188
Reivich, K., 261, 265
Rempel, J. K., 122–123, 130–131
Resick, P. A., 178, 188
Resnick, B., 43, 61
Resnick, S. G., 84, 92, 95, 97
Reynolds, C. R., 251
Rhoades, G. K., 127, 130
Richardson, C., 167, 170, 171, 188
Richardson, G. E., 75, 80
Richardson, H. A., 208, 222
Richardson, J., 17, 24, 274, 280, 283
Richmond, V. P., 271, 283
Riedel-Leo, C., 284
Riggs, M. L., 123, 129

Righetti, F., 178, 189
Rigo, T. G., 268, 282
Roberts, L. M., 7, 16, 24
Robinson, J. D., 269, 283
Robinson, V. M., 46–48, 52–53, 61
Robles, T. F., 30, 40
Rodrigues, A., 131
Rogge, R. D., 130
Rolland, J. S., 101, 112
Roloff, M. E., 178, 187–188, 237
Ronning, R. R., 251
Rosenberg, L., 53, 61
Rosenberg, M., 133, 147, 193–194
Rosenheck, R. A., 84, 92, 95, 97
Rosenthal, R., 268, 283
Ross, M., 122–123, 131
Rossi, D. C., 216, 221
Rossi, D., 216, 222
Roter, D. L., 43, 49, 59–61
Roy Morgan Research, 239, 251
Ruby, N. L., 188
Ruch, W., 40
Rude, M., 215, 222
Ruiz, J. M., 32, 41
Rusbult, C. E., 119, 124, 129, 131, 169, 188–189
Russek, L. G., 118, 131
Russell, J. C., 143, 147
Ryan, E. B., 268–269, 272–273, 282–283
Ryff, C. D., 34, 41, 118, 131

•S•

Sachs, L. A., 270, 283
Sala, F., 43, 47, 49, 53, 55, 57, 61
Salas, E., 221
Saleebey, D., 65, 81
Salisbury, M. M., 221
Salovey, P., 258, 265
Salvador, S., 72, 80
Sapir, E., 183, 189
Sarmany-Schuller, I., 41, 45, 62
Saunders, P. A., 53, 55, 61
Sawyer, R. K., 241, 251
Sayre, J., 47–48, 54, 61
Scheier, M. F., 227, 235, 263, 265
Schlosser, F., 227–228, 235
Schmidt, F. L., 208, 219, 282
Schneider, I. K., 178, 189

AUTHOR INDEX

Scholl, J. C., 6, 12, 46, 48–50, 52–56, 61
Schopler, J. H., 82, 97
Schroeder, A. B., 269, 284
Schultes, L. S., 46, 61
Schultz, B., 216, 219, 222
Schultz, M., 43, 45–46, 48, 52–55, 57, 61
Schutz, P. A., 256, 265
Schutz, W. C., 180, 189
Schwartz, G. E., 118, 131
Schweitzer, M., 293, 299
Scott, C. K., 122, 129
Scuka, R. F., 149–150, 165
Seagal, J. D., 120, 122, 126, 131
Sebes, J. M., 149, 164
Seeger, M. W., 228–231, 237
Seeman, T. E., 118, 131
Segrin, C., 118, 122, 131
Seibold, D. R., 154, 165, 215, 222
Seiffer, S., 270, 281
Sekerka, L. E., 267, 275, 277, 280, 284
Seligman, M. E. P., 2. 4–7, 9–10, 12–13, 17–19, 24, 29, 41, 59, 64–65, 70, 75, 78, 80–82, 84, 90–93, 95, 97, 134–136, 145–147, 158–159, 165, 170–171, 175, 177, 179, 181–182, 184–185, 189, 201, 203, 223, 227, 237, 238, 249, 251, 253–258, 260–263, 265, 268, 273, 278, 283–284, 286, 289, 292, 298–299, 304–305
Sellnow, T. L., 228–229, 237
Shaner, J. L., 269, 282
Shanock, L., 243, 250
Shearer, R., 45, 59
Sheehan, R., 150, 163
Shelby, R. A., 99, 13
Sheldon, K., 187
Shelton, C. M., 84, 96
Shepard, C., 269, 284
Sheridan Burns, L., 247, 251
Sherman, S., 185, 189
Shibutani, T., 85, 97
Shumovich, M. A., 283
Shumway, S. T., 125, 131
Shutz, P. A., 256–257, 265
Siegel, J. E., 113
Siegler, I. C., 38
Sigmon, S. T., 237
Sikand, C., 66–67, 79
Siler, C., 123, 129

Simmons-Mackie, N., 43, 45–46, 48, 52–55, 57, 61
Simon, J. M., 43–44, 47, 49, 61
Simon, R. R., 221
Singer, B., 34, 41, 118
Sirimangkala, P., 213, 221
Skill, T., 269, 283
Skoner, D. P., 38
Slatcher, R. B., 120–121, 131
Sloane, P. D., 271, 284
Small, W., 229–230, 237
Smith, A. D., 288, 293–294, 299
Smith, C. A., 137, 147
Smith, C. W., 47, 62
Smith, D. M., 38
Smith, J., 272, 281
Smith, S. M., 131
Smith, T. B., 31, 39
Smith, T. W., 32, 41
Snyder, C. R., 77, 81, 96, 227, 235, 237, 251
Snyder, D. K., 121, 129, 132
Snyder, M., 149, 165
Socha, T. J., 1, 7–8, 13, 22–25, 29, 40–41, 45, 58, 60–62, 64, 75, 80–81, 135, 146–147, 149–150, 156, 163–165, 178, 182, 188–189, 193, 201, 203, 207, 221–222, 266
Soldati, P., 267, 284
Soliz, J., 269, 284
Solly, R., 239, 251
Sorensen, S., 36, 40
Sparks, L., 53–55, 62
Spence, G. B., 276, 280–281
Spiegel, D. K., 31, 41, 99, 113, 188
Spitzberg, B. H., 131, 154–155, 163, 165, 184, 189, 207, 219
Spitzeck, H., 7, 23, 25
Sprenkle, D. H., 150, 163
Spry, T., 289, 299
Stack, E., 125, 129
Stafford, L., 196, 202
Stajkovic, A., 226, 237
Stanley, S. M., 127, 130
Staw, B. M., 227, 280, 284
Steen, T. A., 4, 19, 24, 46, 59, 64–65, 81
Steers, R. M., 236
Stefanek, M., 31, 38
Steger, M. F., 187, 275, 284

Steinfatt, T. M., 154, 165
Steinwachs, D. M., 59
Sternberg, R. J., 242, 250–251
Stewart, C. J., 183, 189
Stewart, J., 154, 165
Stewart, S. L., 100, 11
Stiffler, D., 106, 113
Stockdale, G. D., 269, 282
Stocker, S. L., 131
Stone, A., 130
Stones, M., 268, 281
Strachman, A., 169, 187
Strauss, A. L., 103–104, 112–113
Street Jr., R. L., 187
Street, H., 21, 25
Stroul, B. A., 65, 80–81
Stryker, S., 147
Stucky, N., 293, 300
Suh E., 118, 129
Suinn, R. M., 112
Sunwolf, 86, 89, 96
Sutton, R. I., 277, 280, 284
Sutton, S. K., 34, 41
Sweet, J. M., 188
Swift, A., 134, 147
Syme, L., 31, 38

• T •

Tajfel, H., 284
Tan, S. A., 36, 38, 58
Tangney, J. P., 146
Tapsall, S., 251
Tassinary, L. G., 42
Taylor, E. H., 65, 81
Taylor, K. L., 113
Taylor, M. S., 143, 146
Taylor, M., 131
Taylor, S. E., 32, 39, 100, 112, 119–120, 126, 132
Teasdale, J. D., 136, 146
Tedeschi, R. G., 78, 79
Teeri, S., 269, 270, 274
Ternestedt, B. M., 271, 281
Tesser, A., 33, 41
Tharenou, P., 143, 147
Thibaut, J. W., 189
Thiessen, J. D., 150, 163
Thomas, D. L., 133, 146

Thomas, L. J., 174, 189
Thomas, M. G., 126, 131
Thompson Hays, M. E., 153, 166
Thompson, R., 187
Thompson, S. R., 54, 62
Thompson, T. L., 188
Thompson, W., 299
Thomson, K., 100, 111
Thorson, J. A., 36, 41, 45, 62
Thorsteinsson, E. B., 32, 41
Tiffen, R., 247, 251
Tighe, E., 242, 244, 250
Torrance, E. P., 251
Travis, S. S., 53, 54, 62
Trenholm, S., 176, 179, 181, 189
Trivette, C. M., 65, 66, 71, 75, 79, 80
Tsai, F., 131
Tsang, J., 35, 40, 41
Tsao, M. N., 31, 38
Tugade, M. M., 228, 237
Turkel, S., 303, 305
Turkkan, J., 130
Turner, G., 251
Turner, J. C., 269, 284
Turner, J. W., 269, 283
Turner, R. B., 38

• U •

Uchino, B. N., 29–32, 41
Ulmer, G. L., 288, 300
Ulmer, R. R., 228, 229, 230, 231, 237
Ulrich, D., 267– 268, 271, 273, 275, 280, 284
Umberson, D., 29, 37, 39, 42
Underwood, L. G., 30, 38
Useem, J., 229, 237

• V •

Valimaki, M., 269, 284
Van Wormer, K., 45, 62
Vandenberg, R. J., 208, 222
VandenBos, G. R., 112, 228
Vangelisti, A. L., 181, 188–189
Varley, C., 251
Verette, J., 119, 131
Veroff, J., 8, 22, 118, 122, 130, 132
Vinokur, A. D., 38, 143, 147
von Kimakowitz, E., 7, 23, 25

Vuori, J., 143, 147

•W•

Waldo, M., 150, 164, 165
Waldron, V. R., 51, 52, 62
Wallston, K., 131
Walumbwa, F. O., 232, 237, 267, 277, 280, 281
Wampler, R. S., 125, 131
Wanzer, M., 36, 42, 43, 53, 62
Ward, M., 209, 220
Ware, B. L., 229, 237
Warren, J. T., 257, 264
Watson K. W., 181, 189
Watson, B. M., 209, 220
Watzlawick, P., 153, 166
Wears, R. L., 221
Weaver, J. B., 181, 189
Webb, L. M., 153, 166
Weber, K., 305, 306
Weiner, B., 136, 138, 147
Weinman, J., 131
Weiss, A. D., 268, 284
Wells, R. A., 165
Wells-Di Gregorio, S. M., 113
Wender, R. C., 46, 62
Wernsing, T. S., 267, 277, 280–281
West, M. A., 17, 24, 274, 280, 283
West, R., 131, 203
Wheeless, L. R., 258, 265
Wheeless, L. W., 256, 264
White, A. B., 7, 23
White, A., 155, 157, 159, 163
Whitecap, V. G., 216, 221
Whitley, B. E., 269, 282
Whitton, S. W., 127, 129, 130
Whorf, B. L., 183, 189
Wiemann, J. M., 154, 166, 183, 188, 284
Wiener, E. L., 220
Wieselquist, J., 129
Wiesman, M. H., 60
Wigley, C. J., 212, 213, 220
Wilhelm, K., 120–121, 126, 128
Wilkinson, S., 99, 109, 113
Wilkum, K., 4, 24, 73, 80, 170
Williams, A., 269, 282
Williams, J. K., 101, 112
Williams, M. L., 214, 219

Williams, P., 174, 189
Williams, R. B., 38
Wills, T. A., 170, 187
Wilson, E. O., 304–305
Wilson, K. A., 221
Wilson, M. G., 208, 222
Wilson, S. R., 7, 25
Wimmer, C., 300
Winke, J., 154, 163
Winograd, S., 113
Withorn, A., 82, 87, 89, 97
Witt, P. L., 256, 258, 264, 265
Wolff, H. A., 47, 62
Wolff, J., 241, 251
Wong, N. C. H., 6, 22
Wong, P. T. P., 47, 62
Wood, A. M., 35, 42
Wood, B., 208, 221
Wood, J. T., 196, 203
Wood, J. V., 100, 112
Worchel, S., 284
World Health Organization, 8, 25, 29, 42
Wrench, J. S., 43, 62
Wright, K. B., 222
Wright, K., 101, 112, 183, 189
Wright, M. O., 134, 147
Wright, S. M., 209, 219
Wright, T. A., 237
Wu, M. Y., 211, 222

•Y•

Yang, J. L., 230, 237
Yerby, J., 154, 163
Yingling, J., 190, 192–194, 197, 202
Young, S., 13, 127, 132
Youssef, C. M., 17, 25, 225–227, 234–235, 237, 267, 271, 273, 276, 279, 283, 284
Yovetich, N. A., 119, 131

•Z•

Zachary, G. P., 229, 237
Zack, M., 299
Ziebland, S., 37, 38
Zillman, D., 47, 62
Zimmerman, S., 284
Ziv, A., 49, 62, 125, 132

Subject Index

•A•

abundance
  organizations, 267–268, 271, 273–275, 278–281
  personal, 185
  relationships, 13
abuse
  see also alcohol/alcoholism
  humor, 46
  physical, 66
  sexual, 66, 93–94
  spousal, 136
  substance, 66, 88
acceptance
  and change, 151–152, 158
  diagnosis, 145
  end-of-life, 191, 194–195, 197–199, 200–201
  feelings of, 135, 180
  self-acceptance, 89, 94
accommodation, 119, 126, 160, 269, 272
accomplishment, 170, 176–177, 287, 290, 292, 296
  and coaching, 181–183
  and education, 255–256
  and flow, 260
  and strengths discourse, 72, 77
  and successful aging, 271–272
  and well-being, 10–11, 20
accountability, 15, 176–177, 137
achievement, 10, 50, 88
  academic, 17, 252–259, 263–264
  and flow, 238, 246, 248–249, 260
  and goals, 14–15, 69, 73–74, 124
  and hope, 227
  and life coaching, 171–173, 174–176
  and relationship enhancement, 157, 162

achieving life, 10–11
active participation in education, 258
actor/acting, 285–298
adaptive positive communication, 102, 104–106, 107
adverse events, 209
advice, 19, 72–73, 87, 169, 198
  popular culture, 149, 154
advocates
  for healthy communication, 305
  patient, 44
  of positive psychology, 65–66
affection, 4, 32, 109, 123, 180
  affection exchange, 169
affirmation, 14, 117, 122–124, 214, 295
  and coaching, 180
  readings, 105, 109
  self-affirmation, 78
affirming communication, 123–124, 127, 194–195, 200
  communicator style, 214–215, 216
  expression, 11, 16, 214–215, 217
  intervention, 217–218
ageism, 269, 272
agency, 15, 77, 227
age-related differences, 268
aggression, 70, 178, 182, 207, 212–216
  and humor, 46, 53
aging, 268–269, 271–273
Al-Anon, 12–13, 96
  12–steps, 84, 85
  history, 82–83
  literature, 85–90, 95
  and positive psychology, 90–95
alcohol, 31, 85
  alcoholic, 12–13, 83, 88–90, 150
  alcoholism, 83, 91, 95, 118
Alcoholics Anonymous, 84–84, 89–90, 96

anti-social communication, 208, 212
anxiety, 46, 178, 213, 244, 246
   classrooms, 257, 261–262
   and humor, 37, 55
   illness, 101, 104–105, 110
appraisal theories, 136–139, 141–142, 143–145
appreciation, 8, 35, 92, 94–95, 108, 110
   diversity, 274, 208
   feeling appreciated, 168, 217
   and final conversations, 198, 200, 201
   see gratitude
   for learning, 255–256, 260, 264
appreciative inquiry, 224, 267
apprehension, 207
   see uncertainty
approach behavior, 34
argument, 168, 178, 215–216
   argumentation training, 215–216
argumentativeness, 212–213, 214–216
arousal-relief theory, 47
aspirations, 86, 168, 291, 296
assisted living, 17, 266–276
assurance, 13, 102, 107, 109
   see reassurance
attitudes
   ageist, 269
   caring, 276, 280
   change, 83–84, 91, 92
   classroom, 242
   coping, 90–91
   employee, 235, 208–281
   gratitude, 92
   and humor, 44, 46–47, 49, 52
   identifying, 70, 75
   negative attitude, 270–271
   positive attitude, 13, 64, 77, 102, 108
   and relationship enhancement, 149, 150–152, 154–155, 158, 160–161
   see resilience
   responsibility, 90–91
attribution, 119, 123, 141–142, 144–145
audience, 239–240, 241–242, 248, 288–289, 296–298
Australian journalism, 239–240, 249
authentic communication, 193–194, 201, 304
   authenticity, 6, 89, 289
   goals, 253
   self, 20
authentic leadership, 267, 277, 280
autotelic experience, 243, 246
avoidance, 106, 253
   see uncertainty

•B•

baby boomer generation, 266
balance
   positive-negative, 127
   skills-challenge, 248
   work-life, 167–169, 175, 177–178
behavior change, 154, 161
bereavement, 33, 168, 194
   see death
   see dying
best practices
   interventions, 272–273
   organizational communication, 214
   instruction, 262
   with older adults, 17, 266–268, 279
   positive organizations, 273–276
body image, 104, 107
boredom, 243–244, 259–260
borrowing strengths, 69, 73, 77
BP, 230
bright side of communication, 95, 127, 184, 201, 223
   see positive communication
business organizations, 223–224

•C•

cancer, 30, 31, 36, 37, 302
   adaptive communication, 104–106
   adjustment, 13, 107–108
   body image, 104, 107
   breast cancer, 6, 11, 31, 56, 98–113
   coping, 98, 101–102, 110
   humor, 56
   interactive approach to coping, 99
   maladaptive communication, 106–108
   optimism, 99–100
   positivity, 98–101, 104–106
   related death, 198
   survival, 98, 99
capitalization, 33–35, 37, 125
cardiovascular, 30

SUBJECT INDEX 335

benefits, 31–32, 118
disease, 30, 32, 37
and humor, 36, 45
caregivers, 67, 269–271, 276
celebrate, 15, 34, 181–182
celebratory support, 4–5, 14, 32–35
CEO, 16–17, 181, 223–235
cheerful, 100, 254
Child and Family Branch of the Center for Mental Health Services (CMHS), 66–67
children
    abuse, 90
    classroom, 15, 177, 180
    final conversations, 15, 190–203
    mental health, 6, 11, 12, 63–81
    self-esteem, 133–134
Chinese humor scale, 47
classroom, 17, 73, 175, 186, 252–265
close relationships, 13, 29–34, 37, 117–128, 179
closeness, 34, 101, 126, 179, 195, 271, 303
    see intimacy
coaching, 5, 11, 14–15, 167–186
    accountability, 176–177
    celebrating, 181–182
    empowerment, 170–174
    future of, 183–186
    goal-setting, 174–176
    listening, 181
    and organizations, 216, 276, 280
    positive language, 182–183
    reframing, 179
    validation 180
    values, 179–180
    whole-person approach, 177–179
cognition
    and cancer, 99–100
    cognitive uncertainty, 119
    and communication competence, 154–155
    esteem-threatening, 139
    and health, 263
    and hope, 227
    and humor, 36, 44
    and knowledge, 216
    positive cognition, 14, 117, 128
    see positive thinking
    resources, 226–227
    structures of, 242

cognitive dissonance, 126, 179–180
cognitive model of learning, 256–258
cognitive-emotional theory of esteem support messages (CETESM), 14, 135–146
collaboration/collaborative
    instruction, 159
    theater, 17–18, 285–298
    work teams, 65, 208–209, 274, 280
collectivist culture, 210–211
commitment
    relational, 34, 118–119, 121, 125, 196
    organization, 210, 231, 278
    theater, 285–298
communication accommodation theory, 269
communication coaching model, 184–185
communication competence, 14, 169, 101, 149, 154–156
communication enhancement of ageing model, 272–273
communication excellence, 6, 13, 14, 149, 156
communication predicament of ageing model, 272
communicator style, 16, 212–216
compassion, 6, 14, 95, 156, 193, 231
confirmation, 194–197, 200–201
conflict
    family, 101
    health teams, 209
    interpersonal, 156, 169, 180
    inventional system, 215–216
    positive, 178, 179
    resolution, 13, 151–152, 161–162
    situations, 16, 181
constructive thinking, 171–172
contempt, 176–177
contentment, 4, 168, 181, 201, 254
control, 71, 126, 158, 184, 229
    behavior, 73
    controllability, 136
    crisis control, 230–231
    and humor, 55
    perceptions of, 119–120
    personal, 254
    self-control, 6, 90–92, 95, 193
coping
    alcoholism, 83, 90
    breast cancer, 6, 98–111

conflict, 178
coping potential, 137–139
end-of-life, 192, 199
flow, 243, 296
future threats, 135
hope, 227–228
humor, 36, 46, 47–49, 53, 55
mental illness, 46
negative emotions, 13
and positivity, 98–101
stress, 118, 181
core strengths, 286–289, 298
see character strengths and virtues
counseling, 57, 169–170
see coaching
see therapy
courage, 13, 93, 95
as a virtue, 6, 14, 84, 90,156, 179
creativity, 240–242
art, 286
character strength, 6, 286–287
coaching, 1710172
flow, 243–249
humor, 47
motivation, 242–243
outcome, 240, 242, 245
thought, 53, 86, 258, 261, 263
workplace, 17, 228, 234, 238, 239–249
crew resource management (CRM), 208–210, 218
crisis
crisis communication, 224, 229–232
family, 70
management, 11, 16, 228–231
organizational crisis, 223–235
situation, 226, 229
critical thinking, 6, 258
criticism, 152, 176–178, 195, 262
culture, 8, 210–212
collectivist culture, 210–211
dimensions, 211
family, 65, 74
fridge culture, 304
humor, 47
individualistic, 252–235
organizational, 210, 273, 276–277, 278
popular culture, 99, 111, 184, 305
and positive thinking, 126

and self-esteem, 134
and virtues, 179
curiosity, 6, 278

•D•

daily communication, 124–126, 153, 159, 162, 195, 305
daily living, 3, 167, 179–180, 266, 289, 305
daily readings, 87–89, 93, 105, 109
dark side, 29, 52, 99, 184, 201, 213
death
acceptance, 197–199, 201
see dying
see end-of-life
good, 201
journey, 190, 197, 199, 200
peaceful, 191, 192
permission, 199–200
positive communication, 193–194, 271
preparation, 101
process, 191, 201
unexpected, 33, 190
deception, 54, 155
decision-making, 56, 91, 211–212, 215, 217
deficit model, 65, 268
depression, 64, 66, 121, 178, 182
and humor, 36, 46
protection, 30, 37
social support, 118
developmental perspective, 2, 13, 90–91
diagnosis, 223
breast cancer, 100–111
cardiovascular disease, 32
mental illness, 11, 66, 150, 171
terminal illness, 145, 192
dialectics, 75–76, 169, 212
disappointment, 126, 133–134, 152
disclosure, 125, 180, 169
cancer, 98, 104, 107
self-disclosure, 30, 32–38, 55, 89
written, 121
discrimination, 285–286
discussion negotiation skill, 151–153, 161–162
disease adjustment, 13, 100–102, 103, 106, 110
disease–based model of psychology, 29, 64, 65, 223

disempower, 66
dismissive communication, 107
disparagement theory, 47–48
diversity, 31, 37, 227, 270, 274, 280
divorce, 123, 133, 150, 176, 177
dual process, 48, 55
dying, 5, 15, 190–202
    acceptance, 197–199
    enhanced, 193, 194, 200–202
    see final conversations
    peaceful, 192
    permission, 199–200
    process, 190, 192, 193, 201
    with dignity, 191

•E•

Eastern Communication Association, 148
education, 7, 11, 16, 17, 252–264
    benchmarks, 252–255, 256–258
    equality, 295–296
    flow, 260–261
    happiness, 258–260, 263–264
    interpersonal communication, 156
    optimism, 261–262
educational achievement, 17, 252–259, 263–264
effective communication, 155, 268, 270–273, 277–227
efficacy, 126, 138, 139–140, 271
    see self-efficacy
elation, 256–257
elderspeak, 269
embodiment, 292–295
emotion
    and cancer, 100, 107–111
    challenges, 285
    in classrooms, 253–255, 256–259, 261–264
    closeness, 101
    see cognitive-emotional theory of esteem management
    coping, 13, 47
    and death, 199
    emotional energy, 47
    emotional focus, 137–145
    employee emotions, 280–281
    and esteem, 134
    in final conversations, 196, 199
    and health, 33, 34, 43–44, 49, 64
    issues, 46
    and leadership, 277
    managing, 118, 155
    mixed emotions, 290
    see negative emotions
    and others, 94
    and performance, 292, 294–295, 297
    see positive emotions
    positive psychology, 7, 170, 201, 223–224
    quality of life, 9
    and relationship enhancement, 14, 151, 160–161
    resolution, 195
    sharing, 125, 127–128, 290
    state, 208
    subjective, 201
    theories of, 136, 138
    well-being, 95, 194, 302
    and writing, 120–121, 125–126
emotional intelligence, 6, 258
emotional state, 208
emotional support, 30–32, 37, 102–103, 134, 136, 155
empathic skill, 151–152, 159–160, 161
empathy, 47, 180, 193, 215, 272, 293–294
employee training development, 211
employee turnover, 275, 286
employment, 143, 210, 234, 254
empower/empowerment, 18, 21
    classroom, 262
    and coaching, 14–15, 167, 170–176, 182, 185
    discourse, 66, 73, 85, 182
    elder adults, 272
    end–of–life, 15, 191–192, 199
    and performance, 18, 289, 291
    relationship enhancement, 158
    workers, 267
encouragement
    breast cancer coping, 13, 100, 102, 104, 107–109
    and celebrating, 181–182
    classroom, 259, 263
    creativity, 289
    performance, 290, 292, 295
    relationship enhancement, 152
    as support, 83–84, 88, 91, 141

end-of-life conversation, 11, 15, 190–210
end-of-life journey, 190, 201
    see death
engaged life, 9–11, 46
engagement, 9–10, 64
    employee, 267, 277, 280
    and flow, 177, 259, 260–261
enjoyment, 16, 20, 71, 92
    classroom, 254, 255, 260
    work, 239, 240, 243, 245, 249
enrichment, 18, 150–151, 153, 162, 266–267
    communication, 4, 9, 109, 149, 156
    experience, 256, 294
esteem, 177, 180
    dark side, 53
    partner, 120
    see self-esteem
    social support, 30
esteem support, 5, 11, 14, 133–146, 302
    see cognitive-emotional theory of esteem support messages
esteem threat, 134, 137–145
evaluation
    classroom, 258, 261–262
    DSM, 65
    relationship enhancement, 159, 162
    residential, 273–274, 278, 279
    work, 168
everyday communication, 4, 12, 178, 195–197
everyday life, 289, 302–303, 305
    coping with, 181
    domains, 2
    experiences, 52
    humor, 52
    performance, 292
    quality of, 21
exercise, 35
    acting, 287, 288, 292
    coaching, 179, 180, 185
    gratitude, 19, 46, 92
    humor, 46
    relationship enhancement, 156, 159–162
    strengths discovery, 66
expressive skill, 152
expressive speaking, 151–153, 159–161
    storytelling, 126
expressive writing, 14, 118, 120–122

Exxon, 230

•F•

face threat, 55, 119, 138, 140
facilitation skill, 151, 160, 161–162
failure
    to change, 152
    education, 263
    fear of, 257
    intercultural communication, 216
    learn from, 73, 158
    medical, 209, 216, 226
    organizational, 16, 229
    relationships, 133–134
    and supportive communication, 138, 139, 141–142, 144–145
family service planning, 64, 70
family
    Al–Anon family groups, 83, 85
    business, 232–233
    cohesion, 123
    communication, 100–101, 109–110, 149
    elder adults, 17, 271–272, 274, 276–279
    end-of-life, 191–192, 195, 201
    family-work balance, 167
    and gratitude, 35, 46
    happiness, 255
    healing, 100–101, 110
    healthcare, 56
    as positive institutions, 7, 10, 12, 238, 242
    and prisoners, 285, 288, 290, 294, 296
    relationships, 168–169, 303–304
    strengths and resources, 64–79
    support, 144
    treatment, 64–79, 82–83, 150
fear, 9, 91, 93, 199
    cancer, 98, 101, 104, 109–110
    of change, 170
    death, 191
    evaluation, 32, 35
    failure, 257
    speaking, 262
    workplace, 212, 246
fearless, 84, 85, 91
Federal Substance Abuse and Mental Health Services Administration, 66
feedback
    flow, 21, 177, 244, 248

SUBJECT INDEX

humor, 54
leader, 277
nonverbal, 123
positive, 298
teacher, 262
final conversations, 5, 15, 190–203
financial
    health, 177
    necessity and death, 192
    success, 17, 22, 253
    resources, 69, 72
flourish, 1–4, 7, 9–11, 16, 91, 95, 170, 209, 223–225, 235, 276
flow
    accomplishment, 260
    achievement, 238, 246, 248–249, 260
    coaching, 178
    coping, 243, 296
    creativity, 243–249
    education, 256, 259, 260–261
    engagement, 177, 259, 260–261
    experiences, 21, 71, 177, 178, 201
    feedback, 21, 177, 244, 248
    friendship, 178
    institutional well-being, 296, 295–297
    motivation, 243–244
    positive subjective experience, 4, 10, 256, 261, 286
    time, 10, 239, 260
    workplace, 11, 17, 21, 238–241, 243–249
forgiveness, 6, 14, 179, 278
    Al-Anon, 93–95
    virtue, 4, 6, 13, 20, 90
freedom of expression, 210–211
friendship, 16, 22, 168
    Al-Anon, 13, 82–83
    flow, 178
    genuine, 303–304
    happiness, 245, 255
    health, 32–33
    humor, 46
    older adults, 271
    performance and, 288, 291, 294
    and support, 144, 169, 170
fun, 13, 245, 255, 262
    see humor
future, 4, 15
    expectancy, 137, 139, 141

goals, 15, 21, 69, 72–73, 85–86, 287
happiness, 256
hope, 106, 136, 201, 291, 296–297
mindedness, 6, 20, 171, 172, 182
positive, 75, 77–78, 99, 120, 123
rewards, 253, 255
security, 255, 258
threats, 135, 140–141
uncertain, 104

•G•

gatekeepers, 241
generalization skill, 151, 153, 159, 160
genuineness, 34, 90, 161, 184, 302–304
gift of time, 191–193, 198
globality, 136
achievement goal theory, 256
goal/goals, 8, 86
    achievement goal theory, 256
    approach goals, 21–22
    coachable goals, 180
    common goals, 291, 292
    esteem support, 134, 137
    extrinsic goals, 22, 242, 253
    and flow, 21, 177–178, 242, 243–244, 248
    future goals, 69, 72, 120, 287, 296
    generativity goals, 21
    goal achievement, 69, 73, 171–172, 176–177, 227, 256–257
    goal attainment, 78, 186, 255–256
    goal congruence, 136–137
    goal directed communication, 51, 155
    goal implementation, 160–161
    goal orientation, 171, 178
    goal planning, 71, 72, 78, 159–161
    goal relevance, 136–137
    goal setting, 15, 21, 73, 171, 174–176, 274
    goal success, 76
    goal support, 127
    happiness, 45, 50, 255
    and hope, 77, 227
    intrinsic goals, 22, 253
    life goals, 21, 22, 271, 288
    organizational goals, 278, 281
    outcome goals, 17, 77, 161, 253
    partner's goals, 124

personal goals, 14, 15, 74, 124, 157, 161, 227
of positive psychology, 10, 91
recovery, 83, 85, 94
relational goals, 14, 21, 150, 157, 260
relationship enhancement, 151–153, 159, 162
self-help, 87
SMART goals, 175
spirituality goals, 21
therapy goals, 46
gratification, 11, 148, 150, 255, 275–276
gratitude
and Al-Anon, 90, 92, 95
exercises, 19, 46, 92
expression, 30, 35, 84
happiness, 254
health, 12, 35–36, 37–38
positive state, 302
response to, 13
as virtue, 6, 13, 90, 260, 278
grief/grieving, 177, 190–192, 197

• **H** •

habits, 31, 153, 255, 302–305
happy/happiness
attainment, 9–10
Authentic Happiness, 9–10, 20, 254
classrooms, 252–264
celebrating, 181
citizens, 252
cultivating, 258
destination, 253
end-of-life, 195–201
eudemonic, 75, 266, 267
feelings of, 18, 254
flow, 17, 239, 243, 260–261
health, 4, 18–20, 29, 37, 105
hedonic, 75
humor, 44, 45, 50, 56–58
immediacy, 45
individual vs. collective, 145
life, 258, 264
and money, 255
positive communication, 1, 109, 150, 272
positive emotion, 4, 9–10, 253–256, 258, 289
positive psychology, 4, 9–10, 75, 254

probe, 19
realism vs. happiness, 145
relationships, 118–119, 122–123, 127, 168–169
resilience, 75
self-esteem, 133
set point, 256
support groups, 84
sustaining, 253, 254, 258, 264
workplace, 17, 168, 249, 271
healing
cancer, 6, 13
coaching, 171
courage, 93
final conversations, 199
happiness, 19
humor, 43
places of, 8, 13
positive communication and, 99–101, 102, 225, 302
recovery, 92, 94
health delivery system, 267
Health Insurance Portability and Accountability Act (HIPAA), 275
health management, 120
health outcomes, 14, 30, 37, 44, 120, 267
health problems, 30, 32, 37, 118
health risk factors, 29
health
cancer, 100–102
close relationships, 117–118
coaching, 183
definition, 29
employee, 208
end-of-life, 193, 194, 200
enhancement, 3, 167, 186
and esteem support, 14, 133
everyday, 2
and flourishing, 9
flow, 21
and gratitude, 35–36, 38, 92, 149–150
happiness, 19, 253, 258, 263
see healthcare
health-related humor, 6, 43–47, 49–58
humor, 36–37, 43–58
laughter, 36–37
see mental health
optimism, 263

organizational, 1, 15–18
outcomes, 14, 29, 37, 43–44, 120, 267
physical, 8, 44, 118, 120–121, 135, 144, 150, 167, 169, 177–179, 302
positive communication and, 1–4, 11–13, 19, 29–38, 100, 110, 135, 149–150, 273, 301–305
positive emotions, 5
positive illusions, 126–127
positive institutions, 7, 11, 15–18, 286, 288, 298
positive psychology, 173
positive thinking, 117, 118–122
and positivity, 101
and productivity, 224
promoting, 49, 100, 106, 108, 110
psychological, 2–3, 8, 29, 118, 121, 135, 150, 200
quality of life, 9, 305
recovery, 95
relational, 11, 13–15, 118–119, 127, 144, 149–150, 167–169, 173, 178, 186, 200
social health, 8
social support, 30–35, 37, 169–170
strategies, 18–22
strengths-based health communication strategies, 69–75, 78–79
support groups, 82, 86, 95
treatment and maintenance, 3, 301
see well-being
see wellness
health-based relationships, 45
healthcare
organizations, 7, 16, 45, 201–219, 266–281
outcomes, 218
positive communication and, 2, 18
practitioners, 50
professionals, 3, 18
providers, 45, 70, 70
settings, 50
system, 58, 69, 216
teams, 209
health-related humor model, 49–56
healthy
adjustment, 110
argumentativeness, 212–213
communication habits, 304–305

communication contexts, 11
coping, 98–99, 101, 105
institutions, 2–3, 11, 15–18, 223–224, 286, 298
living, 3, 22, 194, 196
mental states, 223
people, 3
positive communication, 38, 101, 156, 302
positive psychology, 90–91, 93
relationships, 2–3, 11, 84, 118, 120, 127, 168–170, 184
responses, 91
self-esteem, 133
social integration, 31
helping others change, 151, 152–153, 161
hidden strengths, 66, 68, 70, 74
hierarchy of human needs, 133
higher education, 254, 258
high-quality relationships, 117–118, 122, 170, 260, 277, 280
high-stakes environment, 208, 217
historical strengths, 66, 68, 73–74
holistic approach to coaching, 177
holistic health, 37, 43, 52, 65
holistic thinking, 99, 258
hope
construction of, 77–78
discourse, 65, 77–79
end-of-life, 15, 191
future, 106, 136, 201, 291
hopeful communication, 95, 98
idealization, 119
positive emotion, 181, 286
positive organizations, 17, 224–229, 232, 234–235, 271
probing for, 18, 19
recover, 83–84, 93
theory, 77, 227
virtue, 4, 6, 90, 95, 278
hospice, 191, 192, 201
human error, 208
humility, 6
humor
benefits, 12, 30, 36–38, 45–47
comedy, 47, 52
defined, 44–45
end-of-life, 196

•SUBJECT INDEX•

enhance positivity, 44
happiness, 49
harmful, 32–33, 49, 53, 57
health, 43–58
jokes/joking, 36–37, 47, 50–56, 291
see laughter
see sense of humor
model, 6, 49–56, 56–58
positive communication and, 6, 12, 302
and relationships, 36–37, 43
strength, 6
teasing, 47, 53, 55,
theorizing, 47–49
typologies, 49, 57
well-being, 43
hurtful communication, 127

•I•

ideal self/ideal partner, 14, 119–120, 124
idealization, 14, 119–120, 122–123, 126, 179
identity, 14
  age, 269, 271
  anonymity, 89
  character, 292
  couple, 123
  end-of-life messages, 195, 197
  patient, 55
  positive identity, 65
  prisoner, 285
illness, 1, 9, 98, 168, 177
  adjustment, 100–101
  alcoholism, 83
  breast cancer, 101
  humor, 37, 45, 53–55
  mental illness, 46, 65, 66, 77, 170
  terminal, 190, 194
immediacy, 45, 256, 258, 271–272
immune systems, 30–33, 36, 45, 118, 120, 263
incarceration, 285–298
incongruity theory, 48
independence, 8, 266, 272
individualism, 210–211, 253
individualized care, 272, 273
industrial training approach, 208
information sharing, 273
Institute for Professional Excellence in Coaching, 174

integrated model of positive individual and organizational traits, 273, 276
interdisciplinary, 2, 156, 172, 209
International Coach Federation, 173, 185
interpersonal relationships
  healthy, 3, 183
  idealized, 179
  positive communication and, 1, 64, 150
  rewarding, 34
  support, 30, 134
  workplace, 208
interpersonal skills, 155, 157, 159, 270
inter-professional communication, 209
cooperation, 160
  workplace, 267, 274, 275, 280
interventions, 302
  affirming communication, 217–219
  behavioral, 65, 69, 73
  coaching, 173–174
  esteem support, 144
  humor, 45, 57
  positive psychology, 7, 16, 18, 37–38
  social support, 31
intimate, 37, 117–118, 177, 255, 294, 296
intimacy, 4, 14, 34, 121, 125, 195
  goals, 21
  workplace, 16
intrapersonal communication, 153–156
  elder adults, 269, 272
  goal–directed, 175
  health, 11–12
  positive interpersonal communication, 1, 13
  relationship enhancement, 149–150, 153–159
  skills, 5, 153–159, 174
  support, 169
inventional system, 215–216

•J•

Japan, 210
jealousy, 127, 151
job loss, 134, 143–144
job search, 143–145
Joint Commission on Accreditation of Healthcare Organizations, 209
journalism, 238–249
joy, 9–11, 18–19, 175, 238–249, 254

•K•

kin support, 101
Korea, 210

•L•

Laramie Project, The, 288
laughter, 36–37, 47–49, 52, 57–58
    effects of, 45, 125, 127, 196
    eliciting, 46, 50, 54–56
    stimulates, 52, 53
learning, 3, 20–21, 76, 173, 227, 229
    process of, 93
    how to communicate, 101, 149, 155–162
    in the classroom, 255–264
    service–learning, 287, 293
leisure activities, 254, 289
life enhancement, 256
life skills, 258
life span, 8, 9, 101, 102, 109
life transition, 133
life-threatening illness, 45
life-work balance, 175, 178
linguistic determinism, 183
listen, 19, 280, 302–304
    listening, 6, 14–15, 148, 181
    appreciative, 149
    behavior, 155, 158
    empathic, 151, 159, 161, 302
    listener, 50, 125
locus of control, 254
loneliness, 32, 33, 36, 302
loss, 94, 133, 134, 197
    see death
    life, 209
    loved one, 191, 194, 195
love, 6, 18–19, 91, 120, 179, 193
    confirmation, 195–196
low-context communication, 210

•M•

maintenance skills, 151
maladaptive positive communication, 102, 106–108, 109
Malden Mills, 16, 230, 232–234
management, 12, 67, 120, 209, 228, 302
    practices, 210, 212, 272
    techniques, 86, 183, 231

marital distress, 127
meaning of life, 193
meaningful communication, 208, 217
meaningful life, 9–11, 15, 21, 46
Medicaid, 266
medical humor, 44, 46
medical team, 16, 44, 208, 216, 217, 272
medicine, 172, 191–192, 208–209, 216
memory, 125, 289, 294
mental health, 32, 65, 99, 120, 170, 287
    children, 6, 12, 63–79
mental illness, 46, 65, 66, 77, 170
mercy, 6
    see forgiveness
message episodes, 301
message extensiveness, 138, 139
models of health
    biopsychosocial model of health, 29
    diseased-based, 29, 64, 65, 223
    medical model, 29, 64, 65
    traditional, 64, 65, 156, 171
model of humor in health communication, 12, 44, 49
modesty, 6
money, 17, 177, 234, 242–243, 253, 255
mood, 57, 109, 182, 254, 268
    elevate, 36, 52, 64
    negative, 106, 107, 171, 259
    positive, 56, 120, 277, 280
morale, 49, 286
morbidity, 30, 118
mortality, 30–31, 98, 118, 177
    see death
    risk factors, 29, 31, 272
mother-daughter relationship, 99, 101–102, 109
    see family
motivation, 17, 34, 57, 77, 155, 175
    employee, 238, 240, 242–243, 280
    extrinsic, 242
    and flow, 243–244
    inspirational, 232
    intrinsic, 242
    and self-efficacy, 226–227

•N•

narrative, 17–18, 64, 74, 120–126, 294–295
National Cancer Institute, 101

National Institute of Relationship Enhancement, 163
negative affect, 108, 124, 126, 213, 253, 257
negative communication, 111, 127, 272, 279
negative emotions, 9, 13, 34, 46, 104, 107–111, 127, 136–137, 199
  in class, 253
  distress, 137, 171
  see emotions
  see fear
  final conversations, 99
  hurt, 179
  words, 121
negative events, 30, 33, 122, 123, 263
negative feelings, 98, 108, 111, 168
negative social relationships, 29
negative work environment, 239
nonverbal communication, 1, 20, 54, 56, 160
novel experiences, 261
nursing care, 52, 266, 274, 276
nursing homes, 266–281

•O•

older adults, 31, 54, 266–281
  communication experiences, 54
oncological care, 31
openness, 6, 45
operational leadership, 209
opportunity, 84, 110, 121, 190–192, 229
optimism, 17, 98, 100, 120, 227–228, 261–263
  forced, 99, 100
optimists, 185, 263
oral communication, 154
organizational antecedents, 273
organizational communication theory, 208
organizational crisis, 223–235
organizational culture, 210, 273, 276–277, 278
organizational effectiveness, 208, 270, 273
organizational efficiency, 208, 273
organizational health and wellness, 1, 15–18
organizational productivity, 210
organizational relationships, 211, 214–216
organizational research, 208, 225
other-awareness, 208

•P•

pain, 100, 197, 198, 213
  pain reduction, 45
palliative care, 191
  medicine, 192
parent-child communication, 72
  see family communication
  see mother-daughter
passion, 245
pathological, 207
pathways thinking, 65, 77, 227
patient safety, 208, 209
patient-care transfer, 209
pedagogy, 254
performance–oriented students, 257
permission, 194, 199–201
personal accomplishments, 287
personal control, 193
personal development, 267
personal fulfillment, 261
personal growth, 156, 162, 261, 277, 280
personal satisfaction, 277
personal strengths, 46, 95
personnel, 217, 268, 279
pessimism, 98
pessimists, 185, 263
Philip Morris, 230
physical health and wellness, 44, 135, 302
physician-patient communication, 271
Piedmont Regional Jail, 285, 287, 297
pleasant life, 9, 10, 11, 46
pleasure, 8–10, 34, 148, 255, 264
  awareness, 255
poor communication, 209
positive affect, 9, 34, 124, 127
positive change, 64, 78, 231, 262
positive cognition, 14, 117, 128
positive communication habits, 302–304
positive communication
  adaptive positive communication, 104–106
  and cancer coping, 99–101
  character strengths and virtues, 82
  decline, 127
  defined, 1–2
  developmental perspective, 2
  in education, 252–264

SUBJECT INDEX

elder adults, 167–268, 271–273, 279
end of life, 190–202
esteem support as, 134–135
expression, 207, 208–209, 214, 218
extra-hospital setting, 216–218
flourishing, 4, 29
flow, 239
habits, 302–305
happiness, 266
harmful, 128
healing potential, 99, 101, 108–109, 110–111
in health and wellness, 2–3, 29, 302
health promoting, 110
and health, 11–13
and healthy institutions/organizations, 15–18, 208, 223–224, 231, 281
history, 7–8
humor/laughter, 36–37
life coaching, 167, 174, 184
maladaptive positive communication, 106–108, 109–110
and positive psychology, 2, 4–7, 84, 90–95, 134–135
positivity, 102
prisoners, 286, 288
project, 1
quality of life, 7–9
and relational wellness, 13–15, 30, 37–38, 149
relationship enhancement, 149–150, 155–156, 159, 162
in relationships, 127–128
routines, 3
social support, 30–35, 37
strategies, 18–22, 218, 252
and strengths approach, 64
symbolic, 85–87
positive deviance, 224, 225, 231
positive emotions, 7, 13–14, 33–34, 64, 77, 134, 148, 196, 223, 256, 261–262, 286–287, 302
see emotion
enhanced positive emotions, 144–145
gratification, 148–149
gratitude, 13, 35–36
happiness, 9–11, 19, 253–255, 259–260
positive emotion words, 121

positive emotions and coaching, 171–172, 176, 179, 181–182
positive emotions as pillar of positive psychology, 2, 4–5, 70–71, 134, 146
positive emotions in organizations, 267, 276, 277–278, 280
resilience, 228
validating, 180
positive energy, 171–172
positive expectations, 201, 259
positive expression
workplace, 208–209, 218
positive illusions, 11, 119, 120, 126–127
idealization, 123
positive impressions, 118
positive institutions, 7, 70, 135, 223, 266, 278
positive interactions, 37, 117
positive language, 182–183
positive messages, 200, 301–304
positive organizational behavior, 224–227, 231, 235
positive organizational scholarship, 16, 224
positive organizations, 7, 15–17, 277, 224–235, 266–281
positive psychology, 4–7
the good life, 1
authentic happiness theory, 9–10
character strengths and virtues, 5–6, 13, 83–84, 90–93, 95, 179, 223, 289
and coaching, 171–175, 182, 184, 186
courage, 93
defined, 2
developmental, 90–91
education, 252–264
emotions, 4–5, 201
engagement, 260–261
flourishing, 2, 7, 10, 91, 223
flow, 238, 292
forgiveness, 93–94
gratitude, 92
happiness, 254–259
and health and wellness, 95
humor, 46
and mental health, 64–66, 78, 170
optimism, 259, 261–263
pillars of, 2, 4–7, 18, 70, 135, 146, 223, 266

in positive communication, 2, 4–7, 82, 84, 90–95, 134–135, 252, 254
positive institutions, 7, 72, 223–235, 238–249, 266–267
positive organizational scholarship, 7, 15–17, 277, 224–235
quality of life, 4
recovery, 84, 95
resilience, 228, 292
responsibility, 91–92
savoring, 8
self-efficacy, 226–227
tension, 145
well-being theory, 9–10
positive regard, 124, 141, 304
positive relationships, 13, 18, 223, 235, 274, 278
positive states of mind, 302
positive talk, 5, 98, 104, 106–110, 117–128
positive thinking, 14
    cancer, 98–99
    coping, 109
    moral norm, 99
    optimism, 228, 263
    relationships, 117–122, 126–128
positive traits, 2, 70, 119, 134, 259
    see traits
positive turn in communication, 2, 128
positive work environment, 239, 277
positivity
    cancer, 98–101, 104–107, 110–111
    coaching, 185
    end-of-life, 15, 195
    expression, 207, 214
    health–related practice, 44
    higher education, 254, 259, 263
    humor, 44–45, 50, 56–58
    and illusions, 117
    "Positivity," 254
    realistic, 100, 110
    and relational well-being, 126
    as relationship, 13
    storytelling, 125
    unrealistic, 100
post-traumatic stress disorder, 121
potential complications, 209
power of positivity, 207, 231
power-distance, 211

practical skills, 258
present time, 69, 77, 122, 230, 255, 260, 263
    end-of-life, 15, 193–194, 198–199
    esteem messages, 139, 141
    positive emotions, 4, 201
pride, 10, 18, 73, 296–297
    workplace, 279, 290
print journalists, 17, 238–249
Prison Communication, Activism, Research, and Education (PCARE), 286
prison staff, 285–288, 296, 297–298
prisoners, 17–18, 285–298
problematic behaviors, 269–270
problematic features of communication, 207–208
problem-conflict resolution skill, 150–152, 161–162
problem-solving (solve problems), 126, 150–151, 224, 286
productivity, 24, 156
    classroom, 258–259
    organizational, 210, 214, 224
    relationship, 3, 168
    self, 162, 208
    workplace, 225, 238, 247, 249, 277–280
professional performance, 209
promoting health and wellness, 18–19, 82, 301–302
pro-social communication, 207–208, 212–213
psycap measurement, 234–235
psychological capital, 234–235
psychological distance, 45
psychological health and wellness, 2–3, 29, 118, 135, 200
    see well-being
psycho-oncology, 98–99, 101
punishment, 263

•Q•

quality of communication, 269–270
quality of education, 253
quality of life, 2–9, 15
    flow, 21
    humor, 36
    older adults, 268
    women, 103–104
quality messages, 36

•R•

rapport, 44, 286
ratio of positive to negative messages
    3:1, 271
    5:1, 127
realistic positivity, 100–101, 110–111
reassurance, 100, 104–105, 138
reattribution, 137, 139, 141–144, 145–146
recovery, 54, 82–84, 87–88, 90–96
reflection, 154–155, 169, 192–193, 287
    messages, 141
    organizational, 231, 243
reframing, 15, 74, 105–111, 179, 229
    humor, 45
    language, 65, 78–79
rehearsal, 18, 125, 153, 287–288, 291–297
reinforcement, 57, 71, 122, 152–153, 208
rejection, 141–142, 144–145, 168, 179, 248
relational development, 5, 16, 30,
relational expectancy, 211
relational health and wellness, 11, 13–15, 119, 149–150, 167–169, 200
relational quality, 178
relational skills, 149, 258
relationship enhancement, 5, 11, 174
    approach, 14, 148–162
    background, 156–158
    instruction, 158–162
    skills, 5, 151–153
religious, 30–31, 75, 85, 197–198, 254
    character strength, 6
relocation, 169, 266–267
remembering, 73–74
reminiscing, 70–71, 73–74, 124–125, 127
resilience, 17, 77, 286–287
    building, 263, 292
    family, 66, 68, 70, 75
    organizational, 17, 224–226, 228, 232–235, 271, 278
    positive communication, 77
resources
    available, 69, 72–73, 74, 77, 170
    cognitive, 226
    family, 64, 66, 72
    identify, 175, 224, 225–226
    lacking/limited, 101, 216
    optimism, 100, 227–228, 232, 271
    producing/building, 13, 34, 78
    psychosocial, 101
    self-help, 87
    to succeed, 145
    team, 66, 68
    workplace, 238, 241–242, 249
respect, 3, 16, 51, 214, 293–295
    patient, 270, 271, 278, 280
responsibility, 3, 6, 13
    one's actions, 90–93, 95, 176–177, 182, 185
    organizational, 230, 234, 279
    student, 261
    transgression, 145
retirement, 234
    facility, 271, 275–277
reward, 18, 169–170, 242–243, 264, 277–278
    classroom, 255
    financial, 239
    rewarding, 34–35, 117, 214–215, 260, 289
    vs. cause, 253
rhetorical sensitivity, 14, 149, 154–156
role plays, 159, 161–162, 216
role reversal, 101–102
roles, 101, 154, 305
    coaching, 175, 181–182, 185–186
    end-of-life, 191, 202
    organizational, 229, 241, 276, 280
    patient, 55, 79
    relationship, 51, 168
    team, 274
routine, 153, 158, 228–229, 302–304
    daily, 3, 297
    end-of-life, 194
    routine interactions, 196
rural trauma team development course (RTTDC), 217–218

•S•

safety, 72, 93, 133, 208, 209
satisfaction, 4, 34, 64, 210–211, 291
    customer, 267
    flow, 243–246, 249
    humor, 43, 45, 56–58
    job, 213, 238, 249, 277, 280
    life, 9–11, 49, 271
    marital, 32
    patient, 53, 55

workplace, 16, 19, 20
satisficing, 244
satisfying organizational experience, 210–211
savor/savoring, 7–8, 18–19, 125, 255, 259–260
schizophrenia, 118
school performance, 133, 139, 253, 257, 261
self-change, 150–152, 161
self-awareness, 199, 277, 280, 294–295, 298
self-changing skill, 152, 161
self-confidence, 286, 290, 295, 298
self-control, 6, 90, 91, 95
self-determination, 211–212, 269–270, 289
self-efficacy, 226–228, 234–235
    job search, 143–144
    positive organizational behavior, 225–226
    strength, 19–20, 174–175
self-esteem
    adults, 269
    capitalization, 33–34
    children, 133–134
    culture, 134
    esteem support, 133–145
    health, 33
    humor, 36, 45, 52–53
    individual, 119–120, 168–169, 184–185
    protection, 119
    strength, 19–20
    state, 14
    trait, 136, 254
self-disclosure, 30, 32–38, 55, 89
self-fulfilling prophecy, 259
self-help
    books/literature, 87, 99, 149
    support groups, 6, 11, 12–13, 82–95
self-reflective, 277–278, 280–281
self-regulation, 6
self-worth, 289
sense of humor, 36, 75
service-learning, 261, 287
setbacks, 185, 228, 234, 263, 291–292
shared understanding, 209
sharing positive events, 33–35, 124–126, 127–128
sick role, 78–79
silence, 108, 109–110, 289
silencing effect, 106–108, 109–110

situational humor response questionnaire, 47
six-dimensional model of competence, 272
small talk, 196
smoking, 29, 31, 63
social capital, 35–36
social cognitive processing, 226–227
social connections, 8, 30–31
social exchange theory, 170, 176
social identity theory, 268–269
social integration, 30–31
social intelligence, 6, 90–91, 95
social support
    Al-Anon, 12–13, 82–95
    capitalization, 34
    see cognitive–emotional theory of esteem support messages (CETESM)
    during difficulty, 13
    enacted, 167, 173
    end-of-life, 193–194
    see esteem support
    in health, 11–12, 30–32, 37–38, 118
    job search, 143
    see self-help
    sources, 169–170
    stress, 118
    teams, 274–280
    validation, 180
social ties, 30–32, 37, 117–118
social-historical context, 257
socialization, 54, 133–134, 136
socially isolated, 29, 30–31
sophisticated support, 144
sorrow, 200–201
spiritual, 43, 58, 75
    coaches, 183
    spiritual awakening, 85, 88, 95
    spiritual connection, 197–198
    spirituality, 6, 21, 172, 179, 278
stability, 5, 90–91, 135
    CETESM, 136
    relationship, 34, 121, 168
    financial, 258
stakeholders, 228–233, 239, 267–273, 276–277, 281
stereotypes, 272
    challenge, 288, 293–294, 297–298
    humor, 52, 53
    negative, 183, 216, 268–269

stories, 120, 122
  Al-Anon, 88
  end-of-life, 201
  as humor, 52, 54
  life stories, 3, 287–289, 291, 294, 296
  see narrative
  news/journalism, 229, 242, 245, 248
  and positive illusions, 119, 126–127
  survivor stories, 13, 105, 109
storytelling, 14, 46, 117, 123–127, 229–230
  see narrative
strategic rhetoric, 257
character strengths and virtues, 2, 4–7, 12–13, 19, 75, 83–84, 90–95, 179, 223, 226, 278
strengths deficit, 64–65, 75–77
strengths discovery, 66, 71, 75
strengths-based communication, 6, 12, 63–79
stress
  academic, 255, 257
  cognitive dissonance, 179–180
  and conflict, 178
  end-of-life, 198
  listening, 181
  positive talk, 104
  reduction, 32, 35, 45, 48, 57, 180
  related disorders, 37
  relational, 169, 176
  release, 110
  response, 31–32, 102
stressors, 30, 31–32, 118, 124, 168–169
success
  behavior control, 73
  as benchmark, 17, 253, 257, 264
  coaching and, 171, 185
  financial, 17, 22
  happiness, 253
  organizational, 210, 229
  outcome goal, 17, 171, 253
  relationship, 32, 133
  strength spotting, 20
  student, 257
  team, 208–209
successful aging, 271–272
superiority theory, 47–48
support groups, 12–13, 31, 82–90, 95, 103
support network, 98–100

supportive communication, 32, 33–34, 72–73, 181–182, 280–281
  cultures of, 280, 281
supportive organizations, 276–277
survivors, 13, 105, 109, 98–99, 190
symbolic interactionism, 85–87
symbols, 51, 85–87
sympathetic nervous system, 31–32
sympathy, 36–37
system of care, 64–68, 78, 79
systems model of creativity, 240–247

•T•

talent, 242
team
  building, 203
  healthcare, 12, 44, 63–79
  medical teams, 207–219, 272–273
  workplace, 208–209, 274–276, 280
technological advances, 191–192, 208
temperance, 6, 84, 90, 179–180
terminal time, 193
theater of testimony, 287, 295
theory of independent mindedness, 208, 209, 210–214, 216
therapeutic episodes, 303
therapeutic humor, 44, 45
therapy
  and coaching, 170–171, 186
  couples, 150
  psychotherapy, 64
  stigma, 170
threat
  abuse, 93
  communication-related, 209
  esteem threat, 134–135, 136–137, 138, 139–145
  evaluation, 32
  organizational, 228–229, 231, 234, 235
  self-threat, 134
  violence, 93
time constraints, 242, 244, 247
time, 10, 69, 72, 77
tolerance, 171, 211, 263
training programs, 157, 215, 270, 275, 280
training
  coach training, 174, 185
  crew resource management, 208–209

employee, 211, 214–218
interpersonal skills, 134
in nursing homes, 268, 270, 275–276, 278–280
organizational, 225–227, 242
relationship enhancement, 14, 149, 153, 157–159, 161–162
rural trauma team development course, 217–219
savoring, 19
strengths-based communication strategies, 70, 79
see training programs
traits, 74, 78, 215, 225–226
argumentativeness, 212, 215–216
communication, 210, 213
individual, 247, 267, 268, 286
optimism, 227
organizational, 273, 276–277, 278–279
personality, 70, 75, 242, 254, 261
see positive traits
psychological, 36, 70, 232
self-esteem, 136
verbal aggressiveness, 216
transcendence, 6, 21, 84, 90, 92, 93, 179
transformational leadership, 232
transformative cooperation, 267, 275, 280
transgression, 135, 141–142, 144, 145
transition, 132, 134, 231, 266, 269
trauma
and breast cancer, 99–102, 106
events, 32–34, 95, 288–289, 302
medical teams, 16
trauma medicine, 207–208, 216–218
and validation, 180
trust, 14, 125–126, 181, 286
anonymity, 89
capitalization, 34, 125
difficulty, 178
expressive writing, 121
humor, 51, 58
positive illusions, 120
trusting, 75, 168
trustworthy, 118, 182
Tylenol, 230

•U•

uncertainty, 104, 106, 120, 155, 228

avoidance, 211
cancer, 104–106
cognitive, 119
reduction, 153, 193–194, 231
unemployment, 136, 143
unhappy classrooms, 255–256
unhealthy behaviors, 30, 91, 101
uninspired workforce, 210

•V•

Valdez, 230
validation, 6, 11, 34, 110, 195–196, 303–304
empowerment coaching, 15, 179–180
feelings, 109–110, 212
not validating, 107–111, 214
in organizations, 207–219
Values in Action Inventory of Strengths, 84
values
see character strengths and values
verbal aggressiveness, 212–213, 214, 216
violence, 66, 93, 285
virtues, 2–6, 19, 65, 75, 82–84, 90–95, 179, 226, 259–260, 289
see character strengths and virtues
communication excellence, 14, 156
partner, 119
in organizational crises, 17, 223, 231
vitality, 6, 18, 19, 20

•W•

wealth, 255
see money
well-being
cancer, 101
coaching, 168, 171–173, 175–178, 183–186
collective, 145
communication strategies, 18–22
education, 17, 254–259
employee, 208, 238–239, 278
end-of-life, 193–197, 201
esteem support, 133–135, 141, 144
everyday, 2–4
expressive writing, 120–122
family communication, 101
flow, 240, 243–244, 249, 295–297
happiness, 17, 75, 238, 254–255, 258–259

see health
health and wellness, 12, 37, 44, 179
humor, 49, 56
individual, 1–2, 11, 36
life domains, 1
older adults, 272–273
organizational, 1–2, 11, 224–225, 238–239, 249, 271, 280, 286, 295–298
patient, 271
positive communication and, 2, 7–11, 18–22, 29
positive emotions and, 34, 271, 276, 278
positive illusions, 126–127
positive psychology and, 4–7
positive talk, 122–124
positive thinking, 118–120
positivity, 46–47
prisoner, 288, 292, 298
recovery, 92
relational, 1–2, 11, 13–15, 36–37, 117–128, 146, 150
self-disclosure, 32–33
sharing positive events, 124–126, 127–128
social support, 30, 169
support groups, 82
validation, 180
well-being theory, 2, 9–10
see wellness
wellness, 17, 20, 43, 50, 100–101, 162
cancer, 100–102
coaching, 183
employee, 208
health, 156, 173, 301–305
humor, 50
organizational, 1, 15–18
physical health, 44, 135, 302
positive communication, 1–4, 11, 13, 273, 303–305
positive emotions, 5
positive psychology, 173
psychological, 2–3, 29, 118, 135, 200
recovery, 95
relational, 11, 13–15, 119, 149–150, 167–169, 200
strategies, 18–22
see well-being
wisdom, 6, 84, 88–89, 90, 179

Wise Ways Program, 84
work practices, 239, 244, 249
Workforce Investment Act, 143
workload, 168
workplace
    flow, 11, 21, 238–241, 244–249
    positive psychology, 7
    quality of life, 9
    relationships, 15–17, 183
    women, 216
World Health Organization, 8, 12, 29

Gary L. Kreps, Series Editor

This series examines the powerful influences of human and mediated communication in delivering care and promoting health.

Books analyze the ways that strategic communication humanizes and increases access to quality care as well as examining the use of communication to encourage proactive health promotion. The books describe strategies for addressing major health issues, such as reducing health disparities, minimizing health risks, responding to health crises, encouraging early detection and care, facilitating informed health decisionmaking, promoting coordination within and across health teams, overcoming health literacy challenges, designing responsive health information technologies, and delivering sensitive end-of-life care.

All books in the series are grounded in broad evidence-based scholarship and are vivid, compelling, and accessible to broad audiences of scholars, students, professionals, and laypersons.

For additional information about this series or for the submission of manuscripts, please contact:

Gary L. Kreps
University Distinguished Professor and Chair, Department of Communication
Director, Center for Health and Risk Communication
George Mason University Science & Technology 2, Suite 230, MS 3D6
Fairfax, VA 22030-4444
gkreps@gmu.edu

To order other books in this series, please contact our Customer Service Department:

(800) 770-LANG (within the U.S.)
(212) 647-7706 (outside the U.S.)
(212) 647-7707 FAX

Or browse online by series:
www.peterlang.com